AMERICAN BUDDHISM

Methods and Findings
in Recent Scholarship

CURZON CRITICAL STUDIES
IN BUDDHISM

General Editors:

Charles S. Prebish
Pennsylvania State University

Damien Keown
Goldsmiths College, University of London

The Curzon Critical Studies in Buddhism Series is a comprehensive study of the Buddhist tradition. The series explores this complex and extensive tradition from a variety of perspectives, using a range of different methodologies.

The Series is diverse in its focus, including historical studies, textual translations and commentaries, sociological investigations, bibliographic studies, and considerations of religious practice as an expression of Buddhism's integral religiosity. It also presents materials on modern intellectual historical studies, including the role of Buddhist thought and scholarship in a contemporary, critical context and in the light of current social issues. The series is expansive and imaginative in scope, spanning more than two and a half millennia of Buddhist history. It is receptive to all research works that inform and advance our knowledge and understanding of the Buddhist tradition. The series maintains the highest standards of scholarship and promotes the application of innovative methodologies and research methods.

BUDDHISM AND HUMAN RIGHTS
Edited by Damien Keown, Charles Prebish, Wayne Husted

THE REFLEXIVE NATURE OF AWARENESS
A Tibetan Madhyamaka Defence
Paul Williams

ALTRUISM AND REALITY
Studies in the Philosophy of the Bodhicaryāvatāra
Paul Williams

WOMEN IN THE FOOTSTEPS OF THE BUDDHA
Kathryn R. Blackstone

THE RESONANCE OF EMPTINESS
A Buddhist Inspiration for Contemporary Psychotherapy
Gay Watson

AMERICAN BUDDHISM

Methods and Findings in Recent Scholarship

edited by
Duncan Ryūken Williams
and
Christopher S. Queen

CURZON

First Published in 1999
by Curzon Press
15 The Quadrant, Richmond
Surrey, TW9 1BP

Editorial Matter © 1999 Duncan Ryūken Williams and Christopher S. Queen

Typeset in Sabon by LaserScript Ltd, Mitcham
Printed and bound in Great Britain by
TJ International, Padstow, Cornwall

British Library Cataloguing in Publication Data
A catalogue record of this book is available from the British Library

Library of Congress in Publication Data
A catalogue record for this book has been requested

ISBN 0–7007–1204–6 (Pbk)

To Masatoshi Nagatomi
whose broad-minded approach to Buddhist studies
helped to inspire the study of American Buddhism

CONTENTS

FOREWORD

Diana L. Eck

Wat Buddhanusorn is a jewel, a beautiful new Thai Buddhist temple dedicated in 1997 in Fremont, California, near San Francisco. It is one of several Thai temples in the Bay area and one of dozens now scattered throughout the United States. Its story is not unlike that of hundreds of new Buddhist communities in America. For over ten years, the Thai community of the Fremont area had gathered in a large bungalow house on Niles Boulevard. It converted the house into quarters for resident monks and classrooms for an education program ranging from instruction in Buddhism and the Thai language to instruction in music and dance. A converted garage had become its Buddha hall. Over the course of a decade, the community had come to include Laotian, Vietnamese, and Cambodian Buddhists as well.

When I first visited Wat Buddhanusorn in 1995, the new temple was under construction in the lot immediately behind the bungalow on Niles Boulevard. The foundation had been laid and a skeleton of two-by-fours framed. By the time of my next visit in late 1997, the stunning new temple had already been dedicated. With its graceful roof line and elaborate ornamentation, this temple is a striking and highly visible new addition to the religious landscape of Fremont. The drive down Niles Boulevard will never be the same.

Inside the Buddha hall of the new temple, a fine golden image of the seated Buddha graces the raised altar, and just behind it is a colorful mural, painted by a local Thai artist, depicting scenes of the three worlds – the heavens, this world, and the netherworlds. The most remarkable part of this complex mural might well serve as a visual icon of the two-way traffic of influence and interaction constitutive of Buddhism in America. It is a painted depiction of Wat Buddhanusorn itself and, just above it, the city of San Francisco, represented by the unmistakable Golden Gate Bridge. The image gives vivid expression to the religious reality of this Thai Buddhist community. Just as Wat Buddhanusorn is now a visible part of the religious life of Fremont and the greater Bay area, so the Bay area is a visible part of the religious life of this Thai Buddhist community – inscribed, so to speak, in the iconography of its altar. And just as Wat Buddhanusorn will have a role in reshaping the context of American public and civic life, so will the context of American life gradually reshape this Buddhist community.

This temple is one of more than one hundred fifty Buddhist temples and centers in the San Francisco Bay Area, documented by the Pluralism Project. In addition, there are new Hindu temples, Islamic centers, and Sikh gurdwaras. In Fremont alone, just down Niles Boulevard from Wat Buddhanusorn, there is a graceful Japanese Jōdo Shinshū temple built by the first Buddhists in this area. A new Sikh gurdwara has been constructed nearby on Hillside Terrace, now renamed Gurdwara Terrace. The largest of the Hindu temples in Fremont shares its facility with a Jain congregation. Across town, the Islamic Society of the East Bay and St. Paul's United Methodist Church have just completed a mosque and a church, built side by side on the frontage road they named Peace Terrace. It is in this context that the Abbott of Wat Buddhanusorn participates in a Tri-City Ministerial Association, bringing together the 'clergy' and leadership of an increasingly diverse area.

The new and more complex religious diversity that has become part of the American scene in the past thirty years, since the passage of the 1965 Immigration Act, has raised a range of new research questions for those of us who study religion. A single community, like Wat Buddhanusorn, becomes the site for investigating the dynamic processes of cultural and religious change. How is a Thai Buddhist community like Wat Buddhanusorn negotiating a new identity in the American context? What does it mean to be Thai? American? Buddhist? How will the sense of cultural, national, and religious identity change with the second and third generations? How will their sense of what it is to be Buddhist change in the encounter with Japanese, Lao, Cambodian, Vietnamese, Korean, or Euro-American Buddhists? How will the relation of monks and laity evolve? Will the monks or laity participate in a pan-Buddhist council? In what ways will this Thai Buddhist community participate in such interreligious groups as the Tri-City Ministerial Council, and what changes might that encounter generate? What aspects of Thai Buddhist culture and tradition will prove most durable or most dynamic in the American context? The investigation of these and a multitude of other questions will require the sustained attention of a new generation of scholars.

Whatever the term 'American Buddhism' may come to mean, the communities constituting the fabric of Buddhist life in America today are manifold and complex, probably more so than in any other nation on earth. There are new and old immigrant Buddhist communities from all the Buddhist cultures of Asia. Some, like the Japanese, have been here for generations, while others, like the Khmer, have put down roots only recently. Some have come as economic migrants, others have come as political refugees. Immigrants from all over Asia have encountered one another – often for the first time – here in the United States, and they have also encountered native-born American Buddhists and a growing infrastructure of Dharma centers for teaching and practicing traditions of meditation. The encounter of these diverse Buddhist worlds with one another is truly just beginning, and the study of what evolves will take time and patience.

The conference that gave rise to this volume was a landmark in Buddhist studies and in American studies, bringing together scholars from both fields of study to focus on new research in American Buddhism. The papers presented here provide a sample of a rich research agenda for both scholars of Buddhism and American religious history. As the field of Buddhist studies begins to take the reality of American Buddhist communities seriously, and as scholars of American religion begin to wrestle with the presence and the significance of old and new Buddhist communities, the dialogue of disciplines represented by this volume will become increasingly necessary, and increasingly fruitful.

PREFACE

Duncan Ryūken Williams

The present volume has its origins in a conference, *Buddhism in America: Methods and Findings in Recent Scholarship*, held at the Harvard Divinity School in May 1997 and convened by Christopher S. Queen and Duncan Ryūken Williams. Sponsored by the Harvard Buddhist Studies Forum and organized by its associate director, Karen Derris, the conference brought together scholars from a variety of disciplinary backgrounds to give papers on new research findings on American Buddhism. In addition to the presentation of original research, the conference also served as a forum to discuss methodological issues in the emerging field of studies on American Buddhism. This volume includes a number of papers presented at the conference as well as additional chapters solicited from other scholars.

The editors wish to acknowledge the assistance provided by the following individuals and organizations without whom this volume could not have come to fruition. Harvard Divinity School, the Harvard Buddhist Studies Forum, the Harvard Pluralism Project, the Boston Research Center for the 21st Century, and the Boston University Institute for Dialogue among Religious Traditions, institutionally, and Ronald Thiemann, Virginia Strauss, and John Berthrong, individually, provided crucial support for the May 1997 Buddhism in America conference. The editors would like to thank Diana Eck for her participation as a keynote speaker at the conference, sharing her recent CD-ROM, *On Common Ground: World Religions in America*, and the film *Becoming the Buddha in L.A.* with the conference participants. A particularly strong word of thanks also goes to the 1997 associate director for the Harvard Buddhist Studies Forum, Karen Derris, who went well beyond her duties in organizing the logistical aspects of the conference.

Charles Prebish, the editor of the Curzon Press Critical Studies in Buddhism Series and a pioneer in the study of American Buddhism, provided important feedback on substantive matters from the earliest stages. Other members of the Curzon Press staff were highly professional in their part in putting the volume together. In addition, the expert assistance of Kit Dodgson of the Harvard Center for the Study of World Religions, who prepared the manuscript, and Jonathan Lawson of Harvard University, who prepared the index, was invaluable. We thank Don Farber for the cover photograph.

The editors have attempted to preserve standard transliteration of foreign terms, except in quoted passages in which alternative systems are used; diacritical marks may be omitted in the latter case. In keeping with the practice of a growing number of scholars in the fields of diaspora and immigration studies, the editors have omitted the hyphen in terms such as Asian American, Japanese American, etc. Euro-American and Afro-American, on the other hand, remain hyphenated. Italic type is used for most foreign terms. Curzon Press uses the British system of quotation, with single quotes for first citation, and double quotes for secondary citation.

This volume is dedicated to Masatoshi Nagatomi, Professor Emeritus at Harvard University, whose broad-minded approach to Buddhist studies helped to create the climate for the study of American Buddhism.

INTRODUCTION

Christopher S. Queen

Once again people went around the circle identifying themselves, 'I am So-and-so and I'm a such-and-such.' Just before my turn approached, I heard a voice – who knows who, my psyche, my maggid – a voice that said 'Go for it.' I said, 'My name is Sylvia. I am a Buddhist.' Nothing happened. Lightning did not strike. The circle of identification continued. I felt good.[1]

This is a book about religious identities in transition, and the ways scholars have attempted to understand them. The author of the statement above, co-founder of the Spirit Rock Meditation Center in Woodacre, California, used to say, 'My name is Sylvia Boorstein. I grew up as a Jew, and I teach Buddhist meditation.' But something prompted her to present herself as a Buddhist on the occasion she recounts. Now she writes, 'I am a real Buddhist, I'm not an ethnic Buddhist, but I'm a real Buddhist, and I'm also a Jew. I'm not a person without a country. I am a person who has dual citizenship.' She concludes that American Buddhism is not so different from any other slice of modern America: 'Women and men. Old and young. Some monastics. Mostly lay people. Some people interested in incorporating Buddhist ritual practice into their lives. Some people (most, I think) interested in studying what the Buddha taught, dedicated to practicing clarity and loving-kindness. Some people are not connected to another religious tradition. Some, like myself, are connected. This is how American Buddhism looks.'[2]

Or, this is how *part* of American Buddhism looks. The profiles of the new Buddhists in this volume confirm this author's assessment. The typical convert to Buddhism identified in the studies of James Coleman, Phillip Hammond and David Machacek is a 46-year-old white female from a mainstream religious background, with a masters degree and personal income of $50,000. She spends between thirty and sixty minutes a day in meditation or chanting and holds liberal views of life and politics. At the same time, she is turned off by a good deal that passes for modern culture and is inclined to try new beliefs and practices. She is likely to be single or divorced, living away from her parents and siblings, and 'at a turning point in life.'

Sylvia Boorstein is quick to point out that she is not an 'ethnic Buddhist.' By one account, there are between 3 million and 4 million Buddhists in the United States (about 1.6% of the population), of which about 800,000 are converts.[3] This means that the majority of American Buddhists have brought their religious identity with them from Asia, recently or generations ago. Most are of Chinese and Japanese ancestry, with recent immigrants from Vietnam, Cambodia, Laos, and Tibet swelling the Asian American Buddhist ranks. In this volume we look at Asian American Buddhists first, both because they are more numerous and because they have been practicing Buddhism in North America for longer. Consider the authority of these voices in the annals of American Buddhism:

> I rejoice to see that the best intellects of the day have all approved of your grand scheme. Twenty centuries ago, just such a congress was held in India by the great Buddhist emperor Asoka, in the city of Pataliputra, modern Patna, and the noblest lessons of tolerance therein enunciated were embodied in lithic records and implanted in the four quarters of his extensive empire.
> – *Anagarika Dharmapala, in a letter to the organizers of the World's Parliament of Religions, held in Chicago in 1893.*[4]

> Many important ideas have come from these meetings. Now it is time to put them into action. The world is full of problems that money and technology cannot solve. The world's religions must cooperate to find the solutions. Tolerance and altruism are taught by the great religions and by secular ethics; indeed our capacity for compassion, kindness, and peace may have a biological basis. But in the end, we must all affirm that a good heart and a good brain are essential to secure our common future.
> – *Tendzin Gyatso, the 14th Dalai Lama, in closing remarks at the Parliament of the World's Religions, held in Chicago in 1993.*[5]

Buddhism has been a part of the American cultural experience for more than a century now, growing, for the most part, in an environment of toleration, punctuated by episodes of true enthusiasm and deep suspicion. Its leaders and representatives have not been, as the editor of a popular Buddhist magazine wrote in 1991, 'almost exclusively, educated members of the white middle class.'[6] More often they have been educated and talented missionaries from the growing Asian Buddhist diaspora, Buddhists who chose North America for their home. They include the Japanese teachers D. T. Suzuki, Sōkei-an, Nyogen Senzaki, Shunryū Suzuki-Rōshi, and Taizan Maezumi-Rōshi, the Mongolian Geshe Wangyal, the Tibetan

Chögyam Trungpa Rinpoche, the Vietnamese Thich Thien-an, and the Korean Seung Sahn, to name only a few. Even the Sinhalese Anagarika Dharmapala and the present Dalai Lama of Tibet, who did not settle in the North America, but saw it as a critical mission field, became, by the powerful influence of their travels here, founders of American Buddhism. The vision of these Asian missionaries, of a protean, living tradition, attracting new sympathizers and adherents, accepting and transcending sectarian differences, and entering into dialogue with other faiths and with scientific and social thought, has deeply shaped the character of the new Buddhism.

The choice of 'American Buddhism' for the title of this volume, over the non-committal 'Buddhism in America,' reflects a major finding of our contributors, namely that *recognizable patterns of American Buddhism are emerging in every quarter.* The attributes of this new Buddhism transcend both the unprecedented multiplicity of traditions and lineages that coexist here, and more generally, the cultural and religious divide that has been called 'the two Buddhisms': Asian American Buddhist immigrants on one hand, and Euro-American Buddhist converts on the other.[7] The religious outlooks and institutions that appear in the following essays on Asian American identity, new convert communities, inter-Buddhist associations, environmentalist literature, virtual *sanghas* on the Internet, and the scholar's role in the classroom and the community, point to a vibrant *American Buddhism* in the making.

American Buddhist Studies: A Question of Method

How should we go about the study of American Buddhism? The scholarly techniques required to understand cultural developments that are going on in the present and in the neighborhood, as it were, are different from those needed to understand traditional texts in Pali, Sanskrit, or Chinese, or events that happened centuries ago in Asia. But the techniques of American Buddhist studies must not be confused with the daily flood of journalistic accounts of American religious life, including popular book and film reviews, special theme issues in the mass print media, and interviews of Buddhist 'personalities' in the broadcast media. While some of these accounts are responsibly reported and may reflect significant aspects of American Buddhism, they cannot take the place of historically informed, critical Buddhist studies.

Academic theses and dissertations on topics related to Buddhism have been written by American scholars since 1892, and those on American Buddhism have begun to appear since 1947, as the appendices of this book attest. Yet no study has offered the range of methodological approaches and critical perspectives presented here. These include *interview-based fieldwork* in settings such as Lao Buddhist temples (Van Esterik), Euro-

Introduction

American Buddhist dharma centers (Seager), local inter-Buddhist associations (Numrich) and the Naropa Institute (Goss); *survey-based studies* of the Buddhist Churches of America (Tanaka), new convert communities (Coleman, Hammond/Machacek), and scholars of Buddhism (Prebish); *database sampling* of Japanese American Sōtō Zen Temple financial records (Asai/Williams) and Buddhist chat-groups on the Internet (Hayes); *participant observation* in the Buddhist Churches of America (Tanaka) and the Fokuangshan and Hsi Lai Temples in Taiwan and California (Chandler); *literary criticism* of the writings of Buddhist poet/activist Gary Snyder (Strain); and *methodological analysis* of interpretive categories in American Buddhist studies (Tweed), the field-researcher's role (Chandler), the selection of materials and categories in textbook writing (Seager), survey formulation and data-sampling issues (Hammond/Machacek), and critical issues in the study of American Buddhism (Prebish).

If one interpretive category may be said to pervade the findings of these studies, it is that of *multi-layered religious identities in transition*. Consider the composite persona of Sylvia Boorstein, 'a faithful Jew and a passionate Buddhist'; the creole faith of Anagarika Dharmapala, raised an observant Buddhist but trained in Episcopalian mission schools in colonial Ceylon; and the wonderfully laminated psyche of his mentor, the American-Protestant-Spiritualist-Theosophist-Buddhist Henry Steel Olcott, whose version of the Buddhist dharma was a catechism of questions and answers reminiscent of his Sunday school years in New Jersey.[8] Consider the exuberant syncretism of Gary Snyder, whose 'Pacific Buddha' combines native American and Chinese wisdom with ecosystems theory and the cool-hip stylishness of the San Francisco Beats (Strain), and the expression of complex identities in hybrid *institutional* forms: the Sunday schools and basketball leagues of the Buddhist Churches of America (Tanaka); the growing reliance on English language in the otherwise conservative social and ritual life of the Japanese American Sōtō Zen Temples of Hawaii and California (Asai/Williams); and the rapid growth of university courses and scholarly publications taught and written by lay Buddhist scholar-practitioners, who sometimes assume roles reminiscent of those played by eminent scholar-monks in traditional Asian societies, informing and guiding the new American *sangha* in the theory and practice of Buddhism (Goss, Prebish).

In order to make sense of the studies offered here, it is necessary to understand and accept the religious and methodological situation that Thomas Tweed describes so plainly in his discussion of 'night-stand Buddhists, sympathizers, and adherents, and other creatures':

[If] we ignore those who affiliate with hybrid traditions, engage in creole practices, or express ambivalent identities, there would be no one left to study. Most of the religions I know emerged in contact and exchange with other traditions, and they continued to change over time–always in interaction. Scholars cannot locate a pristine beginning or pre-contact essence to use as a norm to define orthodoxy or orthopraxis. There is hybridity all the way down.

This situation is not the by-product of a cultural promiscuity peculiar to the New World, where spiritual refugees sought freedom from interference in their tightly-defined communities, only to splinter and recombine in a new welter of cults, sects, churches, and denominations.[9] If Tweed is correct, *such fermentation and effervescence is the mark of religious life in all times and places.* It would be careless, therefore, of historians to postulate a static, pristine Asian Buddhism that is sullied in the marketplace of American religion. Indeed, as much as other traditions, Buddhism has grown by fits and starts amid unholy alliances from the beginning. We recall that the Buddhist council convened by King Asoka in the third century BCE and praised by Dharmapala for its 'noblest lessons of tolerance' was the occasion for the mutiny of the *Vibhajyavādins* (Distinctionists) and *Sarvastivādins* (All-is-ists) from the *Mahāsanghikas* (Great Assemblyites) and *Pudgalavādins* (Personalists), who had earlier split from the *Sthaviras* (Elders).[10] Can anyone doubt the overwhelming evidence of cultural mingling and universal hybridity found in the Buddhist annals of Central and East Asia, where acculturation, accommodation, syncretism, and eclecticism were always the rule, never the exception?[11]

Yet, some commentators have expressed impatience with the hybridity of Buddhism in the West, lamenting that 'even the doctrine of rebirth, which is one of the few common denominators among the various Asian traditions, is controversial in Western Buddhist circles,' and warning that 'as long as there continues to be this inability to define or agree on what in the tradition is distinctively and essentially Buddhist, any attempted reforms will probably further fragment Western Buddhism rather than provide it with a distinctive, unified form.'[12]

It is here that the authors of these chapters may contribute to the growing consensus that a recognizable pattern of American Buddhism – not a 'unified form,' certainly not a canon of 'essential' beliefs and practices – is emerging amidst the pluralism and dissent of American society. Many commentators, both practitioners and scholars, have reflected on the still-fuzzy outlines of such a pattern, while citing an increasingly consistent list of features. In 1988, the Theravāda-trained *vipassana* meditation teacher, Jack Kornfield, wrote that the emerging American Buddhism is characterized by democratization ('Western Buddhists are trained to think and understand for themselves and are less suited to the hierarchical models of Asia'), feminization ('to develop the Dharma as a practice of relationship to the body, the community, and the earth, and to stress interdependence and healing rather than conquering or abandoning'), and integration ('not a withdrawal from the world, but a discovery of wisdom within the midst of our lives').[13] In 1997, the Tibetan-trained American teacher, Lama Surya Das, offered his own list of characteristics at a conference in Boston. Included were non-dogmatic teachings, lay-based organizations and leadership, experiential practices such as meditation and chanting, gender equality, non-sectarian/ecumenical/eclectic affiliation, simplified beliefs and rituals, egalitarian/democratic/non-hierarchical institutions, psychologically or rationally based beliefs and practices, experimental/innovative/protean tendencies, and social engagement.[14]

Taken together, these features of the emerging American Buddhism may be grouped under three broad categories as follows:

Democratization, a leveling of traditional spiritual and institutional hierarchies, entailing both *laicization* (the emphasis on lay practice and the de-emphasis of ordained and monastic vocations), and *feminization* (the rise of women in membership and leadership);

Pragmatism, an emphasis on *ritual practice or observance* (particularly meditation, chanting, devotional and ethical activities) and its benefit to the practitioner, with a concomitant de-emphasis of beliefs, attitudes, or states of mind (*agnosticism*); and

Engagement, the broadening of spiritual practice to benefit not only the self, but also family and community (*domestication*), and society and the world, including the social and environmental conditions that affect all people (*politicization*).[15]

These marks of the emerging American Buddhism are not intended to be definitive or complete, but they may serve as useful touchstones as we turn to a survey of findings in the present volume.

Asian American Buddhist Identities

Our opening studies offer evidence of what might be called the cultural and religious *activism* of Asian American Buddhist communities in North America, in contrast to popular perceptions of their passivity and marginality. As we shall see, this activism most often takes the form of cultural assimilation, in this context 'Americanization,' which we shall interpret in terms of democratization, pragmatism, and engagement, as defined above. To be sure, there is a continuum here, from the strongly assimilative impulse of the Buddhist Churches of America (BCA) and the Taiwanese Fokuangshan Order and its California branch Hsi Lai Temple, on one hand, to the cultural conservatism of the Lao refugees in Toronto and the Japanese American Sōtō Zen temples in Hawaii and California, on the other. On such a continuum, the national origin of the groups is not a predictor of Americanization, as the two Japanese American communities occupy the extremes of assimilation (the Protestant-style ecclesiology of the BCA, for example) and cultural preservation (traditional death rites and culture festivals for the Sōtō temples). Nor is the degree of innovation and social engagement a predictor of the success of assimilative strategies, as the sad tale of the Hsi Lai Temple fundraising scandal reveals.

We have in these contrasting studies a testament to the Asian American Buddhists' resolute will to survive *as Buddhists* in a society that still pledges allegiance to 'one nation under [the Judeo-Christian] God.'[16] 'Hyphenated Americans' experience hybridity even before considering religious identity; when religion is introduced their dilemmas are often compounded. The FBI's arrest of Rev. Issei Matsuura of Guadalupe, California, along with dozens of other Jōdo-Shinshū clergy in February 1942 followed a period in which Buddhist leaders attempted to convince their neighbors and members of Congress that they were not 'Emperor worshippers' (thus sympathetic to the Japanese military ambitions) and that they believed in the separation of religion and politics, 'an ideal long held by the citizens of the United States of America.' Such sentiments failed to stay the passage of the Alien Laws (prohibiting Japanese Americans from owning property) and the Oriental Exclusion Act (cutting off immigration) in 1924, and the incarceration of tens of thousands of Japanese Americans in internment camps during World War II. Similarly the founders of the Hsi Lai Temple in Hacienda Heights, California have had to mollify suspicious and occasionally hostile neighbors in their quest for a place on America's Main Street.

Asian American identity is made up of ethnic and cultural components, with religion predominating on the cultural side. Buddhist temples have served as the cultural centers for immigrant communities since the last century, and religious ritual offers frequent occasions for families to come together. Whether to honor the dead, as in Sōtō Zen's *sōshiki Bukkyō* or 'funerary Buddhism,' or to reenact the ceremonies of the giant temple complex in the old country, as in the Lao *That Luang* ceremony, the immigrant community is reconstituted and reconnected in time and space to its roots – ancestors, buildings, monks, the king, and the earth. In a new land, however, the old rituals may be seasoned by new ingredients: Japanese folk drumming, *taiko,* which was offered by the priest as an opportunity to learn about Buddhism, has now been taken over by a layperson who appeals to the musical and social tastes of his young students, while the eight-foot replica of the Vientiane *stūpa* used in the Lao ceremonies in Toronto is made of yellow styrofoam draped in Christmas tree lights. Twinkies, Coke, and Oreo cookies are offered to attract wandering spirits back to the offering tray in the Lao *Soukhouan* ceremony, while the deep-hued maple leaves of Autumn are substituted for Lao buds and banana stalks in the New England version of the rite.

Not all experiments in acculturation are successful, of course. The long, steady decline of membership in the Buddhist Churches of America is the result of a 50 percent outmarriage rate and the 'cultural rejection' this implies for Japanese American Buddhists. Tanaka reports that attrition through outmarriage is exceeded by a dropout rate for young people estimated at about two-thirds. At the same time, the increased presence of multi-racial families and Euro-American convert members is regarded as a disturbing 'erosion of homogeneity' by traditionalist members. As these centrifugal forces threaten the future of the BCA, it is contemplating another name change. While the adoption of 'Buddhist Churches of America' and English usage in ceremonies seemed a prudent move in 1944 following the bitter internment experience, now a fear of death-by-assimilation has prompted another name-change proposal, to 'Jodo-Shinshu Buddhists of America,' to be voted on in 1999.

The Hsi Lai Temple fundraising scandal of 1996, in which Vice President Al Gore attended a dinner at which tens of thousands of dollars were donated to the Democratic National Committee by members of a Taiwan-based Buddhist sect, was a public relations debacle for American Buddhism rivaling the sex-with-teachers revelations of the 1980s. When questions arose about the likelihood and appropriateness of Buddhist nuns having disposable income to spend on political influence, about the legality of political fundraising at a non-profit site, and about the ultimate source of the moneys raised, the matter was taken up by the United States Justice Department, two oversight committees in Congress, and, perhaps worst, the news media. As a doctoral student conducting research at the Fokuangshan headquarters in Taiwan, and as an unofficial advisor to Master Hsing Yün, the head of the order, Stuart Chandler was in an ideal position to interpret the motives of the principal actors in this Asian American Buddhist drama.[17]

We learn that in approving the fundraiser, Master Hsing Yün acted out of a deep sense of gratitude to the American people for their material and moral support for the Republic of China since its secession from the Mainland, and for their growing tolerance of Asian Americans at home.

> The United States should not consider us to be aliens. I am also an American, I have residency status. I always try to encourage Chinese Americans to assimilate into American society. It is not right to go to the States but try to still live like a Chinese or Japanese. When you are in America, be American. When you come to Fokuangshan, be a part of Fokuangshan. When you are in a family, be a member of that family.

Mingled with feelings of gratitude are two more traditional Buddhist sentiments, according to Chandler, those of generosity (expressed in spontaneous gifts, *dāna*) and of establishing 'friendly relations' (*chieh-yüan*). The latter virtue is associated with the spread of the *dharma* and with planting the seeds of one's own future enlightenment. At the suggestion that large gifts to the American political party that occupies the White House is a form of influence peddling, Master Hsing Yün strongly denies that any material or political benefits were sought.

In the aftermath of the scandal, with its predictable talk-show barbs, late-night humor, and political cartoons showing members of the Clinton administration with slanted eyes and wearing traditional Chinese garb or Buddhist robes, Master Hsing Yün and the leaders of numerous Chinese American organizations expressed fear of a return to the anti-Asian prejudice of the internment years during World War II. At publication time for this volume, the pressure of investigations, indictments, and convictions of persons connected with political fundraising among Asian Americans continues.

In spite of setbacks such as these, Asian American Buddhists have manifested many of the signs of the emerging American Buddhism. Distinctly *democratic*, communitarian, or anti-authoritarian trends may be seen in a general shift from clergy-led ritualism to lay-organized community gatherings, culture classes, and festivals that are open to the non-Buddhist public. The stability of membership (counted in families, not individuals) in the Sōtō Zen Temples has been independent of changes in leadership, Asai and Williams point out, in contrast to the precipitous drop in the Euro-American membership of the Zen Center of Los Angeles after the death of the beloved Taizan Maezumi-Rōshi in 1995. The appearance of lay leadership in two of the more conservative communities (for the *Soukhouan* services in the Lao community of Toronto, and the *taiko* classes at the Zenshuji Sōtō Temple in Los Angeles), and of female leadership at the Hsi Lai Temple may not confirm Jōdo Shinshū Bishop Koyu Uchida's declaration before the House Committee on Immigration in 1924 that 'Buddhism is Democratic,' but it does point to structural changes in Buddhist practice and institutionalization which are congruent with American cultural values.

The *pragmatism* of Asian American Buddhism is abundantly reflected in an emphasis on practice and observance over study and education, and in the openness of most Asian American Buddhists to modify traditional patterns of religious life. The top-to-bottom review of organizational structures, educational programs, and ministerial training currently under way in the BCA is perhaps the most dramatic example of a commitment to reinvention, while the shift to English language liturgies in most Asian American Buddhist temples has occurred more quietly over the years. A stark example of the emphasis on practice over study was the cancellation of financial support for the Sunday School and Zen School programs at Zenshūji, while expenditures for ancestral services rose to $36,400 per year.

The social and political *engagement* of Asian American Buddhists may be surprising to readers used to thinking of Buddhists as apolitical or marginalized. Yet the political battles of the Jōdo Shinshū and Fokuangshan communities are instructive. For the Japanese Americans, the immigration laws of 1924 caused not a decline in Buddhist affiliation (or a corresponding rush to Christianity) but just the opposite: temple roles swelled with new members and 'the immigration law made them more defiant and bold in asserting what they believed to be their rights.' At the Hsi Lai Temple, Chandler reports, morale is low as some neighbors revive talk of the 'cult' in their midst, and as Master Hsing Yün revises his opinion of Americans. What remains, however, is the Master's belief that 'we are all global' in our desires for 'peace, equality, forbearance, friendship, respect, tolerance, everywhere to everyone,' and that 'political engagement remains one expedient means to attain Buddhist ideals.' Meanwhile Sōtō Zen temples in California and Hawaii engage their local communities in the annual *Obon* folk dance festival, temple tours, and the sale of Daruma dolls and picture postcards. Only the Lao community of Toronto, so recently separated from its troubled homeland, has yet to set out on the path of social engagement.[18]

The most successful and consistent record of social engagement among the Asian American Buddhists studied here is that of the Buddhist Churches of America. Kenneth Tanaka summarizes their remarkable accomplishments:

(1) The publication of *The Light of Dharma* journal in English that reached a thousand mostly non-Japanese subscribers for several years beginning in 1901; (2) the establishment of a Buddhist Sunday school system in 1914; (3) the hosting of the 1915 World Buddhist Conference in San Francisco, drawing delegates from East Asia, Southwest Asia, Mexico and Hawaii; (4) the ordination of a number of Caucasian priests in the 1930s; (5) the establishment in 1949 of the Buddhist Study Center in Berkeley which served as one of the country's few centers of Buddhist academic learning; (6) the development of the Buddhist Study Center into the Institute of Buddhist Studies in 1966 as a graduate school, which in 1986 evolved a formal affiliation with the Graduate Theological Union in Berkeley; and (7) the 1978 decision by the U.S. Army to grant the BCA the right to train and certify Buddhist chaplains for its forces.

Certainly, in light of the internment of Japanese Americans during World War II, the appointment of Japanese American Buddhist chaplains to the Army in 1978 must be credited as a stunning achievement.

'Who represents true American Buddhism?' The answer is that Asian American Buddhists are as actively engaged in transforming the practice of ancient Buddhism to fit the social realities of North America as are the 'new Buddhists' who receive the fond attentions of the media. In spite of their higher visibility, however, the complex identities of Euro-American Buddhists have been as little studied and understood as those of the

Asian Americans. It is to these new Buddhists that we now turn our attention.

Profiling the New Buddhists

The three studies in this section expand our understanding of the dynamics of conversion to Buddhism by Americans raised in other religious traditions. Thomas Tweed cautions us not to see conversion as a binary process in which the old identity is switched off as the new one is activated. 'Sympathizer' is his term for the countless spiritual seekers whose partial conversion retains elements of the old and new identities. James Coleman offers summary findings from his new study of 359 practitioners at seven Buddhist centers across the country. Remarkable here is that the common demographics, practices, and attitudes of his subjects transcend their affiliation with the three traditional 'vehicles' of Buddhism: *Hīnayāna,* represented by the Vipassana (Theravāda) meditation centers; *Mahāyāna,* represented by the Zen centers; and *Vajrayāna,* encompassing Tibetan practice centers. The implication is that American Buddhism points in the direction of a new, fourth vehicle, which might be styled *Navayāna* ('new vehicle') or *Lokayāna* ('world vehicle') Buddhism. Phillip Hammond and David Machacek, also reporting preliminary findings from a new national study, sample survey data collected from 401 practitioners of Nichiren Buddhism in the Sōka Gakkai International (SGI) organization. While these observations correspond to or parallel those of Coleman, they go more deeply into the psychology and motivation of those Americans who embrace Buddhism during their adult years.

Readers of Tweed's *American Encounter with Buddhism: 1844–1912* are familiar with the rich selection of interpretive categories he brings to the study of late Victorian society. Americans attracted to Buddhist teachings and culture were often drawn by what they perceived to be *rational, esoteric, and romantic* elements in the tradition; they devoured new translations of Asian scriptures, epic presentations of the Buddha's career (such as Edwin Arnold's 1879 best-seller, *The Light of Asia*), and letters and travel diaries of Americans like Ann Haseltine Judson, William Sturgis Bigelow, and Ernest Fenollosa; they became *sympathizers* by incorporating Buddhist attitudes and ideas into their own ways of thinking or behaving, or *adherents* by embracing the tradition more formally. While many were willing to leave the theism and personalism of their Western religious heritage behind, most reached the 'limits of dissent,' in Tweed's view, when they encountered reports of Buddhist pessimism and passivity. Their faith, whatever its pedigree, must share the *social optimism* and *activism* of Biblical salvation and the American national spirit. A new Adam and Eve required a new Eden (nature) and a new Jerusalem (society) in which justice, equality, and social harmony are available to all.

A century after the Victorians' first flirtations with the Dharma, record numbers of Euro-Americans are taking up the practice of Buddhist meditation, chanting, and devotionalism. Colemen's study polls members of some of the oldest, largest, and best-known Buddhist practice centers in the United States: the Rochester (NY) and Berkeley Zen Centers (founded, respectively, by Philip Kapleau Rōshi and Shunryū Suzuki Rōshi, who redirected 1960s Buddhist sympathizers from the aesthetic-intellectual Zen of Alan Watts and the Beats to the austere practice of 'just sitting' and 'beginner's mind'); Karma Dzong, a large practice center in Boulder, Colorado founded in the 1970s by the Tibetan *tulku*, Chögyam Trungpa Rinpoche; the Dzogchen Foundation, founded in Boston by the Tibetan-trained American, Lama Surya Das; two Vipassana groups affiliated with the Spirit Rock Center, co-founded by Jack Kornfield and Sylvia Boorstein; and the non-denominational White Heron Sangha in San Luis Obispo, California. Although the findings Coleman offers here are only frequency distributions (cross-tabulations and discussion will have to await his monograph), the high return rates for his surveys (between 50 and 90 percent), the geographical and sectarian representativeness of his subjects, and the sharp profile of the new Buddhists that emerges even at this stage of interpretation, makes this study a landmark in American Buddhist studies.

Among Coleman's most striking findings is his confirmation that the new American Buddhists are *'the most highly educated religious group in the United States.'* While only a single member of his sample had failed to finish high school, 94 percent had attended at least some college, and more than half (51 percent) had earned graduate degrees. Small wonder that most of these respondents, like their Victorian forebears, had come to know about Buddhism by reading a book. Small wonder, also, that these Buddhist practitioners have incomes that place them comfortably in the middle to upper-middle class (or 'path' as some enjoy saying). These practitioners are politically liberal, disproportionately from Jewish and Catholic back-grounds (though ex-Protestants outnumber the others), and are seeking religious experience and personal transformation over social stimulation and affiliation.

In 'Supply and Demand: The Appeal of Buddhism in America,' Phillip Hammond and David Machacek have taken a closer look at the social and psychological predispositions of American Buddhists. The 'supply' of the study's title is the presence of religious options that 'pull' potential converts in a new direction; pluralistic, cosmopolitan societies will have a greater supply of such alternatives. The 'demand' for a new religious experience is generally a level of dissatisfaction with one's present identity and a degree of social and intellectual openness to change. By examining these dimensions of the new Buddhists, the researchers underscore Coleman's findings and offer finer detail. The higher education of SGI members (59 percent have a bachelor's or graduate degree), for example, 'weakens certainty' about life's meaning and 'weakens social relationships' which would hold one within a particular religious identity. Eighty percent of the Nichiren practitioners were unsatisfied with the religion of their families prior to conversion, and 66 percent had traveled outside the U.S. Sixty-nine percent were single or divorced, and only 37 percent considered being married to be important (compared to 50 percent of the general population).

Not surprisingly, these studies offer new support for the profile of American Buddhists that has been emerging in recent years. In terms of *democratization,* 57 percent of Coleman's subjects were women, with the ratio of women-to-men highest in the Vipassana communities. Neither study reported on the role of ordained clergy in American Buddhism, but the schism of the lay-founded-and-led Sōka Gakkai International from the clergy-led Nichiren Shōshū branch of Japanese Buddhism in 1991 forms the historical backdrop of SGI identity in the 1990s. Eighty-three percent of SGI members joined the organization at the invitation of a friend or family member (not, as in former years, at the urging of a proselytizing stranger), and 60 percent continue to practice Buddhism because of its egalitarian social benefits.

This finding should not be interpreted to mean that SGI members are less committed to the *practice* of Nichiren Buddhism, the daily chanting of *Namu-myoho-renge-kyo,* 'Praise to the Lotus Sūtra.' Indeed, just as 90 percent of the Zen, Vipassana, and Tibetan practitioners surveyed by Coleman meditate daily and attend at least one intensive meditation retreat per year, so SGI members in the United States and Britain place daily chanting and other ritual activities ahead of academic study and assent to doctrinal tenets of the tradition.[19] Such *pragmatism* is extended to other ritual activities for Coleman's subjects, including walking meditation, the use of visualizations and *kōan* in meditation, and attendance at as many as nine religious services per month. Reading about Buddhism remains important for Euro-American Buddhists, as mentioned above, but this is apparently not regarded as intrinsic to Buddhist *practice* per se; similarly, a substantial majority believe in traditional Asian doctrines of *karma* (93 percent) and rebirth (80 percent), but these beliefs are not necessary for the practice of Buddhism.

The new Buddhists report a range of attitudes and opinions that are consistent with social *engagement.* Sixty-three percent of Coleman's respondents support increased involvement of their *sangha* in 'social activities,' 61 percent supported increased 'charitable activities,' and 33 percent believed that their group should become more 'politically active.' Hammond and Machacek go beyond the liberalism of Coleman's new Buddhists to describe what they call the *'transmodernism'* of their subjects. These Baby-Boomers (57 percent in SGI, compared with 39 percent in the general population) are *more benevolent, less cynical, more optimistic, and more idealistic* than the (mainly non-Buddhist) respondents of the General Social Surveys of the National Opinion Research Center. Compared to non-Buddhists, SGI members are more likely to blame society for social and environmental problems, but to assume personal responsibility for their solution, to value personal freedom over law and order, to de-emphasize materialism, technology, and the benefits of the Federal Government, and to believe that true happiness and personal transformation come from the individual.

In spite of American Buddhism's brief detour into the hedonism and misogyny of the Beat Generation, the profile of its sympathizers and adherents at the end of the 20th century may be seen as a further development of the optimism and activism of the Late Victorians – with the addition of a strong ethic of 'spiritual work' in the form of ritual practice and community service. How are these values disseminated, both within the evolving communities of American Buddhism, and to the society at large?

Modes of Dharma Transmission

The common thread in the collection of studies that follows is that American Buddhists have found innovative means to communicate their unique values and perspectives with one another and with the non-Buddhist world. This should come as no surprise for a religious tradition that early enshrined 'skillful means' *(upāya kauśalya)* as the mark of the superior *dharma* preachers and enlightened beings. Here we consider local inter-Buddhist associations which provide a conduit between Asian American Buddhists, Buddhist converts, and their local communities; the polymorphic activism of poet Gary Snyder; and the virtual *sangha* of Buddhist 'newsgroups' on the Internet. Again, we shall discover the tell-tale marks of emerging American Buddhism in each example.

In *Old Wisdom in the New World: Americanization in Two Immigrant Theravada Buddhist Temples* (1996), Paul Numrich introduced the notion of 'parallel congregations' in his study of Asian American and Euro-American groups that share temple facilities in Chicago and Los Angeles. Now he enlarges the picture in his study of inter-Buddhist associations throughout the country and the world. The cooperation of the member *sanghas* in these groups – such as the nine *sanghas* that comprise the Buddhist Council of the Midwest, or the 22-member groups of the Buddhist Coalition of New England – reinforces again the concept of *one American Buddhism* made up of infinitely varied members. Such groups generally agree to foster Buddhist learning and practice among themselves, to promote understanding and cooperation, to pool resources for mutual support, and to offer information and services to the outside community. In spite of the likelihood of 'fusionist' or 'melting pot' tendencies in organizations whose common commitments might lead to a rounding-off of differences over time, however, these associations are in fact staunchly pluralist in character, respecting and celebrating their cultural and religious differences, and sharing this rich variety with the public. Even influential fusionists like Jōdo Shinshū Bishop Yemyo Imamura and Rev. Julius Goldwater, and the Theravāda leader, Ven. Dr. Havanpola Ratanasara, president of the Buddhist Sangha Council of Southern California and the American Buddhist Congress, have been notably unsuccessful in persuading others of the advantages of 'one vehicle,' or *ekayāna*. In a remarkable flourish, Numrich closes his essay by surveying inter-Buddhist associations outside of the United States and in ancient and medieval history.

Charles Strain's study of Gary Snyder places the poet's work in a much larger interpretive context than it is usually found. Beginning with reference to a burgeoning American literature on Buddhism and the environment,[20] Strain suggests that Snyder represents a unique brand of Buddhist environmentalism, somewhere between 'eco-spirituality and eco-justice,' an 'artful rummaging in cultural woodlots' which include Chinese and Japanese Buddhism, philosophical Taoism, animism and paganism, ecosystem theory and environmental science, and 'the twentieth century syncretism of the "Turtle Island" view' – all articulated in a Mahāyāna idiom that maintains 'the strictness and rightness of its own training method' and 'operates primarily at the level of actual practice and secondarily at the level of theory.' Were Snyder's works, dating back to the 1950s, not so accessible in both the literary and Buddhist worlds, Strain's analysis might imply that the poet-activist had been a dilettante or madman. Rather, the final impression is of a genius who has done more for American Buddhism and *belles lettres* – if not for Buddhism and ecology – than any other figure.

Richard P. Hayes of McGill University has served as the longsuffering (and outspoken) moderator of the Internet newsgroups *Buddha-L* and *Buddhist* for many years. He has compiled what is now a massive database of 'intimate, immediate, and anonymous' exchanges among Buddhist sympathizers, practitioners, adherents, and scholars. As he puts it, the Buddhism that lives in the electronic nether-realm of the World Wide Web functions like Carl Jung's 'shadow,' where 'rejected characteristics of the psyche continue to have an effect, although usually not in ways that the person fully acknowledges.' From among the tens of thousands of postings to these Buddhist newsgroups, Hayes selects a few to illustrate the hardiness of four 'themes from the shadows' in North American Buddhism (though one must quickly note that postings come from foreign countries as well as the United States and Canada): Authority, Doctrine, Practice, and Identity. As these are the very issues that have preoccupied us in this introduction, let us compare Hayes's findings with those of Numrich and Strain.

Tendencies toward *democratization* in these studies take the form of communitarian models of decisionmaking and responsibility, and anti-authoritarian attitudes toward officially sanctioned knowledge and religious experience. The pluralist ethos of the inter-Buddhist associations was tested in Toronto in the early 1980s when some member groups attempted to 'Canadianize' the Toronto Buddhist Federation by jettisoning 'ethnic baggage' to achieve a more unified public face. 'Alienation over this push for "Canadianization" still runs high within the ethnic-Asian Buddhist commmities of greater Toronto, to the extent that the new Sangha Council struggles to remain a viable organization,' Numrich concludes. Meanwhile, Gary Snyder's communitarian vision is frequently expressed in the Buddhist metaphor of Indra's Net and the Native American conception of a Council of All Beings – both applied to the political question of decisionmaking in a postmodern world and to the cosmological/soteriological question of man's place in the world. For denizens of the cybersangha, anti-authoritarian sentiments are expressed through the frequent invocation of a minor Buddhist scripture, the *Kālāma Sutta*, in which the Buddha warns his hearers not to be persuaded by hearsay, expertise, or respect for teachers, but rather to rely and act upon their own experience of what is healthy, admirable, and beneficial. This teaching, above all others, has become a kind of manifesto for American Buddhism. Who says that individualism was a negotiable facet of the American character?

The *pragmatism* of these modes of Dharma transmission is also manifested in somewhat predictable ways. The pluralist ethos of the inter-Buddhist associations virtually guarantees that no sectarian teachings will dominate the life of the collectivity; rather the groups are committed to 'promote among the members strict observance and practice of the teachings of the Buddha' and 'to organize and carry on social, educational, and cultural activities' such as the annual, association-sponsored 'Buddha Day,' 'Buddhist Fair,' or *Visakha* celebrations, to which the wider community is invited. Meetings of the associations are also held on a rotating basis at member temples and *dharma* centers, where group practice may be shared in the style of the hosts. In the life and thought of Gary Snyder, the notion of Buddhist *practice* must be wrested from its traditional monastic setting by lay practitioners:

> Practice simply is one intensification of what is natural and around us all the time. Practice is to life as poetry is to spoken language.... One of the first practices that I learned is that when you're working with another person on a two-person crosscut saw, you never push, you only pull; my father taught me that when I was eight.... We have to learn to change oil on time or we burn out our engines. We all have to learn how to cook.

For subscribers to the Buddhist newsgroups, no agreement seems possible on matters of practice, dogma, authority, and lifestyle. Yet, according to

Hayes, *orthopraxis* may still hold a slight edge over *orthodoxy* for American Buddhists. 'Regardless of what one sees as the goals, or absence thereof, of Buddhist practices, there seems to be general agreement to the proposition that it is a good idea to observe some precepts along the way.'

Social and political *engagement* is attested in the inter-Buddhist associations' commitment to provide a watchdog function for media portrayals of Buddhism, and to cooperate in a wide range of community service activities, including youth outreach, AIDS projects, prison ministries, assistance to poorer temples, and lobbying the Immigration and Naturalization Service on behalf of refugees. While Snyder's 'practice of the wild' may be short on political strategy, he has consistently supported and endorsed environmentalist causes in the Northwest, from anti-logging and endangered species campaigns to anti-nuclear activism. Indeed, his *Smokey the Bear Sutra* must stand as the first overtly environmentalist *gatha* in the history of Buddhist literature. Finally, Richard Hayes reports the willingness of American Buddhists to voice support of the Gulf War in 1991, arguing 'on Buddhist principles that warfare is sometimes necessary and unavoidable.'[21]

At the close of his discussion of the *dharma*'s cacophonous transmission on the Internet, Professor Hayes voices the hope that 'If someone in a hundred years does dig down to see what impact we scholars have collectively had in the formation of American Buddhism, I hope they will be able to see that we have done our best to bring them out of the shadows.' Surely this admirable sentiment of an engaged Buddhist scholar provides the perfect *segue* to our final collection of essays.

The Scholar's Place in American Buddhist Studies

It is rare in the history of scholarship that a new academic specialty appears with sufficient self-consciousness to examine its *own image* in the picture it is attempting to paint. This is not to say that field methodology and hermeneutics have not been the preoccupation of cultural anthropologists since Malinowski's Trobriand Island sojourns and Claude Lévi-Stauss's *Tristes Tropiques*, or that post-colonialist and post-modernist writers on Asian themes have not labored mightily since Edward Said's *Orientalism* to identify their own motives and assumptions as scholars.[22] But in the chapters by Charles Prebish, Robert Goss, and Richard Seager offered here, we have three examples of an effort to assess the interaction between American Buddhists and their scholarly critics from a place very near the beginning of American Buddhist Studies.

As a pioneer of American Buddhist Studies – his publication of *American Buddhism* nearly twenty years ago reflected and arguably shaped the direction of such a phenomenon – Charles Prebish is in a rare position to reflect on its evolution. Here he writes about the emergence of Buddhist

Studies in the American academy, and about the role that Buddhologists may potentially play for American Buddhists in the absence of traditional scholar-monks. Tweed and Coleman have already documented the central role that reading and higher education play in the identity formation of Euro-American Buddhists and sympathizers. Prebish's contribution is two-fold: he estimates that between 25 percent and 50 percent of American scholars of Buddhism are practicing Buddhists (though not all are, like himself, willing to disclose it); and he reports some of the roles these scholars have played as mentors and guides for Buddhist practitioners both on campus and in the public domain.

One role of Buddhist scholars (the *double entendre* is intentional here, for a change) in the life of American Buddhism is their increasingly frequent participation in non-academic conferences. Prebish cites the involvement of Robert Thurman (Columbia University) at the 1997 Boston conference on American Buddhism. Its sequel, scheduled for San Diego in 1998, adds Rita Gross (University of Wisconsin at Eau Claire) and Judith Simmer-Brown (Naropa Institute), also practicing Buddhists. Such participation is not without its pitfalls. During a week-long conference on 'World Buddhism in North America' held in a Buddhist temple in Ann Arbor in 1987, sponsored by the Zen Lotus Society and attracting more than 300 Buddhist leaders, scholars, and practitioners, both Carl Bielefeld (Stanford University) and Donald Lopez (University of Michigan) offered historical interpretations that angered non-academic members of the audience. In both instances (as a videotape of the conference reveals), Prof. Luis Gómez (University of Michigan) jumped up to defend his colleagues – both as a scholar, and as a Buddhist practitioner: 'Scholars must stand back from the tradition in order to understand it. This is very valuable. But sometimes my scholarship, like my Zen Master, tells me "You're wrong!"'[23]

Robert Goss's discussion of the place of the Naropa Institute, both in American Buddhism and in American higher education, offers another example of complex cultural identities in transition. Naropa may be seen as a private, religiously-affiliated institution of higher learning committed to values and training that foster spirituality, personal transformation, and social change in a liberal arts context. Such a perspective recalls the critique of higher education by neoconservative Christians like George Marsden – except for Naropa's commitment to provide *a pluralist, non-sectarian* environment for liberal education. As Prof. Judith Simmer-Brown says, 'I don't care whether people are Buddhist, but I really do care whether they practice some mediatation and that they come to know something about who they are.' Thus Naropa has been identified as a 'participant-friendly' post-secondary institution for Buddhist Studies, where at least a third of its students are practicing Buddhists, and where Buddhist psychology, philosophy, arts education, and theories of social engagement are placed at the heart of the curriculum.

Richard Seager's candid discussion of his own evolving identity as an Americanist interested in East-West encounters and willing (at last) to take up the saga of American Buddhism offers another angle on the field. As he points out, his own Roman Catholic roots made the Protestant Christian triumphalism implicit in much American studies both apparent and odious to him as a graduate student, and also attuned him to the *Heilsgeschichte* ('sacred history') subtext of Rick Fields' *How the Swans Came to the Lake*, the reigning narrative treatment of American Buddhism. This is not to say that Fields, a Jewish Buddhist, intentionally constructed an American Buddhism that favors the Zen side of Euro-American Buddhism, but rather to suggest that a birds-eye view of the territory is not easy to achieve. In his preview of his own *Buddhist Worlds in the U.S.A.*, the first commissioned textbook on American Buddhism, Seager shares with us some of the dilemmas he faces in attempting to produce a representative and impartial account.

To trace the 'three marks' of American Buddhism one last time in these chapters poses a special challenge, for, although the existence of Buddhist scholar-practitioners is as much a part of American Buddhism as are, say, Buddhist subscriber-practitioners on the Internet, we are not provided with as much information on the religious practices of these Buddhists as our authors have provided in previous sections of this book. Nevertheless, there are sufficient indications of the presence of *democratization, pragmatism, and engagement* among the scholars treated here to suggest that these tendencies in American Buddhism also motivate those who study Buddhism for a living. That is to say, most American Buddhist scholars are at least as *American* by temperament as they are Methodist Buddhist (as in my case) or Jewish Buddhist (or *Buddhish,* as in Charles Prebish's case).

The *democratization* of American Buddhism is reflected in the overwhelmingly *lay* context of the discussions of Buddhist scholarship and education. Even those well-known scholars who received monastic education in the process of becoming monks in Asia (such as Professors Robert Thurman, Jeffrey Hopkins, Georges Dreyfus, and Robert Buswell) have long since returned to lay life. 'Practice-friendly' institutions of Buddhist studies are defined as those that may offer Buddhist priestly training, Buddhist practices along with academic study, and a normative presentation of the Buddhist tradition.[24] Yet there is no discussion of what 'Buddhist priestly training' might entail in North America. The editors of this volume must bear some responsibility for this omission, for the contributors to the conference and the volume were not expressly invited to comment on monastic life and education in America; yet it is perhaps telling that no such reflections came up in many discussions of 'the scholar's role in American Buddhist Studies.' Another story that deserves to be told is that of the American scholar-practitioner *women* who have contributed to a modern understanding of the dharma through their feminist readings of Buddhist history and literature; one thinks of Rita

Gross, Janet Gyatso, Anne Klein, Jan Nattier, Miranda Shaw, Judith Simmer-Brown, and Jan Willis, among many others.[25]

The *pragmatism* of American Buddhism may be glimpsed, perhaps indirectly, in Prebish's observation of a 'shift away from Buddhist texts and philosophy (the Buddhist "theology" which some of us have been accused of propagating), toward an investigation of Buddhism's contextual relationship with culture,' meaning, as José Cabezón adds, 'oral and vernacular traditions, epigraphy, ritual, patterns of social and institutional evolution, gender, lay and folk traditions, arts, archaeology, and architecture. . . .' That is to say, Buddhist scholar-practitioners – whether they came to Buddhism through their studies, or to their studies through Buddhist practice – are likely to be more attuned to the cultural expression of Buddhism, that is, to its *practice*, than their linguistically-trained non-Buddhist colleagues are likely to be. At the Naropa Institute, Robert Goss tells us, this openness to the richness of culture and to the contribution of multiple lineages and traditions, is emblematic of the *Rimed* (Tibetan *ris med*) or 'non-sectarian' movement of Eastern Tibet, which Naropa founder Chögyam Trungpa introduced to American Buddhism in the form of Shambhala Training. But for a more celebrated source of Buddhist pragmatism, Naropa leaders cite the life of their root *guru*, the eleventh-century teacher Naropa, who left his position as Abbot of Nalanda Monastic University in India to become an itinerant *yogi*, claiming that knowledge in the absence of practice is sterile.

If teaching is the paradigmatic form of Buddhist *social engagement,* then the scholar-practitioners of these chapters may already be treading the well-worn path of Shakyamuni. Such a connection is spelled out in Prebish's argument for the role of Buddhist scholar-practitioners as modern stand-ins for the *gantha-dhura* or 'book-wielding' scholar-monks of Asian history; or Richard Hayes's hope that he brings historical balance and accuracy to some of the discussions he moderates on the *Buddha-L* and *Buddhist* newsgroups; or Malcolm David Eckel's proposal, floated at the Harvard conference on American Buddhism, that scholars of Buddhism (practitioners or not) volunteer their time and expertise as *consultants* to American *sanghas* obviously in need of solid information about Asian Buddhism. But these wishes may prove illusory. For if the anti-authoritarian and anti-intellectual ethos of most American *sanghas* is recalled, the role of American Buddhist scholars may remain limited to the settings we have already sketched: the university classroom and computer keyboard, the podium at public conferences on religion and spirituality, and at the end of the phone as 'background source' for yet another short-deadline media piece on 'American Buddhism.'

Here perhaps the faculty at Naropa and other 'practitioner-friendly institutions' are the exception. They may pursue a socially engaged spiritual/educational career of which the solitary Buddhologists at traditional liberal arts institutions may only dream. As the anthropologist and engaged Buddhist priest, Joan Halifax, declared at the recent Spirituality in Education Conference at Naropa, paraphrasing the vows of the Zen Peacemaker Order, 'We need to revision education in the West in the twenty-first century as a way to enter the unknown, bear witness to joy and suffering, and heal ourselves and the world.'

Conclusion

In our informal pre-amble through some of the methods and findings of this book, we have encountered a wealth of unsolved mysteries as well as the shimmering outlines of an emerging pattern of American Buddhism. In sampling and previewing the new research offered here, I have attempted to show the presence of three themes that others have identified before, but never attempted to *operationalize* and *contextualize* in any systematic fashion. These themes are interesting, someone says, but are they Buddhist? In the process of tracing the lineaments of democratization, pragmatism, and engagement through the pages that follow, I have been struck by their congruence with the ancient Buddhist refuge-formula, the Three Jewels.

For it is in the *democratization* of American Buddhism, its laicization and feminization, that we see the face of a new kind of 'Buddha' ideal, i.e., one in which training, gender, and institutional position are less important than simple participation and regular effort. Such effort takes the form of some kind of practice – meditation, chanting, temple devotions, and the observance of ethical precepts – more often than it does some special knowledge, belief, or state of mind. This is a new 'Dharma,' in step with a perennial American *pragmatism*, a reliance on action over reflection. And finally, the American Buddhist conception of community, of relationship and affiliation, of 'Sangha,' is shaped by a sense of responsibility for others, and for the ways in which becoming a Buddhist must transform society as well as oneself; this is the attitude of *engagement*. So when American Buddhists 'go for refuge' to the Three Jewels, they still affirm the ideals of a religion now 2,500 years old, but they do so in a new way.

Perhaps American Buddhism will continue to exemplify these patterns – or perhaps it will not. In the final words of this book, Richard Seager offers a perspective worth considering before we begin:

> We are now witnessing only the immediate aftermath of the first, large-scale fluorescence of Buddhism in America. The rapid turning of the wheel of *dharma* in the last three decades churned up great clouds of New World dust, much of which still remains suspended in air. It is too early to make a call on what American Buddhism is. And historical precedents in Asia suggest that there is a great deal more yet to come.

Notes

1 Sylvia Boorstein, *That's Funny, You Don't Look Buddhist: On Being a Faithful Jew and a Passionate Buddhist* (San Francisco: Harper San Francisco, 1997), 8.
2 Ibid., 9, 164–165.
3 Martin Baumann, 'The Dharma Has Come West: A Survey of Recent Studies and Sources,' *Journal of Buddhist Ethics* 4 (1997): 198.
4 John Henry Barrows, ed., *The World's Parliament of Religions: An Illustrated and Popular Story of the World's First Parliament of Religions, Held in Chicago in Connection with the Columbian Exposition of 1893*, vol.1 (Chicago: Parliament Publishing Company, 1893), 8.
5 H. H. the Dalai Lama, 'The Closing Plenary Address' (Chicago: Council for a Parliament of the World's Religions, 1993), edited transcript.
6 Helen Tworkov, 'Many Is More,' editorial, *Tricycle: The Buddhist Review* 1, no. 2 (Winter 1991): 4.
7 Charles Prebish introduced the expression 'the two Buddhisms' in *American Buddhism* (North Scituate, MA: Duxbury Press, 1979), 51–53. Following the controversy created by Tworkov's *Tricycle* editorial, Prebish returned to the question in 'Two Buddhisms Reconsidered,' *Buddhist Studies Review* 10, no. 2 (1993): 187–206, arguing that the distinction was religious and not ethnic. The typology was expanded by Jan Nattier in 'Visible and Invisible' (*Tricycle* 5, no. 1 [Fall 1995]: 42–49) to encompass the 'evangelical' or 'export' Buddhism of Sōka Gakkai, the Japanese lay Buddhist movement that spread rapidly in the West in the 1970s and 1980s, and which is analyzed in Chapter 7 below.
8 See Stephen Prothero, *The White Buddhist: The Asian Odyssey of Henry Steel Olcott* (Bloomington: Indiana University Press, 1996) for the application of the linguistic term 'creolization' to the Olcott's Victorian Buddhism. It may be argued that, just as Olcott superimposes a Buddhist lexicon on the Protestant syntax of his rapidly evolving faith, so the reverse was the case for Dharmapala, whose Biblical lexicon burnished and embellished his Buddhist homilies at the World's Parliament of Religions and in his editorials for the Maha Bodhi Society journal.
9 Ann Felt Tyler cites Ralph Waldo Emerson's description of the 1840 meeting of the Friends of Universal Reform: 'If the assembly was disorderly, it was picturesque. Madmen, madwomen, men with beards, Dunkers, Muggletonians, Come-outers, Groaners, Agrarians, Seventh-Day Baptists, Quakers, Abolitionists, Calvinists, Unitarians, and Philosophers – all came successively to the top, and seized their moment, if not their hour, wherein to chide, or pray, or preach, or protest.' *Freedom's Ferment: Phases of American Social History from the Colonial Period to the Outbreak of the Civil War* (New York: Harper and Row, 1962), 46.
10 See Nalinaksha Dutt, *Buddhist Sects in India* (Delhi: Motilal Banarsidass, 1978), and Anuradha Seneviratna, ed., *King Asoka and Buddhism* (Kandy, Sri Lanka: Buddhist Publications Society, 1994). For a summary of current scholarship in the history of Buddhism, see Richard H. Robinson and Willard L. Johnson, *The Buddhist Religion: A Historical Introduction*, 4th ed., with extensive rewriting by Sandra A. Wawrytko and Thanissaro Bhikkhu (Belmont, CA: Wadsworth Publishing Company, 1997).
11 For a timely argument for the revival of 'syncretism' as a central category in religious historiography, with detailed application to Chinese history and the Ming-dynasty figure Lin Chao-en (1519–1598), see Judith A. Berling, *The Syncretic Religion of Lin Chao-en* (New York: Columbia University Press,

1980). For a social anthropological treatment of the pervasive role of syncretism in the history of religions, see Charles Stewart and Rosalind Shaw, eds., *Syncretism/Anti-Syncretism: The Politics of Religious Synthesis* (London and New York: Routledge, 1994).

12 Robinson and Johnson, *The Buddhist Religion*, 309.

13 Jack Kornfield, 'Is Buddhism Changing in North America?' in Don Morreale, ed., *Buddhist America: Centers, Retreats, Practices* (Santa Fe, NM: John Muir Publications, 1988), xi-xxviii; see also Prebish, op. cit., 173-193; and Rick Fields, *How the Swans Came to the Lake*, Third Edition (Boulder, CO: Shambhala, 1992), 371–380. Further support for this emerging picture is provided by four forthcoming volumes: Charles Prebish and Kenneth Tanaka, *Faces of Buddhism in America* (Berkeley: University of California Press, in press); and Charles Prebish, *American Buddhist Studies* (Berkeley: University of California Press, forthcoming); Richard Seager, *Buddhist Worlds in the U.S.A.* (New York: Columbia University Press, forthcoming); and Christopher S. Queen, ed., *Engaged Buddhism in the West* (Boston: Wisdom Publications, forthcoming).

14 Lama Surya Das, 'Emerging Trends in Western Dharma,' keynote address, 'Buddhism in America' conference, Boston Park Plaza Hotel, January 19, 1997 (available on videocassette from Sounds True, Box 8010, Boulder, CO 80306).

15 The difficulty of characterizing American Buddhism at this stage in our understanding is illustrated by this simple exercise, in which the meaning of certain elements – *democratization* and *feminization*, for example – shifts when we regroup the characteristics. In Kornfield's assessment, democratization refers to a style of decisionmaking in Buddhist communities, while feminization refers to certain ideological shifts in the presentation of the Buddhist *dharma*. In my version, both traits may be taken to describe a pervasive shift in the institutionalization of Buddhism – a leveling of spiritual, gender, and organizational roles – which may also be seen to encompass the salience of lay leadership in American Buddhism.

16 *The New York Times Magazine* for December 7, 1997, ran a special issue on 'God Decentralized,' devoted to the premise that while 'Americans are still among the most religious people on the planet … they're busy inventing unorthodox ways to get where they're going.' Gabrielle Glaser's 'Scenes From an Intermarriage' features the Ono family, in which 18-year-old Alistair and 22-year-old Sarah are raised in their Japanese American father's Jōdo Shinshū tradition, while their Middle-Western-Dutch-Lithuanian-German mother retains her Roman Catholicism. The article is excerpted from Glaser's *Strangers to the Tribe: Portraits of Interfaith Marriage* (New York: Houghton Mifflin, 1997).

17 The editors are grateful to Mr. Chandler for publishing his reflections here and not in another form for the *New Yorker*.

18 This is not to say that the rituals van Esterik documents do not have deep significance and therapeutic value for members of the Lao community, or that such teachings as the transfer of merit earned in the ritual to deceased loved ones, or the nestedness (*emboîtment*) of the individual in the widening circles of family, community, and world, do not do not remind participants of their interdependence with others; it is rather to say that the Lao community has not reached the stage of outreach, service, or political activism that is implied by the term 'engagement,' as it is used here.

19 See Jane Hurst, *Nichiren Shoshu Buddhism and the Soka Gakkai in American: The Ethos of a New Religious Movement* (New York and London: Garland Publishing, 1992); and Bryan Wilson and Karel Dobbelaere, *A Time to Chant:*

The Soka Gakkai Buddhists in Britain (Oxford: Clarendon Press, 1994). It is significant in this connection that SGI Buddhists stress the invocation (*daimoku*) of the title of the *Lotus Sūtra* and not its reading and study.

20 The reference is to Ian Harris, 'Getting to Grips with Buddhist Environmentalism: A Provisional Typology,' *Journal of Buddhist Ethics* 2 (1995): 173-190. For the most comprehensive scholarly volume on the subject, see Mary Evelyn Tucker and Duncan Ryūken Williams, eds., *Buddhism and Ecology: The Interconnection of Dharma and Deeds* (Cambridge: Harvard University Center for the Study of World Religions, 1997).

21 Most engaged Buddhists are indeed non-violent, so the predilections of these newsgroup subscribers cannot by taken as characteristic. See Christopher S. Queen and Sallie B. King, eds, *Engaged Buddhism: Buddhist Liberation Movements in Asia* (Albany: State University of New York Press, 1996).

22 See Clifford Geertz, *Works and Lives: The Anthropologist as Writer* (Stanford: Stanford University Press, 1988); and James Clifford, *The Predicament of Culture: Twentieth-Century Ethnography, Literature, and Art* (Cambridge: Harvard University Press, 1988). In Buddhist Studies, Donald S. Lopez, Jr., ed., and colleagues have taken a similar leap in applying post-colonialist criticism to the fathers of the field and to themselves, in *Curators of the Buddha: The Study of Buddhism under Colonialism* (Chicago: University of Chicago Press, 1995). See Jan Nattier's review for a more balanced view of the 'dangers' of Orientalism in Buddhist Studies: 'Buddhist Studies in the Post-Colonial Age,' *Journal of the American Academy of Religion* 65, no. 2 (Fall 1997): 469–485.

23 'World Buddhism in North America.' Videocassette (Ann Arbor, MI: Zen Lotus Society, 1987). Among the other scholars who took part in this conference were Alan Sponberg (University of Montana), Anne Klein (Rice University), and Richard Hayes (McGill University).

24 As defined by Duncan Ryūken Williams in 'Where to Study?' *Tricycle* 6, no. 3 (Spring 1997): 68.

25 Among the many fine studies by and about women scholars in American Buddhism are Sandy Boucher, *Turning the Wheel: American Women Creating the New Buddhism* (Boston: Beacon Press, 1988, 1993); Rita M. Gross, *Buddhism after Patriarchy: A Feminist History, Analysis, and Reconstruction of Buddhism* (Albany: State University of New York Press, 1993); Sallie B. King, trans., *Journey in Search of the Way: The Spiritual Autobiography of Satomi Myodo* (Albany: State University of New York Press, 1993); Anne C. Klein, *Meeting the Great Bliss Queen: Buddhists, Feminists, and the Art of the Self* (Boston: Beacon Press, 1995); Diana Y. Paul, *Women in Buddhism: Images of the Feminine in the Mahayana Tradition* (Berkeley: University of California Press, 1979, 1985); Miranda Shaw, *Passionate Enlightenment* (Princeton: Princeton University Press, 1994); Liz Wilson, *Charming Cadavers: Horrific Figurations of the Feminine in Indian Buddhist Hagiographic Literature* (Chicago: University of Chicago Press, 1996).

Part One

Asian American Buddhist Identities

CHAPTER ONE

Issues of Ethnicity in the Buddhist Churches of America

Kenneth K. Tanaka

February 18, 1942, early morning, still in our night clothes and huddled by the heater, we listened grimly to the news over the radio. There was a loud rapping on the back door. Three men stood there. They were the FBI. 'We came to arrest Rev. Matsuura,' said one, as they came through the door.[1]

This paper is concerned with the issues of ethnicity within the Buddhist Churches of America (BCA). The paper will be descriptive in nature, based on interviews, surveys, and personal observation.[2]

As the institution representing the Nishi-Hongwanji branch of Jōdo-Shinshū in the continental United States, the BCA will celebrate its centennial in 1999.[3] In 1997, the BCA is comprised of a national headquarters located in San Francisco and sixty temples served by sixty-one priests.[4] Total membership in 1996 stood at 16,902, a figure that represents a gradual attrition from the 1988 figure of 20,021 and a 1977 count of 21,600.[5] The number of priests reveal a parallel decline from its peak of 123 in 1930, to 71 in 1981 and to the 61 priests in 1997.[6]

The choice of this topic, ethnicity, is partly motivated by my desire to clear up some points concerning the common perception of the BCA as, at best, a paradigmatic ethnic Buddhist institution and, at worst, an 'ethnic fortress.' The focus is also a response to the ongoing debate on the issue of two kinds of Buddhism in America as reported by Charles Prebish and others: the one 'ethnic' or 'Asian American' and the other 'white' or 'Euro-American.' The two are seen as mutually isolated and very distinct in their membership and focus.[7] Ethnic temples have served not only the spiritual but also the cultural and social needs of their members, particularly among the most recent of the immigrant population. In contrast, many observers note that Euro-American groups focus primarily on spiritual practices. We should, however, remain cautious about the underlying implication in these observations that ethnic groups are less spiritual. Cultural activities have always played a vital part of Buddhist temples in Asia and were integrated with the spiritual life of the larger communities. Perhaps a deeper, more nuanced analysis will reveal their spiritual significance in the lives of practicing Buddhists.

This division has also contributed to the smoldering debate concerning the question, 'Who represents true American Buddhism?' Some Asian American Buddhists are offended at the suggestion that white Buddhists are the sole contributors to the creation of American Buddhism while ethnic Buddhists are seen as having played virtually no role in it. Helen Tworkov, the editor of *Tricycle: The Buddhist Review*, for example wrote 'Asian American Buddhists ... so far ... have not figured prominently in the development of something called American Buddhism.'[9] This viewpoint ignores the history of contributions made by groups of Asian American Buddhists, some entering their second century of roots in American soil. What is implied, according to Asian American critics, is that Buddhism becomes truly American only when white Americans become seriously involved. This form, then, is called 'American Buddhism,' distinguished from simply 'Buddhism in America,' i.e., Buddhism as a foreign religion practiced by Asian American Buddhists.

In contrast to the two-category dichotomy, Jan Nattier has proposed a three-category model using an economic paradigm: the Buddhists are elite, missionary, or immigrant, and their Buddhism is respectively an 'import,' an 'export,' or 'baggage.' 'Elite Buddhists' belong to a higher socio-economic class, are highly educated, and overwhelmingly of European descent. Due largely to their economic prowess, they were able to actively 'import' their preferred brands of Buddhism, primarily the 'meditative' Tibetan, Vipassana, and Zen traditions. 'Missionary' or 'evangelical Buddhists' are chiefly represented by the Sōka Gakkai organization in the United States, whose conscious missionary activity was funded and directed from its headquarters in Japan since the 1960s. The Sōka Gakkai has a substantial percentage of African American, Latino, and Asian American members; in 1983 55 percent of its members came from non-European ethnic backgrounds. Lastly, 'ethnic Buddhists' entered the United States as Asian immigrants. Nattier regards their form of Buddhism as 'the most complex and sophisticated' due to its concern with the entire fabric of life, spanning many generations, rather than a focus on the individual search for enlightenment.[10] The BCA would fall under this 'baggage' category.

In this paper, 'ethnicity' is seen as possessing two dimensions: culture and race. Culture is further distinguished into traditional arts and shared values. The arts refer to any number of Japanese-inspired fine arts and martial arts: flower arrangement, tea ceremonies, *shigin*, *kendō*, *jūdō*, *karate*, *aikidō*, etc. Also included here is instruction in the Japanese language, which traditionally includes calligraphy and appreciation of Japanese literature. 'Values' refers to the shared worldviews that were especially prevalent among the *issei* (first generation) immigrant population. These values are best represented by gratitude (expressed as *arigatai; kansha*), frugality (*mottai'nai*), industriousness (*kinben-sa*), responsibility (*sekinin*), and obligation (*giri*).[11]

The racial aspect of ethnicity is evidenced in many ethnic groups by their members' powerful drive to associate with others of the same national background. This need was, in the case of BCA members, accentuated by external forces that impacted the Japanese Americans before World War II, including their incarceration during the war. The Buddhist temple served as refuge within a hostile social environment.

Historical Background to the Ethnic Nature of the BCA

Religion and ethnicity are closely related phenomena in North America. Much of the development of religion in the New World could not be fully understood without taking into consideration immigration patterns and the role of ethnic bonding. The BCA certainly fits this pattern. For a non-Christian and non-European immigrant population such as the BCA membership, the role of ethnicity was perhaps even more crucial and enduring. I will mention here some developments from the first fifty years of BCA history that contributed to the strong ethnic nature of this religious institution.

The arrival in 1899 of the first missionaries, Dr. Shūye Sonoda and Rev. Kakuryō Nishijima, took place within an atmosphere that was far from friendly or receptive. For example, a combative attitude can be detected in the *San Francisco Chronicle* caption to the photograph of their arrival as it noted, 'They will teach that ... pure Buddhism is a *better* moral guide than Christianity' (emphasis added). The reporter goes on to describe Buddhism as challenging the ultimacy and nature of the Christian concept of God as nothing more than a 'figment of the human imagination.'[12]

Similar attitudes existed even within the Japanese community. The groundwork for the arrival of the official missionaries had begun several years earlier. One year before their arrival, a Buddhist representative met with the Japanese Consul in Seattle, but, according to existing records, this government official was not favorable to the idea of bringing Buddhism to the United States. He feared that the introduction of a 'foreign religion' would cause numerous problems for the Japanese and Americans who were, for the present, coexisting peacefully. The Consul was annoyed by the idea and inquired whether the American government would allow the entrance of a 'foreign religion.' He saw Buddhism as a threat to the relationship between the two peoples.[13]

Thus, it is no great surprise to learn that the Jōdo-Shinshū priests sent from Japan, though called *kaikyōshi* (missionaries or, literally, 'emissaries

5

[*shi*] who open up [*kai*] the teachings [*kyo*]'), rarely carried out active propagation activities beyond the existing Japanese American communities. This was due partly to political considerations. It appears that, prior to World War II, the Japanese governmental attitude noted above fostered a tacit understanding among the 'missionaries' that they were to stay confined to the Japanese American communities.[14] This understanding was further reinforced by the fact that these priests had been invited to existing Japanese American communities in order to serve their cultural, social, and spiritual needs. Consequently, the priests found themselves being discouraged by their lay 'hosts' from actively propagating beyond their communities. The lay members needed their priests to help create a social oasis within the sea of racial hostility.

The hostilities aimed at the Japanese in the society at large contained ample references to the Buddhist temples. For example, testifying before a subcommittee of the House Committee on Immigration in 1921, Senator James D. Phelan of California explained:

> There are seventy-six Buddhist temples in California and I am told that they are regularly attended by 'Emperor worshippers' who believe that their Emperor is the over-lord of all.[15]

Similar claims were voiced by Valentine S. McClatchy, publisher of the *Sacramento Bee*:

> The Japanese hold that their Mikado is the one living God to whom they owe their very existence, and therefore all obedience.... Buddhism, which is tolerated in Japan, has Shintoism grafted onto it.[16]

Bishop Kōyu Uchida did not allow these accusations to go unanswered, as attested to in his statement to the House Committee:

> We wish to strongly emphasize that our Churches have nothing to do whatsoever with Shintoism, politics or any imperialistic policy formulated by the Japanese government. Our mission is to elevate the spiritual life, not to dictate politics, or policies of any government. We should also like to point out that Buddhism is democratic, an ideal long held by the citizens of the United States of America.[17]

It requires mentioning here that it was Bishop Uchida who had pushed for all the temples to refer to themselves as a 'church,' presumably to blunt the appearance of being too foreign.[18] However, anti-Japanese sentiments continued to crescendo, culminating in the 1924 Alien Land Laws and the Oriental Exclusion Act. According to the new laws, Japanese nationals could no longer own property, and new immigration from Japan was terminated.

Ironically, the Exclusion Act proved to be a windfall for the Buddhist temples. Many *isseis* interpreted the law as extremely unjust. As a result, many of them, including those who were 'fence-sitters,' became members of the Buddhist temples. The Buddhist temples came to be perceived as bastions of Japanese culture and refuges from the storms of a hostile society. This is reflected in an observation made during that period about the Gardena Buddhist Church near Los Angeles:

> After the passage of the Immigration Law of 1924 discriminating against the Japanese, the number of Buddhists increased rapidly, and so did that of the Buddhist churches. Before that event, some of them had been hesitant in declaring themselves Buddhists, considering such an act impudent in a Christian country. But the immigration law made them more defiant and bold in asserting what they believed to be their rights; it made them realize the necessity of cooperation for the sake of their own security and welfare, and naturally they sought centers of their communal activity in their Buddhist churches.[19]

Eighteen years later World War II dealt the ultimate blow to the Japanese American communities: the internment. Of the approximately 110,000 people interned, 60 percent were Buddhists, and the vast majority of them belonged to the Jōdo-Shinshū school. Among the first to be rounded up in the early days of the war were the Buddhist priests. Among them was Rev. Issei Matsuura of Guadalupe, a small farming community in central coastal California. Mrs. Matsuura, a highly respected spiritual and community leader in her own right, later recalled those terrifying events in her book, *Higan* (Compassionate Vow).

> February 18, 1942, early morning, still in our night clothes and huddled by the heater, we listened grimly to the news over the radio. There was a loud rapping on the back door. Three men stood there. They were the FBI.
>
> 'We came to arrest Rev. Matsuura,' said one, as they came through the door. I had a foreboding that something like this would happen. But when the time actually came, I felt crushed. I was instructed to pack a change of clothing for my husband. Hurriedly, I put his underwear and toiletries in a bag. Separately, I wrapped his *koromo* (priest robes) and *kesa* (a miniature version of the original monastic robes that is worn around the neck), *seiten* (book of sacred writings) and *Kanmuryōjukyō sūtra* (the Contemplation Sutra).
>
> 'Only bare necessities,' they said, but he being a minister, the extra religious articles were allowed. My husband walked the long corridor to the *hondō* (Buddha hall), lit the candle and incense and quietly read the *Tanbutsuge*. Our youngest daughter, Kiyo, and I bowed in *gassho* (the placing the palms together as expression of reverence), realizing this may be our last parting. The FBI stood at attention through the sutra chanting.[20]

7

In April 1942, Mrs. Matsuura was evacuated to the camps, along with the entire Japanese American community in the Guadalupe region. She would later write:

> Whatever land and property were acquired in the almost fifty years of immigrant history leading up to that day were to be sold at any price or just abandoned. We were told to leave with only what we could carry. Bearing numbered tags identifying us as 'enemy aliens,' and steeped in uncertainty, we tearfully left our home.[21]

Ironically, the most critical step in the Americanization of Jōdo-Shinshū Buddhism took place in the internment camps located in Topaz, Utah. The great change started with a series of meetings at the Topaz camp in early 1944 and climaxed with a conference in Salt Lake City (east of the quarantined zone) in July of that year. A new constitution was adopted that called for a shift to English as the primary language and a change of the name from 'North American Buddhist Mission' to 'The Buddhist Churches of America' (BCA).

But at the same time, these events reflect the forces that would shape the strong ethnic character of the BCA. This historical background served to galvanize the BCA communities to cohere around issues of ethnicity, which at times eclipsed the religious motivation in many of the churches' members.[22] Many BCA members came to equate being Japanese Americans with being Buddhists. In other words, their ethnically driven political identity and religious affiliation were intimately connected. By making this connection, they risked being seen as more foreign and less patriotic since, as we saw above, the American political establishment regarded Buddhism as foreign.

I now wish to examine the BCA's current situation in the 1990s by enumerating what I regard as ethnic preservation and ethnic rejection trends.

Ethnic Preservation Trends

A recent questionnaire surveying the opinions of teachers and parents of Dharma School (Sunday School) children in three temples in California, included the question, 'Why do you take or send your child/children to Dharma School?'[23] Following are some of the answers entered by the respondents:

— 'Learn Buddhism; fellowship with other Dharma School children and staff; association and linkage with other Japanese American families and friends'
— 'Expose them to Buddha Dharma; expose them to other Buddhist children'

— 'Exposure to Buddhist teachings and Japanese culture'
— 'To be exposed to Japanese culture and Buddhist thought'

These responses reveal motivations that are rooted in the parents' desire either to instill Japanese culture or to foster association with other Japanese Americans. In my own experience, these responses are representative of the *sansei* (third generation) who are now in their mid-thirties to mid-fifties.

This interest among the *sansei* parents may very well support the 'ethnic revival' thesis discussed by sociologists.[24] They maintain that in immigrant populations in general, those of the third generation take a deepened interest in their ethnicity and cultural heritage as compared to their parents, whose interests were financial stability and social acceptance. From their more privileged position, particularly in their educational background, the third generation is able and can afford to look back toward its ethnic heritage.

This thesis, in my view, does apply in great measure to *sanseis* in the BCA. We need not look very far to find examples of 'ethnic revival' cultural expression, such as the music group, *Hiroshima*, whose unique integration of Japanese instruments with contemporary American rhythm catapulted them to national recognition. In the political arena, the redress movement for the financial reparation of World War II internees was largely initiated and carried through by the ethnically inspired third generation. The success of this movement, which virtually everyone considered an improbability, could not have been accomplished by the second generation alone.

The BCA's high level of ethnicity can be discerned in the manner in which the temples also function in ways that sociologists call the 'base-institution.' The temples serve as legal umbrella organizations, providing facilities for clubs and sub-organizations engaged in cultural programs such as Japanese language school and martial arts.

It appears that cultural activities at the temples will continue to flourish, abetted in part by the sustained interest in both Asian martial arts and fine arts shown not only by Jōdo-Shinshū members but also by the public at large. The interest in Asian culture shows no signs of abating, since for a growing number of Americans it no longer carries the stigma of being foreign. Furthermore, this interest in Asian culture has gone beyond the traditional artistic forms to include values that are associated with or emerge directly from Buddhism. Many parents speak of the hope of instilling in their children such values as interdependence and cooperation, which they see as based in Buddhist or Japanese culture.

One major category of sub-organizations demonstrating a high degree of 'ethnicity as race' are the athletic groups, particularly basketball leagues. These leagues exist throughout the state of California wherever a large concentration of Japanese Americans is found; at least half of the Buddhist temples field teams and serve as sponsors or are affiliated with them in one form or another. Today, these athletic groups, starting with kindergartners, marshall a huge following with active participation of their *sansei* parents. Tournaments are held annually that take these teams considerable distances and include overnight stays with parental participation.

Such athletic events show no signs of waning. I predict that these groups will continue to be among the most vigorous affiliated organizations of the BCA temples. They attract a cohort of active, younger parents and a sizable number of children and youth. What makes the athletic organizations interesting to our study are their ethnic ties. Their common bond is not Buddhism or religion, but being Japanese American, since Christian churches and secular community groups also field teams within these leagues.[25] In my view, these athletic organizations have an enormous impact in reinforcing ethnic preservation.

Ethnic Rejection Trends

Compared to a heightened cultural awareness among members of the BCA, its racial composition will be increasingly diversified. Much of this is attributable to the large percentage of out-marriages among Japanese Americans, which hovers around 50 percent. No official statistics are available but I would estimate the percentage of biracial and biethnic[26] children in the Dharma schools throughout the BCA to be approximately 40 percent. Temples east of the Rocky Mountains report even higher numbers that are closer to 50 percent. Euro-Americans account for approximately 3 percent of the participant youths within all the BCA temples.

This trend toward racial and ethnic diversity is accentuated by the large percentage of former members who have dropped out. The younger generations who have remained in the temples are in reality a small segment compared to the group that has left the temples. While no official figures are available, it is my estimation that perhaps only one-quarter of the regular Dharma school students in the 1960s continue to be temple members. In the San Francisco urban area, for example, a temple member laments that out of twenty-five old friends only two have remained members, even though most of them were still living in the area. This is not uncommon. Even if we took the most optimistic figure, I would estimate that two-thirds of the *sanseis* who attended the temples in their youth are no longer regular members or attendees.

Already the percentage of non-Japanese American membership is estimated to be approximately 15 percent nationally; the figures will be higher outside California. Even within California, certain events such as the summer *Obon* bazaar festivals are attended by non-temple members of the larger community, often constituting as much as 70 percent of the crowd, as in the case of the Marysville temple in Northern California.

The leadership is also showing signs of change. A few years ago the BCA governing body, the National Board of Directors, included three non-Japanese American lay directors out of a total of forty-one.[27] Of the sixty-one current BCA ministers, five are Euro- Americans.[28] In my estimation, the number of non-Japanese interested in the ministry as a career will remain high in proportion to the general membership. This trend began around 1980 after which four of the five Euro-American priests were ordained. In the future, the percentage of non-Japanese Americans among the BCA seminary students at the Institute of Buddhist Studies (IBS) in California or in training in Japan will most likely continue to be high. Of the three IBS students closest to ordination, one is of Caucasian-Japanese parentage, another is of Hispanic and Filipino background, and the third is a Japanese American who was born in Japan and came to this country in his adolescence. Of the next group of students interested in the priesthood, one is biracial (Caucasian-Japanese parentage) and the other is Japanese American.[29]

In the area of cultural values, while the first two generations of Japanese Americans placed a premium on gratitude and obligation, younger generations clearly do not cherish them to the same degree. These traditional Japanese values are often at odds with their lives in the suburbs and particularly in their places of work, where self-assertiveness and self-preservation are required in order to survive and prosper. This conflict is often at the root of their questions concerning their attempts to live a Buddhist life in the modern world. Although younger generations may turn to the temples for cultural solace and a sense of community, it seems by all indicators that the community may not be effectively sustained by the values of gratitude, obligation, frugality, etc., as was so in the past.

Continual insistence on the use of Japanese language will undoubtedly be a source of hindrance and even annoyance for some. This sentiment can be discerned in the mixed responses in the above-mentioned survey to the chanting of *sūtras* in Jōdo-Shinshū services. While some find chanting (which is still predominately in Japanese) to be part of the services they enjoy, others clearly expressed unhappiness with not being able to *understand* what is being chanted.[30] The survey asked:

> When attending temple services, what part or aspect of the services gives you a 'good' feeling, or makes you feel good? Or what part or aspect of the service do you like the best? What aspects of temple services do you like the least? Why?

Examining responses to what aspects of services members liked the *least*, we find the following (S/B/W = temples: S = San Francisco, B = Berkeley, W = Watsonville; age; gender):

— 'Sutra chanting in foreign language.' (S, 46F)
— 'Chanting.' (B, 45F)

— 'Probably chanting, for I don't understand the purpose of repeating words I don't understand. When I read the translation, I'm not sure I want to say them. I generally feel uncomfortable with ritual practices.' (B, 44F)
— 'Basic rudimentary religious part: chanting.' (S, 43M)
— 'Sutra chanting, I don't understand the meaning of the sutra.' (W, 48F)
— 'Chanting. I can't relate too well. Not as meaningful, unless in English, but then it's awkward in English. It feels so mechanical or something. I think I'm not disciplined enough of a person to appreciate it!' (B, 38F)

These responses can be interpreted in many ways, but, in my view, they express dissatisfaction with participating in a liturgy rooted in another culture, whose language they do not understand. Members would be inclined to enjoy services more if they could understand more of the liturgy. As one member explained, 'I particularly enjoy "Gassho to Amida" (in English) because I can relate to it and understand what I am reciting or chanting' (S, 39F).

The use of Japanese language will continue to diminish as older Japanese-speaking members fade from the scene, and Japanese immigration to the United States remains low. And there are no signs that BCA temples will begin to attract in any significant numbers the non-immigrant Japanese nationals residing in this country on work visas. Those temples that still continue to hold separate services in Japanese are sparsely attended, mostly by English-speaking second-generation members who find the Japanese sermons nostalgic and more comforting. Use of the Japanese language is headed for an inevitable decline in most of the temples.

Restructuring Jōdo-Shinshū Education

Another major development taking place is the move to strengthen the temples' religious dimension. Spearheaded largely by a core group of younger American priests in their forties and early fifties,[31] the BCA leadership has begun serious deliberation on 'restructuring,' with the intent to better align the overall institution with the religious needs of a changing membership in the various temples. This proposal seeks to work on three areas: (1) the Institute of Buddhist Studies, (2) Buddhist education, and (3) BCA organizational structure.

The changes in the first two areas aim to enhance the quality of education of ministerial trainees and lay members, respectively. A more sweeping proposal in the third area seeks to change (1) the manner in which business is carried out at the BCA national level, (2) the role of the Bishop to one that is primarily a spiritual leader or an administrative manager of the ministers, (3) the way in which the limited number of ministers is allocated effectively among the temples, and (4) the role of the traditional hierarchy of main temples (*betsuin*) and its head minister (*rimban*).

This restructuring is part of the BCA attempt to clarify and define its identity as a Jōdo-Shinshū institution. One explicit manifestation of this attempt can be seen in a proposal by the Ministers Association to change the organization's name from 'Buddhist Churches of America' to 'Jōdo-Shinshū Buddhists of America.' After being submitted at the annual meeting of the BCA in February 1994, this proposal was tabled for further study. We must wait at least until February 1999 to know the final decision. Whether the name change passes or not is less significant than the proposal itself, for it reflects the institution's ongoing reappraisal of its identity in response to the changing membership pattern within as well as to other Buddhist and religious communities in the continental United States.

Whatever changes occur, the ethnic elements of the BCA will certainly not be completely eliminated. As stated above, they will continue to persist but will no longer be the defining or core elements of the BCA temples. Many within the BCA realize that ethnicity can no longer be the common bond that holds together the religious communities. They are calling for the religious dimension to assert itself as the common bond and the unchallenged primary purpose of the temples.

This is not to imply, of course, that the BCA was somehow bereft of educational and propagation efforts. To the contrary, history reveals a series of endeavors that were quite progressive in content. They include (1) the publication of *The Light of Dharma* journal in English that reached a thousand mostly non-Japanese subscribers for several years beginning in 1901; (2) the establishment of a Buddhist Sunday school system in 1914; (3) the hosting of the 1915 World Buddhist Conference in San Francisco, drawing delegates from East Asia, Southwest Asia, Mexico, and Hawaii; (4) the ordination of a number of Caucasian priests in the 1930s; (5) the establishment in 1949 of the Buddhist Study Center in Berkeley which served as one of the country's few centers of Buddhist academic learning; (6) the development of the Buddhist Study Center into the Institute of Buddhist Studies in 1966 as a graduate school, which in 1986 evolved into a formal affiliation with the Graduate Theological Union in Berkeley; and (7) the 1987 decision by the U.S. Army to grant the BCA the right to train and certify Buddhist chaplains for its forces.[32] Aside from these benchmark developments, the BCA has conducted religious education since its inception. It was in these Jōdo-Shinshū settings that some Buddhist scholars and thinkers received early Buddhist teaching and inspiration, including Richard Robinson, Alex Wayman, Leo Pruden, Gary Snyder, and Jack Kerouac.

This push toward Dharma-centered temples is partially due to an increased desire to understand Buddhist teachings on the part of a growing number of members, including newer converts. The younger generation is better educated and less ethnically isolated and lives in a religiously pluralistic world. Their family makeup is often one of religious diversity. They feel a need to better understand their religion for themselves and to explain their teaching in an intelligent manner to those of other faiths.

In actualizing the new education reforms, the BCA leadership will need to reconcile the growing push to emphasize Jōdo-Shinshū teaching (as manifested in the proposed name change) with so-called general Buddhism, represented by the teachings of the Four Noble Truths and the Six Paramitas. In the past, these teachings had been stressed, in the opinion of many, at the expense of Jōdo-Shinshū teachings, which were felt to be understandable only after the basics were mastered. As it turned out, a large segment of the second generation was educated primarily in these general Buddhist teachings with only an emotional appreciation of Jōdo-Shinshū.[33]

There will inevitably be a renewed focus on Jōdo-Shinshū teachings in order for the BCA to define its identity within the American context. One of the questions to be resolved is the degree to which the basic Buddhist teachings are included or excluded in this process. This task is intimately related, in my view, to the incessant requests by lay members to be instructed in ethical guidelines from a Jōdo-Shinshū point of view. There is a growing need to be able to apply the spiritual teachings to everyday concerns. Further, such core Jōdo-Shinshū doctrine as Amida and Pure Land will require, as a recent survey of the BCA membership suggests, presentation other than literal explanation.[34] Moreover, efforts also will be needed to clarify the teachings centered on *shinjin* (often rendered 'faith') in relation to the Protestant emphasis on faith. Undoubtedly, scholars have dealt with these issues in the past, but the time has now arrived for the BCA to undertake a concerted effort in 'Shinshū-ology' in the rapidly changing American social and religious milieu.

At stake in the restructuring of Jōdo-Shinshū education is the fundamental question: can the BCA make the effective transition from being traditionally ethnic-centered to becoming more Dharma-centered? The co-existence of the religious and ethnic dimensions in the BCA from its inception, as seen above, is approaching a threshold for a major change in balance and direction.

Some Concluding Thoughts

The projected changes within the BCA will further call into question the adequacy of a simplistic binary model of Buddhism in America. It will become increasingly unsatisfactory to subsume the BCA under the traditional ethnic model, given the 'Americanization' process that has taken place for nearly one hundred years. This holds true even for the tripartite model (elite or import, missionary or export, and immigrant or baggage) proposed by Jan Nattier; given its century of existence in North America, 'furniture' appears more appropriate a category than 'baggage.'

Within the context of the controversy initiated by Helen Tworkov's view that 'Asian American Buddhists ... so far ... have not figured prominently in the development of something called American Buddhism,' the accomplishments of the BCA, as seen, for example, in its role as the only certifying institution for the U.S. Armed Forces Buddhist chaplains; or its seminary, the Institute of Buddhist Studies, forging a relationship with a consortium of Christian seminaries (the Graduate Theological Union, Berkeley) to confer a joint M.A. degree, warrant further evaluation and consideration.

The intimate connection between ethnicity and religion applies to virtually all religious groups in North America. The BCA certainly fits this pattern. However, the role of ethnicity was even more critical and enduring for a non-Christian and non-European immigrant population such as the BCA membership, whose Buddhist identity was specifically equated with ethnic origin and, in the eyes of the dominant society and political leadership, even with a foreign government, i.e., the Japanese emperor. For a Japanese American to be Buddhist before the Second World War came at the risk of being perceived as un-American and even anti-American.

Projecting our view into the near future, although ethnicity will continue to be a salient feature of the BCA, it will diminish in importance, particularly in its racial dimension due to the high level of inter-marriages, new converts, and to the coming of age of the less ethnic-oriented fourth-generation membership. Even the cultural dimension will undergo a process of selection in which only those arts that are in accord with the popular American taste – such as Taiko drumming – will survive and prosper. This development will bring about greater heterogeneity within the BCA, and as a result, ethnicity will play a lesser role as the bonding force of the community. The BCA leadership will be severely challenged by the erosion of homogeneity based on ethnicity. In response to the changing times, efforts will be made to move the Dharma more to center stage as the foundation of the institution. Consequently, religious education will be strengthened, which should bring about greater inclusivity and diversity. In defining its indentity, the BCA must inevitably address the issue of the boundaries of the Jōdo-Shinshū tradition and its uniqueness in relation to other Buddhist schools.

Selected Bibliography

Annual Report (compiled and maintained by the Buddhist Churches of America since the 1950s, they serve as valuable resource).

Bloom, Alfred. 'Shin Buddhism Plants Roots in America: A Socio-Historical Perspective.' In Charles Prebish and Kenneth Tanaka, eds., *The Faces of Buddhism in America*. Berkeley: University of California Press, forthcoming.

Kashima, Tetsuden. *Buddhism in America: The Social Organization of an Ethnic Religious Organization.* Westport, CT: Greenwood Press, 1977.
____. 'The Buddhist Churches of America: Challenges for Change in the 21st Century,' in *The Pacific World*, n.s., 6 (Fall 1990): 28–40.
Matsuura, Shinobu. *Compassionate Vow.* Berkeley: Matsuura Family, 1986.
Munekata, Ryo, ed. *Buddhist Churches of America.* Vol. 1: *75 Year History, 1899–1974.* Chicago: Nobart, Inc., 1974.
Tanaka, Kenneth. 'Symbolism of Amida and Pure Land in the American Context.' *The Pure Land*, n.s., 8–9 (December 1992): 64–87.
____. *Ocean: An Introduction to Jodo-Shinshu Buddhism in America.* Berkeley: WisdomOcean Publications, 1997.
Tuck, Donald. *Buddhist Churches of Canada: Jodo Shinshu.* Lewiston, NY: The Edwin Mellen Press, 1987.
Wheel of Dharma (a monthly publication of the Buddhist Churches of America).
Yoo, David. 'Enlightened Identities: Buddhism and Japanese Americans of California, 1924–1941.' *Western Historical Quarterly* (Autumn 1996): 281–301.

Notes

1 An account of a wife of a BCA minister residing in the central coast region of California. See below for a fuller citation of her description. Shinobu Matsuura, *Compassionate Vow* (Berkeley: Matsuura Family, 1986), 63.
2 My role within the BCA has been that of an active participant since adolescence as a Dharma (or Sunday) school student, a youth leader, a seminarian, and a BCA minister. My academic role as a faculty member of the Institute of Buddhist Studies has also permitted me to be involved in academic activities at the Graduate Theological Union and the University of California, Berkeley.
3 Nishi-Hongwanji (or Hompa Hongwanji-ha) and Higashi-Hongwanji (or Ōtani-ha) are by far the two largest among the ten existing branches of the Jōdo-Shinshū school in Japan and are the only ones represented in the United States. Of these two, Nishi-Hongwanji is overwhelmingly larger, with approximately 175 temples, fellowships, and branches, compared to approximately ten belonging to Higashi-Hongwanji.
4 *1997–1998 Directory* (San Francisco: Buddhist Churches of America, 1997), 2–10.
5 *1996 Annual Report* (San Francisco: Buddhist Churches of America, 1997), 29. Due to the method of determining membership, the actual 1996 membership population is significantly larger. These figures do not include children and even adult, married children who may continue to participate in the temple activities as part of the *family* headed by their dues-paying parents. There are also Japanese American families who are not official members but participate in many of the cultural programs held at the temples. Further, actual statistics are even more difficult to obtain since temples maintain differing sets of criteria for determining membership.
6 Donald Tuck, *Buddhist Churches of Canada: Jodo Shinshu* (Lewiston, NY: The Edwin Mellen Press, 1987), 78, 96.
7 For an excellent discussion of this debate, see Charles Prebish, 'Two Buddhisms Reconsidered,' *Buddhist Studies Review* 10, no. 2 (1993): 187–206. This issue surfaced in essays for the general readership by Victor Sōgen Hori and Rick Fields in *Tricycle: The Buddhist Review* (Fall 1994): 48–52, 54–56.
8 Realizing this 'hidden' treasure of these cultural expressions, some Euro-American writers such as Rick Fields and Jan Nattier have suggested that

Euro-American Buddhists re-evaluate and even learn from the rich complex of cultural-religious heritage practiced in the ethnic temples. See essays by Fields cited above and by Nattier mentioned below. See also Rick Fields and Don Farber, *Taking Refuge in Los Angeles: Life in a Vietnamese Buddhist Temple* (New York: Aperture Foundation, 1987).

9 *Tricycle: The Buddhist Review* (Winter 1991): 4. Ryo Imamura sent a rebuttal, and the controversy intensified when the rebuttal was not printed. His letter and Tworkov's reply were printed in *The Sangha Newsletter* (Newsletter of the Wider Shin Buddhist Fellowship), 7 (Summer 1994): 2–10.

10 Jan Nattier, 'Visible and Invisible,' *Tricycle: The Buddhist Review* (Fall 1995): 42–49. The quotation appears on p. 49a. A more academic treatment of this subject will appear in her essay included in a volume co-edited by Charles Prebish and myself, *The Faces of Buddhism in America,* (University of California Press, 1998.)

11 The most prominent among these has been 'gratitude,' which Robert Bellah not only cited as the hallmark of Tokugawa religious value but one noticeably prominent among Jōdo-Shinshū followers.

12 Ryo Munekata, ed., *Buddhist Churches of America:* Vol. 1, *75 Year History, 1899–1974* (Chicago: Nobart Inc., 1974), 47.

13 Tetsuden Kashima, *Buddhism in America: The Social Organization of an Ethnic Religious Organization* (Westport, CT: Greenwood Press, 1977), 14.

14 This is based on a personal conversation with a BCA minister who knew several older ministers who had experienced their government's admonition. It does not appear to be a documented policy but more in the realm of an 'unwritten rule.' Rev. Julius Goldwater further corroborated this in a phone interview in November 1994. He was one of the few Caucasian Jōdo-Shinshū priests who served the BCA community in the years immediately prior to and during World War II in the Los Angeles area and served as custodian of temples during the incarceration of the Japanese Americans.

15 Kashima, *Buddhism in America,* 32.

16 Ibid., 32.

17 Ibid., 32.

18 Ibid., 17–18; Ryo Munekata, *Buddhist Churches of America,* 49.

19 Kosei Ogura, 'A Sociological Study of the Buddhist Churches in North America, with a Case Study of Gardena, California, Congregation,' Master's Thesis, University of Southern California, 1932, 85–86.

20 Matsuura, *Compassionate Vow,* 63. I have taken the liberty of affixing brief explanations of the Buddhist terms in the parentheses that follow the terms.

21 Ibid., 65.

22 Kashima, *Buddhism in America,* 20–21. He cites San Diego and Guadalupe as examples of temples that had a strong sense of ethnic community. In San Diego, it was the 1916 overflow of the nearby dam that served as a catalyst to consolidate the community toward the founding of the temple. The Guadalupe community was Buddhist due to pragmatic reasons; it turns out that the Buddhist missionaries in Los Angeles responded positively one day earlier than their Christian counterparts to the request for the establishment of a religious center. This sealed the Buddhist affiliation of their religious center.

23 As part of Shinshū History II course in the spring semester 1993, four students at the Institute of Buddhist Studies conducted a survey based on a questionnaire at Berkeley, San Francisco, and Watsonville BCA temples. The survey's objectives were to determine 1) profiles of the pupils, parents, and teachers of the Dharma schools, 2) the parents' reasons for taking their children to Dharma

school, 3) their reasons for belonging to a BCA temple, 4) their level of knowledge about the basic teachings, and 5) the degree to which their Buddhist understanding was actually connected to Japanese cultural beliefs, customs, and practice.

24 Marcus L. Hansen, 'The Third Generation in America,' *Commentary* 14 (1952): 492–503.

25 For example, in the San Francisco Bay area the East Bay League includes teams from three Buddhist temples (Berkeley Sangha, Berkeley Otani, and Southern Alameda County), two Christian churches (El Cerrito Free Methodist and Buena Vista in Alameda), and three community organizations (Mt. Eden in Hayward, Oakland, and Diablo in Concord).

26 The term 'biethnic' here refers to children of marriage between a Japanese American and an American of another Asian descent.

27 *Buddhist Churches of America: 1994–1995 Directory* (San Francisco: Buddhist Churches of America, 1994), 12–14. Since 1994, this number has dropped to one in 1996 and 1997.

28 *Buddhist Churches of America: 1997–1998 Directory* (San Francisco: Buddhist Churches of America, 1997), 2–10.

29 These figures are as of September 1997.

30 The following are *positive* responses toward chanting: Chanting is a good feeling. Listening to the message is expanding. (W, 39F); Enjoy sutra chanting and sermon. (S, 35M); Chanting and meditation. (B, 30F); Chanting and the meditation. (S, 28M); The chanting (especially when there is a large congregation) is very stimulating. I also enjoy singing, and actually wish that we would sing more songs during service. (B, 26F); I enjoy Dharma talks that are applicable to me and my life. Also enjoy chanting. (B, 21M); Sutra chanting, sermon, interaction after the service. (W, 47F)

   The positive nature of these responses does not necessarily mean, of course, that the respondents are in favor of chanting in Japanese over English or that they support the use of Japanese language in the temples.

31 Approximately half of the sixty-one priests are missionaries from Japan, most of whom are committed to living permanently in the United States as permanent residents or naturalized citizens. The other half are Americans of Japanese heritage, with the exception of the five Euro-American priests previously mentioned. The American-born (second) group is generally younger and, unlike virtually all of the Japan-born priests, come from families where the father was not a priest.

32 For this to be realized, the BCA had to fulfill two primary requirements, the existence of a national organization and a qualified seminary program. BCA's long experience as a nationally organized system with headquarters in San Francisco fulfilled the former requirement. The Masters program at the Institute of Buddhist Studies fulfilled the latter.

   This Buddhist chaplaincy received ample coverage in the media, particularly in the California press, including the *Los Angeles Times*, *San Jose Mercury and News*, and the *San Francisco Chronicle*. Such media attention was proof that the general American public recognized the significance of the program. This development was not without a controversy within the BCA, however. The supporters saw it as the recognition of the legitimacy of Buddhism in this country, while the opponents objected to the affiliation with the military on spiritual and moral grounds. The training program has yet to produce a single candidate and has attracted very little interest within the BCA. Nevertheless, the BCA role in the chaplaincy program is ironic given its historical past, for it was in the Topaz, Utah relocation camp, administered and guarded by the army, that efforts began to restructure the original organization under a new name, the Buddhist Churches of America.

33   The emphasis on general Buddhism and teachings within the BCA was due in part to their ethical and 'logical' qualities. These were perhaps easier to grasp for the lay teachers and members and also served to instill moral values among the young. Further, these basic teachings were presented as philosophy rather than as religion, which proved palatable to the members who regarded Buddhism as 'a system of thought and way of life,' not as a religion in the usual sense.

34   See Kenneth K. Tanaka, 'Symbolism of Amida and Pure Land in the American Context,' *The Pure Land,* n.s., 8–9 (December 1992): 64–87. An informal survey taken in 1990 shows that the BCA respondents prefer a symbolic rather than a literal understanding of Amida and Pure Land.

CHAPTER TWO

Japanese American Zen Temples: Cultural Identity and Economics

Senryō Asai and Duncan Ryūken Williams

Zen Temples, Centers, and Monasteries

The American 'Zen boom' of the 1950s and 1960s and the subsequent proliferation of Zen centers and monasteries between 1970 and 1990 has been well documented.[1] However, the first American Zen temples, built by Japanese immigrants for the Japanese American community, were established nearly fifty years earlier, in 1913 in Hawaii and in 1922 on the mainland United States. Despite these roots in early-twentieth-century American history, traditional Japanese American Zen temples have received little scholarly attention and have been overshadowed by the Zen centers formed during and after the 'Zen boom.'

The Zen centers and monasteries built in the United States after 1960, with a primarily Euro-American membership,[2] have focused on Zen meditation as a major activity. In this paper, we will refer to these meditation-focused institutions as *Zen centers* (found largely in urban areas) and *Zen monasteries* (more often located in rural settings). In the approximately 250 Zen centers and monasteries in the United States,[3] Zen meditation is the foremost activity, and membership is comprised mainly of Euro-Americans. These Zen centers and monasteries offer regular daily, weekly, and monthly schedules of practice. Insofar as the Zen tradition has often been characterized as 'the meditation school' within Buddhism, that Zen centers and monasteries stress meditation is not surprising. In this paper, however, we will show how meditation is not, and never has been, a major focus at the traditional Japanese American *Zen temples*. Instead, the Zen temple has served as a Japanese American community center with its major activities geared toward the maintenance of community and familial ties through death rites and 'Japanese culture' activities, including tea ceremonies, folk dancing, and other Japanese cultural events.

Rather than meditation centers or training monasteries, these Japanese American institutions are better termed Zen temples as they closely resemble the *dankadera* (parish temples) of Japan. *Dankadera*, which constitute over 90 percent of Zen temples in Japan, also rarely offer Zen meditation practice; they instead focus on death rites such as funerals and ancestral memorial services. In this paper these institutions will be termed 'temples,' as they correspond to the average Japanese *'tera'* or *'ji'* (temple) as opposed to a *'sōdō'* (training monastery). Training monasteries, which offer Zen meditation, constitute less than 1 percent of Zen institutions in Japan.[4] Through an analysis of the economics of Japanese American Zen temples, focusing on revenue sources and expenditures, we will show how death rites along with the maintenance of 'Japanese culture' are the chief activities of these Japanese American temples.

Temple Membership and Cultural Identity

There are fourteen Japanese American Zen temples of the Sōtō Zen tradition in the United States; of these, nine are in Hawaii and five are on the mainland.[5] In this chapter, we examine three of the oldest and most representative of these temples: Shōbōji, the headquarters of the Hawaiian Sōtō school, founded in 1913 in Honolulu; Zenshūji, the headquarters of the North American Sōtō school, founded in 1922 in Los Angeles; and Sōkōji, founded in 1934 in San Francisco.

All of these temples were established for Japanese American immigrants who had belonged to the Sōtō Zen school in Japan. Japanese Sōtō Zen priests were sent to establish these temples for the Japanese American community as branch temples of the two Japanese headquarter temples, Eiheiji (Fukui Prefecture) and Sōjiji (Kanagawa Prefecture).

In the Sōtō tradition, religious affiliation is not an individual matter but a larger familial and community concern.[6] Thus, the official membership at the Japanese American Sōtō Zen temples has been based on the numbers of families rather than on individuals. Euro-American Zen centers have departed from this practice, tabulating their membership on individual members.

In 1997, the combined membership of the two largest American temples was 1,100 families, 800 families at Shōbōji in Hawaii and 300 at Zenshūji in Los Angeles. The number of families belonging to these Zen temples has not fluctuated very much over the past several decades, though all Japanese American temples (particularly those of the American Jōdo Shin tradition) have experienced a slight but steady decline in membership over the past two decades as first- and second-generation members pass away.[7] At Shōbōji in Hawaii, this decline has been more pronounced in the 1990s, given its longer history (see the Membership Dues line in Table 1).

However, this decline is slight compared to the larger picture, which shows that membership has been remarkably stable over the past fifty years.[8] This stability is based on the fact that family and community obligations to the temples, in the form of death rites and cultural activities,

21

Table 1 Shōboji's Revenue

	1980	1983	1986	1989	1992	1995	96 Estimated	96 Actual	97 Estimated
Memorial Services	$17,125.00	$23,015.00	$27,043.00	$29,185.00	$33,907.82	$31,718.63	$31,000.00	$29,172.50	$30,000.00
Funeral Services	$11,140.00	$18,820.00	$19,345.00	$17,785.00	$21,900.00	$21,350.00	$21,000.00	$18,350.00	$20,000.00
Donations	$5,677.00	$12,505.00	$15,658.00	$22,218.22	$34,736.35	$25,063.03	$30,000.00	$20,008.51	$20,000.00
Membership Dues	$34,673.00	$41,914.00	$45,230.00	$47,467.00	$52,892.00	$49,149.00	$50,000.00	$46,823.00	$47,000.00
Crematorium	$1,694.00	$1,727.00	$2,097.00	$1,612.51	$1,679.00	$2,482.00	$1,500.00	$1,506.00	$1,500.00
Dormitory	$21,567.00	$21,782.00	$35,028.50	$50,745.00	$62,445.00	$38,480.00	$40,000.00	$31,778.00	$35,000.00
Wedding	$2,180.00	$2,727.00	$1,780.00	$1,325.00	$1,450.00	$375.00	$500.00	$975.00	$500.00
Hall Rental	$5,863.00	$7,440.00	$3,560.00	$1,804.50	hall closed	---	---	---	---
Incense Sales	$1,907.00	$1,589.00	$1,611.50	$2,757.70	$1,991.00	$1,694.00	$1,700.00	$1,783.00	$1,700.00
Sōtō Radio Show	$2,417.00	$2,200.00	$1,890.00	$1,500.00	$1,285.00	$1,500.00	$1,500.00	$1,500.00	$1,500.00
Women's Association	$332.98	$412.13	$460.10	$325.02	$287.96	$204.42	$200.00	$195.23	$200.00
Tea Sales	$272.00	$257.00	$212.00	$76.00	sales stopped	---	---	---	---
Obon Service	$16,340.41	$19,932.25	$17,916.56	$22,613.00	$22,331.00	$25,819.00	$30,000.00	$25,726.00	$30,000.00
Higan Services	$4,722.50	$7,600.00	$5,862.00	$7,171.00	$7,131.00	$6,407.00	$6,500.00	$6,500.00	$6,500.00
Sutra Reading	$892.00	$1,168.54	$897.00	$1,277.00	$1,198.00	$1,196.20	$1,000.00	$995.00	$1,000.00
Jpn. Lang. School	$23,877.39	$24,000.00	$15,000.00	$14,800.00	$16,000.00	$12,000.00	$12,000.00	$12,000.00	$16,000.00
Health Insurance	$878.12	$4,656.28	$10,531.26	$13,699.08	sales stopped	---	---	---	---
Offering Box	$2,549.70	$2,757.89	$2,833.47	$3,301.20	$3,802.86	$3,240.00	$3,000.00	$3,228.00	$3,000.00
Postcard Sales	$1,480.45	$551.52	$122.00	$160.50	sales stopped	---	---	---	---
Vending Machines	$5,184.50	$4,041.00	$5,392.17	$5,232.45	sales stopped	---	---	---	---
Misc. Commission	$162.22	$131.16	$218.15	$293.76	$316.80	$189.18	$200.00	$118.05	$200.00
Judo Instruction	$348.00	$211.00	$525.00	$375.00	class stopped	---	---	---	---
Miscellaneous	$4,217.11	$4,071.55	$2,894.50	$2,033.50	$2,122.00	$7,458.32	$3,000.00	$12,248.96	$12,000.00
Bazaar Fund Raising	$9,943.50	$11,000.00	$12,716.44	$12,896.00	$12,000.00	$12,000.00	$12,000.00	$12,000.00	$12,000.00
Interest (Checking)	$1,018.62	$1,191.00	$3,962.06	$1,728.85	$988.36	$400.39	$350.00	$362.08	$350.00
Interest (Savings)	$17,293.74	$14,585.42	$6,271.29	$5,000.00	$8,666.43	$8,000.00	N/A	N/A	N/A
Stands at Bon Dance	$2,027.00	$2,290.00	$2,293.00	$1,772.00	$1,500.00	$2,411.00	$1,500.00	N/A	N/A
New Year Service	$1,519.00	$3,546.00	$3,578.36	$5,431.00	$5,481.00	$5,000.00	$5,257.00	$5,000.00	N/A
New Year Party	$1,096.00	$782.00	$750.84	$415.00	$709.00	$530.00	$800.00	$970.00	$800.00
TOTAL	$177,558.50	$218,001.32	$239,109.55	$285,959.39	$301,482.57	$254,780.46	$245,750.00	$242,614.76	$253,750.00

override personal faith in Zen Buddhism or the practice of Zen meditation. This is in contrast to the relative instability of membership at Euro-American Zen centers. At the Euro-American Zen Center of Los Angeles, for example, while there has been a core group of members, there has been a high turnover rate outside this core group.[9] In addition, following the 1995 death of Taizan Maezumi, the founder and head abbot of the Zen Center of Los Angeles, there was a significant drop in membership (from 150 active members to 70 members after his death).[10] What this suggests is that Euro-American Zen centers revolve around a core group of individuals with a high percentage of temporary members whose main allegiance is to the head teacher. This prompts a decline in membership when the charismatic leader passes away. In contrast, Zenshūji, the Japanese American Zen temple in Los Angeles, has maintained a stable membership of 300 families despite a constant turnover of the head priest. The charisma of the priest, or the lack thereof, has a neglible effect on membership because, as we shall see below, it is not mystical experiences found in Zen meditation or erudite interpretations of Zen *kōans* which are important at Japanese American Zen temples, but rather the performance of death rites and the maintenance of Japanese cultural identity as a community center.

Temple Economics: Death Rites and Japanese Culture

The examination of temple economics is a relatively neglected approach to American Buddhist studies.[11] Tracking temple activity through an analysis of temple revenues and expenditures allows us to utilize quantitative data to compare and balance the somewhat more subjective approaches – such as participant-observation or interviewing – generally used to study American Buddhism.

In Zenshūji temple in Los Angeles, for example, the income and expenditures from 1979 to 1995 reflects an economic situation that has been remarkably stable (see Table 2). Since 1981, income has exceeded expenditures with an average of a 7 percent increase each year. The mean annual income during this sixteen-year period was $136,187, while the mean annual expenditure was $126,400. This fiscal stability has been maintained by most Japanese American temples through two major sources of revenue: death rites and Japanese culture activities.

As in parish temples in Japan, the performance of death rites, or what Taijō Tamamuro, the historian of Japanese Buddhism, has called '*sōshiki Bukkyō*' (funerary Buddhism),[12] is the single largest source of revenue at Japanese American Zen temples. A more detailed analysis of Zenshūji's income (Table 3) reveals that donations from funerals and memorial services for the dead is the biggest income source in any given year (for example, 37 percent of the total income, $61,420, in 1991).[13] These donations are, in effect, fees for the performance of ancestral rites which

Table 2   Accounts at Zenshūji

	1979	1980	1981	1982	1983	1984	1985	1986
REVENUE	$90,000	$82,000	$101,000	$104,000	$100,000	$120,000	$115,000	$133,000
EXPENSES	$82,000	$86,000	$93,000	$95,000	$95,000	$113,000	$115,000	$125,000

	1987	1988	1989	1990	1991	1992	1993	1994	1995
REVENUE	$136,000	$162,000	$153,000	$170,000	$166,000	$172,000	N/A	$185,000	$190,000
EXPENSES	$130,000	$145,000	$149,000	$158,000	$155,000	$169,000	N/A	N/A	$186,000

Table 3   Zenshūji's Revenue

	1980	1988	1989	1990	1991	1992	1994	1995
Memorial Services	42%	24%	27%	26%	24%	29%	32%	30%
Membership Dues	18%	12%	13%	13%	15%	14%	19%	18%
Room Rental	18%	12%	13%	10%	11%	11%	10%	8%
Funeral Services	7%	9%	8%	10%	5%	6%	7%	7%
Special Donations	6%	9%	7%	12%	13%	7%	4%	6%
Altar Accessories	5%	4%	5%	3%	3%	4%	2%	4%
Miscellaneous	4%	5%	4%	6%	6%	6%	1%	5%
Carnival		16%	14%	11%	11%	11%	11%	11%
Parking Fees	3%	2%	2%	4%	4%	3%	3%	
Daruma & Mochi		2%	3%	3%	5%	4%	5%	4%
Other	10%	4%	4%	4%	3%	4%	6%	4%

include funerals as well as memorial services.[14] Memorial services in the Japanese American Zen temples are of three types: 1) those held for one's own deceased family members at regular intervals after their death (Year 3, 7, 13, etc.); 2) a monthly service for every temple member who died in a particular month; and 3) seasonal services for family ancestors (*Obon* in August and *Higan* in March and September). Since these death rites are the most frequent activities at the temple, it is not surprising that the temples earn their greatest revenue from them. The figures from 1996 are: Zenshūji (Los Angeles), 37 percent (Table 3); Shōbōji (Honolulu), 41 percent (Table 1); and Sōkōji (San Francisco), 31 percent (Table 4).

It is not only ancestral rites that characterize the main activities of Japanese American temples, but also their commitment to maintaining Japanese culture. We can see the temple's function as a community center as part of a larger pattern among Asian American temples as a whole; studies on more recent immigrant groups, such as Laotian and Thai, show a parallel function of the temple.[15]

In Asian American temples, one of the key vehicles of maintaining cultural identity has been language instruction. While this has been

Table 4   Sōkōji's Revenue 1996

Funeral/Memorial Services	31%
Membership Fees	12%
Hall Rental	15%
Parking Fees	19%
Food Bazaar	17%
Rummage Sale	2%
Shichi-Go-San Fees	3%
Other	1%

historically the case at Japanese American Buddhist temples, there has been a shift from a focus on language to broader cultural activities in the past decade. This is due to the fact that an increasing number of younger Japanese Americans are not learning Japanese because, unlike first-generation immigrants, they are first and foremost Americans, and few plan to return to Japan. The shift from Japanese to English among second- and third-generation Japanese American families is reflected at the Los Angeles Zenshūji in the language used in services such as funerals and weddings. Up until 1965, services were conducted solely in Japanese, but from 1965 to 1980 both Japanese and English were used; finally, since 1985 these ceremonies have been performed solely in English. In addition to English services, another indication that interest in Japanese language has diminished at Japanese American Zen temples is the decline of the temples' Japanese language schools. The Japanese language school at Hawaii's Shōbōji, called Wakei Gakuen, has seen a steady decline in students and revenue since the mid-1980s (see Table 1, Japanese Language School line). The Los Angeles Zenshūji language school, Terakoya, was closed in 1996 when it failed to attract enough students.

Thus, it is not Japanese language, but Japanese culture, that is the second organizing activity of Japanese American Zen temples. These activities include 'culture classes' in subjects such as the Japanese tea ceremony, calligraphy, flower arrangement, and Japanese folk song and dance. Both young people and adults attend. The most popular activity for the youth at both Zenshūji and Shōbōji is Japanese folk drumming, called *taiko*. Although drumming was originally presented in 1986 as an activity for the Buddhist priest to teach young people about Buddhism, Buddhist education took a back seat when the priest who started the drumming group returned to Japan and its leadership shifted to a layperson.[16] What this suggests is that Japanese cultural activities, not Buddhist religious education or practice, draw the membership to the temple.[17]

The interest in Japanese culture can be seen in both the revenue and the expenditures of the temple. In addition to the culture classes, which bring in fees assessed for the use of temple space (see Table 3, Room Rental line), a number of cultural activities with some connection to Buddhism make up a significant portion of the temple's income. These include the *Obon* dance and carnival, originally related to a Buddhist memorial service honoring one's ancestors, and now simply a traditional summer event in Japan. Members gather with their extended family at the temple to participate in folk dancing and to enjoy Japanese food and music.[18] This summer event is also a big fundraiser for the temple as family members, their friends, and non-Japanese Americans visit the temple. In 1996, for example, Hawaii's Shōbōji attracted 5,000 visitors during the ten-day *Obon* festival. Los Angeles's Zenshūji raised 11 percent of its total budget – amounting to $20,900 – from the *Obon* festival stalls (Table 3, Carnival line). Another recent Buddhist-inspired Japanese cultural source of revenue is the sale of 'Daruma' dolls at Zenshūji (Table 3, Daruma and Mochi line). 'Daruma' is the Japanese term for Bodhidharma, the first patriarch of Zen in China, but the meaning has lost its Zen Buddhist connection in modern Japan.[19] Although Daruma is a Chinese Zen figure, the general Japanese and Japanese American public know Daruma mainly as a red doll which symbolizes tenacity and determination to accomplish goals. The dolls are used by everyone from politicians, business executives, and high school students who paint in one of Daruma's eyes while making a pledge to accomplish a goal, such as winning an election, successfully conducting a business negotiation, or getting into a college. The practice is concluded with the painting of the other eye when the goal is accomplished. These dolls, while originally having a Buddhist inspiration, have become a cultural commodity rather than a religious object of devotion for most Japanese Americans.

Japanese culture is so central to Japanese American Zen temples that even cultural activities with no relationship to Buddhism have become major activities at the temple. For example, a full 17 percent of San Francisco's Sōkōji's total income in 1996 came from a food bazaar held in conjunction with a cherry-blossom festival in April (Table 4, Food Bazaar line). Food seems to be an important aspect of maintaining Japanese culture in other events as well: the *Obon* festival and the New Year period, when *mochi,* or rice cakes, are sold (Table 3, Daruma and Mochi line). While not everyone at the temple may speak Japanese anymore or believe fervently in Buddhism, Japanese food remains a consistent aspect of Japanese American Zen temple culture.

Another temple ceremony that is not related to traditional Buddhism is the performance of *Shichigosan* (literally, seven-five-three) service, a celebration of a child's rite of passage commonly held at Shintō shrines in Japan. Sōkōji began offering this service in 1990 (1996 at Zenshūji) because it is one of the most popular rituals in Japanese culture.[20] These types of cultural events, of course, have their parallel in Christian confirmation or Jewish bar/bat mitzvah services, and in such events as church bazaars.

The temple as a locus for Japanese culture is also exemplified by the Zen temples' role in representing Japanese culture for non-Japanese Americans. For example, until 1989 one substantial source of income at Hawaii's Shōbōji was a guided temple tour for visitors and tourists to Hawaii who wanted to 'experience Japan' without having to go there (Table 1, Postcard Sales, Vending Machines, and Tea Sales lines). In the 1980s, several bus loads of tourists would come on package tours from the mainland on a daily basis for a guided tour of the temple grounds and an opportunity to purchase such items as Japanese tea and postcards. As such, the temple represented Japanese culture while at the same time raising revenue through vending machines and the sale of postcards and Japanese green tea. The role of representing culture was not unique to Shōbōji and can be seen at other Asian American temples, such as the Eastern States Buddhist Association in Chinatown (New York), which has long been a destination on the Shortline Sightseeing Bus tour of New York.[21]

A shift to a more secular arena for maintaining the temple's economy can be seen after 1990 when Japanese American temple leaders recognized the slow, but sure, decline in the amount of revenue raised from ancestral memorial rites. In 1990 the abbot of Hawaii's Shōbōji, Jihō Machida, responding to a 5 percent annual drop in membership, rebuilt the social hall to serve as a local non-denominational elementary school. This new Sōtō Academy flourished in the open market for private elementary schools in Hawaii. Indeed, the 1996 net income was nearly $100,000, which allowed for a $20,000 contribution back into the temple's finances (Table 6).[22] Even though it is non-religious, one of the attractions for Japanese American parents is its connection to Japanese culture.

This strong emphasis on Japanese culture is also reflected in the way the Japanese American Zen temples prioritize expenditures. For example, the temples' efforts to teach Buddhism, especially to young people, has become a remarkably low priority. At Zenshūji, for example, the budget of the Young Buddhist Association for teaching Buddhism at 'Sunday school' and 'Zen school' has hovered close to just 1 percent of the total budget (Table 5, Young Buddhist Association line). Indeed, after allocating $1,600 in 1990 and $750 in 1991, the temple decided not to allocate any money for Buddhist education in stark contrast to the $36,400 allocated to support ancestral services in 1995 (Table 5, Service Related Items line).

Thus, unlike Euro-American Zen centers that focus on the study of Buddhism and the practice of Zen meditation, Japanese American Zen temples revolve around death rites and cultural activities.

Table 5   Zenshūji Expenditures

	1988	1989	1990	1991	1992	1993	1994	1995
Tax & Insurance	22%	19%	15%	10%	10%	N/A	N/A	7%
Utilities	14%	15%	15%	15%	13%	N/A	N/A	10%
Office Supplies	5%	8%	10%	9%	9%	N/A	N/A	10%
Staff Saaries	34%	37%	39%	42%	41%	N/A	N/A	41%
(Ministers' Salaries)	(19%)	(21%)	(29%)	(31%)	(31%)	N/A	N/A	(30%)
Cleaning & Maintenance	5%	5%	9%	8%	6%	N/A	N/A	7%
Service Related Items	18%	15%	12%	15%	19%	N/A	N/A	20%
Church Activities	1%	1%	2%	1%	2%	N/A	N/A	5%
Young Buddhist Association	(0%)	(0%)	(1%)	(0.5%)	(0%)	N/A	N/A	(0%)

Table 6   Sōtō Academy, 1995-1996

	1994–95 Actual	1995–96 Budget	1995–96 Actual
REVENUE			
Tuition	$564,926.50	$520,000.00	$572,719.48
Cafeteria	$37,974.95	$45,000.00	$41,490.09
Textbooks	$14,318.65	$20,000.00	$20,413.00
Facility Fees	$1,832.00	$1,400.00	$1,230.00
Computer Classes	$7,300.00	$30,000.00	$22,745.50
Other	$11,689.83	$1,000.00	$239.45
Total	$638,041.93	$617,400.00	$658,837.52
TOTAL EXPENSES	$566,384.88	$556,400.00	$563,038.63
DIFFERENCE	$71,657.05	$61,000.00	$95,798.89

Zazenless Zen in America

In his now-classic piece on contemporary Zen in Japan, Ian Reader coined the phrase 'Zazenless Zen' – Zen Buddhism devoid of *zazen,* or Zen meditation – to characterize modern Zen Buddhist institutions.[23] The phenomenon of 'Zazenless Zen' characterizes Japanese American Zen temples as well. Unlike Euro-American Zen centers, which commonly hold daily or even twice-daily Zen meditation sessions, the Zen meditation groups (*Zazenkai*) at the temples hold meditation sessions less frequently; Los Angeles Zenshūji (three times a week), San Francisco Sōkōji (once a week), and Honolulu Shōbōji (once a week). In other words, even though all three are considered Zen temples, engagement in Zen meditation is not a central activity.

That these Japanese American Zen temples are, to a large extent, 'zazenless' is reflected even in the architectural layout of the temples. Unlike Euro-American Zen centers which have the *zendō* (Zen meditation hall) at the center of their facilities, Japanese American Zen temples have Zen meditation on the periphery. San Francisco's Sōkōji and Honolulu's Shōbōji, for example, don't have a meditation hall, and in the case of Los Angeles's Zenshūji, the *zendō* occupies a small space in the basement of the main building. Instead, the *hondō* (main hall for services) is the architectural center of Japanese American Zen temples. Many of these *hondō* are lined with pews, much like a typical Christian church and are thus quite unsuitable for traditional Zen meditation, which requires a flat surface upon which a meditator can sit on a black meditation cushion (*zafu*). Sōkōji makes do with outfitting a section of the *hondō* with meditation cushions with a seating capacity of eight. In the case of Zenshūji, even when the temple basement underwent reconstruction in 1987 with the hopes of expanding the Zen meditation hall, the seating capacity of the hall was increased by five (from 20 to 25). At the center of this same basement is the 'social hall' in which community meetings and classes are held, both of which attract more people.

This combination of a social hall in the basement and a *hondō* for services upstairs at Zenshūji reinforces our contention that Japanese American Zen temples serve primarily as cultural community centers and places to honor one's ancestors through memorial rites. But what of the few members who do take part in Zen meditation? In 1997, 20 people belong to the Zen meditation group led by the priest at Zenshūji (Sōkōji's group has eight members), but approximately 90 percent of these members (70 percent at Sōkōji) are not Japanese American. Since at Zenshūji non-Japanese Americans make up only 5 percent of the temple membership as a whole, this means that almost all non-Japanese Americans participate in the Zen meditation group, while Japanese American participation is almost nil. This delineation between the majority of Japanese Americans who don't participate in Zen meditation and the minority of non-Japanese Americans (including African Americans, Euro-Americans, and Hispanics) who do, had been institutionalized until 1994 because the meditation group operated independently of the temple both in terms of membership and finances. In 1994, to increase opportunities for interaction between these two groups, meditation group participants were encouraged to become members of the temple and most did. This split between Japanese American and non-Japanese American participation in Zen meditation is not unique to these temples. Paul Numrich observed a similar split in his study of Theravāda temples in several American cities and termed it 'parallelism.' He found two separate yet parallel groups shared the use of Theravāda temples: immigrant South/Southeast Asian Buddhists who used the temple as a cultural center, and convert (primarily Euro-American) Buddhists who used the temple for meditation with the head monk.[24] This data strongly suggests a kind of parallel world between Asian American Buddhism and primarily Euro-American Buddhism, with the former focusing on cultural rites and the latter on meditation. However, in both scholarly work and the mainstream media, the Asian American groups are either ignored or conflated with a monolithic Buddhism.

It is not surprising that many scholars and members of the general public perceive Zen Buddhism as consisting primarily of Zen meditation. This perception persists because of the emphasis scholars and journalists writing about Zen Buddhism have placed on Zen meditation centers. Indeed, Zen meditation is not only central to the Euro-American Zen center's daily schedule and its members' motivations for coming to the center, it is the backbone of the center's economics. Looking at Tables 7, 8, and 9 (which list the revenue sources for three Zen centers: Zen Center of Los Angeles, Minnesota Zen Meditation Center, and Nebraska Zen Center), one can see that the main revenue sources of Euro-American Zen centers derive from

Table 7   Zen Center of Los Angeles

Revenue 1989	
City Center Resident Fees	35%
Fundraising	20%
Non-Resident Fees	18%
Mountain Center Activities	11%
Publications & Bookstore	10%
Loan Interest	6%

Table 8   Minnesota Zen Meditation Center

Revenue 1/1/92–9/30/92	
Membership Fees	$18,609.00
Other Contributions	$14,911.00
City Center Programs	$18,157.00
Hōkyōji Programs	$4,769.00
Sales (Books, etc.)	$5,270.00
Other	$4,160.00
Total Revenue	$65,876.00

Table 9   Nebraska Zen Center

Revenue 1994	
Activities	$3,417.00
Bellevue College Honorarium	$600.00
Donations	$10,487.71
Bank Interest	$40.12
Membership Fees	$690.00
Newsletter	$971.00
Overnight Fee	$35.00
Pledges	$6,922.00
Reimbursible Fees	$468.96
Resident Fees	$685.00
Total Revenue	$24,316.79

programs related to Zen meditation (especially retreat charges) and Zen study (especially the sale of books related to Buddhism and charges for classes). This vastly contrasts with the revenue and expenditures of Japanese American Zen temples. At Los Angeles Zenshūji, for example, the total amount of income and expenses from the Zen meditation group is less than 5 percent of the total temple budget (see Table 10). Another

Table 10   Zenshūji Zazen-kai

1/1/92–9/20/92	
Revenue Total	$4,098.28
Donations	($2,773.28)
Membership Pledges	($1,325.00)
Expenditures Total	$5,737.45
Lecture Honorarium	($816.50)
Gifts to Clergy/Temple	($2,750.00)
Meditation Retreats and Miscellaneous	($2,170.95)

important source of income is the resident fee charged to those who live at a Zen center, which, for example, was 35 percent of the total revenue for the Zen Center of Los Angeles (see Table 7). Conspicuously absent from these Euro-American Zen center budget tables is revenue derived from death rites or Japanese culture classes.

In conclusion, this study of Japanese American Zen temples and their economics has shown that, rather than Zen meditation, the primary activity of these under-researched temples are ancestral death rites and Japanese culture events. In contrast to Euro-American Zen centers, the members of Japanese American Zen temples expect that the temple will provide them with familial and cultural identity rather than with a space to meditate.

References

Bloom, Alfred. 'The Western Pure Land.' *Tricycle* 4, no. 4 (Summer 1995): 58–63.

Eck, Diana L. (with the Pluralism Project at Harvard University). *On Common Ground: World Religions in America*. New York: Columbia University Press CD-ROM, 1997.

Finney, Henry C. 'American Zen's "Japan Connection".' *Sociological Analysis* 52 (Winter 1991): 379–396.

Gernet, Jacques. *Buddhism in Chinese Society: An Economic History from the Fifth to the Tenth Centuries*. New York: Columbia University Press, 1995.

McFarland, Horace Neill. *Daruma: The Founder of Zen in Japanese Art and Popular Culture*. Tokyo: Kodansha International, 1987.

Numrich, Paul David. *Old Wisdom in the New World: Americanization in Two Immigrant Theravada Buddhist Temples*. Knoxville: University of Tennessee Press, 1996.

Ogden, Tara Keiko. 'Gambarimashō! Religion among the Japanese in America during World War II.' M.A. Thesis, University of California, Santa Barbara, 1995.

Ōkuwa, Hitoshi. *Jidan no Shisō* [The Idea of Temple Parishioners]. Tokyo: Kyōikusha, 1979.

Pitkow, Marlene. 'A Temple for Tourists in New York's Chinatown.' *Journal of American Culture* 10, no. 2 (Summer 1987): 107–114.

Preston, David L. *The Social Organization of Zen Practice*. Cambridge: Cambridge University Press, 1988.

Reader, Ian John. 'Zazenless Zen? The Position of Zazen in Institutional Zen Buddhism.' *Japanese Religions* 14, no. 3 (December 1986): 7–27.

____. 'Images in Sōtō Zen: Buddhism as a Religion of the Family in Contemporary Japan.' *Scottish Journal of Religious Studies* 10, no. 1 (Spring 1989): 5–21.

Sangha Letter [*Zen Center of Los Angeles*] (Feb.–Dec. 1990; Jan. 1991): 2; (Oct.–Nov. 1992): 2.

Tamamuro, Taijō. *Sōshiki Bukkyō* [Funerary Buddhism]. Tokyo: Daihōrinkaku, 1963.

Tworkov, Helen. *Zen in America: Profiles of Five Teachers*. San Francisco: North Point Press, 1989; rpt. New York: Kodansha, 1994.

Van Esterik, Penny. *Taking Refuge: Lao Buddhism in North America*. Tempe, AR: Arizona State University, Program in Southeast Asian Studies, 1993.

Vryheid, Robert Edward. 'An American Buddhist Monastery: Sociocultural Aspects of Soto Zen Training.' Ph.D. diss., University of Oregon, 1981.

Williams, Duncan Ryūken. "Re-presentations' of Zen: An Institutional and Social History of Sōtō Zen Buddhism in Edo Japan.' Ph.D. diss., Harvard University, forthcoming.

Yanagawa, Keiichi, ed. *Japanese Religions in California*. Tokyo: University of Tokyo, 1983.

ZCLA Year End Review (November 1990).

Zenshūji. Los Angeles: Kenkō Yamashita, 1995.

Notes

1 See David L. Preston, *The Social Organization of Zen Practice* (Cambridge: Cambridge University Press, 1988); Helen Tworkov, *Zen in America* (San Francisco: North Point Press, 1988; rpt. New York: Kodansha, 1994); and Robert Vryheid, 'An American Buddhist Monastery,' Ph.D. diss., University of Oregon, 1981.

2 We are, of course, somewhat hesitant to use the term Euro-American because some centers have up to 5 percent non-Euro-American (including African American, Latino, and Asian American) membership and leadership. Nevertheless, over 95 percent of the membership of most Zen centers and monasteries are persons of European descent.

3 See the listing compiled by Duncan Williams for the Pluralism Project in *On Common Ground: World Religions in America,* ed. Diana Eck and the Pluralism Project (New York: Columbia University Press CD-ROM, 1997). This number includes centers affiliated with both the Sōtō and Rinzai Zen traditions from Japan, as well as centers belonging to the Ch'an/Sön traditions from China and Korea.

4 See Ian Reader, 'Zazenless Zen? The Position of Zazen in Institutional Zen Buddhism,' *Japanese Religions* 14, no. 3 (December 1986): 7–27, and 'Images in Sōtō Zen: Buddhism as a Religion of the Family in Contemporary Japan,' *Scottish Journal of Religious Studies* 10, no. 1 (Spring 1989): 5–21, for an analysis of this phenomenon in contemporary Japan. Duncan Williams argues in his forthcoming Ph.D. dissertation, "Re-presentations' of Zen: An Institutional and Social History of Sōtō Zen Buddhism in Edo Japan,' that this is not simply a modern phenomenon in that less than 1 percent of the approximately 17,000 Sōtō Zen temples in the eighteenth century offered Zen meditation as a temple activity.

5 There are no Japanese American Rinzai Zen temples, although there are a number of Rinzai Zen centers and monasteries.

6 For the most comprehensive overview of familial affiliation at Buddhist temples in Japan, see Hitoshi Ōkuwa, *Jidan no Shisō* [The Idea of Temple Parishioners] (Tokyo: Kyōikusha, 1979).

7 See Alfred Bloom, 'The Western Pure Land,' *Tricycle*. 4, no. 4 (Summer 1995): 62, where he discusses the drop in membership of the Buddhist Churches of America, the American Jōdo Shinshū tradition, from 21,600 families in 1977 to 17,755 families in 1994.

8 In any given year, if we examine new membership rolls, there has never been a decline or an increase of more than 5 percent.

9 For example, in 1990, the Zen Center of Los Angeles reported a membership size of 350 in *ZCLA Year End Review* (November 1990): 1, which included fifty new members as reported in *Sangha Letter* [*Zen Center of Los Angeles*] (Feb.-Dec 1990; Jan. 1991): 2. One way to determine if the new membership is joining the core group is to track these new members for three years following their initial membership. This is because this Zen center has a policy of giving its members voting rights after three consecutive years of membership. Of the fifty new members who joined in 1990, only six received these rights in 1992: *Sangha Letter* [*Zen Center of Los Angeles*] (Oct./Nov. 1992): 2. This means that forty-four out of fifty individuals had drifted away from the center, suggesting a high percentage of temporary members – a phenomenon not found at Japanese American Zen temples.

10 From interview with the abbot of Zen Center of Los Angeles in 1996.

11 In the study of East Asian Buddhism, for instance, it is only in the past fifteen years that we have seen the intersection of economics and Buddhist studies. The work of Jacques Gernet on medieval Chinese temple economics, *Buddhism in Chinese Society: An Economic History from the Fifth to the Tenth Centuries* (New York: Columbia University Press, 1995), is representative of this recent trend.

12 Taijō Tamamuro, *Sōshiki Bukkyō* [Funerary Buddhism] (Tokyo: Daihōrinkaku, 1963).

13 All figures are taken from treasury records held at Zenshūji with the exception of the figures for 1980, which can be found in Keiichi Yanagawa, ed., *Japanese Religions in California* (Tokyo: University of Tokyo, 1983), 61.

14 The temple held 239 memorial services in 1989, 292 in 1990, 184 in 1995, and 184 in 1996, while the number of funeral services held were 30 in 1989, 38 in 1990, 34 in 1995, and 30 in 1996. There has been little change in the number of funeral services, though the number of memorial services decreased slightly even though the cost of a memorial service increased.

15 See for instance, Paul Numrich's *Old Wisdom in the New World: Americanization in Two Immigrant Theravada Buddhist Temples* (Knoxville: University of Tennessee Press, 1996) on Thai American temples and Penny van Esterik's *Taking Refuge: Lao Buddhism in North America* (Tempe, AR: Arizona State University, Program in Southeast Asian Studies, 1993) on Lao American temples.

16 In an interesting adaptation of the *taiko* drumming in Hawaii, Shōbōji's drumming group has also incorporated Hawaiian hula dancing as part of the drumming group's activities.

17 The temple itself acknowledges this fact in this statement on *taiko* drumming, found in a temple pamphlet which makes no mention of Buddhist education: 'Through the art of taiko (drumming), one can experience and comprehend the

traditional cultures and history of one's ethnic background': in *Zenshūji* (Los Angeles: Kenkō Yamashita, 1995), 12.

18 In the case of San Francisco's Sōkōji, the *Obon* dance and carnival are jointly sponsored by the Japanese American Buddhist temples under the auspices of the nonsectarian Japanese Buddhist Association.

19 On Daruma in modern Japan, see Horace McFarland's *Daruma: The Founder of Zen in Japanese Art and Popular Culture* (Tokyo: Kodansha Intl., 1987).

20 Indeed, in Hawaii, where there are over ten Shintō shrines, Japanese American community members hold this rite of passage at the Shintō shrine.

21 See Marlene Pitkow's 'A Temple for Tourists in New York's Chinatown,' *Journal of American Culture* 10, no. 2, (Summer 1987): 107–114, which discusses several Chinese American temples in New York and their relation to tourism.

22 Another example of a nonreligious source of revenue since 1990 is income earned from renting out parking lots in Los Angeles (see Table 3, Parking Fees line).

23 Reader, 'Zazenless Zen?' 7–27.

24 Numrich, *Old Wisdom in the New World*.

CHAPTER THREE

Placing Palms Together: Religious and Cultural Dimensions of the Hsi Lai Temple Political Donations Controversy

Stuart Chandler

Placing Palms Together and the American Spirit

When Vice-President Al Gore arrived at Hsi Lai Temple in Hacienda Heights, California, on 29 April 1996, he was greeted at the main gate by Master Hsing Yün and other senior monastics of the Fokuangshan ('Buddha's Light Order'). Master Hsing Yün led his guest past a 150-piece high school marching band to the temple's main shrine to pay respect to the Buddha, then took him to a reception. Gore and his host next proceeded to the dining room, filled with about one hundred guests at twelve tables. After the two men exchanged Buddha figurines, the vice-president spoke briefly to the gathering. His remarks did not directly deal with American politics. Instead, he praised the Buddhist practice of greeting others by pressing one's palms together. 'The placing of palms together is very much in the American spirit,' he said, 'To bring together, one, two, three, four, so so many, is simply wonderful. It is an act of cooperation, union, mutual respect, and harmony.'[1]

In light of the furor that has subsequently erupted over the funds raised at the event, one wonders if Vice-President Gore and his audience weren't thinking that the gesture of joined palms is even better when there is a $5,000 check pressed in between. Ever since the *Wall Street Journal* reported that the Hsi Lai banquet netted $140,000 for the Democratic National Committee (DNC), and that over a quarter of this was donated by Fokuang monastic and lay members, journalists and others have not only questioned the event's legality, but have also tried to puzzle out why a Chinese Buddhist organization would be delving so deeply into American presidential politics. Some, doubting that the monastics could have come up with the money on their own, have conjectured that they were acting as a front for Taiwan's business interests, or even government. Others have presumed that the Fokuang Buddhists had more admirable intentions in entering campaign politics, but have remained at a loss as to what exactly those motives could have been. Because of language and cultural barriers, mystery continues to enshroud the event. In this essay I hope to dispel some of that mystery by analyzing the Hsi Lai banquet controversy from three angles: (1) the Fokuang explanations for inviting Gore to their Hacienda Heights temple and donating funds to the DNC; (2) the treatment of the incident by U.S. media and politicians; and (3) my own role in acting as liaison between Fokuangshan, the U.S. media, and governmental agencies. In order to set the scene, however, let me begin by providing some historical context.

'Come Eat Vegetarian Food With Us ... I'll Treat'

Al Gore first met Master Hsing Yün in 1989 during a three-day excursion to Taiwan. The trip, sponsored by Fokuangshan, was organized by Maria Hsia, who, along with John Huang, would eventually play a leading role in putting together the Hsi Lai fund-raiser. It included meetings with Taiwanese and U.S. officials and a visit to the Fokuangshan headquarters. Reflecting back on the event, Master Hsing Yün recalls casually remarking to Gore, then still a senator, 'Hey, you could be president.' Gore replied, 'Do I look presidential?' 'Very much so, very much.'[2] It was from this meeting, states Master Hsing Yün, that he and the future vice-president established a relation.

When Gore and Master Hsing Yün met, the present Hsi Lai Temple had only recently opened its doors. Master Hsing Yün had first visited the United States in 1976, at which time he participated in some of the bicentennial celebrations. Impressed by the can-do attitude of Americans, and optimistic about the possibility of spreading the Dharma here, he soon sent a team of monastics to find a suitable location for a temple. The scouting group was discouraged at first; the exorbitant Californian real estate market seemed beyond the organization's reach. When the monastics eventually found a church for sale at a reasonable price, Master Hsing Yün instructed them to purchase it. He found the idea of transforming a Christian property into a Buddhist temple especially appealing since Protestant and Catholic organizations had often acquired temple lands in Taiwan to build churches.[3]

The former church building essentially served as a preparatory site from which to plan a much more ambitious temple. In 1978, fourteen acres were purchased in Hacienda Heights and plans drawn for a large monastery, including an eight-story statue of the Buddha. Gaining approval from the local government to build the complex, however, proved much more difficult than anticipated. Local residents feared that allowing a Buddhist 'cult' into their midst would endanger their children and destroy the value of real estate. Finally, after six public hearings and over one hundred negotiation sessions, permission was granted to build the temple, although the complex was on a smaller scale than originally envisioned and no outdoor statue of the Buddha would be constructed. The cornerstone was laid for the structure in January 1986. Two and one-half years later, Master Hsing Yün made the journey from Taiwan to conduct the temple's consecration ceremony. According to one account, bright lights were seen coming from the back of the main hall during the ceremony and 'Auspicious clouds gathered around the temple forming into the shape of Kuan Yin riding on a dragon.'[4]

Despite the felicitous signs that accompanied the consecration of the temple, there were still hardships to overcome for the fledgling community. Soon after the temple was built, the local Chinese Chamber of Commerce invited Hsi Lai Temple to provide a float for the town's Fourth of July parade. It was a terrible experience for those who participated: they were booed and heckled much of the way. For many years following that debacle, the Hsi Lai community maintained a low public profile while quietly contributing to service projects (such as providing Thanksgiving and Christmas food baskets for poor families) and launching various public relations campaigns. The traffic congestion which occurs during large festivals is a potential source of tension with immediate neighbors, so the temple makes a concerted effort to include them in the celebrations. Several days before the Chinese New Year, for instance, at which time thousands of pilgrims visit the temple, a special banquet is held for the neighborhood. Some five hundred people attend the feast each year.

As another means to establish Hsi Lai Temple as a legitimate, fully accepted member of the community, Master Hsing Yün and the temple's various abbots have consistently sought to secure 'friendly relations' with local and national political leaders. California Secretary of State March Fong Eu was invited to view the Hacienda Heights property just as construction got underway. Apparently, it was she who arranged for Master Hsing Yün to perform purifying services to start the December 1988 session of the California legislature. Fokuang literature proudly states that this is the first time that a Buddhist monastic has performed this rite on government premises in the United States. (Master Hsing Yün later conducted such services in New York City and Chicago as well.) That same year, the mayors of Austin and Houston, Texas, honored Master Hsing Yün as a Friendship Ambassador. Letters of congratulations have been sent to the temple by numerous Californian politicians, including Governor Pete Wilson, Senator Alan Cranston, Representative Matthew G. Matinez, and Los Angeles Mayor Tom Bradley.

Hsi Lai Temple has from its inception maintained at least nominal links with the White House. President Reagan both wired a telegram and dispatched a representative to the temple in honor of its opening in 1988. President Bush invited Master Hsing Yün to his inauguration and, when Fokuangshan's lay organization, Buddha's Light International Association

(BLIA), was founded in 1992 in Los Angeles, he sent a letter, praising the group for its compassionate tenets and devotion to relieving the suffering of all beings. Such contacts with the Oval Office increased and became more direct with the Clinton administration. In September 1993, three Fokuang monastics attended a vice-presidential fund-raiser (organized by Maria Hsia) in Santa Monica, California, donating a total of $15,000 to the DNC. An additional $5,000 was given to the party at a 1995 event attended by both Clinton and Gore, and $25,000 was contributed in February 1996, when Ven. Tz'u Jung, present abbess of Hsi Lai, led a team of Fokuang members to meet President Clinton at a DNC fund-raiser at the Hay Adams Hotel in Washington, D.C.[5] One month later, John Huang arranged for Master Hsing Yün to make a ten-minute 'courtesy call' on Vice-President Gore at the White House.[6] It was during this meeting that Master Hsing Yün invited Gore to visit Hsi Lai Temple for a banquet in his honor. At first, the vice-president was merely going to stop by the temple for a brief tour. 'When Vice-President Gore was coming to Los Angeles,' recalls Master Hsing Yün,

> he was going to go somewhere else for a fund-raising dinner. When he called, I said, 'Don't go there, come eat vegetarian food with us.' ...
> Al Gore declined the invitation, saying that the other place was already set up for the event so it was unlikely that he could come to Hsi Lai Temple for lunch ... I said, 'No problem, you come here to eat. I can prepare twenty tables. I'll treat.'[7]

In the end, Gore did not have to choose between the two venues. The other luncheon, a fund-raiser sponsored by the Asian Pacific American Leadership Council did not attract the anticipated number of donors, so John Huang decided to combine the two events.

Gore's staff wasn't quite sure what political ramifications there might be in having the vice-president visit a Chinese Buddhist temple. On 15 April 1996, John J. Norris, a member of Gore's national security staff, sent an e-mail message to Robert L. Suettinger, an Asia affairs specialist for the National Security Council. In response to Norris's query whether there could be any problems with Gore participating in the event, Suettinger replied: 'This is *terra incognita* to me. Certainly from the perspective of Taiwan/China balancing, this would be clearly a Taiwan event, and would be seen as such. I guess my reaction would be one of great, great caution. They may have a hidden agenda.'[8] Despite this warning, Vice-President Gore decided to make the trip. In order to minimize any risk of negative reaction from the Chinese government, his staff worked with the organizers of the luncheon to de-emphasize the temple's connection to Taiwan. There was to be no display of Taiwanese flags or political symbols and no politicians from Taiwan were to be allowed to 'exploit the event.'[9]

Those investigating the April 29 banquet have wondered about the degree to which its participants regarded it as a fund-raiser. Al Gore has steadfastly asserted that he considered it to be 'community outreach,' although one also 'finance-related' and designed for 'donor maintenance.'[10] Master Hsing Yün has characterized it as an opportunity to reaffirm 'friendly relations' with the vice-president. Many of the other participants, however, came with checks in hand. All those contacted by the Asian Pacific American Leadership Council knew from the outset that money was being collected. Charlie Woo, a California businessman later told the *Washington Post* that 'I was at a table of people who understood that it was a fund-raiser. People had to pay to attend.' David C. Hwang, head of the Taiwanese-American Citizens League, recalls handing Huang a $1,000 check at the temple.[11] Fokuangshan devotees who attended had similarly been asked by Abbess Tz'u Jung to contribute funds to the DNC. The combined donations of the Asian Pacific American Leadership Council and Fokuangshan members, however, only came to approximately $85,000, far below the $200,000 John Huang had predicted would be raised. To increase the take, the day following the banquet he had Maria Hsia contact Rev. Man Ho (the Fokuang monastic in charge of coordinating the event) to press the temple to raise more money. Rev. Man Ho forwarded this request to Master Hsing Yün, who readily agreed, personally providing $5,000. Rev. Man Ho then bid temple treasurer Ven. Yi Chu to round up fifteen devotees – eleven monastics and four lay-monastic followers[12] – to also contribute, thereby raising a total of $55,000. Hence, it appears that neither Master Hsing Yün nor Vice-President Gore were aware that the event was to be a fund-raiser. The Hsi Lai monastics in charge of organizing the banquet (including Abbess Tz'u Jung, Ven. Man Ho, and Ven. Yi Chu), some Gore staff members not present, and many of the participants in the luncheon, however, did recogize it as such. Master Hsing Yün was approached for funds the day following the event. Al Gore knew that donors were present but seems to have remained unaware that money actually changed hands during and immediately after the event until Phil Kuntz of the *Wall Street Journal* broke the story the following October.

Upon discovering that the Hsi Lai banquet had served as a fund-raiser for the Democratic National Committee, Kuntz questioned the event's legality on three fronts. First, by law no political fund-raising may occur at a tax-exempt religious organization. Second, it appeared that not all of the contributors were U.S. citizens. Master Hsing Yün certainly was not, and there were doubts about others as well. Third, the ultimate source of some of the money was unclear. Kuntz wondered how Buddhist monks and nuns living on $40 monthly stipends could come up with $5,000 contributions. When he posed this query to Ven. Man Ya, one of the monastics who had provided the DNC with $5,000, she replied that the money was not, in fact, her own.[13] She stated that a woman she recognized as a Democratic activist and Buddhist devotee, but whose name she could not remember, had approached her at the temple fund-raiser, handed her $5,000 in cash and asked her to write a check to the DNC for the same amount.[14]

Kuntz was right to raise doubts about the event's legality. Soon after the *Journal* article came out, the DNC reimbursed Hsi Lai Temple $15,000 to protect its tax-exempt status. Further research conducted by reporters of the *Los Angeles Times* revealed that the banquet for Gore may not have been the first instance in which the temple has been the location for a political fund-raiser; according to one article it also served in this capacity for a Connecticut gubernatorial candidate in 1990.[15] Any fund-raising on the premises clearly contradicts federal election laws. The legality of non-citizens donating funds to a political party proves to be more problematic. Non-citizens may give if they are permanent residents, i.e., have a 'green card,' and are living in the United States at the time. Legal experts have been less certain about whether those with residency status may give funds while living outside the United States. It appears that under current laws such donations are permissible, although there is legislation being drafted to change this. The third legal question, that concerning the unknown source of the funds donated not only by Ven. Man Ya but by all of the monastics became the central question of investigations undertaken by the U.S. Justice Department, the Senate's Governmental Affairs Committee (GAC), and the House Reform and Oversight Committee.

Ven. Man Ya soon admitted to the Federal Election Commission that there had never been a mysterious devotee who had stuffed a wad of small bills into her hand. She wrote in a two-page statement to federal agents that she had told the 'harmless lie' merely as a ploy to get Kuntz off the phone.[16] Ironically, although it was Ven. Man Ya's white lie that instigated the subsequent investigation, it turns out that she was one of the few monastics to use her own money. An audit of temple bank records revealed that Master Hsing Yün and all of the other monastics and lay monastics who had contributed funds to the DNC on April 30 were reimbursed that same day by the International Buddhist Progress Society (the incorporated name of Hsi Lai Temple). When Venerables Man Ya, Man Ho, and Yi Chu were all called to testify before the Governmental Affairs Committee on 4 September 1997, Venerable Yi Chu not only testified that she had reimbursed all fifteen Fokuang disciples but also admitted to having subsequently doctored some of the checks to make it appear that they had come out of the persons' personal accounts rather than the temple's general fund. Both she and Ven. Man Ho also admitted having destroyed lists of banquet participants, saying that they did so shortly after the newspaper accounts came out in October 1996.[17] Both, however, steadfastly asserted that all of the moneys reimbursed had been raised here in the United States through devotee donations and bookstore sales. None had come from Taiwan.

The underlying question that continues to baffle many Americans about the event remains: what were these Chinese Buddhists with only a tenuous formal tie to the United States hoping to gain by feting the vice-president at a banquet and donating large sums of money to the DNC? To answer this, we must now look more closely at the Fokuang perspective on wealth and politics.

'I Am Also American, I Have Residency Status'

Politicians and journalists have suspected that Master Hsing Yün and his followers were acting as some kind of clandestine agents for the Taiwan government or business interests. The fact that the master has a close relationship with Republic of China (ROC) political and corporate leaders adds fuel to such speculation. Since the 1970s, a steady stream of top governmental officials have called on Master Hsing Yün, including Presidents Chiang Ching-kuo and Lee Teng-hui. The master has also served for nearly a decade on the Central Advisory Committee of the ruling Kuomintang (KMT) party. Although the post is largely ceremonial and involves no policy making (its 210 members attend funerals and weddings on the party's behalf), it nonetheless signifies the imprimatur of KMT approval. The same year he received this post, Master Hsing Yün was also invited to propagate the Dharma and confer the Three Refuges among soldiers stationed on Jinmen and Ma-Tzu islands, a task he has continued to perform periodically at various army bases and military academies. Government sanction of Master Hsing Yün and Fokuangshan activities has also taken the form of awards. In 1985, he became the first Buddhist leader to gain recognition for meritorious service from the Education Department. Both the Ministry of the Interior and Ministry of Foreign Affairs in May 1997 conferred upon Master Hsing Yün medals of commendation, the highest honor bestowed by these offices upon ROC citizens.

Master Hsing Yün also has considerable clout among Taiwan's business leaders: Fokuangshan benefactors include some of the island's wealthiest families and a variety of industries utilize the monastery complex as a location for conferences. One such international symposium sponsored by the China Steel Corporation led to Fokuangshan being offered twenty-six acres virtually free of charge in Wollongong, Australia (just south of Sidney), home of the BHP Steel Company. Fokuangshan has subsequently erected a US$35 million temple on the site. Because of these contacts with the business world, and in reaction against the organization's own considerable wealth, other Buddhists have criticized Fokuangshan as being too commercial, little more than a business enterprise with but a veneer of religious cultivation. Master Hsing Yün counters that such comments arise from jealousy and a misplaced suspicion of money.

Based on these political and corporate connections, it is possible that Master Hsing Yün was surreptitiously acting on behalf of Taiwan's power elite when he invited Al Gore. It nonetheless remains highly improbable that he was directly given funds by them in an attempt to influence the U.S government. Neither journalists nor investigators for the House, Senate, or Department of Justice have found any evidence that funds were transferred from Taiwan into Hsi Lai coffers (as with all Fokuang branches, Hsi Lai Temple is financially independent from the Fokuang headquarters). On the other hand, the fact that in February 1997 Master Hsing Yün accepted a position on the ROC cabinet's Overseas Chinese Commission indicates that, even if he was not acting as some kind of agent for the government, he certainly had its relationship with the overseas Chinese community in mind.

Another possible motive behind the largess of Master Hsing Yün and his followers was to benefit their own organization, Fokuangshan. Whether in the United States, Europe, or Australia, creating friendly ties with local and national political leaders can help ease bureaucratic red tape for Fokuangshan branch temples. Even more importantly, such ties with the political elite provide prestige, both in the country of the branch temple and back at home in Taiwan. The symbolic import of having one's photograph taken with government officials should not be underestimated. What could better legitimize Fokuang Buddhism and signify its compatibility with American values than a picture of the abbess of Hsi Lai Temple with President Clinton and an American flag in the background, or a photo of Vice-President Gore offering a bouquet of flowers to an image of the Buddha? Back in Taiwan, what could better display the global importance of Fokuangshan than an album filled with pictures of Master Hsing Yün, not only with the Dalai Lama and the Pope, but with Vice-President Gore, President Diosdado Macapagal, and His Excellency Sir Clarence Seignoret as well? Furthermore, contributing funds to the DNC would amplify this symbolic importance. All Taiwan citizens are well aware of the enormous amount of money and resources that the United States sank into the ROC economy in the 1950s and 1960s. For the DNC to request donations from one of Taiwan's leading religious figures gives concrete evidence that the two societies are no longer patron and beneficiary, but peers. Those living in Taiwan take great pride in the fact that they now dispense charity worldwide rather than receive it. Certainly, such dynamics were at work when Master Hsing Yün pledged to donate what will amount to thousands of New Taiwan dollars to a hospital run by Protestants, or when Fokuangshan has run social service programs in the Philippines, Bangladesh, India, Nepal, South Africa, and the United States. The satisfaction of being able to give money to others and the prestige that accompanies such generosity is reward enough. No future restitution or favors are necessary or expected.

Master Hsing Yün would not agree with either of the motives proposed above. He chafes at any mention of 'influence peddling.' He also strongly denies that he and his followers acted to gain benefit or prestige for themselves. Instead, he has proffered three explanations for sponsoring the banquet. First, Master Hsing Yün insists that he provided the donation to express his deep gratitude to the United States. The master often emphasizes gratitude as an essential virtue for those engaged in Buddhist cultivation. Such gratitude must be pure, however, neither sycophantic in nature nor driven by any ulterior aim. During the interview conducted by GAC investigators, he explained:

> I must play the role of elder to you since you are all young. Thirty or 40 years ago President Truman ordered a fleet to protect Taiwan. The living standard was very low at the time. The United States usually asked Catholics and Protestants to give relief food. I told myself that, when Buddhism has the ability, I want to repay the United States. No matter what it may be, I want to help. Many disciples see me take the lead, so they emulate.[18]

In fact, this sense of gratitude has led Master Hsing Yün generally to favor the Republicans over the Democrats, for it has been the former who have pushed harder over the years to maintain military aid for Taiwan. The master's donation to the DNC, therefore, was an expression of his sincere appreciation for all that the American political system represents and all that it has done for his country. His generosity was motivated by gratitude, not thoughts of prestige.

Master Hsing Yün has also said that he invited the vice-president on behalf of the entire Asian American community. He told a group of international Buddhist youth:

> Over the past ten years or so, I have often been invited to attend presidential elections or breakfast meetings, but I think it is much too far to travel just to eat breakfast! This time, when Vice-President Gore was coming to Los Angeles, he was going to go somewhere else for a fund-raising dinner. When he called, I said, 'Don't go there, come eat vegetarian food with us.' ... Al Gore declined the invitation, saying that the other place was already set up for the event so it was unlikely that he could come to Hsi Lai Temple for lunch. I thought, 'Since America is a democracy, presidents and vice-presidents often go to eat at the homes or places of other ethnicities. If one were to come to an Asian place, especially a Buddhist place, this would certainly have an influence. I ought to do my best for all Chinese and Asians.' I said, 'No problem, you come here to eat. I can prepare twenty tables. I'll treat.'[19]

If Master Hsing Yün was trying to 'peddle influence,' he was not doing so to benefit the government of Taiwan, but rather the Chinese American community. After Ven. Tz'u Jung attended a DNC fund-raiser at the Century Hotel in Los Angeles in July 1996, a Fokuangshan publication praised Clinton for being 'the first U.S. president to pay particular attention to Asian Americans.'[20] The article went on to state that, under Clinton, 197 Asian Americans had already been appointed as top government officials and a bill allowing one million Asians to immigrate to the U.S. had recently been ratified. Master Hsing Yün and his followers hoped to express their gratitude to the administration and to encourage the continuation of such policies. The primary people gaining influence through the Hsi Lai banquet were Chinese, but also American.

The question that arises is that of determining when a person of Chinese heritage can also claim to be an American. Master Hsing Yün assumes that any Chinese who spends time in the United States is more or less 'American.' Hence, he considers himself to be an American:

> The United States should not consider us to be aliens. I am also American, I have residency status. I always try to encourage Chinese Americans to assimilate into American society. It is not right to go to the States and try to still live like a Chinese or Japanese. When you are in America, be American. When you come to Fokuangshan, be a part of Fokuangshan. When you are in a family, be a member of that family, when you are in a country, be a part of that nation.[21]

The perimeters of the Chinese American community are therefore murky. The general American public tends to consider citizenship as a minimum requirement for identifying oneself as 'American.' That this is the case became quite evident when, even after it became general knowledge that permanent residents have the right to donate funds to political parties, news reports continued to emphasize that the donations to the DNC by Fokuang members were suspect because most of these people were not citizens. Legally, the debate has centered on whether or not residents can still donate such funds if they spend most of their time in their country of origin rather than in the United States. Culturally, the issue is one of identity: when does a person truly have the right to wave the American flag?

Establishing Friendly Relations

Beyond trying to help the Chinese American community, Master Hsing Yün has repeatedly asserted that the overriding reason that he invited Al Gore to Hsi Lai Temple and subsequently donated funds to the DNC was to establish 'friendly relations.' This explanation is not as simple as it may first appear since the term 'friendly relations' is a rather unsatisfactory English translation for the Chinese Buddhist term *chieh-yüan*. To fully appreciate the dynamics underlying the Hsi Lai incident, we must therefore spend a few moments considering this concept.

The *Fokuang Dictionary* states that *chieh-yüan* refers to the situations in which: 'although there is no way that cultivation in this life can result in liberation, there can be an initial point of contact for fruition some time in the future.'[22] In other words, a particular person may have no hope for enlightenment in this lifetime but, by having the seed of the Dharma planted in his or her consciousness, it can bear fruit in a future reincarnation. Historically, *chieh-yüan* has been applied to describe those undertakings that serve to attract people to Buddhism: building a temple or *pagoda*, printing scriptures or books, or donating funds. In its contemporary usage, the term especially describes any activity that establishes or strengthens a personal relationship in such a way as to spread the Dharma. *Chieh-yüan* is often accomplished by drawing people, especially children, to Buddhist practice through distributing candies, treats, or money. It is said that the T'ang dynasty Pure Land master Shao-k'ang (8th century C.E.) first attracted followers by giving children one coin for each invocation of Amitabha Buddha. Within a month, many people started doing it, so he reduced payment to one coin for every ten invocations. By year's end, all in the region were following the practice with no expectation of monetary reward.[23] Ven. Yi K'ung, currently head of Fokuangshan's Cultural Council, tells how, at age four or five, she originally went to Master Hsing Yün's Lei-yin Temple solely to enjoy the 'gifts of affinity' (*chieh-yüan-p'in*) inevitably offered. At first she may have come for these snacks of peach-shaped longevity buns or Buddha's hands made of flour, but as she participated in the various temple activities, she found herself increasingly drawn to the Dharma.[24] This understanding of *chieh-yüan* emphasizes that, to effectively plant the seed of the Dharma so that it may flourish in the future, one must first create appropriate conditions (*yüan*). The goal of 'establishing friendly relations' is to create a positive predisposition toward Buddhism so that, later, when the time is ripe, people will be that much more likely to find resonance with its teachings.

A very important element in creating such nurturing conditions is to establish a relationship of trust and mutual admiration between the two parties. *Chieh-yüan* is not merely the transmission of abstract teachings but, rather, refers to the spontaneous creative energy that arises through direct interaction between people. In explaining the concept *chieh-yüan*, Master Hsing Yün observes:

> When positive energy is applied to friendship, untold good forces are released. There is nothing in the world more beautiful than the positive energy which can be generated between people and among friends. This kind of energy is like water which can wash away bad *karma*. It is like an oil which smooths the progress of good *karma*. Positive energy among people is the single greatest force for bringing good into this world.... [25]

There are three components to creating such positive energy: the giver, the recipient, and the gift. The most precious gift of all is the Dharma itself, but if such a gift would not yet be appreciated by the recipient, more mundane presents will serve the purpose better. In providing the gift, the pure intention of the giver is of utmost importance if merit is to be gained from the act. He or she must have no selfish aim in establishing a relationship with the recipient. Chinese Buddhists therefore distinguish *chieh-yüan* from *p'an-yüan*, which generally signifies the clinging of the wayward mind to external phenomena and, as the opposite of *chieh-yüan*, refers specifically to providing favors or establishing ties with some ulterior motive in mind.[26] In the pure giving of *chieh-yüan*, whether or not the recipient of the gift can assist the giver in some fashion in the future is of no concern. In fact, those who practice *chieh-yüan* in its highest form do so with no concept of giver, recipient, or gift. All are regarded as radically inter-related aspects of ever-changing reality.

This background about *chieh-yüan* clarifies an important motive Master Hsing Yün had in establishing ties with Vice-President Gore. The seed of the Dharma has only recently been planted in the United States. Creating a positive impression with government leaders makes it that much more likely that the seed will enjoy nurturing circumstances. No fruit may emerge in the immediate future, but in due time it will develop. Gore and others who now come to Hsi Lai Temple to garner political or financial support will eventually realize more noble intentions for visiting. And because of the prestige such leaders hold in American society, their favorable impression of Buddhism will affect a great number of others as well.

A Picture Is Worth a Thousand Words

The Hsi Lai donations controversy has clearly shown that, even if Master Hsing Yün is right and America does hold great promise for Buddhist practice, very few in the country are anywhere close to seeing it in such terms. A primary reason that the Hsi Lai banquet has received so much attention is that the series of photographs showing Vice-President Gore strolling alongside robed, tonsured monastics in an ornate building filled with exotic statues succinctly encapsulates the fear that underlies the entire political donations scandal: a foreign people of radically different values is attempting to infiltrate our government. One could say that the Hsi Lai affair primarily has been about images. The very same photographs that are displayed with pride at the Fokuangshan headquarters in Taiwan have created unease among much of the American public and have been gleefully utilized by Republicans to embarrass Gore. During the GAC panel hearings, committee Republicans displayed on easels and television screens sixteen huge color photograph enlargements of the vice president's visit to the temple. Gore was shown clasping his palms together, offering flowers to the Buddha, and surrounded by two hundred saffron-robed monastics.[27] Not surprisingly, the episode's visual component has been exploited by cartoonists. Bill Mitchell created three cartoons of a seated

Gore in Buddhist robes. 'Late this afternoon,' states the caption heading all three cartoons, 'Vice-President Gore offered yet another explanation for his attendance at a Buddhist monastery fund-raiser. . . .' In the following screen Gore is made to say, 'What is the sound of one hand donating?' or 'If a donation is made, but no one is there to see it, did it really happen?' or 'Ich bin eine Buddhist.'[28] The *National Review* placed on the front cover of its March 1997 issue a caricature of Bill and Hillary Clinton and Al Gore, all with slanted eyes and in traditional Chinese garb – the president as a peasant, the first lady in Maoist uniform, and Al Gore as a Buddhist monk.

Master Hsing Yün believes that the entire controversy has been fueled by anti-Asian prejudice:

> You certainly know that not only Asians have donated money, other ethnic groups have as well. Why hasn't this issue been raised about them? The Asian community in America has not received equal treatment or respect. This contradicts the American spirit, which is supposed to be one of equality and righteousness. This incident arose because the media needed to find some news to make a show of it. The situation has been blown way out of proportion.[29]

The leaders of a wide range of Chinese American organizations have held the same view. Shortly after the GAC committee hearing testimony given by the three Fokuang nuns, former Los Angeles Councilman Michael Woo told the press: 'Asian Americans are now facing the most profound crisis we have seen since the internment of Japanese Americans over 50 years ago.' Woo, Daphne Kwok (representing the Organization of Chinese Americans), and Edward Chen (American Civil Liberties Union) all called for hearings by the U.S. Commission on Civil Rights to remind people that the emerging story of fund-raising was no excuse for discrimination.[30]

There is great validity to these complaints. Such a high profile investigation into possible illegal contributions by people and organizations with ties to Asia has provided the perfect pretext for fanning latent hostilities. Such prejudices have been further inflamed through the rhetoric of politicians and commentators. The day after the *Wall Street Journal* first broke the story about the Hsi Lai banquet, Bob Dole quipped during a campaign rally that the Democrats had had a fund-raiser at a Buddhist temple in Los Angeles and '[Gore] showed up and ate vegetables. You have to take a vow of poverty to be in that temple. . . . Next thing you know they're going to have fund-raisers at homeless shelters.'[31] During the July 10 session of the GAC campaign finance hearings, Sam Brownback (Rep-Kansas) said, 'No raise money, no get bonus' (he later apologized, saying that no racial slur had been intended).[32] Not surprisingly, arch-conservative spokespeople such as Rush Limbaugh have been ruthless in their commentaries of the event.

That the *National Review* and Rush Limbaugh would seize upon the Hsi Lai banquet as an opportunity to further their own agendas could be expected. More surprising in my view was the coverage of the Hsi Lai controversy in *Tricycle: The Buddhist Review*. The editors opened their brief article, 'Paper Traces,' by asserting that, not only had members of Hsi Lai Temple apparently broken federal campaign law, but they also violated the Vinaya, which forbids monastics from using or handling money. They also observed, 'Another donor listed in the DNC reports was Master Shing Yun, a name that bears striking similarity to Master Hsing Yun, the founder of Hsi Lai temple.'[33] The article was accusatory in tone. The unnamed author of the piece apparently neither speaks Chinese nor knows much about Chinese Buddhism. For instance, the debate over whether or not a monk may handle money dates from as early as the Second Council, which took place in Northern India some time during the fourth or third century B.C.E. The Central Asian Buddhist missionaries who introduced the tradition to China during the early centuries C.E. represented schools that permitted monastics to receive gold and silver. This has continued to be the standard practice through the centuries for not only Chinese but Korean and Japanese monastics as well.

Similarly, to point out the misspelling of Master Hsing Yün's name makes his intentions sound much more sinister than they were. He has never denied having made a contribution. In fact, Kuntz's *Wall Street Journal* article, from which *Tricycle* learned of the differences in spelling, made no such inference of intentional subterfuge. Most likely it was the person who recorded the donation in the DNC records who was responsible for transposing the 'h' and 's' in the name 'Hsing.' (Those unfamiliar with the Wade-Giles system of transliteration often make this mistake.) *Tricycle* did run a letter of response from Master Hsing Yün in its next issue. Unfortunately, they prefaced his remarks with the snide headline, 'Dow of Poverty.'[34] Such reporting does little to increase understanding between America's Euro-American and Asian Buddhist populations. If the magazine truly wants to be the voice for all Buddhists in the United States, they should pay closer attention to possible biases creeping into their reportage of so-called 'Ethnic Buddhism.'[35]

Despite the short-term notoriety suffered by his own organization, Master Hsing Yün, ever the optimist, believes that the controversy itself may in the long run serve the positive function of dispelling misconceptions and introducing a wide range of Americans, especially those in the media and political circles, to Buddhist teachings. He may be right. The general assumption that Buddhist monastics take a 'vow of poverty,' for instance is gradually being dispelled, at least in some quarters. Although many news agencies (including *ABC News*, *Businessweek*, and the *New York Post*) continued to mention this supposed vow even through the GAC hearings, others, such as the *Washington Post*, eventually corrected themselves on this point. For Master Hsing Yün, even such minor and fleeting glimpses into the Buddhist world may be all that is necessary to plant the seed of the Dharma so that it can sprout forth in a future life.

Political Controversy and Scholarly Responsibility

Although I have no aim of spreading Buddhism in America, I like to think that I have played at least a small role in dispelling some of the misunderstandings and misconceptions that have characterized the Hsi Lai episode from the start. I had been at the Fokuangshan headquarters in southern Taiwan for only three weeks when the *Wall Street Journal* initially published the Hsi Lai donations story in October 1996. I had chosen this organization as the topic for my dissertation because, although it was only thirty years old, it already boasted a monastic community 1,300 strong and a worldwide lay membership over one million. The charisma of its leader, Master Hsing Yün, and his willingness to foster friendly ties with political and corporate figures had already made him a well-known, if controversial, figure not only in Taiwan, but throughout the Chinese diaspora. Little did I realize, however, that my dissertation topic would soon be the subject of political debate in congressional committees, news rooms, and coffee shops throughout the United States.

My own understanding of the Hsi Lai controversy developed in a rather uneven fashion: living half a world away, I often acquired news reports of the investigation several months after their publication; on the other hand, living at Fokuang headquarters as the Hsi Lai banquet controversy unfolded provided a wonderful opportunity for me to witness first-hand how Master Hsing Yün and the organization as a whole responded to such scrutiny. Such issues as Fokuangshan's financial system (especially individual monastic accounts) and Master Hsing Yün's reasons for delving into national and international politics were raised time and again for over a year. I was not only permitted to attend meetings in which Master Hsing Yün explained what occurred at the banquet to monastic and lay followers but was even allowed to observe the interview of Master Hsing Yün conducted by a fact-finding team sent to Taiwan by the U.S. Senate's Committee on Governmental Affairs. Such privileged access is any researcher's dream come true.

This access provided insight, but it also placed me in a precarious position as an impartial observer. I could not simply be a non-participating witness who played no role in how the events unfolded. As time went by, I found myself becoming increasingly involved in the process itself, acting as both an advisor and press liaison for Fokuangshan. This active involvement began almost immediately after the *Wall Street Journal* broke the story. Shortly after the *Wall Street* article, reporters from both the *Washington Post* and the *Los Angeles Times* arrived at Fokuangshan to interview

Master Hsing Yün. Ven. Man Hua, the nun in charge of international affairs, also arranged for the journalists to meet with me so I could provide an 'objective,' scholarly answer to any general questions they had about the organization. At this point, my role was still marginal: I had not been present at the banquet and had only arrived at Fokuangshan a month earlier, so my knowledge of the incident and even the group as a whole was still too superficial to add much insight into Fokuangshan's financial structure or possible political intentions.

Immediately recognizing the importance of this incident for my own research, I henceforth kept a careful eye on the Internet for any updates in the American press. I did so not only for my own benefit, however; I also passed on any article I found to Ven. Man Hua. I did this because I felt that Fokuangshan had a right to know what others were saying about them. By so doing, however, I also put myself in the position of unofficial press liaison for the group. Hence, when several newspapers published articles portraying Fokuangshan in a very negative light, Ven. Man Hua asked me to draft a letter of response to be sent by Master Hsing Yün. Since the articles based their criticisms on a distorted understanding of Buddhist practice (especially in regards to whether or not monastics take a 'vow of poverty'), I agreed to write the draft. I felt uneasy doing so, however, since this placed me dangerously close to acting as an advocate for the group.

My role as active participant rose to a new level in late May 1997, when the GAC sent a fact-finding team to interview the master. Soon after Ven. Man Hua received the request for an interview by the committee, she asked me if I thought the master should accept it. My immediate response was to agree to meet with them. I advised to do so both as a strong believer in openness and, taking at face value Master Hsing Yün's insistence that neither he nor any of his followers had intentionally done anything wrong, I felt cooperation with the investigating committee would be for the best. When Ven. Man Hua discussed the GAC's request with Master Hsing Yün, she related my advice as well. The master also thought openness the best policy and so agreed to the meeting, despite strong reservations being voiced by senior Fokuang monastics and Master Hsing Yün's U.S. legal councilors. Having agreed to the meeting, Master Hsing Yün wrote a statement for the investigators, which I translated. I was more than just a translator, however, since I gave advice when asked about possible legal ramifications of certain wording. In addition to providing such advice, I was actively involved in two other ways as well. First, I agreed to Ven. Man Hua's request that I provide Master Hsing Yün and the investigators with a copy of the paper I had recently presented about the Hsi Lai controversy for the Buddhist Studies Forum of Harvard University. Second, once the investigators arrived, I was part of the group escorting them on a tour of the mountain and then sat in on the interview they conducted for Master Hsing Yün, acting as scribe on behalf of his legal councilors.

My willingness to participate actively as both press liaison and advisor for Fokuangshan will certainly raise eyebrows in the scholarly community. Some will argue that I have seriously compromised my ability to remain 'objective.' I am highly aware of the dangers of my position. Such precariousness, inherent in any project heavily reliant upon the participant-observation method of collecting information, gains special saliency under politically-charged circumstances such as those encountered during my research. According to the participant-observation model, instead of simply observing rituals and daily events from the sidelines, making one's own presence as little felt as possible, the fieldworker is to engage in the activities with the group under study. Such a tactic has two advantages. First, the researcher benefits from a more 'existential,' first-hand knowledge of the activity. To understand just what significance a particular rite or activity may have for the participants, the researcher undertakes the same actions. Simultaneously, by engaging in the course of events alongside everyone else, the sense of the researcher as outside intruder diminishes, at least slightly. And yet, as one participates, one is supposed to do so in such a way as to make little or no impact on the process itself. One participates, but from the periphery.

In my own experience as participant-observer in a politically sensitive episode, I most certainly broke the taboo against influencing outcome. Although I was far from a central figure in the case, my unofficial roles as press liaison and advisor affected, if ever so slightly, the progression. I don't know, for instance, if Master Hsing Yün would have still met with the GAC team if I hadn't advised him to do so. Probably he would have. On the other hand, most of the Fokuangshan leadership felt strongly that he should not. I also noticed that, after reading my paper about the episode, Master Hsing Yün gave much greater saliency than he had previously to his sense of gratitude to the United States for its past assistance to Taiwan as a primary motivating force behind the Fokuang donations to the DNC.

Participating in a controversial public incident of a group that one is still actively researching has very definite risks. If the GAC interview had gone badly, for instance, Master Hsing Yün and the rest of Fokuangshan's leadership would have, rightly, resented my advice, which perhaps would have negatively affected our future interactions. Fortunately, the interview went off well, giving a boost to my ongoing quest for access to meetings, interviews, and documents. This became evident almost immediately. While there had still been some uncertainty about whether or not to permit me to attend meetings between Master Hsing Yün and monastics, after the GAC interview I was openly welcomed for all such gatherings. Shortly thereafter, when my family and I moved from Fokuangshan headquarters in southern Taiwan to Nan Tien Temple (a Fokuangshan branch in Australia), Master Hsing Yün personally called the abbess upon our arrival to ensure that we would be taken care of, thereby ensuring a smooth transition into the community.

A potentially negative outcome resulting from advice one has given is not the only risk inherent in participating in politicized controversy. What if, during my fieldwork, the evidence had suggested to me that Master Hsing Yün was acting as an agent for Taiwan's government? Would I have made this public at once, thereby essentially terminating any hope of further fieldwork? In such a case, my duties as an American citizen would have to outweigh those associated with my scholarly endeavors. A more difficult decision would occur if my findings were equivocal, for instance if I had found that Fokuangshan personnel had not been completely straightforward. As scholars, we cannot act as personal relations agents. We must describe the blemishes we have found as well as the beauty marks. But to make public even minor blemishes while still researching a group can have a detrimental effect on subsequent interactions. On the other hand, when one's interpretation of the group is essentially positive, there is the risk that people will question one's scholarly 'objectivity.' Because one is giving a sympathetic appraisal of the group, it appears as though one is acting as advocate for the group. In fact, what one is advocating is not the group's perspective or interests, but the truth, i.e., an accurate understanding of that group and the incident in question. So long as one regards the organization in a positive light, it therefore seems not only permissible, but desirable for the scholar to portray it in this light to the general public, especially when the perception is otherwise. In other words, when the public has an unduly negative perception, it is one's duty as both scholar and citizen to correct that perception. Similarly, when the public has an overly positive perception of an organization that one is studying, one has the responsibility to point out flaws and abuses.

The question of whether, to what degree, and how one should participate in political or controversial aspects of a religious organization one is studying takes on greater salience as Buddhist communities take root in American soil. My advice would never be sought for Taiwanese political issues. It is, however, very natural for the Fokuangshan community to ask my opinion as an educated American about things American, especially when the group is feeling confused and threatened by them. We seek entrance into Buddhist communities as 'participant-observers' with the aim of increasing our own scholarly community's understanding of that group. To the degree that we acquire the trust and respect of the group we study, they will naturally also hope that we can both help them to understand mainstream American society and act as a liaison between them and the general public. So long as one does this in the proper way, with full understanding of the potential risks and liabilities, it provides an excellent opportunity for us scholars of religion to fulfill our obligation of providing a sophisticated and multifaceted understanding of human religious behavior.

On Being Chinese, American, and Buddhist

Did Master Hsing Yün invite Vice-President Al Gore to Hsi Lai Temple to benefit Taiwan business and political interests, his own organization, the Chinese American community, or to express his gratitude and to enhance America's potential as a place for Buddhist practice? Only he can know the answer for sure. All five motives may very well have played a role. As a Buddhist master, however, it makes sense that his primary goal in engaging in international politics has been Buddhist in nature. Some may argue that he was being used, either directly or indirectly, by politicians to further their agenda. On the other hand, one may also contend that Master Hsing Yün regards political engagement as one expedient means to attain Buddhist ideals. In this particular case, political involvement has proved counter-productive. Morale of the Hsi Lai community is at an all-time low, certain of their neighbors have renewed concerns about the 'cult' in their midst, and Master Hsing Yün himself has become more pessimistic about American society.

On the surface, the 'Hsi Lai scandal' was about money and politics. As one considers the event in more depth, however, it becomes apparent that the underlying issue has been that of identity. Who is an American? To what degree can a person be culturally an American even if not legally one, i.e., not a citizen? Do American ideals transcend territorial and juridical boundaries? These are difficult questions. For Chinese, especially those who constitute the Chinese diaspora, cultural factors are much more important than territorial or political considerations in constituting one's identity. Because these factors are so fluid, a person can participate in multiple cultures simultaneously. Hence, Master Hsing Yün finds no incompatibility in claiming himself to be both thoroughly Chinese and fully American. Ultimately, however, he considers such appellations as inconsequential:

> I don't feel that you are Americans. I also don't feel that I am a Chinese. We are all global. We are all the same.... If we could join together with one another with no regard to nationality or race, it would be wonderful. So [the] global character [of Fokuangshan] doesn't simply mean building temples in various places, we want to spread peace, equality, forbearance, friendship, respect, tolerance, everywhere to everyone.[36]

Although Master Hsing Yün may say that 'We are all global,' his call to de-accentuate national identity serves to shift a person's primary allegiance to the vehicle that allows such de-emphasis to occur, i.e., to Buddhism. We are all global in that we all have Buddha Nature. Only when we recognize this will national and other local allegiances fade away. Herein lies the irony of the Hsi Lai Temple incident: Master Hsing Yün invited Al Gore to the temple as part of an idealistic program to lead people toward a more global sense of identity; in the short-term, however, the event has served to accentuate further people's sense of national and cultural differences.

References

Akers, Mary Ann. 'More Events, Funds Linked to Hsi Lai Temple,' *The Washington Times*, Sept. 14, 1997 [Internet].

'Buddhist Nuns Admit Destroying Documents' *AllPolitics*, Sept. 4, 1996 [Internet Site].

'Dow of Poverty,' *Tricycle: The Buddhist Review*, Spring 1997, 10–11.

Fokuangshan. *The 16th General Conference of the World Fellowship of Buddhists: The Grand Opening of Fo Kuang Shan Hsi Lai Temple, U.S.A. Souvenir Magazine*. Hacienda Heights, CA: Hsi Lai Temple, 1988.

Franken, Bob. 'Asian Americans Fight Fund-Raising Scandal Backlash.' *AllPolitics*, Sept. 11, 1997 [Internet site].

'In the News: Paper Traces.' *Tricycle: The Buddhist Review*, Winter 1996, 86–88.

Kovalesk, Serge F. 'Buddhist Nun Changes Story on US$5,000 Donation.' *China Post*, Dec. 7, 1996, 1, 15 (reprinted from *Washington Post*).

____. 'Temple Reimbursed Some Contributors to DNC.' *China Post*, May 27, 1997, 1 (reprinted from *Los Angeles Times*).

Mitchell, Allison. 'Gore Staff Cleared Temple Fete, Aide Says.' *New York Times*, Feb. 15, 1997, 10.

'Mixing Religion, Politics' *AllPolitics*, Oct. 22, 1996 [Internet site].

Sun, Lena H., and John Mintz. 'Nuns Tell of Panic About Fund-raiser.' *The Washington Post*, Sept. 5, 1997, A1.

Tumulty, Karen. 'Gore's Turn to Squirm.' *Time Magazine*, Sept. 15, 1997 [Internet].

Weisskkopf, Michael, and Lena H. Sun. 'Gore Community Outreach Touched Wallets at Temple: April L.A. Event Raised Funds and Questions.' *Washington Post*, Oct. 25, 1996, A1, A20, A21.

Yu, Chun-fang. *The Renewal of Buddhism in China: Chu-hung and the Late Ming Synthesis*. New York: Columbia University Press, 1981.

Yün, Hsing, general editor. *Fokuang Ta Tz'u-tien* [*Fokuang Encyclopedia*]. Taiwan: Fokuang Publishing House, 1989.

Notes

1 This is a translation of Master Hsing Yün's Chinese version of Vice-President Gore's comments.

2 Master Hsing Yün, Address, 'BLIA Buddhist Youth Conference,' Jan. 3, 1997.

3 Master Hsing Yün, Address, Fokuang Disciples Meeting (including all Fokuang monastics and Fokuang college students living in Taiwan), Jan. 27, 1997.

4 *The 16th General Conference of the World Fellowship of Buddhists: The Grand Opening of Fo Kuang Shan Hsi Lai Temple, U.S.A. Souvenir Magazine* (Published by Fokuangshan, Hsi Lai Temple, U.S.A., 1988), preface, ii.

5 Mary Ann Akers, 'More Events, Funds Linked to Hsi Lai Temple,' *The Washington Times*, Sept. 14, 1997 [Internet].

6 Michael Weisskkopf and Lena H. Sun, 'Gore Community Outreach Touched Wallets at Temple: April L.A. Event Raised Funds and Questions,' *Washington Post*, Oct. 25, 1996, A1, A20, A21.

7 Master Hsing Yün, Address, 'BLIA Buddhist Youth Conference,' Jan. 3, 1997.

8 Alison Mitchell, 'Gore Staff Cleared Temple Fete, Aide Says,' *New York Times*, Feb. 15, 1997, 10.

9 Ibid.
10 Karen Tumulty, 'Gore's Turn to Squirm,' *Time Magazine*, Sept. 15, 1997 [Internet].
11 Weisskkopf and Sun, 'Gore Community Outreach.'
12 'Lay monastic' is my ponderous translation for *shih-ku*. *Shih-ku* vow to devote their lives to Buddhism. They remain celibate and live at a temple, as do full monastics, but do not take the 350 *Bhiksuni* vows. Hence, they do not shave their heads, wear monastic robes, or need adhere to all rules governing monastic life. There are currently approximately 30 *shih-ku* in the Fokuang organization. The term 'monastic' (*ch'u-chia chung*) refers to monks and nuns. 'Disciples' (*t'u-chung*) covers monastics and lay monastics. 'Devotees' (*hsin-t'u chung*) refers to all followers, lay, lay monastic, and monastic.
13 Ven. Man Ya is the abbess of a Fokuang branch in Richardson, Texas.
14 Serge F. Kovalesk, 'Buddhist Nun Changes Story on US$5,000 Donation,' *China Post*, Dec. 7, 1996, 1,15 (reprinted from *Washington Post*).
15 Serge F. Kovalesk, 'Temple Reimbursed Some Contributors to DNC,' *China Post*, May 27, 1997, 1 (reprinted from *Los Angeles Times*).
16 Kovalesk, 'Buddhis Nun Changes Story.'
17 'Buddhist Nuns Admit Destroying Documents,' *AllPolitics* [Internet Site], Sept. 4, 1996.
18 Interview of Master Hsing Yün conducted by fact-finding team of U.S. Senate Governmental Affairs Committee, June 15, 1997.
19 Master Hsing Yün, Address, 'BLIA Buddhist Youth Conference,' Jan. 3, 1997.
20 *International Buddhist Progress Society Quarterly*, Winter 1993, 8.
21 Private interview, Dec. 27, 1997.
22 Master Hsing Yün, general editor, *Fokuang Ta Tz'u-tien* [*Fokuang Encyclopedia*] (Taiwan: Fokuang Publishing House, 1989), 5190.
23 Chun-fang Yu, *The Renewal of Buddhism in China: Chu-hung and the Late Ming Synthesis* (New York: Columbia University Press, 1981), 43.
24 Fu Chi-ying, *Ch'üan Teng* [*Passing Down the Light*], 71.
25 Master Hsing Yün (Tr. Tom Graham and Ven. Yi Jih), *A Letter to Members of the BLIA*, chapter 2, 'The Meaning of the BLIA Verses,' 1997.
26 Master Hsing Yün, general editor, *Fokuang Ta Tz'u-tien* [*Fokuang Encyclopedia*] (Taiwan: Fokuang Publishing House, 1989), 6665.
27 Lena H. Sun and John Mintz, 'Nuns Tell of Panic about Fund-raiser,' *The Washington Post*, Sept. 5, 1997, A1.
28 Bill Mitchell, Internet, Sept. 14, 1997.
29 Private interview, Dec. 27, 1996.
30 Bob Franken, 'Asian Americans Fight Fund-Raising Scandal Backlash,' *AllPolitics* [Internet site], Sept. 11, 1997.
31 *Los Angeles Times*, Oct. 18, 1995.
32 Franken, *AllPolitics* [Internet site], Sept. 11, 1997.
33 'In the News: Paper Traces,' *Tricycle: The Buddhist Review*, Winter 1996, 86–88.
34 'Dow of Poverty,' *Tricycle: The Buddhist Review*, Spring 1997, 10–11.
35 Fokuang Buddhists also gained some surprising allies after the Hsi Lai incident. Ralph Reed, executive director of the Christian Coalition said he fully empathized with the Buddhists. The DNC, he continued, were the ones to blame for turning 'a Buddhist temple into a den of thieves.' The Christian Coalition was at the time fighting a legal battle over whether or not they had provided illegal political donations. 'Mixing Religion, Politics,' *AllPolitics* [Internet site], Oct. 22, 1996.
36 Private interview, Dec. 27, 1996.

CHAPTER FOUR

Ritual and the Performance of Buddhist Identity among Lao Buddhists in North America

Penny Van Esterik

The lowland Lao first entered North America as refugees around 1978 following the take-over of the Royal Lao government by the Pathet Lao and the establishment of the Lao People's Democratic Republic (Lao PDR). By 1985, 102,783 Lao had resettled in the United States and 12,793 in Canada.[1] The Lao Lum or lowland Lao are the largest ethnic group in Lao PDR, and the majority practice Theravāda Buddhism.[2]

This paper examines the transformation of a ritual act, *Soukhouan,* and the celebration of a ritually charged place, *That Luang,* Vientiane, the capital of Lao PDR. Both are key parts of performing Lao religious and ethnic identity in Lao PDR and in North America. Both these rituals reside more or less comfortably within Theravāda Buddhism. I first consider *Soukhouan* rituals, and then the celebrations surrounding *That Luang.* The paper concludes with some speculations with regard to Buddhism and the establishment of Lao national and ethnic identity in North America.

Soukhouan

Soukhouan rituals accompany Buddhist, community, and household celebrations and express the heart of Lao identity. Despite the disruption of war and socialist reconstruction and the changes in the lives of Lao refugees resettled in North America, this ritual celebrates social relatedness in a concrete and powerful way. *Soukhouan* reasserts and strengthens social bonds by helping individuals 'pull themselves together' and by tying individuals to their communities.

Soukhouan rituals literally invite the thirty-two components of an individual's spirit essence, or *khouan,* to reside comfortably and permanently in the hair whorls on the crown of the head. If the *khouan* leaves the body for any length of time, physical or mental illness or even death might result. The prerevolutionary, or feudalist, form of *Soukhouan* was probably the most elaborate, although Ananda Rajah argues that this feudalist 'traditional' image of the *Soukhouan* ceremony reflects a romanticized, idealized view.[3]

Soukhouan ceremonies vary in complexity, with weddings and New Year's being the most elaborate. The basic *Soukhouan* structure includes a set of actions, objects, and words that accomplish a ritual task. That task is to strengthen an individual's morale by attracting and binding the wandering souls firmly into the individual's body.

Soukhouan rites celebrate rites of passage, such as marriage, pregnancy, birth, and ordination; mark the start of an undertaking, such as a trip or military service; celebrate someone's return to the community after an absence; strengthen someone suffering from a long or serious illness; dispel bad luck; and welcome officials or guests to a community or a celebration.[4]

The term *Soukhouan* is in most general use; the term *baci* refers specifically to the conical tray-like structure for the 'auspicious rice' used in the ritual. The Cambodian origin of the word hints at the more formal or royal context of the term *baci*, compared to the more informal term, *Soukhouan*. The *khouan* are attracted back to the body by the beauty of the words and by the flowers and offerings built up on a tree-like structure on a tray or in an offering bowl. Here, the talent, wealth, and imagination of the sponsors of the ritual can be fully displayed. Precut lengths of white string are draped from the branches of the *baci*. The structure is decorated with fresh flowers, and beneath the *baci* are dishes of rice, boiled eggs, bananas and other fruit, alcohol, and delicacies to attract a wandering soul.

The officiant is not a monk but a lay elder who probably spent some time in the monkhood. While relatives and friends surround the candidate to be honored, the officiant takes a few strings from the *baci* and recites prayers to entice the wandering souls back into the body of the candidate. These prayers include the Pali verses honoring the Buddha, Dhamma, and Sangha, the Invitation to the Deities (*Anchern Theweda*), and other prayers appropriate to the context.

Following these invocations, the cotton threads are carefully picked off the *baci* and used to bind, first, the wrist of the celebrant, and later, others participating in the *Soukhouan*. While the elders tie strings around the wrist of the celebrant, they recite a formulaic wish for long life, wealth, happiness, and the success of the current undertaking – ordination to the monkhood, a journey overseas, marriage, or school exams. Following the *Soukhouan* and the ceremony of which it forms a part, such as the ordination of a new monk, participants share a festive meal.

Soukhouan may also be performed in much less elaborate settings, as, for example, when a young man who finds he must leave his village suddenly goes to his elderly relatives for their blessings and good wishes for his safety and success. But he still carries with him the strings on his wrist for at least three days and nights to remind him of the strength of his family's concern and to boost his morale.

When the Pathet Lao established the Lao PDR in 1975, they were unable to purge all remnants of royalist ritual, including *Soukhouan*. The Pathet Lao, after their unsuccessful efforts to destroy religion altogether, are now skilled in pulling apart the strands of ethnic and religious identity to emphasize some and downplay others. Since there is no longer a Lao king, royal symbols have largely disappeared or been reinterpreted in Lao PDR.

In contemporary socialist Laos, *Soukhouan* ceremonies still form the basis of wedding ceremonies, along with government authorization for the marriage of its cadre. Martin Stuart-Fox notes that *Soukhouan* persist in the new regime as ceremonies of welcome or farewell for guests, to mark an auspicious occasion, or to prepare for an important event.[5] Lao refugees leaving camps to be repatriated in Laos are given a *Soukhouan* ceremony to wish them luck on their return to Laos. Although some of the more magical or feudalistic language may be altered for officials, *Soukhouan* rituals are not described as needing to be purged from Lao culture. That is, they are not seen as superstitious, feudalistic remnants, but as expressions of egalitarian reciprocity and generosity. In fact, Mayoury Ngaosyvathn sees *Soukhouan* as strengthening the moral stance of the new regime by emphasizing marital fidelity and the respect of children for their parents. Less ostentatious and expensive ceremonies also enhance the equality-oriented policy of the new government.

Soukhouan rituals have also thrived in refugee camps and in Lao refugee communities in North America. They have been successfully adapted to meet new needs in new contexts. Their core meaning remains intact, although the acts are reinterpreted. Lao refugees from New England, for example, comment on constructing *baci*:

> Here in America we make the floral offerings with leaves and flowers that we gather. At home in Laos we used to arrange the flowers differently, just the buds in rows, stuck into a banana stock. Here we don't have banana stalks so we do it this way now... We arrange flowers in a beautiful silver bowl. On the leaves are many strings to bless our loved ones. You tie a string around the person's wrist and say a blessing for strength, health, and long life. There are different blessings for different people. When your wrists are tied in the *baci* ceremony you must keep the strings on for three days and nights.[6]

In North America, the delicacies under the *baci* include cans of Coca Cola, Twinkies, and Oreo cookies, which are later eaten by children.

In North American communities, Lao continue to celebrate their ethnic identity with *Soukhouan*, particularly for weddings. During Buddhist services, parents may approach Buddhist monks to tie threads around the wrists of a sick child. Following a motorcycle accident, a very acculturated-looking young Lao couple requested the monk and elders to perform an abbreviated *Soukhouan* for them to rid them of bad luck. For these individuals, the strings tied by monks or elders around the wrist of the person for whom the ceremony is performed reestablish the psychological equilibrium of the individual, bring blessings, and promote good health.[7]

As the strings help individuals 'pull themselves together' in the face of challenges, so too the strings tie individuals more tightly into their communities. *Soukhouan*, as a joint social activity, affirms core Lao values of reciprocity and sociability. Ngaosyvathn writes that *Soukhouan*

> expresses traditional Lao values of avoidance of conflict and aims at promoting consensus within the social fabric and strengthening social ties. As a key element of Lao culture, the ritual is a microcosm of Lao values serving to integrate the individual both spiritually and socially. In these terms, the ritual may be seen as the quintessential expression of conceptualizations of Lao identity.[8]

Soukhouan rituals present great analytical challenges for anthropologists because they require examination once again of the relations between different aspects of religious and cultural practice; *Soukhouan* encompasses animistic, Buddhist, and court Brahman concepts in a single ritual event.

The problem of where spirits and Hindu deities fit into Theravāda Buddhist practice is epitomized in *Soukhouan* rituals. To some extent, the potential contradictions are also resolved. For in the practice of *Soukhouan*, the strands are truly interwoven and bound together in the performative act. The question raised by scholars regarding whether *Soukhouan* is a Buddhist, animist, or court Brahman ritual is not raised by participants because it is not relevant to them. The act of performing a *Soukhouan* integrates and demonstrates the interdependence of all the strands of Lao religion.

The historical, textual, and contextual strands of Theravāda Buddhism, spirit worship, and court Brahmanism are all intertwined in *Soukhouan*. In different contexts, one strand predominates or provides the dominant symbol for religious activities. Currently, the symbols of court Brahmanism are effectively purged from the Lao religious scene. Kingship no longer exists as the pivotal reference point for ritual behavior as it still is in Thailand. Nevertheless, the more formal *baci* invoke the Hindu gods to observe and participate in the *Soukhouan*.

The greatest contradiction between the various strands in Lao religion concerns the person. Theravāda Buddhism is based on concepts of *anatta* (non-self) and *anicca* (impermanence). How can these concepts provide the basis for stable social and political hierarchies and institutions of some permanence? *Soukhouan* fixes the temporary manifestation we perceive as humans long enough to 'tie down' this human illusion with all its suffering and imperfections and gives it a fixed bounded identity. Building on the insightful work of G. Condominas,[9] we can use the concept of 'enboîtment' to stress the importance of the body or person as the first 'box,' surrounded sequentially by the household, village, and *muang* (political realm, principality, or city). It is the body that is most immediately addressed in *Soukhouan* rituals.

Soukhouan, the most basic Lao ritual, stresses the integrity and identity of persons and offers ritual protection to keep mobile 'souls' trapped within a person's body. Only then can a person act (morally or immorally) within a Buddhist social order. Lao Buddhists are not ambiguous about non-self and impermanence as guiding principles. They place priority on the integrity of the person as a social actor. Thus, they have been able to carry the ritual guaranteeing this integrity across revolutions and resettlement virtually unchanged.

The loss of 'soul,' vital essence or *khouan,* is a powerful metaphor for the experience of Lao Buddhists in North America, as individuals were separated from their homeland and loved ones and faced painful disruptions to every aspect of their lives. Like the wandering souls unable to return to their homes, refugees wander without homes, facing dangerous and unknown conditions. *Soukhouan* rituals are particularly necessary when the social order has been disrupted, as in the experience of refugee flight and resettlement. For Lao refugee communities throughout North America, it is the strength of these social bonds that can tie souls into bodies, and reintegrate individuals into new community settings in North American cities and, for repatriated Lao, into the transformed villages of the Lao PDR.

That Luang

The festival of *That Luang*, celebrated in late November or early December around the *stūpa* (reliquary) outside of Vientiane has been described as 'the most important occasion in the Lao religious calendar.'[10] The *stūpa* housing Buddha relics was built around 1567 when the Lao capital was shifted to Vientiane. The French restored the monument after its burning in the 1870s. It has since become an important pilgrimage center. But without the Lao king, the ritual has become more of a 'national ceremony' in Lao PDR as well as in North America.

More so than most Lao rituals, *That Luang* celebrates a place as well as an event. Since the ritual of *That Luang* is so intimately connected with the *stūpa* outside Vientiane, it is surprising that it has been transferred to North America so successfully. In the Kingdom of Laos, government officials used to pledge allegiance to the Lao king during *That Luang* rituals. However, the ritual of *That Luang* was secularized during the revolution and served as a central rallying ground for official post-liberation rallies in 1975. Its symbolic importance was further exploited when Lao PDR officials offered food and robes to the resident monks at the site in 1979. In 1995, a number of NGOs produced a calendar widely distributed in Vientiane. The cover showed two temples flanking a large rendering of *That Luang* with a procession of men and women from a number of different ethnic groups playing instruments and dancing together. This is particularly noteworthy, since the midland Khmu and upland Hmong head the procession beside the lowland Lao, who are not Buddhists. *That Luang* is clearly becoming a sign of national identity rather than religious identity.

Photographs of *That Luang* are prominently displayed in Lao homes and at Lao community events in North America. The festival of *That Luang* was first celebrated in Toronto as a Buddhist merit-making occasion in the late 1980s. Dominating these celebrations was a model of the *stūpa* at Vientiane built out of bright yellow-painted styrofoam. The model, standing about eight feet high, was decorated with Christmas tree lights and flowers. The model stood in the middle of the hall, with the laity sitting on all sides of the model, facing the monks on the stage at the front of the room.

A merit-making service preceded the celebration of *That Luang*. Following the monks' meal and final chants, community members and visitors from New York State joined in a procession around the model of *That Luang*. The procession formed behind four money trees (*Kalapra-pruk*), to the accompaniment of drums and cymbals, with guests and important male community leaders leading the procession in three clockwise circumambulations of the *stūpa*. As the procession passed the monks on the stage, the monks sprinkled holy water on the crowd. The demeanor of the chanting monks and the sedate male marchers – eyes downcast and hands folded in front of chests – contrasted strikingly with the joyous singing and dancing of the middle-aged women who broke out of the throng to dance, 'hoot,' sing, and entice participation from embarrassed teenage males sitting on the periphery of the room smirking or trying to ignore the antics of their mothers, sisters, and aunts. 'You would think they were drunk,' muttered one black leather-jacketed youth in English.

Following the procession, the merit accrued by participating in the ritual and giving generously was shared with others. Merit transference is stressed whenever there is a rupture in the social order, such as during funerals and ordinations; for refugees, the rupture in the social order is particularly obvious. Transferring merit is one of the ten traditional good deeds of Theravāda Buddhism.[11] The sharing of merit with the gods and with the wandering ghosts (Pali: *peta*, the only non-humans who can acquire merit) is mentioned in Buddhist scriptures (*Anguttara-Nikāya*, *sutta* 50; *Dīgha-Nikāya*, *sutta* 16). In practice, the act of sharing merit is a very human response to the loss of loved ones and the uncertainty of their rebirth status. While the monks chant the verse to share merit with all sentient beings, all present slowly pour water from a small bottle into pedestal bowls. By this act, those who perform meritorious acts generously wish that others –

particularly their deceased relatives – could reap the benefits of their meritorious deeds. For the Lao, this wish is most intensively directed towards deceased parents in Lao PDR.

This act of generosity is particularly poignant for refugees who may have left their parents behind. For others, close relatives remain missing and presumed dead. Few refugees in North America can afford to return to Laos at short notice in time for their parents' funerals, which is why the act of transferring merit is more significant for Lao refugees than for Lao Buddhists in Laos. During a service at a temple in Vientiane, Laos, in July 1989, the act was performed very quickly with water poured onto plants and over cobblestones much more casually than at the Toronto services. There was not the emotional intensity and tension during the chanting that one feels among Lao refugees in Toronto.

This practice also reflects core Lao values regarding responsibilities to elders and parents. These responsibilities do not end with resettlement in a third country. In fact, they become more complex, as the Lao in North America must deal with missing parents, parents whose funerals and memorial services were incomplete, and caring for elderly relatives. For example, an unmarried Lao refugee in Toronto who could not support his elderly parents placed his parents in a subsidized seniors' apartment where neither he nor their grandchildren could stay overnight for a visit. The old couple felt imprisoned – isolated and useless because they were cut off from their relatives. Regulations in the apartments made it impossible for the unmarried son to fulfil his responsibilities to his parents.

Merit-making through water pouring (*Kruat nam*) is a metaphor of loss and death. It expresses one of the dominant ethical preoccupations of Lao refugees and exemplifies the kind of problems they face in adapting to their new home. With the loss of their parental and ancestral generations, they lose the direct continuity with their past that is at the core of Lao identity. For Lao Buddhists in North America, the practice of transferring merit to deceased relatives helps bridge the distance between Laos and North America, past and present, old and new responsibilities.

Following the *That Luang* ritual procession, the food offered to the monks is redistributed to the laity in the form of a communal meal. This is more than just the commensality of most Lao social occasions. For it is considered a particular blessing to share the food given to and accepted by the monks. Anyone participating in the ritual occasion is welcome and encouraged to join the groups of friends sitting around raised bamboo trays laden with special Lao food dishes. Even those who have not contributed food are actively encouraged to share the meal, as if the sharing of food may cause the intention to give generously to arise among all partaking of the meal. Leftover food is carefully wrapped and taken to those who were unable to attend the ceremony, so that they too may participate in the blessings created by the communal merit-making.

This shared meal of Buddhist merit-makers is a model of reciprocity, redistribution, and generosity and actually creates groups. The act of eating together and sharing each other's food constitutes a group, even if this group identity can only be maintained for a short period of time and must be reconstituted on the next ritual occasion. However, it is a concrete and reliable means of establishing a moral community where people know they can develop relations of trust with others and cooperate in joint activities within the domain of religion.

The centrality of food in Lao ceremonies cannot be overemphasized. Yet the relations between food and religious practice have been transformed in North America. On ritual occasions, there is an excess of food donated to the monks. This is in the form of cooked glutinous rice, unpeeled fruit, and special dishes such as curries and soups to be served with the rice. The rice and fruit are placed directly into the alms bowls of the monks. The other dishes are arranged on trays and presented to the monks. In fact, the monks take only a small amount from the dishes displayed on the trays, although they symbolically accept all the food presented. This excess of food is redistributed to the laity in the form of a communal meal following the service. This is an important social and political occasion in North America, as it is one of the few occasions when Lao from distant communities get together.

Adapting Buddhism

It is difficult to be a Lao in North America, difficult to form a Lao community, and difficult to be a Buddhist in a Judeo-Christian context. Lao who arrive in North American cities together may not have known each other in the camps in Thailand let alone in Laos. They share a national origin and the refugee experience, but little else. From this commonality, they must construct Lao identity and Lao community. Buddhist ritual occasions provide special opportunities for forming and strengthening groups. The problem of dealing with strangers is a problem of trust. Who is trustworthy? Who shares your personal standards of morality? Who is a true friend? Buddhist merit-making is an opportunity for displaying one's moral worth and demonstrating one's trustworthiness.

But focusing on Buddhist rituals emphasizes solidarity of ethnic communities rather than cleavages along class and religious lines. Buddhist temples are also sites of conflict over power, resources, and cultural change.[12] Any Buddhist temple established in a North American city can no longer be the 'hub' of community life; the physical space of the temple no longer dominates the landscape nor serves the multiple functions performed by a Lao temple in Laos. In Laos, the temple and Buddhist activities were totally integrated into everyday life. In North America, the temple loses its centrality – spatially, cognitively, and socially – because of the dispersed population and the economic effort Lao refugees need to expend to survive and prosper in North America.

The timing of communal celebrations in North America must be integrated with work weeks. Services are generally held on Sundays, when Buddhist and Christian services compete within the community. That is, it is not easy to participate in both ritual systems on a single weekend. However, in some communities, Buddhist services are held on Saturdays, freeing refugees to attend Christian services, often with their sponsors, on Sundays.

In North America, ritual events are condensed in time. Rituals that lasted three days in Laos take one day in North America. All-day rituals in Laos are condensed to two or three hours in North America. This is partly related to the shift in the use of the weekend, when there are other alternative ways to spend time. Rituals compete with sports and other leisure activities, carried out on weekends, where in Laos, ritual time replaced work time. In North America, other social, economic, and political activities are embedded within ritual time. Since there are only a limited number of occasions for widely dispersed Lao families to get together, Buddhist rituals are also occasions for visiting, matchmaking, selling cloth from Lao PDR, and exchanging information about available jobs and apartments. Religious identity becomes secondary to cultural identity, as temples become sites for cultural preservation through music, dance, and language classes. While public funds cannot be used to support religious initiatives, they can be used to support cultural centers and ethnic associations.

When monks are only available occasionally, ritual cycles change to accommodate their schedules. Seasonal rituals may be stressed or unstressed depending on the availability of monks. On the occasion of a single monk's visit to a community, a public ritual might be held on Sunday, a house blessing at a sponsor's home the next day, and a service to dispel bad luck at a third house. This opportunistic scheduling means that ritual acts which may normally never occur together in Laos will be put together in North America.

These changes in scheduling, condensation, and embeddedness in ritual time may be quite disorienting for elderly Lao familiar with the more leisurely pace of ritual time in Laos. However, since most Lao in North America experienced the disruptions of normal time during the war and the suspension of time while in refugee camps, they adapt readily to the temporal structures of future-oriented westerners, even within their religious domain.

The Lao face particularly difficult problems resolving the meaning of Lao cultural identity outside of Laos. Rituals such as *Soukhouan* and *That Luang* provide raw materials from which individual Lao can begin to structure a new identity in North America. From these ritual acts they select those values which are central to their individual and collective identities as *Lao* rather than their identity as Buddhists.

Nevertheless, Buddhism is important to this task because it provides a framework for explaining suffering and for making sense out of an otherwise chaotic world. Buddhist temples also provide material as well as spiritual insurance against unforeseen needs, counseling, alternative healing techniques, crisis intervention, recreational activities, as well as spiritual resources.[13] Buddhist rituals performed in new lands remain an important part of reconstituting identity.

References

Archaimbault, Charles. *The New Year Ceremony at Basak (South Laos)*. Trans. S. Boas. Ithaca, NY: Cornell University Southeast Asia Program, 1971.

Battisti, Rosemarie. 'Preserving the Spiritual and Cultural Heritage of Amerasian and Southeast Asian Families.' In *Reasons for Living and Hoping: The Spiritual and Psycho-Social Needs of Southeast Asian Refugee Children and Youth Resettled in the United States*. Washington, D.C.: The International Catholic Child Bureau, Inc., 1989.

Bernstein, S. 'Reflections on What It Means to be an American Buddhist.' In *Reason for Living and Hoping: The Spiritual and Psycho-Social Needs of Southeast Asian Refugee Children and Youth Resettled in the United States*. Washington, D.C.: The International Catholic Child Bureau, Inc., 1989.

Bliatout, B. T., et al. 'Mental Health and Preservation Activities Targeted to Southeast Asian Refugees.' In ed. T. Owen, *Southeast Asian Mental Health: Treatment, Prevention, Services, Training and Research*. Washington, D.C.: National Institute of Mental Health, 1985.

Berval, René de. *Kingdom of Laos*. Limoges, France: A. Bontemps Co., Ltd., 1959.

Burford, G. 'Lao Retrospectives: Religion in a Cultural Context.' *Journal of Refugee Research* 1 (1981): 50–58.

Burwell, R. J., P. Hill, and J. F. Van Weklin. 'Religion and Refugee Resettlement in the United States: A Research Note.' *Review of Religious Research* 27 (1986): 356–366.

Canda, Edward, and Thitya Phaobtong. 'Buddhism as a Support System for Southeast Asian Refugees.' *Social Work* 37, no. 1 (1992): 61–67.

Condominas, G. 'In Search of a Vat: The Dai Lu in Internal and the Lao in External Exile.' In *Proceedings of the International Conference on Thai Studies*, 445–456. Canberra: Australian National University, 1987.

Diamine, Arthur. *Laos: Keystone of Indochina*. Boulder: Westview Press, 1985.

Evans, Grant. *Lao Peasants under Socialism*. New Haven: Yale University Press, 1990.

Gombrich, R., and G. Obeyesekere. *Buddhism Transformed*. Princeton, NJ: Princeton University Press, 1988.

Gunn, G. 'Theravadins and Commissars: The State and National Identity in Laos.' In ed. M. Stuart-Fox, *Contemporary Laos*, 76–100. New York: St. Martin's Press, 1982.

Halpern, Joel, and Sam Pettengill. *The Far World Comes Near: The Kingdom of Laos and Laotian Americans – An Exhibition of Laotian Arts and Culture*. Amherst, MA: Augusta Savage Gallery, University of Massachusetts, Amherst, 1987.

Hein, Jeremy. *From Vietnam, Laos and Cambodia: Refugee Experience in the United States.* New York: Twayne Publishers, 1995.

Kuamtou, S. 'Lao in Kalihi.' In ed. T. Beng, *New Immigrants.* New York: Pilgrim Press, 1981.

Lafont, P. B. 'Buddhism in Contemporary Laos.' In ed. M. Stuart-Fox, *Contemporary Laos*, 148–162. New York: St Martin's Press, 1982.

LeBar, F., and A. Suddard. *Laos: Its People, Its Society, Its Culture.* New Haven: HRAF Press, 1960.

Lewis, R. E. M., W. Fraser, and P. J. Pecora. 'Religiosity among Indochinese Refugees in Utah.' *Journal for the Scientific Study of Religion* 27 (1988): 272–283.

McIntosh, W., and J. Alston. *Religion and the New Immigrants: Initial Observations Concerning Lao Refugees in Houston, Texas.* Paper presented at the Annual Meeting of the Association for the Sociology of Religion, Toronto, Canada, 1981.

McLellan, Janet. 'The Role of Buddhism in Managing Ethnic Identity among Tibetans in Lindsay, Ontario.' *Canadian Ethnic Studies* 19 (1987): 63–76.

Muecke, Marjorie. 'Resettled Refugees' Reconstruction of Identity: Lao in Seattle.' *Urban Anthropology* 16, no. 3–4 (1987): 273–289.

Ngaosyvathn, Mayoury. 'Individual Soul, National Identity: The *baci*-Sou Khuan of the Lao.' *Sojourn* 5 (1990): 283–307.

Rajah, Ananda. 'Orientalism, Commensurability and the Construction of Lao Identity: A Comment on the Notion of Lao Identity.' *Sojourn* 5 (1990): 308–333.

Stuart-Fox, Martin. 'Marxism and Theravada Buddhism: The Legitimation of Political Authority in Laos.' *Pacific Affairs* 56 (1983): 428–454.

Stuart-Fox, Martin, and Rod Bucknell. 'Politicization of the Buddhist *Sangha* in Laos.' *Journal of Southeast Asian Studies* 13 (1982): 60–80.

Suksamran, Somboon. *Political Buddhism in Southeast Asia.* London: C. Hurst and Company, 1977.

Tambiah, Stanley J. *Buddhism and the Spirit Cults of Northeast Thailand.* Cambridge: Cambridge University Press, 1970.

Van Esterik, John. 'Lao.' In ed. D. Hines, *Refugees in the United States*, 149–165. Westport, CT: Greenwood Press, 1985.

Van Esterik, Penny. *Taking Refuge: Lao Buddhists in North America.* Tempe, AZ: Program for Southeast Asian Studies, Arizona State University, 1992.

____. 'Interpreting Cosmology: Guardian Spirits in Thai Buddhism.' *Anthropos* 77 (1982): 1–15.

____. 'In-Home Sponsorship for Southeast Asian Refugees: A Preliminary Assessment.' *Journal of Refugee Resettlement* 1, no. 2 (1981): 18–26.

____. 'Cultural Factors Affecting the Adjustment of Southeast Asian Refugees.' In ed. E. Tepper, *Southeast Asian Exodus: From Tradition to Settlement*, 151–171. Ottawa: Canadian Asian Studies Association, 1980.

Notes

1 UNHCR statistics, 1986.
2 For a more detailed discussion of the use of the term Lao, see Ananda Rajah, 'Orientalism, Commensurability and the Construction of Lao Identity: A Comment on the Notion of Lao Identity' in *Sojourn* 5 (1990): 308–333. A more complete treatment of the flow of Lao refugees to North America and their efforts to establish Buddhist institutions is found in my *Taking Refuge: Lao*

Buddhists in North America (Tempe, AZ: Program for Southeast Asian Studies, Arizona State University, 1992), from which I have drawn for this paper.

3 Ananda Rajah, 'Orientalism, Commensurability and the Construction of Lao Identity: A Comment on the Notion of Lao Identity,' *Sojourn* 5 (1990): 313.

4 Cf. Stanley J. Tambiah, *Buddhism and the Spirit Cults of Northeast Thailand* (Cambridge: Cambridge University Press, 1970); Mayoury Ngaosyvathn, 'Individual Soul, National Identity: The *baci*-Sou Khuan of the Lao,' *Sojourn* 5 (1990): 283–307; and F. LeBar and A. Suddard, *Laos: Its People, Its Society, Its Culture* (New Haven: HRAF Press, 1960).

5 Martin Stuart-Fox, 'Marxism and Theravada Buddhism: The Legitimation of Political Authority in Laos,' *Pacific Affairs* 56 (1983): 428–454.

6 Joel Halpern and Sam Pettengill, *The Far World Comes Near: The Kingdom of Laos and Laotian Americans – An Exhibition of Laotian Arts and Culture* (Amherst, MA: Augusta Savage Gallery, University of Massachusetts, Amherst, 1987).

7 Mayoury Ngaosyvathn, 'Individual Soul, National Identity: The *baci*-Sou Khuan of the Lao,' in *Sojourn* 5 (1990): 289.

8 Ibid., 300.

9 G. Condominas, 'In Search of a Vat: The Dai Lu in Internal and the Lao in External Exile,' in *Proceedings of the International Conference on Thai Studies*, 445–456 (Canberra: Australian National University, 1987).

10 G. Gunn, 'Theravadins and Commissars: The State and National Identity in Laos,' in ed. M. Stuart-Fox, *Contemporary Laos*, 84 (New York: St. Martin's Press, 1982).

11 R. Gombrich and G. Obeyesekere, *Buddhism Transformed* (Princeton, NJ: Princeton University Press, 1988), 24.

12 Jeremy Hein, *From Vietnam, Laos and Cambodia: Refugee Experience in the United States* (New York: Twayne Publishers, 1995), 8.

13 Edward Canda and Thitya Phaobtong, 'Buddhism as a Support System for Southeast Asian Refugees,' *Social Work* 37, no. 1 (1992): 64.

Part Two

Profiling the
New Buddhists

CHAPTER FIVE

Night-Stand Buddhists and Other Creatures: Sympathizers, Adherents, and the Study of Religion

Thomas A. Tweed

An American Catholic bishop once confided to me with dismay that the Vietnamese who attend mass in his archdiocese are 'not really Catholic.' Initially I was perplexed by this claim. Did he mean that they had not been baptized in their homeland? Something else? 'They're still too Buddhist,' he explained. He meant that the Buddhist influence was great among Vietnamese Catholics, and they carried that hybrid tradition with them to the United States when they fled after the fall of Saigon in 1975. I thought of that conversation as I recently read a newspaper article on 'The Accidental Buddhist,' which called attention to hundreds of thousands of Americans who practice Buddhist meditation but do not affiliate with any Buddhist temple or center. These examples about Vietnamese Catholics and Buddhist meditators raise central questions in the study of religion: How do we define religious identity? Who is Catholic? Who is Buddhist? And how do we view those who have interest in a religion but do not affiliate? In this essay, I focus on the issue of religious identity as it confronts religion scholars, in particular those who investigate the history of Buddhism in the United States. I aim, first, to complicate our view of adherence, as I propose a strategy for establishing religious identity; and, second, I suggest that we add another category – *sympathizer* – to those we use to interpret religious life.[1]

Adherents: Complicating Religious Identity

Even though many monographs have described peoples with creole practices that have changed in interaction with other traditions – as in the religious history of Cuba and Haiti, Thailand and China – most Western scholars of religion still have assumed that religious identity is singular and fixed, and that the subjects of studies fall into two categories: adherents and non-adherents. Further, identifying adherents seems straightforward. For some, an adherent is one who accepts certain defining beliefs and practices, a strategy I call an essentialist or normative approach. Or, for others, an adherent is one who joins a religious organization or participates in its ritual life. But these three standard strategies for defining religious identity – applying norms, counting members, or observing attendance – introduce conceptual confusions and overlook important persons and groups. The normative approach might suggest, for example, that a Buddhist is one who has formally taken refuge in the Three Jewels (the Buddha, the Dharma, and the Sangha), practiced prescribed rituals at a Buddhist temple (chanting), or affirmed defining beliefs (the Four Noble Truths). But this constructs an essentialized notion of the tradition, imagining the religion as static, isolated, and unified. It fails to acknowledge that traditions change, that they have contacts and exchanges with other traditions, and that hybrid traditions emerge with diverse expressions claiming authenticity. Any normative definition of a religion, therefore, excludes many who might want to count themselves as followers. The other two strategies for establishing religious identity – membership and attendance – invite fewer conceptual difficulties since they do not imagine a defining core, but they fail to account for those who have little or no relation with a Buddhist institution yet still understand the world in Buddhist terms, engage in Buddhist practices, or (at least) view themselves as Buddhists. In short, the usual ways of deciding who is Buddhist – or Christian, Hindu, or Muslim – fail to take seriously enough the complexity of religious identity.[2]

And, as some studies have shown, religious identity can be complex in several ways. First, as in Japan, religions can be functionally compartmentalized: you might be married in one tradition, Shintō, and memorialized in another, Buddhism. Second, especially in diverse cultural contexts where religious identity does *not* carry harsh political or economic consequences, some religious women and men self-consciously and unapologetically draw on varied practices from multiple traditions. In some periods and regions in China, for instance, men and women have turned to Buddhist *bodhisattvas*, Confucian sages, and Taoist immortals – along with a host of other human or suprahuman exemplars who have emerged from vernacular religious traditions. In seventeenth-century America, many Massachusetts Puritans combined occult practices, like astrology, with their Protestant piety, just as some who attended Spiritualist seances in the 1850s identified themselves as Episcopalians. And, today, some who turn to the healing powers of crystals during the weekday sing hymns at a United Methodist Church on Sunday.[3]

Third, even in cultural contexts where admitting that you incorporate practices or beliefs from multiple traditions can get you sanctioned by religious leaders, relegated to menial labor, or sentenced to prison, religious identity can be multiple or ambivalent. There can be 'ism'-crossing, a (often less self-conscious) combining in practice of more than one tradition – as in the influence of Santería on Cuban Catholicism or the impact of Shintō on

Japanese Buddhism. In fact, these sorts of religious combinations are so common that, if we ignore those who affiliate with hybrid traditions, engage in creole practices, or express ambivalent identities, there would be no one left to study. Most of the religions I know emerged in contact and exchange with other traditions, and they continued to change over time – always in interaction. Scholars cannot locate a pristine beginning or precontact essence to use as a norm to define orthodoxy or orthopraxis. There is hybridity all the way down. In this sense, religious identity is usually complex. Ambivalence is the norm.[4]

Finally, religious identity also can be complex for converts. Conversion involves a more or less (often less) complete shift of beliefs and practices. The old tradition never fades completely; the new one never shapes exclusively. That was true of Christian converts in colonial Africa, Asia, and North and South America, where indigenous practices colored the religious life of many native 'converts.' It remains true of self-identified Buddhist converts in modern industrialized nations with legislated religious freedom. Conversion also has its social costs and payments, and that affects the character of religious belief and practice. In some colonized nations in nineteenth-century Africa, for example, conversion to Christianity could slightly raise one's social status. On the other hand, in nineteenth-century Britain, conversion to Vedanta Hinduism might prompt derision. In periods and places where conversion has high social *value*, the number of self-announced converts might multiply, even though their spiritual practice might retain many elements of the denounced tradition. Where conversion has high social *costs*, many of the converted who have found their frameworks of meaning and habits of practice profoundly altered by a realignment with another tradition might do all they can to hide that from public view. Some celebrate conversion; others conceal it. Either way, the converts' self-understanding and everyday practice is complex.[5]

If religious identity is as complex as I have suggested, then this has implications for the study of Buddhist adherents in America. As we study 'cradle' Buddhists who were born into the tradition – Chinese immigrants in nineteenth-century San Francisco or Laotians in contemporary Chicago – we should be alert to the ways that their religious practice has been hybrid and their religious identity ambivalent – in the homeland, in transit, and in the new land. In a similar way, as we study converts, we should attend carefully to the evidence in language, artifact, and gesture that their religious life reveals influence from multiple sources, including the tradition they rejected when they joined the Buddhist *sangha*.

Sympathizers and the Story of Buddhism in America

So far I have discussed only adherents, cradle Buddhists who inherited the faith and converts who chose it, those followers who might meet the standard criteria for defining Buddhist identity. But placing the focus there excludes a great deal: it overlooks those who have not offered full or formal allegiance to the tradition.

And many in the United States, and the West, fit that profile. Fifteen percent of the French express 'an interest' in Buddhism and two million describe it as 'the religion they like best,' according to a recent report. Of the 600,000 Buddhists in France less than 100,000 are 'full blown Buddhists.' But, the report continued, 'many millions are said to be influenced by Buddhism.' That recent article about meditators I mentioned at the start of the essay made a similar point about the United States. One scholar quoted in that story suggested – correctly, I think – that we do not know how many Americans use Buddhist meditation practices. But, she estimated, 'the number is large, probably in the many hundreds of thousands, possibly more.' In that same article Helen Tworkov, the editor of the popular Buddhist quarterly *Tricycle*, estimated that half of the publications' 60,000 subscribers do not describe themselves as Buddhists. I call those 30,000 *Tricycle* subscribers and the hundreds of thousands of unaffiliated meditators *sympathizers*, or in a flashier but less precise and inclusive phrase, *night-stand Buddhists*.[6]

What, then, is a sympathizer or night-stand Buddhist? It might be useful to clarify first what it is *not*. *Sympathizer* does not refer to men and women who identify with a tradition self-consciously but fail to practice it vigorously or regularly. Luke-warm adherents are familiar in many cultural contexts and religious traditions. David D. Hall noticed the pattern in seventeenth-century New England. In his *Worlds of Wonder, Days of Judgment* Hall distinguishes 'devout Calvinists' from 'horse-shed Christians.' The latter spent the long intermission between the two services in the horse-shed – yes, those Protestants attended two services on the same day – talking of secular, not religious, matters. Horse-shed Christians, in Hall's account, 'limit[ed] their commitment' to Christianity. They practiced intermittently – more in some seasons or years than others and more at certain points in the life cycle. Horse-shed Christians deserve scholarly attention, but they are not night-stand Buddhists.[7] The term *sympathizer* does not signal the level of commitment among those who identify themselves with a tradition.

Sympathizers are those who have some sympathy for a religion but do not embrace it exclusively or fully. When asked, they would *not* identify themselves as Buddhists. They would say they are Methodist, or Jewish, or unaffiliated. If we could talk with them long enough – or, better yet, visit their homes and observe their daily routine – we would notice signs of interest in Buddhism. They might practice *zazen*, subscribe to a Buddhist periodical, or read books about the tradition. They might attend lectures at the local university. They might visit a Buddhist center's web page or participate in an on-line Buddhist discussion group. They might consciously decorate their homes with Buddhist artifacts. Night-stand Buddhists, then, are those who might place a how-to book on Buddhist meditation on the nightstand – say, Philip Kapleau's *The Three Pillars of Zen* – and read it before they fall to sleep, and then rise the next morning to practice, however imperfectly or ambivalently, what they had learned the night before. If I am right, these sympathizers have been an important part of the story of Buddhism in America since the 1880s – from philosopher Paul Carus and businessman Andrew Carnegie to composer John Cage and artist William Wiley, and, more important, the many ordinary American sympathizers whose names have been lost to us.[8]

These sympathizers have encountered Buddhism in different social sites; or, to put it differently, several cultural practices have created and sustained their interest in the tradition – reading texts, viewing artifacts, and performing rituals. We could consider artifacts (including domestic furnishings and landscape architecture as well as paintings and computers) or analyze ritual practices (including meditation, chanting, or the medical uses of mindfulness practice). Here I will mention only a few textual examples.

Sympathy for Buddhism in America was predominantly a matter of reading texts in the late nineteenth century, and only as Buddhist teachers and institutions multiplied did other kinds of ritual and material contacts with the tradition become possible and important for a wide range of Americans. Still, the text-centeredness of religious sympathy (and conversion) continues in contemporary America, as James Coleman shows in his chapter in this volume: the vast majority of those non-Asians who are drawn to the tradition report that a text was decisive for them.

Several kinds of texts have been influential since the nineteenth century. Since the 1880s, when the first English-language Buddhist magazine appeared in the United States, sympathizers have been drawn to the tradition by periodicals. That first Buddhist magazine, *The Buddhist Ray* (1888–94) had a small circulation and was too idiosyncratic – with its blend of Theosophical, Swedenborgian, and Buddhist themes – for most Euro-American readers. The next English-language Buddhist magazine, *The Light of Dharma* (1901–7) had a slightly larger and more geographically dispersed readership – and it included some very sophisticated accounts of the tradition by Asian Buddhists, mostly Japanese. Some of those authors, like the youthful D. T. Suzuki, would go on to have considerable influence after World War II.

In 1991 another Buddhist periodical appeared, one that consciously linked itself with that first publication from the 1880s. That magazine, *Tricycle: The Buddhist Review*, has drawn criticism as well as praise. Shortly after its appearance, one Euro-American Buddhist teacher from California complained to me that it was an 'East Coast' magazine, and soon after an Asian American Buddhist dismissed it, saying that it was just for elite white Americans. If there are 'two Buddhisms' in America (Caucasian and Asian), as Charles Prebish and others have claimed, clearly *Tricycle* has been less aligned with the interests of Asian American followers. But the magazine has been important for identifying – and maybe creating – European American and African American Buddhist sympathizers in the United States. Its tens of thousands of readers who do not affiliate with Buddhism formally or fully are an important part of the tradition's history in America.[9]

Many sympathizers also have encountered the tradition in books. As I argued in *The American Encounter with Buddhism, 1844–1917*, if we considered the popularity of only three nineteenth-century books we would get a sense of the scope and significance of Buddhist sympathy in the period: Edwin Arnold's *The Light of Asia* (1879), Henry Steel Olcott's *Buddhist Catechism* (1881), and Paul Carus's *The Gospel of Buddha* (1894). Each had sizeable sales. Arnold's poetic life of the Buddha sold between five hundred thousand and one million copies and went through eighty American editions. Olcott's catechism went through more than forty editions before the author died in 1907. Carus's *Gospel of Buddha* went through thirteen editions by 1910, and it introduced many Americans to the tradition.[10]

That pattern continued throughout the twentieth century, as an increasing number of books reached a wide audience and sparked interest among sympathizers. Those include, for example, Dwight Goddard's *A Buddhist Bible* (1938), a work that excited many readers in the post-war period. It was Goddard's book that Jack Kerouac carried in his backpack as he and other 'Dharma Bums' of his generation borrowed some Buddhist ideas and practices. The writings of D. T. Suzuki (along with his public lectures) have had profound influence on some Americans since the 1940s, including his *An Introduction to Zen Buddhism* (1934), a book that continued to sell 10,000 copies each year in the 1990s. Suzuki's influence on sympathizers was both direct and indirect. His indirect influence came through the painters, musicians, therapists, and poets his books inspired.[11]

In recent decades, the number of books with Buddhist themes has multiplied many times. For example, in 1997 *Books in Print* listed 197 titles that began with 'Zen ... ,' 'Zen and ... ,' or 'Zen of...' The list included, by my count, seventy-seven how-to books that apply Zen to one or another aspect of life, from the silly to the sophisticated, including *Zen and Creative Management, Zen and the Art of Kicking Butts: The Ultimate Guide for Quitting Smoking Forever, Zen in the Art of Golf, Zen and the Art of the Internet*, and *Zen and the Art of Changing Diapers*. However we might assess these popular prescriptive texts, which sometimes have little to do with Zen as most scholars and practitioners would understand it, they clearly show the breadth of Buddhist sympathy in the culture.[12]

The list of recent titles on Buddhism also includes fine translations of sacred texts, informed advice about practice, and reflections by American or Asian teachers. Among the latter, Thich Nhat Hanh's *The Miracle of*

Mindfulness (1975) is a good example. Beacon Press reports that the book had sold 'about 125,000' copies by 1997. If we added the publication figures for his other English-language books, from Riverhead Press and Parallax Press, his influence seems indisputable. (For example, his recent text, *Living Buddha, Living Christ,* has sold 80,000 copies for Riverhead Press.) As with all texts, it is impossible to count the proportion of sympathizers included among his readers (or to determine how readers interpreted the books). It seems clear, however, that many of Thich Nhat Hanh's readers do not belong to Buddhist groups or identify themselves with Buddhism.[13]

The Meaning of 'Adherent' in the Scholarship

Some readers might object at this point: but we know this. You have built a monument to the obvious. We know that religious identity is hybrid and that there are Buddhist dabblers. And it is true that some of the best writing about Buddhism in North America has acknowledged the problem of determining identity. In his important 1979 study, *American Buddhism,* Charles Prebish takes on the issue in a two-page section titled 'What Constitutes a Buddhist?' There Prebish acknowledges that 'it has become difficult to know what constitutes a Buddhist today.' He points to the varying ways that Buddhist institutions count members: does membership refer to those who donate, attend, or join? Emma McCloy Layman in *Buddhism in America*, a study published three years earlier, also had noticed the problem as she tried to count American Buddhists. 'There are several reasons for the difficulty in estimating the number of Buddhists in America,' Layman proposed. Among the four she listed were these: that most 'nominal Buddhists' had failed to ritually accept the tradition, while other 'self-styled Buddhists' had not joined any Buddhist institution.[14]

Other more recent reflections on Asian immigrant Buddhists have acknowledged a related difficulty in defining Buddhists, making the point I have emphasized here: religious belief and practice, in the homeland and the new land, has been hybrid. In his study of the Vietnamese in the United States, the anthropologist Paul James Rutledge noticed:

> The religious thought of many Vietnamese has been a *blending* of a number of systems, choosing not to claim one and denounce the others but rather to *mix* the teachings of various faiths in order to meet the particular needs of their community or family. This *syncretistic* practice is deeply rooted in the practice of religion by Vietnamese people.... Although most Vietnamese are Buddhist, either by practice or claim, Vietnamese refugees in America also ascribe [to] Confucianism, Taoism, Roman Catholicism and a variety of Eastern religions less known in the West.[15]

77

Penny Van Esterik, an anthropologist who specializes in Southeast Asia, made a similar point in *Taking Refuge*, her book-length study of Lao Buddhists in Toronto. She notes that Lao religion combines both 'spirit worship' and Theravāda Buddhism. The vernacular tradition of venerating spirits has been strong in Laos, as strong as anywhere in Asia, and for Van Esterik that indigenous tradition has become part of Laotian Buddhism. 'Ghosts and spirits,' she suggests, 'are interacted with as part of the Buddhist world order.' For that reason, 'understanding Lao religion in the past and the present requires close attention to obeisance owed to the spirit world as well as the system of Theravāda Buddhism. The relation between these two systems provides the unique characteristics of Lao religion.' Van Esterik essentializes and isolates the two religious 'systems' a bit too much for me – interpreting them as if they were two originally distinct and self-contained cultural forms that then came into contact with the other – but still, she recognizes the hybrid character of Buddhist identity.[16]

Other scholars have noticed how cradle and convert Buddhists have had complex and ambivalent relationships with American cultural and religious values and practices. Even if he offers an interpretation that is not sympathetic enough to Henry Steel Olcott's self-understanding as a Buddhist, Stephen Prothero's sophisticated book, *The White Buddhist*, centers upon the issue of religious identity. In an imaginative use of linguistic theory, Prothero argues that Olcott's was a 'creole' faith, combining a Buddhist 'lexicon,' a Theosophical 'accent,' and a liberal Protestant 'grammar.' Olcott, according to Prothero, accepted and promoted a Protestantized and Americanized Buddhism. In his study of Americanization in two Theravāda Buddhist temples in Los Angeles and Chicago, Paul Numrich noticed that in Los Angeles temples hold summer camps, and in Chicago monks wear overcoats. In other words, Asian American Buddhists have accommodated American culture, as well as resisted it, and in the process complex forms of the tradition have emerged in this cultural context, where Buddhists meet not only Christians, Jews, and Muslims, but a wider variety of Buddhists than anywhere in Asia.

Many scholars and Buddhists, and some Buddhist scholars, have considered the problems of adapting this Asian tradition to a Western culture. One scholar, writing for an issue of *Amerasia Journal*, exhorted Asians not to be afraid of 'religious symbiosis' as the younger generations seek to revitalize 'Asian American religious identities.' Some Buddhist leaders in the United States have made similar suggestions; while others have held a more traditional line. Either way, observers have noticed that cultural exchanges have happened and new forms of Buddhism have emerged as practitioners make their way in America, as they meditate in chairs, sing Buddhist hymns, bite into burgers, and gather on Sundays.[17]

If some scholars have acknowledged the hybrid character of Buddhist identity, others have not; but even those who note its complexity have not usually explored that fully in their writings. Let's return to one of the first and best books on the subject, Prebish's *American Buddhism*. Prebish acknowledges the problem of defining Buddhist identity in two pages, as I have noted, but then goes on to write as if that were not very complicated as he surveys the Buddhist scene in the 1970s, considering, in turn, the various Buddhist traditions and groups: Buddhist Churches of America, San Francisco Zen Center, Buddhist Vihara Society, Tibetan Nyingma Meditation Center, and so on. Rick Fields, in his lively and important historical narrative of Buddhism in the United States, also shows that he knows that Buddhism has been creole, assuming varied forms in Asian cultures and encountering great diversity in America. He repeats, for example, the common wisdom about Chinese religious blending in China and America: 'The Chinese temples reflected popular Chinese religion, which was a *mixture* of Taoism, Confucianism, and Buddhism.' Still, most of his story overlooks or underemphasizes the hybrid character of Buddhism in the United States, especially among Asian immigrants. My point here – and I want to be clear – is not that these writers, and the rest of us too, have failed to notice the complexity of Buddhist identity. Those of us working in this subfield have not always systematically or fully applied our best insights about the hybrid character of Buddhist identity in our studies.[18]

To shift the focus slightly – and approach the center of my interest in this topic – I think that part of the problem in the subfield of American Buddhist history, and in religious studies more broadly, is that we continue to draw on an essentialist-normative definition of religious identity, those that construct a core or essence of right practice or belief and measure all historical expressions against that. Fields, for instance, suggests that 'Buddhist history is the record of lineage – of who gave what to whom....' To apply this standard means that those who have teachers and affiliate with institutions are authentic Buddhists; others are suspect and (mostly) excluded from our stories about American Buddhist history. Because it avoids the theoretical problems of essentialist definitions and allows more characters into our historical narratives, I suggest that we use self-identification as the standard for identifying Buddhists. Buddhists, in my view, are those who say they are.[19]

Some readers might object that this position is too uncritical, allowing a flood of Buddhist pretenders through the scholarly gates. That concerns Philip C. Almond, the author of a fine study of Buddhism in Britain, and it is occult Buddhists, those connected with the Theosophical Society, who most worry him. His solution: ignore them, even though esoteric Buddhists far outnumbered all other self-identified Caucasian Buddhists in Europe and America during the late-nineteenth century. He explains his stance in a footnote: 'I have not dealt with the Esoteric Buddhism of Madame Blavatsky and her English disciple, Alfred Sinnett. Esoteric, it may have been. Buddhism it certainly was not....' Fields never responds directly to this issue, but he, too, implicitly rejects self-identification as a standard when he emphasizes the importance of lineages and institutions. In his *American Buddhism*, Prebish follows Holmes Welch, the accomplished scholar of Chinese Buddhism, in arguing that 'it is insufficient to simply ask "Are you a Buddhist?"' Because of the interpenetration of religious traditions, and the concomitant overlapping of religious identities, in China, the respondent might say that, yes, he is a Buddhist. In the next minute, however, he might also admit to being a Taoist or a Confucian too. Prebish proposes another strategy for settling Buddhist identity: 'A more appropriate question might be (as Professor Welch suggests): "Have you taken the Three Refuges?" Further, "Do you practice the five layman's vows?"' Prebish then complicates the issue further by pointing out that he has ignored 'a consideration of the *quality* of membership and *commitment* to the tradition.' And here a misleading essentialist-normative definition of Buddhist identity enters. In this view, which I think remains common among scholars and almost universal among practitioners, a Buddhist is someone who meets certain standards of orthodoxy or orthopraxis. She is a Buddhist if she takes refuge in the Three Jewels, accepts the doctrine of no-self, or chants regularly. But Prebish worried that some readers might misinterpret him: 'It might be inferred my sympathies rest with the older, traditional forms of Buddhism; that I assume the only valid form of a religious tradition is its pristine expression. Each claim, however, would simply be ungrounded.' Still, even though Prebish tries to clear a middle path by acknowledging the need for accommodation to the host culture, there are limits on what he (and most scholars and practitioners) will accept as Buddhist: 'Of course there is no *Ur*-Buddhism, but we must ask at what point the "aloha-amigo" amalgam becomes so strange and fantastic that it ceases to be *Buddhist, American,* or a *meaningful combination of the two.*' I see his point, of course: some claims to Buddhist identity seem very odd when measured against the history of the tradition in Asia, or even America. Still, I stand by my proposal that self-identification is the most useful approach for scholars.[20]

Let me support that claim with two examples, one from the turn of the twentieth century and the other from the contemporary period. F. Graeme Davis, a self-proclaimed Buddhist from Vermillion, South Dakota, is one of the characters in the story of Buddhism in America whom we might exclude if we use the usual standards for settling religious identity. Graeme, one of the most memorable figures in the Victorian American encounter with Buddhism, saw himself as a Buddhist. He also subscribed to a Buddhist magazine, *The Light of Dharma*, and even corresponded with the Japanese priests at the Jōdo Shinshū Buddhist mission in San Francisco. 'My sympathies are altogether with you and your work,' Graeme wrote to the Reverend Nishijima in San Francisco in 1901, '[and] it is my hope that I may sometime be able and worthy to aid in working for the same cause, for

I believe Buddhism to be the religion of humanity.' But I have been unable to find evidence that he ever joined, or even attended, a Buddhist institution or ritually proclaimed his allegiance by taking refuge in the Buddha, Dharma, and Sangha. He tried his best to live the Buddha's teachings: he even organized a group, with three other students at the University of South Dakota, which met every Friday evening 'for the purpose of studying Buddhism.' Not enough historical evidence survives to offer a textured interpretation of the meaning of Buddhism for Graeme and his three friends – wouldn't you love to sit in that dorm room in 1901 to hear his study group's conversations about Buddhism? – but he is an important character in the story of American Buddhism, even if essentialist or institution-focused standards for deciding religious identity would lead us to ignore him.[21]

A second example of a self-proclaimed Buddhist who might be excluded if we use other criteria for deciding identity, is, I hope, familiar to you. Margaret – let's give her a pseudonym to protect her – is a middle-aged woman from a suburb just outside a major northern city. When we inquire about her life, we find that she practices zazen intermittently, dangles a crystal from her rearview mirror, watches television programs on yoga, and reads books on Zen and Tibetan Buddhism. At home she is (mostly) vegetarian and, on the mornings she can find the time, she practices tai chi. On some Saturday afternoons, after she finishes with the soccer carpool and before preparing dinner, Margaret visits the local bookstore, lingering around the 'New Age' section, usually leaving with a book on past lives or healthy relationships. On most Sundays she attends St. Mark's Episcopal Church. Margaret never attended or joined a Buddhist group. She has not taken refuge in the Three Jewels. Nor does she seem to meet most formal criteria for Buddhist identity. Still, when we ask her, Margaret insists that she is a Buddhist. Now, why would we want to take her claim seriously? In short, because of what it reveals about her and the culture. It helps us attend to someone – and to a wider cultural pattern – that we otherwise might have missed. It is important to know that in American culture at this particular moment, or at least in that middle-class (mostly white) suburban subculture, some folks want to claim Buddhist identity. Then we can begin to ask a series of questions, beginning with the most basic: why does she say she is Buddhist? We might learn that it is fashionable in her circle to be Buddhist or that she wants to signal, to anyone who will listen, her dissent from the Christian church she visits on Sunday, a church she attends mostly because she feels compelled to raise her children in some faith and the local Buddhist center has no religious education (and joining there would invite too much ridicule from her extended family). And there are other reasons she identifies with Buddhism, ones that we cannot fully or confidently recover. In any case, my point is that a normative definition of Buddhism excludes Margaret, and Graeme, from the historical narrative, and thereby overlooks important characters and significant trends.

These examples, and many others, indicate that there might be reasons to widen our definition of 'Buddhist' to include these self-identified followers, but, I realize, some readers still might have other grounds for rejecting the strategy I propose (self-identification) since personal religious commitments and role-specific obligations can shape our responses on this issue. For practitioners, and especially for religious leaders, it might make sense to draw boundaries, to set limits on acceptable belief and practice. In one sense, religious leaders have a role-specific obligation to disallow certain practices and contest certain beliefs. Some followers might insist, for example, that *authentic* Buddhists do not condone violence or affirm theism. Yet scholars, and practitioners who are working as scholars, do not have the same obligations to establish right practice or right belief. A scholar's duty, I suggest, is to understand as much as possible about religion and culture. For that reason self-identification is the most useful standard for defining religious identity, and not only because it avoids the theoretical problems of essentialist approaches and includes the greatest range of characters. It also uncovers much about the status and meaning of the religion at that historical moment and in that cultural setting.

The Significance of Sympathizers

Whether or not scholars have used self-identification to locate Buddhists – and most have not – some have acknowledged the hybrid character of religious identity, even if they have not always emphasized that in their work. Fewer interpreters, however, have taken seriously the many Americans who have had sympathy for Buddhism but have not self-identified with the tradition. A handful of sympathizers find their way into Fields's long narrative of American Buddhist history – for example, Henry Adams – but Fields (for the most part) ignores those who did not fully identify themselves with the religion. Even some who might be counted as Buddhists by any criteria – for example, William Sturgis Bigelow and Ernest Fenollosa, who both took the precepts at a Japanese temple – enter the historical narrative only as an aside. 'From the viewpoint of American Buddhist history,' Fields explains, 'the period of the *fin-de-siecle* Boston Buddhists remains an interlude... [since] neither of them had the inclination – or the training – to introduce Buddhist practice on a more practical level...neither founded any organizations or left any Buddhist disciples.' With this standard for determining characters' importance, it is not surprising that those who did not profess Buddhist identity are (mostly) ignored. The same is true of Prebish's *American Buddhism*, and most other studies on the topic.[22]

Among those who have written about American Buddhism, Emma Layman did take notice of sympathizers. She called them, alternately, 'inquirers' or 'Dharma hoppers,' and discussed each briefly. By 'inquirers' she meant those 'who are transients at the temple or meditation center, as well as non-Buddhist scholars and Christian clergymen who may be on several Buddhist mailing lists.' 'Dharma hoppers,' in her usage, are 'shopping around for a magic key to happiness and peace of mind, then dropping out.' 'Many have tried several Buddhist sects,' Layman continues, 'some have tried several Christian denominations before becoming Buddhists, and some played around with Yoga, Krishna Murti, or Sufi' [sic]. It is not clear that Layman's 'Dharma hoppers' are actually sympathizers in my terminology, since some (or many) might identify themselves as Buddhists at some point along their religious journey. Still, Layman recognizes that among non-Asians there have been many seekers who have had interest in Buddhism, and some ambivalent entanglement with the tradition, even if these 'hoppers' never self-identify or formally affiliate.[23]

But *sympathizer* is not an interpretive category for most religion scholars, or students of American Buddhism in particular, and so these 'inquirers' and 'Dharma hoppers' are not among the characters in our narratives about the history of Buddhism in the United States. Consider one more example from the scholarship. The Buddhist studies scholar Jan Nattier has offered a very useful typology of American Buddhism and, concomitantly, American Buddhists. 'Religions travel in three ways,' Nattier proposes, 'as import, as export, and as "baggage."' And it is 'these divergent styles of transmission, not matters of doctrine, practice, or national origin, that have shaped the most crucial differences within American Buddhism.' Elite Americans, mostly privileged whites, have sought out the Asian imports, mostly Vipassana and Zen, which emphasize meditation. Other converts have been attracted to Asian exports with missionizing impulses, like Sōka Gakkai International. Other Buddhists in America, according to Nattier's scheme, have been Asian immigrants who have brought their Buddhism along with them as cultural 'baggage.' This typology helps us to see a great deal about American Buddhists that we might otherwise overlook, but it does not account for all that is culturally or religiously significant. I suggest that we keep Nattier's economic metaphor but add another category to her typology. When it comes to the Dharma, there are not only baggage bearers, importers, and exporters, but *shoppers* as well. At least tens of thousands – and probably hundreds of thousands – of Americans have neither inherited the tradition from their parents nor bought it fully in the marketplace of U.S. religion. They shop – purchasing a bit of this and consuming a bit of that, but never buying it all. Our standard typologies (Caucasian Buddhists/Asian Buddhists or import/export/baggage Buddhists) and the usual interpretive categories (adherents/non-adherents) have not accounted for Buddhist sympathizers, who deserve fuller study.[24]

Conclusion: Including Diverse Characters in the Story

I have argued, first, that religious identity is hybrid, which scholars have sometimes acknowledged but rarely emphasized; and that using self-identification to locate Buddhists best accounts for this religious hybridity. Second, scholars have attended even less carefully to those who have sympathy for Buddhism but do not fully or formally embrace it, and these sympathizers – like those who self-identify with the religion but never join – enrich the narrative of American Buddhist history, revealing a great deal about the beliefs and practices of American culture.

To put this differently, a wide assortment of characters have played their roles in the story of Buddhism in the United States, and we should find a place in the scholarly narratives for them all. Of course, we need to consider both *cradle Buddhists*, those born into the faith, and *convert Buddhists*, those who chose it, as we highlight the creole character of their religious life – for example, Asian immigrants who unconsciously blend Laotian spirit-religion with Theravadin practices, or Euro-American converts who unwittingly combine Protestant principles and Vajrayana values. But there are also *not-just-Buddhists*, who (if asked) would openly acknowledge dual or multiple religious identities: the Vietnamese refugee who says she is Confucian and Buddhist, the American Zen convert who claims to be both a practicing Buddhist and a religious Jew. Borrowing the term that Hall used to describe luke-warm Puritans, we also should remember *horse-shed Buddhists*, who practice more at some times of the year than others or, even though they join a temple or center, practice less vigorously than most religious leaders would prescribe. *Dharma hoppers*, to use Emma Layman's term, move from one group to another in their spiritual journey, and some claim Buddhist identity while others, distancing themselves from all institutional piety, prefer the 'seeker' label. Some other non-Buddhists, whom I have not discussed here, play an important role, too, in the story: *Buddhist opponents*, such as evangelical Protestants who dismiss Buddhism as a dangerous 'cult' or try to convert followers in Asia; and *Buddhist interpreters*, journalists, film makers, scholars, poets, painters, and novelists who represent the tradition for American audiences. Most important, I have tried to suggest, we should remember the many *night-stand Buddhists*, who have found themselves drawn to Buddhism, even if they never have gone farther in their practice than sitting almost cross-legged on two folded pillows, imitating an illustration in Kapleau's *Three Pillars of Zen*, silently facing their bedroom wall.[25]

References

Abe, Masao. *A Zen Life: D. T. Suzuki Remembered.* New York: Weatherhill, 1986.
Almond, Philip C. *The British Discovery of Buddhism.* Cambridge: Cambridge University Press, 1988.

Arnold, Edwin. *The Light of Asia; Or, The Great Renunciation; Being the Life and Teaching of Gautama.*1879; Wheaton, IL: Theosophical Publishing House, 1969.

Arsone, Sarah. *Zen and the Art of Changing Diapers.* Ventura, CA: Printwheel, 1991.

Brandon, Brandon. *Santeria from Africa to the New World: The Dead Sell Memories.* Bloomington: Indiana University Press, 1993.

Cage, John. *Silence: Lectures and Writings.* Middletown, CT: Wesleyan University Press, 1973.

Carnegie, Andrew. *Autobiography of Andrew Carnegie.* Boston: Houghton Mifflin, 1920.

Carus, Paul, ed. *The Gospel of Buddha.* 1894; Tucson, Arizona: Omen, 1972.

Colson, Elizabeth. 'Converts and Tradition: The Impact of Christianity on Valley Tonga Religion.' *Southwestern Journal of Anthropology* 26 (1970): 143–56.

Comaroff, John L., and Jean Comaroff. *Of Revelation and Revolution: Christianity, Colonialism, and Coercion in South Africa.* Chicago: University of Chicago Press, 1991.

Dawson, Lorne. 'Self-Affirmation, Freedom, and Rationality: Theoretically Elaborating "Active" Conversions,' *Journal for the Scientific Study of Religion* 29 (June 1990): 141–63.

Desmangles, Leslie G. *The Faces of the Gods: Vodou and Roman Catholicism in Haiti.* Chapel Hill: University of North Carolina Press, 1992.

Fields, Rick. *How the Swans Came to the Lake: A Narrative History of Buddhism in America,* revised and updated edition. Boston and London: Shambhala, 1986.

Gelburd, Gail, and Geri De Paoli. *The Transparent Thread: Asian Philosophy in Recent American Art.* Philadelphia: University of Pennsylvania Press, 1990.

Goddard, Dwight, ed. *A Buddhist Bible.* 1938; Boston: Beacon Press, 1994.

Hall, David D. *Worlds of Wonder, Days of Judgment: Popular Religious Belief in Early New England.* Cambridge: Harvard University Press, 1990.

Hall, G. Stanley. *Life and Confessions of a Psychologist.* New York and London: D. Appleton, 1923.

Hanh, Thich Nhat. *The Miracle of Mindfulness: A Manual on Meditation,* trans. Mobi Ho, rev. ed. 1975; Boston: Beacon Press, 1987.

Kammerer, Cornelia. 'Customs and Christian Conversion among Akha Highlanders of Burma,' *American Ethnologist* 17 (1990): 277–91.

Kapleau, Roshi Philip. *The Three Pillars of Zen: Teaching, Practice, and Enlightenment: Twenty-Fifth Anniversary Edition.* 1965; New York: Anchor, 1989.

Kehoe, Brendan P. *Zen and the Art of the Internet: A Beginner's Guide.* Englewood Cliffs, NJ: Prentice Hall, 1993.

Kerr, Howard, and Charles L. Crow, eds. *The Occult in America: New Historical Perspectives.* Urbana: University of Illinois Press, 1983.

Layman, Emma McCloy. *Buddhism in America.* Chicago: Nelson-Hall, 1976.

Lewis, James R., and J. Gordon Melton, eds. *Perspectives on the New Age.* Albany: State University of New York Press, 1992.

Lofland, John. '"Becoming a World-Saver" Revisited.' *American Behavioral Scientist* 20 (July/August 1977): 805–18.

Low, Albert. *Zen and the Art of Creative Management.* Rutland, VT: Charles E. Tuttle, 1993.

McLaughlin, Joseph D. *Zen in the Art of Golf.* Atlanta: Humanics Trade, 1997.

Marthaler, Dennis G. *Zen and the Art of Kicking Butts: The Ultimate Guide for Quitting Smoking Forever.* Duluth, MN: Dennis G. Marthaler, 1995.

Martin, Walter. *Kingdom of the Cults.* Minneapolis, MN: Bethany House Publishers, 1985.

Moore, R. Laurence. *In Search of White Crows: Spiritualism, Parapsychology, and American Culture.* New York: Oxford University Press, 1977.

Nattier, Jan. 'Buddhism Comes to Main Street.' *Wilson Quarterly* 21 (Spring 1997): 72–80.

Numrich, Paul David. *Old Wisdom in the New World: Americanization in Two Immigrant Theravada Buddhist Temples.* Knoxville: University of Tennessee Press, 1996.

Olcott, Henry S. *The Buddhist Catechism* 44th ed. 1915; Talent, OR: Eastern School Press, 1983.

Prebish, Charles. *American Buddhism.* North Scituate, MA: Duxbury Press, 1979.

____. 'Two Buddhisms Reconsidered.' *Buddhist Studies Review* 10 (1993): 187–206.

Prothero, Stephen. *The White Buddhist: The Asian Odyssey of Henry Steel Olcott.* Religion in North America Series. Bloomington: Indiana University Press, 1996.

Ridenour, Fritz. *So What's the Difference.* Ventura, CA: Regal Books, 1979.

Rifkin, Ira. 'The Accidental Buddhist.' *News and Observer* (Raleigh), 7 February 1997, 1E, 4E.

Russell, James C. *The Germanization of Early Medieval Christianity.* New York and Oxford: Oxford University Press, 1994.

Rutledge, Paul James. *The Vietnamese Experience in America.* Bloomington: Indiana University Press, 1992.

Snow, David, and Richard Machalek, 'The Convert as a Social Type.' In *Sociological Theory,* ed. R. Collins. San Francisco: Jossey-Bass, 1983.

____. 'The Sociology of Conversion.' *Annual Review of Sociology* 10 (1984): 167–90.

Staples, Clifford L., and Armand L. Mauss. 'Conversion or Commitment? A Reassessment of the Snow and Machalek Approach to the Study of Conversion.' *Journal for the Scientific Study of Religion* 26 (1987): 133–47.

Stevens-Arroyo, Anthony M., and Andres I. Pérez y Mena, eds. *Enigmatic Powers: Syncretism with African and Indigenous Peoples' Religions among Latinos.* Program for the Analysis of Religion among Latinos Series, no. 3. New York: Bildner Center for Western Hemisphere Studies, 1994.

Suzuki, Daisetz Teitaro. *An Introduction to Zen Buddhism.* 1934; New York: Grove Press, 1964.

Tambiah, Stanley J. *Buddhism and the Spirit Cults in Northeast Thailand.* Cambridge: Cambridge University Press, 1970.

Tweed, Thomas. *The American Encounter with Buddhism, 1844–1912: Victorian Culture and the Limits of Dissent.* Bloomington: Indiana University Press, 1992.

____. 'Inclusivism and the Spiritual Journey of Marie de Souza Canavarro (1849–1933).' *Religion* 24 (1994): 43–58.

____. 'Identity and Authority at a Cuban Shrine in Miami: Santería, Catholicism, and Struggles for Religious Identity.' *Journal of Hispanic/Latino Theology* 4 (August 1996): 27–48.

____. *Our Lady of the Exile: Diasporic Religion at a Cuban Catholic Shrine in Miami.* New York and Oxford: Oxford University Press, 1997.

____. 'Asian Religions in America: Reflections on an Emerging Subfield.' In Walter Conser and Sumner Twiss, eds. *Religious Diversity and American Religious History: Studies in Traditions and Cultures.* Athens: University of Georgia Press, 1998.

Tworkov, Helen, and Thomas A. Tweed. 'The Original Ray.' *Tricycle* 1, no. 1 (Fall 1991): 6–7.

Van Esterik, Penny. *Taking Refuge: Lao Buddhists in North America*. Tempe: Arizona State University, Program for Southeast Asian Studies; Toronto: York University, Centre for Refugee Studies, York Lane Press, 1992.

Zürcher, Erik. *The Buddhist Conquest of China*. Leiden: E. J. Brill, 1959.

Notes

1 Personal interview, The Most Reverend Agustín A. Román, 9 June 1994, Archdiocese of Miami Pastoral Center, Miami Springs, Florida. Ira Rifkin, 'The Accidental Buddhist,' *News and Observer* (Raleigh), 7 February 1997, 1E, 4E. Another newspaper article that appeared in the same year, and was reprinted in many papers, raised related issues about religious identity. In 1997 the six-hundred-member Union of Orthodox Rabbis declared that the Reform and Conservative branches 'are not Judaism at all.' The rabbis thereby excluded approximately 80 percent of the Jews in North America on the grounds that the Reform and Conservative traditions condoned assimilation and intermarriage. 'Orthodox Rabbis Assail Other Branches: Union Says Movements Are Not Judaism,' *The News and Observer* (Raleigh), 1 April 1997: 6A.

2 Most students of Buddhist history know well that religion is hybrid. It is not only classic studies of Chinese or Thai religion that teach us that: for instance, Erik Zürcher's *The Buddhist Conquest of China* (Leiden: E.J. Brill, 1959) and Stanley J. Tambiah's *Buddhism and the Spirit Cults in Northeast Thailand* (Cambridge: Cambridge University Press, 1970). Throughout Asia, Buddhist religious belief and practice changed as it encountered new cultures and other traditions – for example, combining with vernacular spirit religions, blending with Confucianism, mixing with Shintō, and incorporating Taoism. In a similar way, students of Christian history have emphasized the Hellenization, and later Germanization, of Christianity as it moved throughout the Mediterranean and Europe. On the latter, for example, see James C. Russell, *The Germanization of Early Medieval Christianity* (New York and Oxford: Oxford University Press, 1994). Contact and exchange among indigenous, African, and European religions is especially clear in the Caribbean and Latin America. Consider, for example, studies of religious life in Cuba and Haiti: Leslie G. Desmangles, *The Faces of the Gods: Vodou and Roman Catholicism in Haiti* (Chapel Hill: University of North Carolina Press, 1992); and George Brandon, *Santeria from Africa to the New World: The Dead Sell Memories* (Bloomington: Indiana University Press, 1993). See also Anthony M. Stevens-Arroyo and Andres I. Pérez y Mena, eds., *Enigmatic Powers: Syncretism with African and Indigenous Peoples' Religions among Latinos,* Program for the Analysis of Religion among Latinos Series, no. 3 (New York: Bildner Center for Western Hemisphere Studies, 1994). Many other historical and ethnographic monographs document religious hybridity, too many to cite here, while many theorists in cultural studies have emphasized hybridity in other areas of culture.

3 Howard Kerr and Charles L. Crow, eds., *The Occult in America: New Historical Perspectives* (Urbana: University of Illinois Press, 1983). David D. Hall, *Worlds of Wonder, Days of Judgment: Popular Religious Belief in Early New England* (Cambridge, MA: Harvard University Press, 1990). R. Laurence Moore, *In Search of White Crows: Spiritualism, Parapsychology, and American Culture* (New York: Oxford University Press, 1977). James R. Lewis and J.

Gordon Melton, eds., *Perspectives on the New Age* (Albany: State University of New York Press, 1992).

4 I have made a similar point in my analysis of Cuban religion: 'Identity and Authority at a Cuban Shrine in Miami: Santería, Catholicism, and Struggles for Religious Identity,' *Journal of Hispanic/Latino Theology* 4 (August 1996): 27–48; and *Our Lady of the Exile: Diasporic Religion at a Cuban Catholic Shrine in Miami* (New York and Oxford: Oxford University Press, 1997), 43–55.

5 My view of religious transformation is shaped by many studies in the sociology of conversion, including David Snow and Richard Machalek, 'The Convert as a Social Type,' in *Sociological Theory*, ed. R. Collins (San Francisco: Jossey-Bass, 1983); David Snow and Richard Machalek, 'The Sociology of Conversion,' *Annual Review of Sociology* 10 (1984): 167–90; Clifford L. Staples and Armand L. Mauss, 'Conversion or Commitment? A Reassessment of the Snow and Machalek Approach to the Study of Conversion,' *Journal for the Scientific Study of Religion* 26 (1987): 133–47; John Lofland, '"Becoming a World-Saver" Revisited,' *American Behavioral Scientist* 20 (July/August 1977): 805–18; and Lorne Dawson, 'Self-Affirmation, Freedom, and Rationality: Theoretically Elaborating "Active" Conversions,' *Journal for the Scientific Study of Religion* 29 (June 1990): 141–63. The anthropological literature on conversion is helpful, too, because it is even more sensitive to the wielding of power and the persistence of hybridity. For example see John L. Comaroff and Jean Comaroff, *Of Revelation and Revolution: Christianity, Colonialism, and Coercion in South Africa* (Chicago: University of Chicago Press, 1991); Elizabeth Colson, 'Converts and Tradition: The Impact of Christianity on Valley Tonga Religion,' *Southwestern Journal of Anthropology* 26 (1970): 143–56; Cornelia Kammerer, 'Customs and Christian Conversion among Akha Highlanders of Burma,' *American Ethnologist* 17 (1990): 277–91.

6 'Buddhist Revival French-Style,' *Religion Watch* 12 (December 1996): 7. This piece originally appeared in the *National Catholic Register* for November 17–23, 1996. Rifkin, 'The Accidental Buddhist,' 1E, 4E. I used the term *sympathizers* in *The American Encounter with Buddhism, 1844–1912: Victorian Culture and the Limits of Dissent* (Bloomington: Indiana University Press, 1992). I introduced the phrase *night-stand Buddhists* in 'Asian Religions in America: Reflections on an Emerging Subfield,' in Walter Conser and Sumner Twiss, eds., *Religious Diversity and American Religious History: Studies in Traditions and Cultures* (Athens: University of Georgia Press, 1998).

7 Hall, *Worlds of Wonder*, 15. Hall borrowed the term *horse-shed Christians* from the psychologist G. Stanley Hall, who used it in his memoirs to describe his own male relatives: *Life and Confessions of a Psychologist* (New York and London: D. Appleton, 1923), 58.

8 Roshi Philip Kapleau, *The Three Pillars of Zen: Teaching, Practice, and Enlightenment: Twenty-Fifth Anniversary Edition* (1965; New York: Anchor, 1989). This book, which originally appeared in 1965, has been popular. It had four hardcover printings by Weatherhill (the first publisher) and Harper and Row (the second publisher), as well as fourteen printings in paperback by Beacon Press. In 1989 Anchor Books issued a twenty-fifth anniversary paperback edition. In the contemporary period, other media – videocassette and computer – can function in similar ways for sympathizers. For example, Zen Mountain Monastery in Mt. Tremper, New York, under the leadership of Abbot John Daido Loori, has distributed a how-to video on zazen: *Introduction to Zen Meditation*, produced by John Daido Loori and Dharma Communications, 54 min., 1991, videocassette. That Buddhist community also has an

elaborate web page, sells recordings of Dharma discourses, and maintains an on-line Zen practice training advisor via electronic mail, called 'cybermonk' (cybermonk@mhv.net), where would-be meditators or long-time practitioners can get advice about their practice. Paul Carus wrote many works on Buddhism, even if he never embraced the tradition exclusively or fully, but he expressed his personal religious views (and sympathy for Buddhism) most clearly in his voluminous correspondence in the Open Court Publishing Company Papers, Morris Library, Southern Illinois University, Carbondale, Illinois. On Andrew Carnegie's affection for Buddhism, and Edwin Arnold's poetic life of the Buddha in particular, see Andrew Carnegie, *Autobiography of Andrew Carnegie* (Boston: Houghton Mifflin, 1920), 207. I offer overviews of Carus's and Carnegie's sympathy for Buddhism in *The American Encounter with Buddhism*, 65–67 (Carus), 44–45 (Carnegie). For evidence of Buddhism's influence on Cage's work, see John Cage, *Silence: Lectures and Writings* (Middletown, CT: Wesleyan University Press, 1973). For a helpful autobiographical fragment concerning his relation to Buddhism see 'Where'm Now,' in Kent Johnson and Craig Paulenich, eds., *Beneath a Single Moon: Buddhism and Contemporary American Poetry* (Boston and London: Shambhala, 1991), 43–44. An exhibition catalog helpfully discusses the painter William Wiley's sympathy for Buddhism and the tradition's influence on his art: Gail Gelburd and Geri De Paoli, *The Transparent Thread: Asian Philosophy in Recent American Art* (Philadelphia: University of Pennsylvania Press, 1990), 112–15.

9 *Tricycle* linked itself with the *Buddhist Ray* in its inaugural issue by reproducing the cover of the nineteenth-century periodical and telling the story of the magazine and its editor, Herman C. Vetterling, in its first 'Ancestors' column: Helen Tworkov and Thomas A. Tweed, 'The Original Ray,' *Tricycle* 1, no. 1 (Fall 1991): 6–7. Charles Prebish, 'Two Buddhisms Reconsidered,' *Buddhist Studies Review* 10 (1993): 187–206.

10 Edwin Arnold, *The Light of Asia; Or, The Great Renunciation; Being the Life and Teaching of Gautama* (1879; Wheaton, IL: Theosophical Publishing House, 1969). Henry S. Olcott, *The Buddhist Catechism*, 44th ed. (1915; Talent, Oregon: Eastern School Press, 1983). Paul Carus, ed., *The Gospel of Buddha* (1894; Tucson, Arizona: Omen, 1972). Tweed, *American Encounter with Buddhism*, 46.

11 Dwight Goddard, ed., *A Buddhist Bible* (1938; Boston: Beacon Press, 1994). The first edition of Goddard's volume appeared in 1934, the Beacon edition comes from the enlarged version that first was published in 1938. Daisetz Teitaro Suzuki, *An Introduction to Zen Buddhism* (1934; New York: Grove Press, 1964). The sales figures for the *Introduction* came from the press: Telephone interview, 25 April 1997, Jay Sullivan, Grove Press. The first American edition of the book appeared in 1954 from Grove Press. On the influence of D. T. Suzuki, see Masao Abe, *A Zen Life: D. T. Suzuki Remembered* (New York: Weatherhill, 1986).

12 *Books in Print, 1996–97: Subjects*, vol. 7 (New Providence, New Jersey: R. R. Bowker, 1996). Albert Low, *Zen and the Art of Creative Management* (Rutland, VT: Charles E. Tuttle, 1993). Dennis G. Marthaler, *Zen and the Art of Kicking Butts: The Ultimate for Quitting Smoking Forever* (Duluth, MiN: Dennis G. Marthaler, 1995). Joseph D. McLaughlin, *Zen in the Art of Golf* (Atlanta: Humanics Trade, 1997). Brendan P. Kehoe, *Zen and the Art of the Internet: A Beginner's Guide* (Englewood Cliffs, NJ: Prentice Hall, 1993). Sarah Arsone, *Zen and the Art of Changing Diapers* (Ventura, CA: Printwheel, 1991). Of course, the number of books on Zen is much larger still. On 31 October 1997 the on-line Library of Congress catalog listed 2,624 titles under the subject 'Zen.'

13 Thich Nhat Hanh, *The Miracle of Mindfulness: A Manual on Meditation*, trans. Mobi Ho, rev. ed. (1975; Boston: Beacon Press, 1987). The sales figures for *Miracle of Mindfulness* and *Living Buddha* were provided by Beacon Press in communication with the author: Susan G. Worst, editor, Beacon Press, electronic mail, 14 March 1997.

14 Charles S. Prebish, *American Buddhism* (North Scituate, MA: Duxbury Press, 1979), 42–43. Emma McCloy Layman *Buddhism in America* (Chicago: Nelson-Hall, 1976), xiv–xv.

15 Paul James Rutledge, *The Vietnamese Experience in America* (Bloomington: Indiana University Press, 1992), 47. Italics mine.

16 Penny Van Esterik, *Taking Refuge: Lao Buddhists in North America* (Tempe: Arizona State University, Program for Southeast Asian Studies; Toronto: York University, Centre for Refugee Studies, York Lane Press, 1992), 41.

17 Stephen Prothero, *The White Buddhist: The Asian Odyssey of Henry Steel Olcott*, Religion in North America Series (Bloomington: Indiana University Press, 1996). Paul David Numrich, *Old Wisdom in the New World: Americanization in Two Immigrant Theravada Buddhist Temples* (Knoxville: University of Tennessee Press, 1996). Rudy V. Busto, 'Response: Asian American Religious Identities: Building Spiritual Homes on Gold Mountain,' *Amerasia Journal* 22, no. 1 (1996): 189.

18 Rick Fields, *How the Swans Came to the Lake: A Narrative History of Buddhism in America*, revised and updated edition (Boston and London: Shambhala, 1986), 74.

19 Fields, *How the Swans Came to the Lake*, xiii.

20 Philip C. Almond, *The British Discovery of Buddhism* (Cambridge: Cambridge University Press, 1988), note 10, page 147. Prebish, *American Buddhism*, 43–44.

21 F. Graeme Davis to Rev. Nishijima, 27 April 1901; reprinted in *Light of Dharma* 1 (June 1901): 28–29. On F. Graeme Davis, see Tweed, *American Encounter with Buddhism*, 44.

22 Fields, *How the Swans Came to the Lake*, 153–54, 164.

23 Layman, *Buddhism in America*, xiv, 203. For an analysis of one 'Dharma hopper' – or, in my terms, religious seeker – who actually did ritually align herself with Buddhism in a public ceremony, only to later practice Baha'i and Vedanta Hinduism, see Thomas A. Tweed, 'Inclusivism and the Spiritual Journey of Marie de Souza Canavarro (1849–1933),' *Religion* 24 (1994): 43–58.

24 Jan Nattier, 'Buddhism Comes to Main Street,' *Wilson Quarterly* 21 (Spring 1997): 74.

25 For a contemporary evangelical Protestant interpretation of Buddhism as a dangerous or misguided 'cult,' see Walter Martin, *Kingdom of the Cults* (Minneapolis, MN: Bethany House Publishers, 1985), 261–69. Other evangelical handbooks and pamphlets do not classify Buddhism as a cult but still dismiss it, refuting its major claims and challenging its practices, often as a means of preparing Christians to evangelize. For example, see Fritz Ridenour, *So What's the Difference* (Ventura, CA: Regal Books, 1979), 83–92. That evangelical description and assessmemt of the religions has been popular among conservative Christians: more than 615,000 copies of the first edition were in print when the second edition appeared in 1979. The publisher now claims 'more than 800,000' copies have been sold. Buddhist opponents, then, are an important part of the story. Our imaginary meditator might consult chapter nine of Kapleau's *Three Pillars of Zen*, called 'Postures,' which includes fifteen drawings of meditators in various positions, from the full-lotus to the Burmese posture, on zafus, benches, and chairs. Kapleau, *Three Pillars of Zen*, 327–53.

CHAPTER SIX

The New Buddhism: Some Empirical Findings

James William Coleman

Everything changes. This fundamental fact lies at the marrow of Buddhist realization, and throughout its 2500-year history, Buddhism itself has certainly lived up to this dictum. First in India and then throughout the Asian world, Buddhism has continually adapted to the changing circumstances of time and place. Yet, against the panoramic diversity of the Buddhist tradition, what may be the most sweeping change in its long history is passing largely unnoticed by most of the world. After fading out in the land of its birth centuries ago, and teetering on the edge of twentieth-century extinction in Tibet and China, a new Buddhism is now emerging in the industrialized nations of the West. It is a Buddhism with fundamental sociological differences from anything that has gone before, yet, in the best tradition of Buddhist logic, it is also a Buddhism unchanged from the moment of Siddhartha Gautama's great realization under the *Bodhi* tree. Western Buddhists and spiritual seekers are doing exactly what the Buddha recommended – looking deeply to see the nature of things from their own direct experience – but they are doing it in ways that often contradict centuries of Asian Buddhist tradition.

The Scope of Study: Defining the New Buddhism

Even those with some knowledge of the Buddhist tradition and an awareness of its growing influence in the West often fail to understand the profound sociological differences between Asian Buddhism and the new style of Buddhism emerging in the United States; and the academic community is just beginning to devote its efforts to the systematic study of this important new religious phenomenon. The findings reported here are part of a larger research project that seeks to rectify this deficiency and lay the foundations for a comprehensive sociological understanding of this new Buddhism.

The first step in this undertaking is to define the term 'new Buddhism' a bit more clearly, since it is not intended to apply to the whole range of

91

Western Buddhism, but only to the distinctive new form of Buddhism that is emerging among Western converts to Buddhism. In contrast to the traditional forms of Asian Buddhism, men and women practice together as equals in this new Buddhism. Teachers borrow freely from different Buddhist traditions that are almost completely isolated from each other in Asia. Ceremonies and rituals are simpler and more direct, and few people believe in their ability to produce magical effects. But most importantly, the new Buddhism makes the path of meditation and spiritual discipline available to everyone, not just to an elite group of monks.

The other principal form of Buddhism in the West, which might be termed 'ethnic Buddhism,' is practiced primarily by Asian immigrants and their descendants. Although this ethnic Buddhism has certainly adapted to its new Western environment, it still adheres far more closely to traditional forms than the new Buddhism that is the focus of this paper.

More problematic is the classification of the Sōka Gakkai. Sōka Gakkai is one of the new religious groups that emerged during Japan's immediate postwar period, and it has gained a considerable following in the West. Unlike the ethnic Buddhists, most of Sōka Gakkai's members here are not Asians, and it would seem to qualify as an important part of the new Buddhism we are exploring. But Sōka Gakkai has some glaring differences from the other groups we are studying here. While new Buddhist groups focus on meditation, the repetition of a chant in praise of the *Lotus Sūtra* (*Namu Myōhō Renge Kyō*) is the central practice of Sōka Gakkai. While other Western Buddhist groups tend to display an indifference or even a hostility toward the pursuit of material gain, Sōka Gakkai adherents believe that diligent chanting produces wealth as well as personal happiness. While the attitude in most other groups is that new members will come when they are ready, Sōka Gakkai has been known to pursue an aggressive policy of proselytization know by the descriptive Japanese name, *shakubuku*, which translates as 'break and subdue.' All in all, Sōka Gakkai's practices and beliefs have many significant differences from those of other Buddhist groups that appeal to Westerners; and a separate study would be required to do them justice. I will not attempt that task here or make a definitive statement about whether or not the Sōka Gakkai should be included under the overall rubric of the new Buddhism; the chapter by Hammond and Machacek in this volume treats some of these questions.

Although there is certainly far more eclecticism in the United States then there ever was in Asia, the new Buddhism draws on three principal Asian traditions which still retain their distinct characteristics. The Zen Buddhists of East Asia were the first to develop a significant body of Western students, and it is with them that we find the origins of the new Buddhism. But they were soon followed by Vajrayāna Buddhism from Tibet and the Vipassana meditation movement derived from Theravāda Buddhism from South and Southeast Asia.

Methodology

The data reported in this paper are from a survey which is part of larger study of the new Buddhism that utilizes other methodologies, including in-depth interviews and participant observation. The survey employed a cluster design. Seven Buddhist groups were selected, and then a random sample was made of the membership of each group. The primary objective in selecting the groups for this study was to find representatives of all of the divergent steams of the new Buddhism. The sample therefore has two groups that follow the Zen tradition, two groups that follow the Vipassana tradition, and two from the Vajrayāna tradition. In addition, one more eclectic group was included that does not have an affiliation to any specific Buddhist tradition.

Some effort was also made to select groups that draw upon the most influential lineages within each tradition. The two Zen groups included in the survey were the Berkeley Zen Center in California and the Rochester Zen Center in New York, and each center represents one of the most important Zen lineages in the United States. The Berkeley Zen Center traces its origins back to Shunryū Suzuki Rōshi – the founder of the San Francisco Zen Center and arguably one of American Buddhism's single most influential figures. The Rochester Zen Center was started by Philip Kapleau Rōshi, who was the first Zen master from a Western background to gain prominence in the United States. Kapleau was trained in the Harada-Yasutani lineage, a mixed Sōtō-Rinzai lineage, which has also had enormous influence on Western Buddhism.

The Vajrayāna tradition is represented by two groups with widely divergent approaches. The first is Karma Dzong in Boulder, Colorado, founded by Tibetan Buddhism's most influential teacher in the West, Chögyam Trungpa Rinpoche, and probably the largest local Buddhist *Sangha* with a Western membership. The second Vajrayāna group is the Dzogchen Foundation, centered in Boston and directed by Lama Surya Das, a Western-born teacher of Tibetan Vajrayāna.

Two large Vipassana groups in the San Francisco Bay area were also surveyed. One is headed by Gil Fronsdal and the other by James Baraz; both are affiliated with the Spirit Rock Meditation Center in Marin County, California, which is less traditional than the Insight Meditation Society in Barre, Massachusetts, the other influential Vipassana center in North America. Finally, the survey included the White Heron Sangha in San Luis Obispo, California, a more eclectic Buddhist group without clear denominational affiliations.

Although the leaders of all these groups proved quite cooperative, they were nonetheless reluctant to supply me with official membership lists, so in six of the seven cases the surveys were distributed by group officials at their meetings and returned by mail. The one exception was the Rochester Zen

Center, which included the survey and a return envelope in one of its mailings. This procedure made it impossible to utilize follow-up mailings to maximize the response rate, but, fortunately, the members of these centers proved quite willing to participate. Despite its considerable length, the questionnaire's overall response rate was well above 50 percent, and in one group it ran to over 90 percent. The Dzogchen Foundation was the only group with a response rate below 50 percent, and I was forced to distribute a second round of surveys to bring up the sample size. It is difficult to say how those who filled out the questionnaires differed from those who ignored them, but it does seem likely that more dedicated and involved members were over-represented in my survey, since apathetic members would have been less likely to attend the meetings where the surveys were distributed. The total number of returned surveys was 359.

The Results

It should be pointed out that the following results are from a preliminary analysis of the data and in most cases are based on nothing more than frequency distributions. Nonetheless, this analysis does, I think, provide some very interesting results.

Membership Demographics

Perhaps the most obvious place to start developing a sociological understanding of American Buddhism is with the demographics of its members. So, what kind of a person becomes a Buddhist in the West? About 57 percent of those who responded to this questionnaire were females and 43 percent male. There were, however, some significant differences among the groups surveyed. The Rochester Zen Center, known for its aggressive style of practice, actually had a majority of male respondents, while the highest ratios of females to males tended to be in the Vipassana groups. The bulk of the respondents were from their late 30s to their early 50s. The youngest was 19, the oldest 78, and the mean age was 46. This finding supports the conventional wisdom in the Buddhist community that American Buddhism has its greatest appeal to the 'baby boom' generation.[1] The question of whether there is something unique in the experience of the baby boomers that makes Buddhist practice especially attractive or whether they were simply the first generation to which Buddhist practice was available in North America cannot be answered until we see if later generations become more involved in Buddhism as they age.

Ethnically, the memberships of these Buddhist groups is overwhelmingly white. Only about one in ten respondents identified himself or herself as Asian, Black, or Hispanic, a matter that has been of some concern to Buddhist leaders.[2] When asked about family religious background, 31 percent responded Protestant, 25 percent Roman Catholic, 16.5 percent Jewish, 6 percent said it was non-religious, 2 percent Buddhist, and 19 percent other or no response. A comparison of these findings with the demographics of the entire American population confirmed the observation often made by Buddhists leaders, that Catholics and especially Jews are proportionately more likely to be attracted to Buddhism than other Americans.

These data indicate that American Buddhism clearly has its strongest appeal to the middle and upper middle class. About one-third of the respondents reported their family income to be between $30,000 and $60,000, while another 19 percent fell in the $60,000 to $90,000 range. About 20 percent of the respondent had incomes over $90,000 and about 30 percent fell on the other end of the spectrum, making less than $30,000. While those income figures are somewhat higher than the national average, the educational level of American Buddhists is very high. Of the 353 people who responded to the question on education level, only a single person reported having failed to finish high school, and less than one in twenty said that their education stopped with high school graduation. Eleven percent reported that they had some college experience, 32 percent were college graduates, and, surprisingly, more than half of the respondents (51 percent) had advanced degrees. Thus, it appears that Buddhism continues to have its strongest appeal to the highly educated and culturally sophisticated, just as it did when it was first spreading through Asia.

Just as Buddhists are far more highly educated than the average American, they are far more liberal as well. Almost 60 percent of the respondents said they were Democrats, while the nine persons reporting a Republican affiliation (2.6 percent) were outnumbered by more than three to one by those affiliated with the Green Party (9.9 percent). A self-ranking on a left to right political scale also produced a distribution heavily skewed to the left.

Becoming Involved

Very few of the respondents were born into Buddhism, and several questions in the survey sought to explore the ways they first became involved in Buddhist practice. When asked directly about this, a majority reported that it was through reading a book. Hearing about Buddhism from friends was the only other commonly given response.

The questionnaire also explored two other pathways to Buddhist practice – the use of psychedelic drugs and the martial arts. There are many reports of people becoming interested in meditation because of the altered states of consciousness they experienced while under the influence of a psychedelic drug, and the survey confirmed the importance of such experiences for many practitioners. Sixty-three percent of the respondents said that they had taken a psychedelic drug – a much higher percentage than in the general population – and of those, half said that the use of psychedelic drugs had had some role in attracting them to Buddhism. The martial arts, on the other hand, appears to be a less common route into Buddhist practice. While 34 percent of the respondents had practiced a martial art, two-thirds of those said it did not help attract them to Buddhism. About half as many (12 percent) said Buddhism attracted them to the martial arts as the other way around (23 percent).

A related issue concerns personal motivation for becoming involved in Buddhism. The questionnaire asked respondents about their degree of agreement or disagreement with three statements: 'I became involved in Buddhism in order to help deal with my personal problems'; 'I became involved in Buddhism because of a desire for spiritual fulfillment'; and 'I became involved in Buddhism because I was attracted to the people I met who were involved with it.' The survey found the desire for spiritual fulfillment was by far the most important motivation among the respondents, followed by the attempt to deal with personal problems. Over fifty percent of the respondents 'strongly agreed' that they became involved in Buddhism for spiritual fulfillment (53.5 percent), while 20.6 percent strongly agreed with the statement concerning personal problems, but only about 12 percent strongly agreed with the statement concerning interpersonal attraction.

The Social Dimension

Most sociologically oriented students of contemporary religion would agree that religion serves to meet both the social and spiritual needs of its members. But as might be implied from the responses concerning motivation we just discussed, American Buddhists seem far more interested in the spiritual/experiential side of religious life than in its social dimension. When asked to rank the relative importance of meditation, services and ceremonies, and social relations with other members, well over 90 percent of the respondents ranked meditation as number one. Social relations were generally ranked second, and services and ceremonies were given the least importance.

Although the public often thinks of most Eastern religions as exclusive, all-encompassing cults, the survey shows just the opposite to be true. Rather than the exclusivity and isolation we would expect among cult members, a surprising 41 percent of our respondents reported that few or none of their friends were involved in Buddhism. In contrast, only three of the respondents said that all of their friends were involved in Buddhism, and only about 16 percent said that most of their friends were.

The respondents did, however, express some desire to build a stronger social community. When directly asked, about 63 percent agreed that their group should become more involved in social activities, and almost that many (60.9 percent) agreed that their group should be more involved in charitable activities. However, only one-third felt that their group should be more politically active.

Practice and Belief

The data already discussed clearly show that meditation practice is the heart of Buddhism for most of the respondents. Although the frequency and duration of sitting meditation practice varies greatly from one member to another, the data indicate that most respondents maintained a regular meditation schedule. Only 10 of the 359 respondents said that they meditated less than once a week. The typical respondent reported that he or she meditated almost every day for a mean of a little over 40 minutes at a sitting (median 35 minutes, mode 30 minutes). In addition, nearly 90 percent of the respondents occasionally supplemented their sitting practice with walking meditation, and one-third did so on a regular weekly basis.

Despite the enormous cultural gulf separating the new Buddhists from the tradition of Asian monastics, the style of meditation is directly derived from traditional Asian practices. Some respondents reported practicing visualizations or working on the puzzling riddles known as *koans*, but meditation for most respondents meant focusing on their breath – either by counting breaths one by one or by simply following them with close attention.

Most of the time, the members of these groups meditated at home, but most also regularly attended group meetings at Buddhist centers, rented halls, and private homes. In addition to their daily meditation, over 90 percent of the respondents had also attended an intensive meditation retreat. The typical respondent had been involved in Buddhist organizations for about nine and one-half years and had attended twelve retreats, so they averaged a little more than one retreat a year, most of which ranged from 1 to 10 days.

In addition to their meditation practice, the respondents indicated that they attended some kind of Buddhist religious service approximately 9 times per month. Reading was another important source of contact with Buddhism for most respondents. Sixty-three percent said that they 'frequently' read books or articles relating to Buddhism, and another 32 percent said they 'occasionally' do. In contrast, only 5 percent said they 'rarely' read about Buddhism, and less than 1 percent never read such material.

Although the acceptance of a particular set of doctrines has never been given great prominence in Western Buddhism, there are of course many different ideas and beliefs which are traditionally associated with Buddhist practice. The survey queried respondents on their belief in two key Buddhist ideas – *karma* and reincarnation – and the results indicate that the vast majority of respondents accepted both beliefs. Almost 93 percent of the respondents agreed that 'What happens to us in this life is determined by the kind of *karma* we create,' and over 80 percent agreed that 'After death, we are reborn into another life.'

Conclusions

The results from this preliminary examination of these data can hardly be considered definitive. They do, however, paint an interesting picture of the practitioners of the new Buddhism which is quite consistent with the comments and observations I have gathered in interviews with leaders and senior practitioners in American Buddhist groups around the country. Demographically, the members of these new Buddhist groups tend to be white, middle- and upper-middle-class people in their middle years, with a strong left/liberal leaning in their political views. One of the most striking characteristics of the respondents was their extremely high level of education. It would not seem unreasonable to conclude that these Buddhists constitute the most highly educated religious group in the United States.

Not surprisingly, then, most practitioners first heard about Buddhism through reading books or articles and continue to read new material concerning Buddhism and Buddhist practice. Although the use of psychedelic drugs was instrumental in stimulating an interest in Buddhism in a significant minority of respondents (about 25 percent), martial arts practice seemed to be considerably less important. In contrast to the motives of most traditional American religious congregants, the central focus and *raison d'être* of the new Buddhists is direct religious experience and the personal transformation it produces. Accordingly, respondents gave far more importance to meditation practice than to the social aspects of religious life. Moreover, the respondents carried such beliefs over into their daily lives and carried on a disciplined spiritual practice that includes regular meditation, group meetings and rituals, and extended meditation retreats.

References

Barker, Eileen, ed. *New Religious Movements: A Perspective for Understanding Society.* New York: Edwin Mellen, 1982.

Fox, Stephen. 'Boomer Dharma: The Evolution of Alternative Spiritual Communities in Modern New Mexico.' In Ferenc Szasz and Richard Etalain, eds., *Religion in Modern New Mexico*, 145–170. Albuquerque: University of New Mexico Press, 1997.

Kurtz, Lester. *Gods in the Global Village.* Thousand Oaks, CA: Pine Forge, 1995.

Needleman, Jacob, ed. with George Baker. *Understanding the New Religions.* New York: Seabury, 1978.

O'Dea, Thomas F., with Janet O'Dea. *The Sociology of Religion.* Englewood Cliffs, NJ: Prentice-Hall, 1983.

Roof, Wade Clark. *A Generation of Seekers: The Spiritual Journeys of the Baby Boom Generation.* San Francisco: Harper San Francisco, 1993.

Stark, Rodney, with William Sims Bainbridge. *The Future of Religion: Secularization, Revival, and Cult Formation.* Berkeley: University of California Press, 1985.

Notes

1 See Wade Clark Roof, *A Generation of Seekers: The Spiritual Journeys of the Baby Boom Generation* (San Francisco: Harper San Francisco, 1993), and also Stephen Fox, 'Boomer Dharma: The Evolution of Alternative Spiritual Communities in Modern New Mexico,' in Ferenc Szasz and Richard Etalain, eds., *Religion in Modern New Mexico* (Albuquerque: University of New Mexico Press, 1997), 145–170.

2 The Interracial Buddhist Council, which operated primarily on the West Coast, has been one such forum to support and include people of color in Buddhist centers and retreats.

CHAPTER SEVEN

Supply and Demand: The Appeal of Buddhism in America

Phillip Hammond and David Machacek

Having conducted a survey of American members of Sōka Gakkai International during 1997, we offer here an early glimpse of some of our findings. They bear on the appeal Buddhism may have for Americans.[1]

As a Buddhist sect, Sōka Gakkai traces its roots to the fifth century B.C.E. and the teachings of Siddhārtha Gautama. More specifically, however, it is the teachings of Nichiren Daishōnin, a thirteenth-century Japanese monk, that form the basis of Sōka Gakkai beliefs and practices. Organizationally, Sōka Gakkai is far younger, being the creation of two Japanese educators, Tsunesaburō Makiguchi and Josei Toda, who, in the decade before World War II, founded Sōka Kyōiku Gakkai ('Value-Creating Education Society'), a movement imbued with Nichiren's teachings but dedicated initially to educational reform. Both founders were imprisoned for rejecting the militarism surrounding them in the 1930s. Makiguchi died there, but Toda came out of prison in 1945 and set about rebuilding the movement. Membership expanded rapidly. By the time of Toda's death in 1958, the organization claimed a membership in excess of 750,000 households in Japan. It was at this point that the current president of Sōka Gakkai, Daisaku Ikeda, assumed the leadership position.

By 1975, Sōka Gakkai had associations in many parts of the world and thus changed its name to Sōka Gakkai International (SGI). The first overseas chapter was in the United States, begun and maintained originally by Japanese wives of American servicemen. In the 1960s and 1970s recruits were sought among non-Japanese as well – to the point where Japanese Americans are a clear minority in SGI-USA.

How Our Survey Was Done

The most comprehensive listing of 'members' of SGI-USA is found in the subscription lists of the four publications distributed through the group's

100

headquarters in Santa Monica, California. The largest of the four publications is the weekly newspaper, *World Tribune*, but persons were eligible to be part of the sample by virtue of subscribing to any one or more of the four. Our research budget allowed us to print and mail nearly 1,200 questionnaires. With an estimated 40,000 subscribers from which to select respondents, we randomly chose three percent, stratified to represent proportionately each of the geographic regions of the U.S. where subscribers are found.

This process yielded 1,185 names and addresses, of which 104 were removed from the list, either because they told us they were not members or because they could not be found at the address provided and were presumed by SGI headquarters to be no longer members. Of the remaining 1081, we heard from 401, yielding a response rate of 37 percent. Our book will go into great detail concerning the 'representativeness' of our sample, but as will be shown below, the questions of greatest interest to us can be pursued even if the sample is 'biased' in some way (if, for example, females returned questionnaires at a higher rate than males).

What We Are Looking For

In a broad sense, in this essay we are interested in finding out why there are Sōka Gakkai Buddhists in America. If, for example, one asks why there are Jews in America, the answer is found in the history of Jewish immigration and the formation in America of Jewish families who had Jewish children. The same kind of answer applies to the Greek Orthodox and other groups in which ethnicity or national origin is tied to religious identity. We understand their presence in the United States by understanding the history of immigration.

Sōka Gakkai International, called Nichiren Shōshū Buddhism before 1991, in America revealed a similar pattern in its early years, as the first members were migrants from Japan, often married to American GIs. Indeed about one in ten persons in our sample report being born in SGI, either in Japan or in the United States as a child of someone already a member. But this means that nine in ten converted to SGI-USA.

We can be even more specific, however, because, while only one in ten were born into SGI, others (N=34) converted into SGI from some other sect of Buddhism. And, although this conversion process is interesting in its own right, the question implied in our sub-title – the appeal of Buddhism in America – clearly invites focus on persons who convert to Buddhism in the U.S. from entirely different religious backgrounds. The assumption, then, is that this third category of members made the greatest change in converting to SGI, and the first category of members made the least change, with the second category somewhere in between.

Pushes and Pulls

The three categories just discussed suggest the scheme we follow in this essay and will elaborate in our book – a scheme based on a supply and demand model of behavior. In this case, the behavior is religious identity as a member of SGI, but the model fits many behaviors. Take, for example, the act of voluntarily migrating to a country different from the one in which a person is born. We can see immediately that two kinds of factors may operate – those factors in the native land that make continued living there less desirable, and those in the destination land that make the prospect of living there more desirable. The first factors push, while the second factors pull.

Now consider the example at hand – membership in SGI-USA. Some people find that the religion into which they are born remains desirable, at least to the degree that they do not wish to defect. They feel no push. At the same time, neither are they aware of any alternative religion that appears more attractive than their own. They feel no pull either. We have just described our first category of SGI-USA members. There is little of theoretical interest about them when it comes to the question of *why* they are members of SGI-USA. Neither push nor pull, for them, seems to play much of a role. We will attend to them in our book, of course, but not in this paper.

How about the second category – those who have switched from one kind of Buddhism to Sōka Gakkai? We might expect in these cases to find that a major factor in why they are SGI-USA members is found in the *pull*, or attraction, of SGI over whatever other Buddhism they once practiced. After all, in all probability they have not been 'pushed' out of Buddhism but simply drawn to a variant of the religious perspective they had already adopted. Our theoretical interest tends to focus then on how they were 'pulled' into SGI, not 'pushed' from an earlier kind of Buddhism. They, too, will be ignored here.

It is thus our third category on which the theoretical focus is greatest, because clearly persons in that category have experienced both pushes and pulls – pushes in the sense that they found traditional American religions less than satisfactory, and pulls in the sense that they evidently found in SGI an appealing alternative.

Using again the migration analogy, we can note that persons may be subject to many factors that 'push' them away from their native land and other factors that 'pull' them toward another country. But persons are not equally 'available' to act on those pushes and pulls. First, some will be held back by structural features of their existence: family ties, for instance, or occupational or community loyalties. Others will be held back by ill health or lack of financial resources. Second, certain cultural features may represent barriers to migrating: language incompetence, for instance, or lack of job skills or travel experience. Together, these structural and cultural features may be so inhibiting as to make pushes and pulls irrelevant.

So it is with the 'migration' from one religious identity to another; structural and cultural features may effectively render some people unavailable to the pushes and pulls of their religious existence.

The aforesaid, then, suggests that we consider both the structural and cultural availability of these American SGI converts prior to encountering SGI. And these features should help us to better understand the appeal of Buddhism in America.

Supply and Demand

First, an explanation for our title. By 'supply' we mean essentially the 'pulls' in people's social environments of which they are aware. By 'demand' we mean essentially the 'pushes' in that environment. As many have noted, few converts come out of religious settings they find pleasing, and it should go without saying that persons never convert to a religion they have never heard of. Our category of converts who have experienced both pushes and pulls – which is the largest in number in our sample – therefore offers us a chance to look closely at two major issues in the sociology of religion: (1) What factors altered the demand-side of these SGI-USA members that rendered them dissatisfied with their earlier religious situation and left them open to the appeals of Buddhism? and (2) After discovering their openness to that religious perspective, what factors in the supply-side led them to SGI-USA? The remainder of this essay offers some provisional findings that aim to answer these questions.

Let us begin by considering the religious biographies of converts in our sample. For the purpose of this essay, our analysis is *limited* to those who reported having been raised in one of the four major religious traditions in the United States – Protestant, Catholic, Jewish, and 'none.' As we explained above, the 82 respondents whose original religion was coded 'other' in our data were excluded from this analysis.

What can be said about the structural availability of the 325 converts to SGI-USA? One clue comes from the remarkably high number of those converts who have ever been divorced – 44 percent as compared with 23 percent of the general American adult population.[2] Fully 69 percent were, at the time they first encountered SGI-USA, neither married nor living with a partner. Forty-five percent were not employed full-time, and 43 percent were living outside the region where their parents and/or siblings lived. In other words, they were not greatly encumbered by work, marital, or kinship ties. While we have only the 'ever-divorced' comparison with the general population, it seems safe to say that converts were in a good position to take on new religious commitments because they were structurally free of many social ties.

How about their 'cultural' availability? At least three kinds of cultural availability can be imagined. First is the religious situation of converts prior to their conversion to SGI-USA. The survey tells us they were more likely to have been raised without a religious tradition (7.9 percent) than Americans at large (4.7 percent). More than eight in ten reported being spiritually unsatisfied at the time they encountered SGI-USA. One in three reported a feeling of being 'at a turning point in my life,' and slightly more (36 percent) felt a need for 'guidance and direction.' While these are clear signs of being open to new spiritual paths, remarkably few (14 percent) report that they were actually searching for 'something new and exciting to do with my life.' Just as pushes and pulls are not in themselves sufficient to explain conversion, neither, it seems, is mere availability sufficient. Of course, retrospective questions of the sort reported here must be viewed with caution. Perhaps, for example, it is only *after* one becomes spiritually satisfied with the adopted religion that one realizes the earlier dissatisfaction; the large 81 percent who report retrospective dissatisfaction must thus be weighed against the meager 14 percent who were actively seeking a new path. Nonetheless, taken together, these data suggest a high degree of availability along the spiritual front on the part of these converts. This judgment is reinforced by the fact that 30 percent of SGI-USA converts report that, at some time prior to their conversion, they had been involved in one or more religions other than the one in which they were raised.

A second kind of cultural availability is found in people's openness to 'foreign' things. On this score, SGI-USA converts must be regarded as quite open. In response to the question 'Had you read much about non-Western cultures?' at the time of the first encounter with SGI-USA, a surprising 43 percent said yes, and an even more surprising 66 percent reported having traveled outside the U.S. In this way, too, these SGI converts appear to have been culturally available.

So far, we have looked at evidence of a more-or-less general openness to change on the part of these converts. What about their openness to Buddhism? Here, too, we see signs of availability. Prior to their conversion, 25 percent of our sample reported being 'very interested in Eastern religion and philosophy.' Twenty-seven percent had encountered Buddhism in some form. And 25 percent had encountered some other form of Eastern religion.

In four different ways, then, many respondents tell us that they were available for something new. They were structurally available in the sense that, as best we can surmise, they had relatively fewer ties to other people and institutions. 'Culturally' they were available, too, in that they were not already very embedded religiously, they were mindful of foreign matters, and, finally, they were aware of Eastern religions. There are small correlations among the latter three kinds of cultural availability (for example, a correlation of .363 exists between foreign interest or travel and awareness of Eastern religions, statistically significant beyond the .01 level).

While such relationships are not surprising, it *is* noteworthy that *no* correlation exists between our measure of structural availability and any measure of cultural availability. That is to say, these conditions are independent of each other. Yet each measures a kind of openness to the operation of pushes and pulls.

Moreover, structural availability measures some other features of human existence that have bearing on the conversion process. It is, for example, positively correlated with formal education. Fifty-nine percent of the most available have at least a bachelor's degree, which declines steadily to 37 percent among the least structurally available. It is often noted that education weakens certainty, but it also seems to weaken social relationships. Perhaps for this reason, structural availability is related to feelings of being isolated. Asked if, prior to their first encounter with SGI-USA, they were 'feeling lonely at that time,' only 10.6 percent of the least available said yes, and the percentage nearly triples (to 28.9 percent) as structural availability increases.

We have, thus, a fairly good sense that our converts were, as they first encountered SGI-USA, available in a variety of ways to become converts. The *degree* to which this is true obviously varies, but rather than take more space here to explore the implications of that variation, let us move on to the matter of pushes, or changes, in religious demand.

On the Demand Side

What kinds of Americans would *want* to become Buddhist? Having grown up surrounded by Protestants, Catholics, Jews – indeed, in 92 percent of the cases having themselves been raised in one of those traditions – who would *want* to become a member of SGI-USA? We can make some inferences from our knowledge of the Sōka Gakkai religion itself, for it does not demand of its followers that they flee from the world, that they renounce modernity and material possessions. It has no unusual restrictions on personal behavior, it makes minimal demands on members' collective life, yet offers ready-made friends and social activities.

One way to answer our rhetorical question, therefore, is to look at how SGI converts differ from the American adult public. For example, 53 percent describe themselves as political liberals, as compared with 28 percent of the public, and only 16 percent regard themselves as conservative, as compared with 35 percent of the public. In both populations the modal answer was 'moderate.' Not surprisingly, more than three-fourths of the converts voted for Bill Clinton in 1996, and, by a margin of 6-to-1, prefer the Democratic party over the Republican. In keeping with this 'liberal' theme, SGI converts are twice as likely to respond 'Too little attention' when asked if racial and ethnic minorities receive too much or too little attention in high school and college history classes, as are respondents to the General Social Survey (54 percent vs. 25 percent, respectively).

Another hint at the possibly greater altruism of SGI converts is found in their responses to these two statements:

A. You have to take care of your self first, and, if you have any energy left over, then help other people.
Percentage Agreeing: SGI-USA 41   Public 53

B. People should be allowed to accumulate as much wealth as they can, even if some make millions while other live in poverty.
Percentage Agreeing: SGI-USA 30   Public 58

Other insights into the mindset of people who found themselves drawn to SGI Buddhism can be seen in their leisure activities. Respondents were asked whether they had participated in each of the following activities 'during the last twelve months.' Here are the activities grouped according to the degree converts participated more or less than American adults generally:

SGI-USA Members Participate Much More
1. Visited an art museum or gallery (75% vs. 42%)
2. Went to a live ballet or dance performance (47% vs. 20%)
3. Went to a classical music performance (37% vs. 16%)
4. Taken part in a music, dance, or theatrical performance (30% vs. 10%)

SGI-USA Members Participate Slightly More
1. Made art or craft objects (51% vs. 42%)
2. Went out to a movie theater (85% vs. 73%)
3. Went camping, hiking, or canoeing (51% vs. 45%)
4. Grown vegetables or flowers (64% vs. 61%)
5. Played musical instrument (29% vs. 24%)

SGI-USA Members Participate Slightly Less
1. Participated in any sports activity (55% v. 61%)
2. Videotaped a TV program (56% vs. 63%)
3. Attended a sports event (47% vs. 57%)

SGI-USA Members Participate Much Less
1. Went hunting or fishing (17% vs. 37%)
2. Went to an auto or motorcycle race (6% vs. 16%)

SGI converts attach less importance to domesticity than does the public. Only 37 percent declared that 'being married' is very important, as compared with 50 percent of the public, and 'having children' was very important to 62 percent of the public but to only 46 percent of the converts. By contrast, 'having faith' was very important to 92 percent of the SGI converts but to only 76 percent of the age-adjusted public.

Clearly, then, SGI converts differ from Americans generally by tending to be socially and politically more liberal than the American average. But if, as liberals, they have moved considerably away from conservative traditions, SGI converts have by no means adopted an 'anything goes' position. For example, the environment for them is not to be exploited, and technology is not to be embraced for its own sake. Sixty-two percent of Americans generally regard nature as sacred, but 78 percent of the converts hold that view. One-third of the public agree that 'People worry too much about human progress harming the environment,' but only half that number of SGI converts agree.

Such a benign viewpoint is found in the significantly greater likelihood that SGI converts, as compared with the general public, agree that 'People try to be helpful' (68 percent vs. 48 percent), 'People try to be fair' (62 percent vs. 55 percent), and 'Most people can be trusted' (52 percent vs. 37 percent). Likewise, converts are less cynical about life and society. While 31 percent of them agree that 'In spite of what some people say, the lot of the average person is getting worse, not better,' more than twice that number (64 percent) of the American public agree. To the very despairing statement 'It's hardly fair to bring a child into the world with the way things look for the future,' assent is given by 12 percent of converts, whereas 39 percent (three times the number!) of the public assent.

Our survey asked a question about the causes of poverty, offering four possibilities, and asked respondents to rate each as Very Important, Somewhat Important, or Not Important. This question was taken from the General Social Survey, so we know how the public-at-large answered. Two of the causes find poverty the result of *society's* failure (inadequate schools and inadequate jobs), and the other two find individuals at fault (immorality and lack of effort by the poor themselves.) It was possible for a person to claim that all four are important or that none is important, but in reality some selectivity occurs, and the resulting patterns tell us something interesting about SGI members.

The classic 'conservative' response pattern is to assign little importance to society as the source of poverty but great importance to individual behavior. The classic 'liberal' response pattern is the mirror image of the conservative one; society, not the individual, fails. But there remain two other patterns, one that might be called 'fatalistic' in that neither society nor individuals are found responsible; poverty, so to speak, just is. The fourth pattern – which might be termed a 'human potential perspective' – finds society the cause of poverty and individuals the remedy. This is the modal response by SGI converts, claimed by 35 percent, whereas the modal response by the public is fatalistic (31 percent). The liberal response is second in size (29 percent) among SGI members, with the conservative response the smallest (15 percent). Among the public, the conservative response is second in size (27 percent), and the liberal response smallest (19 percent).

Here again we have evidence that SGI members are liberal but liberal with a slant. Fortunately for us, the study of SGI in Great Britain provided us with a clue, so we were able to include diagnostic questions in our survey instrument. In the Epilogue to their book analyzing SGI members in Great Britain, Bryan Wilson and Karel Dobbelaere suggest that in moving away from conservative traditions associated with the capitalistic work ethic, SGI members at the same time tend also to reject the hedonism and materialism of the consumer society.[3] They write:

> Sōka Gakkai International, whilst drawing on ancient scriptures, none the less has a message which claims special relevance for our own time.... That relevance is manifest in the convergence of the general contemporary climate of economic and social permissiveness with Sōka Gakkai's relinquishment of moral codes and its espousal of general abstract ethical principles which leave adherents free to discover their own form of 'taking responsibility.'

Because they see this stance as transcending the coarser features of materialism, Wilson and Dobbelaere refer to 'post-materialism,' a stance that stresses not economic growth, fighting inflation, and maintaining order but emphasizes instead freedom of speech, more voice to the people, and a less impersonal society. On their scale, an amazing 75 percent of SGI-UK members score as 'pure post- materialists' and another 20 percent as 'mixed post-materialists.' The figures for the British *public* are, respectively, 21 percent and 30 percent.[4]

Prompted by the British study, we included this battery of questions in our survey instrument, one of which also appears in the General Social Survey, enabling us to make the comparison between SGI members and the American public. That question is as follows:

If you had to choose, which of the things on the list below would you say is most important? Which would you consider second most important?

A. Maintaining order in the nation
B. Giving people more say in important government decisions
C. Fighting rising prices
D. Protecting freedom of speech

This question includes two options expressive of 'post-materialism' and two items express 'materialism.' Post-materialism, we argue, is reflected in B and D. By assigning a score of two if the respondent gave one of the two post-materialist responses as the first choice, a score of one if the respondent gave a post-materialist response as the second choice, and a score of zero otherwise, we were able to assign a score to each respondent. A 'pure' post-materialist is one who scores the maximum of 3 points. The study of SGI-UK, using a somewhat different measure, claimed that 75 percent of British members were pure post-materialist. That rate exceeds the SGI-USA rate. Nonetheless with a rate of 51 percent, the American converts are obviously also to be found in the post-materialist camp, with another 25 percent ranked as mixed post-materialist. Perhaps more telling here, among the general American public, only 17 percent rank as pure post-materialist, one-third the rate of SGI-USA members.

To this scale of post-materialism, we added four more items to broaden the measure into an index we call Transmodernism – going 'beyond' modernity as commonly understood. These items are:

1. Agrees with the statement 'I do what is right for the environment, even when it costs more money or takes up more time.'
2. Says it would be good to see reduced emphasis on money and material things.
3. Says it would be good to see a decrease in the importance of work in our lives.
4. Says it would be bad to see more emphasis on the development of technology.

These four items are related, both conceptually and empirically to the post-materialism scale, but they add some subtlety to that scale's starkness – sacrificing on behalf of the environment, de-emphasizing money and the dominance of work, and having reservations about technology. When added to the post-materialism scale, the result is an index with seven categories from Low to High. This Transmodernism Index, we believe, measures what we earlier called a 'demand' for a spiritual orientation represented by Buddhism. It measures, if you please, a 'push' toward that perspective.

How valid is the Transmodernism index? We looked at the relationship between it and a number of other variables, many of which showed high correlations that reveal more of the meaning of transmodernism. Thus, as one looks from those scoring lowest on the index to those scoring highest, one sees:

A lesser likelihood of regarding financial security as 'very important' (from 93 % to 59%).

The greater likelihood of regarding leisure time as 'very important.' (from 47% to 88%).

A decline in the view that a job is the best way for a woman to be independent (from 60% to 11%).

An increase in self-identity as a political liberal (from 7% to 72%).

A decrease of confidence in the U.S. Congress (from 43% to 6%); the U.S. Supreme Court (from 57% to 24%); the Executive Branch (from 53% to 22%); and in major corporations (from 40% to 6%).

An increase in the view that the 'universe is basically friendly' increases (from 36% to 65%).

An increase in the view that 'right and wrong are not usually a simple matter of black and white' (from 14% to 56%).

The decrease in the condemnation of homosexuality (from 67% to 6%); as well as the condemnation of marijuana (from 80% to 28%).

The demand side of our argument is nearly finished. We have constructed a Transmodernism Index, treating it as a measure that predisposes people to look for and adopt a spiritual orientation with Buddhist-like features. The above relationships lend credence to that argument, though of course the substance of those relationships does not reflect Buddhism as such. We conclude, therefore, with three more correlations that come pretty close to expressing the Buddhist philosophy. The higher their Index Score the more persons agree that:

Life, as experienced by most people, is not what it should be (from 64% to 81%).

Happiness cannot be achieved through things external to the self (from 21% to 71%).

Happiness can only be achieved through inner, spiritual transformation (from 50% to 68%).

Might it be concluded, then, that the Transmodernism Index 'predicts' who, among those raised in a Judaic-Christian culture, are more likely to seek out Buddhism? Does it not also identify who, among these SGI members (all Buddhist by definition), are 'more' Buddhist in that they express more, and/ or express more intensely, those qualities that drew these people to Buddhism in the first place? We think it can and does. As we said at the outset, however, it is not enough to experience the 'demand' for a new religious perspective, a 'push' toward a new spirituality. One must also come into contact with the new perspective, and that means that somehow there must be a supplier.

On the Supply Side

The study of religious conversion was, for a long time, the province of *psychologists*, who understandably were interested chiefly in the cognitive and emotional processes that converting people experienced. The emphasis was thus placed on the appeal of new doctrine and new ritual, and on persons' reactions to these things. One of the most significant findings to come out of the research by *sociologists*, once they turned their attention to the various new religious movements that became so visible in the 1970s, was the role of *social*, rather than cognitive or emotional, factors in the conversion process. SGI-USA is no exception to this generalization. Fully 65 percent of these converts told us that they first encountered SGI through a friend, colleague, or acquaintance. Another 18 percent encountered SGI through a spouse or other family member. Only six people out of 325 indicated that it was through a concert or exhibition, or from SGI literature or other publicity. Fifteen percent chose to mark the option 'other,' and many of these also reflect the importance of the social network in acquainting a would-be convert with a new religious perspective. Thus, one woman who marked 'other' told us she encountered SGI through her boyfriend's roommate, another through her hairdresser, and yet another through the 'mother of a boy who played soccer with my son.' Indeed fewer than half of those saying 'other' indicated that they had been approached out of the blue 'by two women in a diner,' or 'on a park bench,' or 'people going door-to-door,' for example.

This information is important because historically Sōka Gakkai practice called for members to engage in aggressive recruitment, a practice known as *shakubuku*. Ethnographic studies of SGI-USA make clear that American members have found the act of confronting total strangers on the street, and inviting them to a chanting session, to be rather distasteful. There has been a decline, therefore, in active, aggressive *shakubuku* and an increased emphasis on a more passive, show-by-example method. When asked if they had observed this change during their SGI years, 97 percent of converts said yes, with only eight persons saying no. When asked if they approve the change, again 97 percent said yes, the other three percent disapproving.

We asked these members how soon after their first encounter they joined SGI-USA. Just over a third (35 percent) reported that they joined within a month, another third joined before a year passed, the remaining third taking longer. It is not surprising to find, therefore, that when asked their first reaction to their first encounter with SGI, only 24 percent chose 'immediate enthusiasm' as a response. Twenty-one expressed 'reluctance' or 'real skepticism,' meaning that the majority (55 percent) may have been favorable but still took some time to get involved. When asked 'Apart from the teachings, can you say what originally attracted you to SGI-USA?' almost everyone answered in the space provided, the vast majority offering a single response. The social nature of the conversion process is underscored by their answers. The most common answer was some variation of 'attracted by the members I met' (48 percent), with another 11 percent mentioning the attraction of a single person. One other answer must be discussed in detail.

The central ritual in SGI is chanting, either alone or in the company of others. Chanting follows a prescribed script and is for the purpose of achieving goals, which may range from quite abstract (for example, world peace) to quite concrete (for example, a pay raise). One important part of the recruitment process therefore consists of visitors hearing testimony about members' successful achievements, and another is encouraging the new visitor to try chanting. The visitor is given a card with the words to chant and invited to chant for his/her own goals. Because these activities occur so early in would-be converts' encounter with SGI, it is understandable that 25 percent of these converts indicated that it was the benefits – for self or others, already received or still hoped for – that were the major attraction for them.

Much smaller numbers mentioned the attraction of the aesthetics of chanting (5 percent), SGI's activities and goals (8 percent), SGI's philosophy (8 percent), a need for spiritual guidance (5 percent), or an interest in Buddhism (3 percent). What seems clear, therefore, is the relatively small role played by so-called doctrinal matters as people convert to SGI-USA. Indeed, when asked if the original attraction is still their main attraction, 40 percent said no, indicating that the benefits of chanting had replaced the winsomeness of members as the major attraction. It is not that SGI-USA converts lose friends among the SGI membership – only 13 percent report having *no* friends among fellow members, and 50 percent even have relatives who are members; it is that the social network that plays such a crucial part in 'pulling' new members and 'supplying' them with knowledge about SGI is no longer so critical to the maintenance of membership.

One special way the crucial role played by social factors in the conversion process is seen, therefore, is the fact that conversion to a new religion can be disruptive of a previous social network. More than half (59 percent) of these SGI converts told us they had experienced negative reactions from relatives or friends as a result of joining SGI-USA. Parents were most often mentioned (34 percent) as the persons being critical, but other family members (30 percent) were also mentioned, as were friends and coworkers (16 percent), and even spouses (11 percent). Under these conditions, it might even be said that the *social* attraction of a new religious movement is a necessary, if not sufficient, component of the conversion process.

Conclusion

How the importance of a social attraction compares with the importance of the other two components – availability and demand – cannot be assessed, of course. In one sense, availability simply fades away as a factor once a member is securely a member. Probably, too, the social attraction diminishes in importance in individual members' lives as they resolve or learn to ignore the objections of others. That leaves the 'supply' component to gain in relative importance, which no doubt has happened to the converts studied here. At first encounter they were but proto-Buddhists, as measured by our Transmodernism scale. It is their active membership that turns them into SGI Buddhists.

Even a cursory glance at the data from our survey of SGI-USA members tells a revealing story about the appeal of Buddhism (at least one form of Buddhism) in America. Structurally, converts to SGI are characterized by loose social ties prior to encountering SGI. They have fewer restrictions on their freedom to move about in the social world. Given that, it is not surprising that the most appealing quality of SGI to newcomers is its membership, which is described by converts as friendly, sincere, and helpful. Culturally, we may infer from the rather large number of former religious 'nones' among the converts, and a pattern of religious shopping prior to encountering SGI, that SGI converts were dissatisfied with the options offered by the American religious mainstream. We discovered a pattern of values among the converts that sets them apart from both religious conservatives and religious liberals – more liberal in their attitudes about sex and the causes of poverty than religious conservatives, and more cautious about science and technology and major social institutions than religious liberals. Taken all together, this value orientation amounts to a kind of 'proto-Buddhist' perspective, which we have shown to be related to three indicators of Buddhist philosophy. In other words, at least part of the appeal of SGI Buddhism may be understood as a function of the cultural availability of converts to non-traditional alternatives and the affinity between Buddhist philosophy and the value orientation of converts.

References

Hurst, Jane. *Nichiren Shoshu Buddhism and the Sōka Gakkai in America*. New York: Garland Publishing Co., 1992.

Metraux, Daniel. *The Lotus and the Maple Leaf: The Sōka Gakkai Buddhist Movement in Canada*. Lanham, MD: University Press of America, 1996.

____. 'The Sōka Gakkai: Buddhism and the Creation of a Harmonious and Peaceful Society.' In Christopher S. Queen and Sallie B. King, eds. *Engaged Buddhism: Buddhist Liberation Movements in Asia*. Albany, NY: State University of New York Press, 1996.

Wilson, Bryan, and Karel Dobbelaere. *A Time to Chant: The Sōka Gakkai Buddhists in Britain*. Oxford: Oxford University Press, 1994.

Notes

1 As of this writing (September 1997), we have just completed the collection phase of our questionnaire study of Sōka Gakkai International in the United States. We have an advance contract with Oxford University Press to publish our book, tentatively titled *Global Citizens: Sōka Gakkai in the United States*. Between now and October 1998, when the book manuscript is due, a much more refined analysis of the survey data will be conducted. Nonetheless, the invitation to contribute a 'reconnaissance'-type paper to the present volume affords us the opportunity to preview the data and make a few provisional statements about SGI-USA, findings that may very well extend to other Buddhist groups in America.

2 Because SGI-USA members are disproportionately baby-boomers, born between 1946 and 1962 (57 percent, as compared with 39 percent of the American adult public), we have adjusted for the age discrepancy when reporting data from the General Social Surveys of the National Opinion Research Center.

113

Since the 1970s, the National Opinion Research Center at the University of Chicago has periodically (annually, as a rule) surveyed a randomly drawn sample of adult Americans. These are the General Social Surveys. Many questions are asked many times, which, when results are added, yields much larger samples than most surveys employ, thus making them excellent 'benchmarks' for comparison purposes.

3 Bryan Wilson and Karel Dobbelaere, *A Time to Chant: The Sōka Gakkai Buddhists in Britain* (Oxford: Oxford University Press, 1994), 220.
4 See table and discussion in Wilson and Dobbelaere, 143–144.

Part Three

Modes of Dharma Transmission

CHAPTER EIGHT

Local Inter-Buddhist Associations in North America

Paul David Numrich[1]

In major metropolitan regions across North America, Buddhists from a variety of ethnic and traditional identities have formed associations to foster cooperative relations and address common concerns. The present essay analyzes this phenomenon by offering an in-depth case study of one such association (the Buddhist Council of the Midwest), a comparative overview of other inter-Buddhist associations on the local, national, and international levels, and a historical perspective on different types of inter-Buddhist interaction. This analysis provides insights into the current state of Buddhism in North America, as well as its possible future development.

As used here, the term *inter*-Buddhist connotes the crossing of significant boundaries of ethnic or traditional identity, for example, interaction among Buddhists from different Asian cultures or among those adhering to different major branches or schools of Buddhism. By contrast, the term *intra*-Buddhist would refer to interaction among Buddhists within the same ethnic group or those adhering to similar traditions or practices. The distinction is sometimes arguable, for example, whether an association comprised exclusively of American converts, but following different meditative lineages, should be considered *inter*- or *intra*-Buddhist. The term interreligious as used in this essay refers to interaction between Buddhists and representatives of non-Buddhist religions.

The Buddhist Council of the Midwest[2]

Buddhism was introduced to the American Midwest by Asian representatives at the World's Parliament of Religions held in Chicago during the Columbian Exposition of 1893. A small but visible Buddhist group was founded in Chicago after the Parliament as part of the larger interest in Buddhism within late-Victorian, Caucasian America. This was a branch of the Maha Bodhi Society, the international, inter-Buddhist association founded by the Sinhalese reformer and missionary, Anagarika Dharmapala.

Attracting mostly professional members, the young organization reportedly held a celebration of the Buddha's birthday in the home of its vice-president, a circuit court judge, in May 1898.[3] In the early decades of the twentieth century, members of two other organizations based in the greater Chicago area kept Buddhism in the American public eye: the Theosophical Society, with permanent headquarters in suburban Wheaton beginning in 1926, and Open Court publishing house in LaSalle (1887–1936), operated by Paul Carus, at which noted Zen writer D. T. Suzuki worked for several years.[4]

Significant numbers of ethnic-Asian Buddhists first settled in the Midwest at the close of World War II, following the release of Japanese internees from the wartime 'relocation centers' created by Executive Order 9066. A handful of Japanese temples appeared in Chicago during the quarter-century between 1944 to 1969, then many other ethnic-Asian groups established temples from 1970 to the present. The total number of such temples in metropolitan Chicago approximately doubled in the 1980s and will likely double again by the end of the 1990s. The conversion of Caucasian Americans to Buddhism after World War II can first be traced to the outreach of two Japanese Buddhist leaders beginning in the mid-1950s. Rev. Gyomay Kubose, founder of the second oldest ethnic-Asian Buddhist temple in Chicago, the Buddhist Temple of Chicago, established in 1944, created the self-styled non-sectarian American Buddhist Association in 1955 to 'study, publish and make known the principles of Buddhism...[a-mong] the general American public.'[5] The other local Japanese leader, Rev. Dr. Soyu Matsuoka, Rōshi, of the Zen Buddhist Temple of Chicago, established in 1949, began to attract Caucasian and African American practitioners in the early 1960s.[6]

Inter-Buddhist cooperation in the Chicago area began in earnest with the formation of the Buddhist Council of the Midwest in the mid-1980s. Yet there were important precedents. The Buddhist Temple of Chicago organized a joint cultural/religious celebration of the Buddha's birth in the 1950s. Until they established their own temple in the mid-1970s, local Thai Buddhists held occasional religious services at the Japanese Midwest Buddhist Temple, an affiliate of the Buddhist Churches of America (Jōdo Shinshū) and the oldest ethnic-Asian temple in Chicago, established in 1944.[7] The impetus for more formal and permanent inter-Buddhist relations through the auspices of a local association emerged from discussions in the summer of 1984 at the American Buddhist Association. Rev. Gyomay Kubose's son and successor, Rev. Sunnan Kubose, and Ven. Dr. Sunthorn Plamintr, a monk from the Thai Buddhist Temple (also known as Wat Dhammaram, established in 1976), took the lead in organizing the new group, which in 1985 sponsored an International Visakha celebration that would become the defining feature of the eventual Buddhist Council of the Midwest.

In late 1986 the group discussed incorporation under the not-for-profit provisions granted by the state of Illinois. A draft constitution for a 'Council of Buddhist Organizations' was drawn up, partly modeled after the constitution of the Vietnamese Buddhist Association of Illinois. Membership in the proposed council would comprise 'all organizations currently involved in the maintaining and promoting of Buddhism' in the area; the council would focus on the following purposes: 1. increasing awareness, understanding, and application of Buddhist principles among the general public; 2. pooling resources and coordinating events in order to 'create an atmosphere of fellowship and cooperation' among Buddhist members; 3. representing the local Buddhist community vis-à-vis the larger society; and 4. serving as an intermediary among members, if necessary.[8]

Taking the name 'Buddhist Council of the Midwest' (BCM), the organization registered with the state of Illinois in October 1987 as a not-for-profit corporation 'organized exclusively for educational, charitable, and religious purposes within the meaning of Section 501(c)(3) of the Internal Revenue Code.' The signatories of BCM's Articles of Incorporation represented nine local temples and meditation centers: Chicago Zen Center, Buddhist Temple of Chicago, Midwest Buddhist Temple, Dharmadhatu Buddhist Meditation Center, Vietnamese Buddhist Association, Zen Buddhist Temple of Chicago, Buddhadharma Meditation Center, Wat Dhammaram, and American Buddhist Association. BCM's stated purposes reflected the earlier draft constitution for the proposed 'Council of Buddhist Organizations':

1. To foster the learning and practice of Buddhism.
2. To represent the midwestern Buddhist community in matters affecting its membership.
3. To pool resources and coordinate efforts by its members to create an atmosphere of fellowship and cooperation.

Note that the internal 'intermediary' function of the initially proposed council was dropped altogether from BCM's purposes.[9]

As an early report to the state of Illinois summarized, BCM's primary goal has been to establish 'a forum for cooperation and interaction between local Buddhist organizations.'[10] Recent editions of its directory of area Buddhist organizations point out that 'The Buddhist Council of the Midwest encompasses a variety of denominations rooted in the many rich traditions in the countries of their origins.... [BCM] constitutes a kaleidoscope of Buddhist philosophies, methodologies, and ideals.'[11] BCM fosters inter-Buddhist relations in numerous ways. The Council's monthly meetings rotate among temples and centers in order to familiarize individual members with Buddhist traditions outside their own. BCM acts as a clearinghouse for news of local Buddhist programs and events through word-of-mouth communication, sharing of information at meetings, and preparation of an on-line monthly calendar. Retreats on topics of mutual interest have been scheduled on an irregular basis; for instance, the well-known Vietnamese Zen master Thich Nhat Hanh led retreats in 1989 and 1991, the latter attracting nearly 200 participants over four days. BCM has always featured interaction between clergy and laity of the various Buddhist traditions. One Japanese lay leader of BCM spoke to me of valuable lessons about respect learned by observing the revered status accorded Theravāda monks.

The annual International Visakha celebration, a rebirth of the celebrations organized previously by the Buddhist Temple of Chicago, has become the primary focus of the Buddhist Council of the Midwest today. Many hours of preparation and coordination go into this event, and virtually the entire agenda of some monthly business meetings may be devoted to fine-tuning its details. In some years the celebration has taken place in public venues in central locations, for example, Northeastern Illinois University and Truman College, but BCM prefers the two large Thai temples on the southwest side of the metropolitan region, Wat Dhammaram and Buddhadharma Meditation Center, both of which offer ample parking and traditional Buddhist interior decor.

Following the south Asian Theravāda tradition, BCM's International Visakha commemorates the three key events in the life of the Buddha – birth, enlightenment, and final passing away – on the closest weekend possible to the full moon of May (the north Asian Mahāyāna tradition commemorates only the birth, a month earlier). BCM takes care not to conflict with major programming of individual temples, and it tries to provide as much variety as possible in the festivities. 'We of the Buddhist Council of the Midwest welcome you to our multi-cultural event,' announces the directory/program for International Visakha. 'Feel free to contact any or all of the temples or centers listed here and see for yourself the diversity available to Buddhists in the Midwest.'[12] The 1997 International Visakha typified this intentionally variform annual gathering, with an inter-Buddhist religious service on Saturday morning, concurrent meditation instruction in six different styles and sequential lectures on four major Buddhist traditions during the afternoon, and an evening cultural program featuring performances from six ethnic-Asian groups. Local temples and meditation centers ran information exhibits throughout the day.

BCM makes strenuous efforts to publicize the International Visakha each year, and attendance typically reaches several hundred. The intent is twofold. First, as one BCM leader explained to me, the event seeks to present an accurate portrayal of Buddhism for the edification of an American public that seems both mystified by and biased against this non-Western religion. 'My fondest hope for the future,' writes another longtime BCM leader closely involved with preparations for the annual celebration, 'is to give the public enough information about Buddhism so that it will be on an equal footing with the other religions. . . .' Thus, the writer continues, 'we won't have to explain ourselves so often, or justify our philosophy to the majority religious community.'[13] Secondly, the International Visakha represents more than a simple provision of accurate information about Buddhism. Many BCM leaders share what might be called a 'missionary' motivation for the event, hoping that through its auspices the Buddha's Dharma might be spread among Americans and might thereby begin to transform American society for the better.

The Buddhist Council of the Midwest explains, defends, and promotes the Dharma outside of the context of its annual International Visakha as well. In the early 1990s BCM engaged in a series of dialogues about personal spiritual experiences with the Office of Ecumenical and Interreligious Affairs of the Roman Catholic Archdiocese of Chicago. BCM co-sponsored the 1993 Parliament of the World's Religions held in Chicago, chairing the Buddhist host committee for that historic convocation, and has actively supported the continuing metropolitan interreligious initiatives coordinated by Parliament organizers. BCM has worked with both the Chicago and Detroit regional branches of the National Conference (formerly the National Conference of Christians and Jews) in the latter's efforts to educate the public about America's growing religious diversity. In connection with the Democratic National Convention that met in Chicago in the summer of 1996, the Buddhist Council of the Midwest filled five tables at the Interfaith Prayer Breakfast with Buddhist monks and laity.

BCM occasionally adopts the role of social watchdog on behalf of Buddhism. Several years ago the Council sent a letter to *Weight Watchers Magazine* protesting a photo of a woman leaning casually on a Buddha statue.[14] At a recent Council meeting one member described an episode of a Saturday morning network television cartoon program which he considered religiously and racially offensive to Buddhists. BCM eventually sent a letter to the local TV station that carries the program requesting a videotape of the episode in order to evaluate its content. 'The Council is very concerned about the way Buddhist people and Buddhist principles are portrayed to the general public,' wrote BCM's president. The discussion surrounding this issue at the Council meeting provides insight into the perceived status of Buddhism in American society. The member who brought the matter to the Council's attention argued that a comparably denigrating portrayal of Christianity would never have appeared on a network television program, since the majority of Americans are Christians. At the close of the meeting the president commented that, as members of a minority in America, Buddhists must join together in their efforts.[15]

Over the years, the Buddhist Council of the Midwest has taken on a variety of social service projects, though some BCM leaders would like to see a more concerted effort in this direction, which has come to be known as 'engaged Buddhism.'[16] BCM's directory calls this 'acts of compassion,' alluding to the basic Buddhist virtue of *karunā*. BCM projects have included youth outreach in immigrant Buddhist temples, refugee assistance within the Kampuchean (Cambodian) and Tibetan communities, cooperation with an organization serving AIDS-affected Asian families, and a meditation program for inmates of the Indiana state prison system. Immigrant temples also appeal to BCM for practical, one-time assistance. Recently, for instance, a small southeast Asian temple required substantial repairs to its facility, and the local Kampuchean association asked for letters of recommendation to bring 35 monks into the country.

BCM's most recent directory lists 50 Buddhist temples and centers in the area (the actual number may exceed this total by a dozen or more). About two-fifths of the 50 are predominantly ethnic-Asian temples, representing Korean, Thai, Chinese, Japanese, Burmese, Kampuchean, Vietnamese, and Laotian groups practicing a variety of Buddhist traditions. The other three-fifths of the total are American-convert meditation centers, mostly in the Zen and Tibetan traditions. Active participation in BCM leadership and events has always featured a nearly half-and-half mix of ethnic-Asian and American-convert Buddhists. Official membership in the Buddhist Council of the Midwest is accorded to temples/centers, though in actuality it appears to be primarily individual-based, that is, interested persons join the association, by virtue of which their respective temples/centers gain representation in the Council.

Three primary factors preclude individuals and/or groups from participating in the Council. The first is practicality – some interested persons simply do not have the time or the means of transportation to attend meetings and events. Second, group insularity and insufficient acculturation to American society render some ethnic Asians incapable of participating in such cooperative social endeavors. Finally, philosophical differences keep certain groups away. The local Nichiren Shōshū Temple, for instance, rebuffed BCM's overtures on religious principle, since to join an inter-Buddhist organization would be to grant equal status to the truths of non-Nichiren Shōshū traditions. One source opined that some 'esoteric' American-convert meditation groups decline to join BCM because they feel they 'practice a superior, purer Buddhism than the rest of us.'[17]

Such an attitude reflects what can be labeled an 'assimilationist' model of group interaction, wherein a dominant group – here a self-defined 'dominance' of religious superiority – expects other groups to conform to its ways. As should be clear from the foregoing description, the Buddhist Council of the Midwest has adopted a 'pluralist' model of inter-Buddhist relations, that is, it respects and encourages the uniqueness of each Buddhist group while seeking common ground upon which all can agree as a basis for united efforts.

Another model of interaction advocated by some North American Buddhist groups and leaders can be labeled the 'fusionist' or 'melting pot' approach, the latter metaphor deriving from Israel Zangwill's play written at the height of the classic American immigration period (1908). The term 'Americanization' is often used in this sense with regard to U.S. immigrant history. According to this model, a completely new creation emerges from the mixture of the best elements from all groups. Some Buddhists in the West invoke the term 'Navayana,' literally a 'New Vehicle' – Robert Ellwood uses the interesting phrase 'fresh vehicle'[18] – forged out of the interplay of the three traditional vehicles of Asian Buddhism (Theravāda, Mahāyāna, and Vajrayāna). Martin Baumann reports efforts at creating an 'integrative Buddhism' in Europe.[19] Some in the U.S. speak of a uniquely 'American Buddhism,' now in its formative stages.[20] The Buddhist Council of the Midwest has considered this topic at least once, prompted by a member's position paper favoring a fusionist approach. BCM's minutes reflect the sense of the group: 'we are not yet ready for this sort of thing.'[21]

Local Inter-Buddhist Associations in North America

My inquiries uncovered nine local inter-Buddhist associations in North America, listed here alphabetically: Buddhist Association of Southwest Michigan, Buddhist Coalition of New England, Buddhist Council of the Midwest, Buddhist Council of New York, Buddhist Council of Northern California, Buddhist Sangha Council of Southern California, Hawaii Association of International Buddhists (here granting Hawaii 'North American' status), Sangha Council of Ontario Buddhist Associations, and Texas Buddhist Council. Additionally, I know of a recent, unsuccessful attempt to form a local inter-Buddhist association in Denver, Colorado, and I suspect there may be other such associations in North America of which I am unaware. A fuller understanding of the phenomenon of local inter-Buddhist associations emerges when we supplement the description of the Buddhist Council of the Midwest given above with pertinent details about these other North American associations.

Although Buddhism's living presence in many North American regions extends back several decades earlier, successful local inter-Buddhist associations of the type under consideration here date only from around the year 1980.[22] This watershed year is not coincidental, as it represents the point in time when the effects of two important and interrelated trends began to consolidate. First, demographic shifts initiated by liberal immigration legislation passed in the United States and Canada in the 1960s became apparent by the 1980s. Largely due to the influx of new immigrants, Buddhism became the fastest growing religion in Canada by 1984,[23] whereas the Asian American population of the U.S. doubled in the 1970s and again in the 1980s, making it the third largest American minority group after Blacks and Hispanics.[24] Secondly, indigenous interest in Buddhism as an alternative religious path reached an all-time high in

North American history beginning in the 1960s, with institutional consolidation in the next two decades.[25] Prior to about 1980, *intra*-Buddhist associations had formed in some regions (e.g., the Buddhist Church Federation of Los Angeles, representing Jōdo Shinshū BCA temples), but the circumstances necessary to form *inter*-Buddhist associations were not in place in most regions until about 1980.

Analysis of formal statements drafted by several of the local inter-Buddhist associations listed above reveals a common core of purposes. Using a variety of phrasing, most of the associations speak of fostering communication, cooperation, and understanding among Buddhist groups in the region. All speak of supporting or facilitating the practice of Buddhism by groups and/or individuals. Some associations identify very specific, often ambitious, means for providing such support. The mission statement of the Texas Buddhist Council calls for acquiring land to build one or more Buddhist retreat centers for use by 'members and other interested parties,'[26] while the general purposes of the Buddhist Council of Northern California include provisions 'to assist Buddhist communities in establishing a Buddhist center of their own' and 'to study, research and provide facilities for Buddhist practices.'[27] The Buddhist Sangha Council of Southern California founded the College of Buddhist Studies in 1983, offering 'students of Buddhism a unique opportunity to experience a comprehensive in-depth study of Buddhism from a non-sectarian point of view, while also promoting knowledge and understanding of the different schools and cultural traditions within Buddhism.' The College sought to address 'the growing desire for more Buddhist education than the [local] temples themselves could provide,' and now grants both academic and ministerial degrees.[28]

Dissemination of the Dharma, in order both to edify the general public and to transform the larger society for the better, appears to be a common motivation underlying the formation of local inter-Buddhist associations, though it is not always stipulated in their formal statements of purpose. The Texas Buddhist Council seeks '[t]o bring the teachings of the Buddha to the mainstream of American life in Texas through education and opportunities for social service.'[29] The Hawaii Association of International Buddhists speaks of developing a 'spirituality' that will improve 'the quality of life among Buddhists as well as humanity as a whole,' and facilitating meditative practices that will contribute 'to inner and outer peace of humankind at the individual and other levels.'[30] A newsletter editorial by the Hawaii Association's founding president expresses appreciation for the freedom of American society, which provides Buddhists the opportunity to 'uplift' that same society: Buddhists can 'creatively develop their religion to suit the present-day needs of American society, such as uplifting the sagging morality evident all around us in America.'[31] A missionary motivation underlay the following appeal for unity given in the presidential address to the first annual meeting of the Buddhist Sangha Council of Southern California: 'Time has come for the Buddhists of all different Sects in America to shun their differences and work together for the greater glory of the Buddhasāsana [the Buddhist religion].'[32]

Some local associations organize an annual Visakha celebration, though I do not know whether these affairs have become as elaborate and time-consuming as that of the Buddhist Council of the Midwest. The Buddhist Association of Southwest Michigan held what it called its first 'Buddhist Fair' in 1997; the associations in both northern and southern California have been holding such events since around 1980. Noted Buddhist scholar Masao Abe gave the keynote address at the twelfth annual 'Buddha Day' celebration sponsored by the Buddhist Council of Northern California in 1990, rousing the audience with these concluding words: 'Let us take on, then, the future task of Buddhism! Let us awaken to the Buddha Dharma ... and in this way let us build a better world where all beings in the ten quarters, including self and others, men and women, nations and races, humans and nature, all may live harmoniously and peacefully.'[33] The Buddhist Sangha Council of Southern California's 'Buddha's Birthday Commemoration ... features a religious service of chanting in various Buddhist traditions, a *dharma* talk and a cultural program of music, dance and arts of the ethnic communities.'[34]

It appears that clergy-laity interaction is typically encouraged in local inter-Buddhist associations. In at least three cases, ethnic-Asian clergy provided the initiative to form an association. In one of these cases, due to the unique circumstances of its origins, a special concern for the ordained Sangha (i.e., the monastic order) has continued to inform the purposes of the association. As I have reported elsewhere, the Buddhist Sangha Council of Southern California coalesced in response to the 1980 ouster of the resident monks at the first Sri Lankan temple in Los Angeles.[35] This context helps to explain the pointedness of the following statement, which goes beyond other local associations' generalities about fostering inter-Buddhist harmony and cooperation: 'The Council continues to act as a mediator in disputes within the Buddhist community and provides support and guidance for Sangha members during times of difficulty or transition.'[36] Also unique among the local inter-Buddhist associations for which I have information is the Sangha Council's stress on monastic ordination and edification; the Council's purposes include these: 'to facilitate ordination into the Buddhist Order' and 'to provide proper education, training and leadership in the Order.'[37] In addition to efforts in these directions through its College of Buddhist Studies (discussed earlier), the Sangha Council has been at the forefront of the controversial movement to reestablish the historically defunct Theravāda Order of nuns, most recently ordaining a Thai woman at the novice (*sāmanerī*) level during the 1997 Buddha's Birthday Commemoration.[38]

Invoking the monastic order's historic role as preserver and teacher of the Dharma, the Buddhist Sangha Council of Southern California organized a one-day conference on 'Buddhism across Cultures,' held at a suburban Los Angeles temple in March 1997. Participants represented the Theravāda, Mahāyāna, and Vajrayāna branches of Buddhism, as well as eight different ethnicities. This convocation harked back to the Conference on World Buddhism in North America held a decade earlier in Ann Arbor, Michigan, though the exact relationship between the two is unclear. As the Ann Arbor conference had also done, the Los Angeles conference reviewed three earlier attempts to attain what it called 'global consensus on Buddhist commitment, practice and purpose': the Theosophist Henry Olcott's 'Common Platform' of Buddhist beliefs, the 'Twelve Principles of Buddhism' proposed by the British Buddhist convert Christmas Humphreys, and a list of 'agreements' from the initial meeting of the World Fellowship of Buddhists. The Los Angeles conference then drafted its own ten-point 'comprehensive statement to reflect the needs and challenges of modern times.' This statement, like those of Olcott and Humphreys but unlike those typically formulated by inter-Buddhist associations, specifies areas of commonly held Buddhist doctrine. Sentiments in this statement more typical of inter-Buddhist associations include commitment to strengthening the practice of Buddhism and honoring and cultivating what it calls 'inter-traditional differences' within the Buddhist religion.[39]

From the information available to me regarding local North American inter-Buddhist associations, only the Buddhist Sangha Council of Southern California expressly identifies interreligious interaction as a formal goal, using these words: 'to engage in ecumenical cooperation with all religious groups.'[40] Other associations, like the Buddhist Council of the Midwest as described earlier, cultivate such interaction to a greater or lesser extent, but subsumed under other goals. For instance, the Buddhist Council of New York is a member of the Interfaith Council of Greater New York, no doubt in part to fulfill the former's goal 'to present the Buddhist Tradition to the general public.'[41] The Buddhist Sangha Council of Southern California participates in the Interreligious Council of Southern California and, since 1982, has co-sponsored conferences on a variety of topics with the Roman Catholic Archdiocese of Los Angeles.[42] Ven. Dr. Havanpola Ratanasara, president of the Sangha Council, gave several presentations at the 1993 Parliament of the World's Religions in Chicago, including one entitled 'Los Angeles: Model of Interreligious Cooperation.' The Sangha Council recently endorsed the stance of the Los Angeles-area Progressive Religious Alliance, a liberal coalition formed to counter the perspectives of the conservative Christian Coalition.[43]

Like the Buddhist Council of the Midwest, other local inter-Buddhist associations have adopted the role of social watchdog on behalf of the rights of the Buddhist minority in society. For instance, the Texas Buddhist

Council's mission statement includes this item: 'To serve as a consultant to and advocate for Buddhist temples, study groups and individuals on matters of cultural, legal and political concern related to the preservation and promotion of the Buddha Dharma in Texas.'[44] The Buddhist Sangha Council of Southern California claims to have 'taken a very active role in assisting temples or communities which are having problems within the larger community,' including the cases of well-known ethnic-Asian temples in the Los Angeles suburbs of North Hollywood and Hacienda Heights.[45] Also, the Sangha Council took the occasion of their 1997 Buddha's Birthday Commemoration to address recent comments by Roman Catholic prelates, including the Pope, considered misrepresentative of Buddhism.[46] Likewise responding to papal misrepresentation of Buddhism, and then taking note of the 'inroads' Buddhism has made in both Europe and America, the founding president of the Hawaii Association of International Buddhists has warned that 'Buddhists should be full of awareness as to the backlash that they could be subjected to unless the Buddhists themselves can practice "Unity in Diversity." '[47] The head of another association wrote me that 'a serious common threat (for example, fundamental[ist] Christians trying to repress Buddhism)' can spur Buddhist groups to concerted action through a local association.[48] Although they make general statements affirming Buddhism's basic compassion and charitableness, it does not appear that most local inter-Buddhist associations promulgate a serious or sustained program of 'engaged Buddhism.'

The ethnic mix of these associations can vary widely. For example, ethnic-Asian groups make up about two-thirds of the listing published by the Texas Buddhist Council, whereas less than one-fourth of the member groups in the Buddhist Council of Northern California are ethnic-Asian. A variety of Asian nationalities seems fairly typical, while the Zen and Tibetan traditions tend to predominate among American convert groups. No doubt the three factors identified earlier as precluding participation in the Buddhist Council of the Midwest obtain for other local associations as well, viz., practicality, cultural insularity, and philosophical differences. As to the first factor, the head of one association explained, simply, that 'temples have their hands full with their own concerns..., ideals alone do not garner membership when many find their plates already full and energy over-extended.'[49]

As to the manner of interaction adopted by such local inter-Buddhist associations, it appears that the pluralist model prevails, viz., respect and appreciation for the uniqueness of each Buddhist group, with agreement upon commonly held concerns as a basis for unity. The first stated purpose of the Texas Buddhist Council is instructive in this regard: 'To preserve and nurture the Buddha Dharma in Texas, realizing and respecting the diversity of Buddhist traditions within the state.'[50] The term 'Buddha Dharma' implies a core of teachings shared by all Buddhist groups regardless of less important differences. This notion of a common doctrinal core is not

127

always expressly stated, however, and its specific contours seem rarely to receive serious examination. In an editorial advocating 'unity in diversity' among Buddhists in America, the newsletter of the Hawaii Association of International Buddhists put forth the four Buddhist virtues of loving-kindness, compassion, sympathetic joy, and equanimity (the *brahmavi-hāras*) as basic to all Buddhist groups. Regarding the diversity of views outside of this shared core, the editorial called for 'respect': 'There should be unity in granting such respect. Unity is not uniformity....'[51] The mission statement of the Buddhist Council of New York includes this typically pluralist sentiment: 'Not favoring any particular sect, the council strives to balance the interests of the three main branches of Buddhism: Theravada, Mahayana, and Vajrayana.'[52]

Fusionist sentiments do not appear in the official purposes of any local, North American inter-Buddhist association for which I have information. In a few cases key individuals harbor such sentiments, but the associations in question seem to function in pluralist fashion. For instance, a 'working paper' circulated prior to the founding of the Buddhist Association of Southwest Michigan stressed the importance of the 'new form of Buddhism ... [that is] already being called American Buddhism,'[53] yet the eventual group's newsletter asserts that this 'association was created to support and encourage Buddhist practitioners of diverse traditions and cultures throughout the area,'[54] clearly a pluralist intention. Likewise, the president of the Buddhist Sangha Council of Southern California, Ven. Dr. Havanpola Ratanasara, has long advocated an Americanized, fusionist form of Buddhism, but, as I have implied elsewhere, his enthusiasm for a new American 'Ekayana' ('One Vehicle') does not seem to have changed the Sangha Council's basic pluralism.[55]

Unsuccessful attempts to establish inter-Buddhist associations in two regions appear to offer a lesson in this regard. Around 1930 in Hawaii, Caucasian convert Ernest Hunt, with support from the head of the Japanese Nishi Hongwanji Mission (Jōdo Shinshū), Bishop Yemyo Imamura, promoted a non-sectarian form of Buddhism. The fusionist philosophy underlying this effort takes clear expression in a statement from a later organization founded by another Caucasian convert associated with Hunt and Imamura in Hawaii, Julius Goldwater: 'In this endeavor there can be no thought of discrimination in sect, race or color; the teachings must be paramount, combining the best of both Hinayana and Mahayana School [sic], and in so doing, reaching that equilibrium so necessary for completeness and growth.'[56] Tellingly, the fusionist efforts in Hawaii were squelched by a staunchly sectarian bishop who relieved Ernest Hunt of his responsibilities in 1935, while inter-Buddhist activities in the Japanese 'relocation centers' on the mainland during World War II tended toward either pluralist accommodation or sectarian tension despite visits to the centers by the fusionist Julius Goldwater.[57]

In the Toronto region, sixteen local Buddhist groups formed the Toronto Buddhist Federation in 1979, sponsoring a joint Visakha celebration the following May that drew over 1,000 Buddhists from a dozen nationalities. Common concerns about their minority status as Buddhists in Canadian society seem to have provided the key impetus for early participation in this association. But, as McLellan reports, the Federation underwent a 'politicization' that included a philosophical push to 'Canadianize Buddhism and rid it of ... "cultural baggage".' As McLellan notes, '[t]he vast majority of Asian practitioners did not agree with this direction.' The Federation changed its name in 1986 to the Buddhist Council of Canada, reflecting a new national focus; in 1989 an association called the Buddhist Communities of Greater Toronto emerged to carry on local inter-Buddhist activities, changing its name in 1994 to the current Sangha Council of Ontario Buddhist Associations. Alienation over the earlier push for 'Canadianization' still runs high within the ethnic-Asian Buddhist communities of greater Toronto, to the extent that the new Sangha Council struggles to remain a viable organization.[58]

Other Inter-Buddhist Associations

The dynamics that led to the formation of local inter-Buddhist associations in North America obtain elsewhere in the contemporary world, though I have seen precious little analysis of such associations. Paul Croucher briefly describes inter-Buddhist efforts in Sydney, Australia,[59] while Baumann mentions local 'umbrella groups' throughout Europe.[60]

Inter-Buddhist associations at the national and international levels share many of the same purposes underlying local associations, as described above. The American Buddhist Congress, established in 1987, represents over 50 Buddhist organizations of various ethnic and traditional identities in the United States. Its stated goals stress inter-Buddhist dialogue and cooperation, propagation of the Dharma, edification of the general public, interreligious dialogue, and humanitarian service. Ven. Dr. Havanpola Ratanasara of the Buddhist Sangha Council of Southern California has served as the executive president of the American Buddhist Congress since its inception, bringing his characteristic views about an emerging and unique 'American Buddhism' to this organization as well, though again it appears that the Congress functions in a pluralist fashion.[61]

The Deutsche Buddhistische Union, established in the late 1950s as a national inter-Buddhist association in Germany, has shown a special interest in political advocacy, and in the mid-1980s drafted a statement of commonly held doctrines and ethics called Buddhistisches Bekenntnis ('Buddhist Confession').[62] A cross-national European association, the European Buddhist Union, established in 1975, stresses dialogue and dissemination of the Dharma. This latter organization may more properly be called an *intra*-Buddhist association, since it has garnered little support from ethnic-Asian Buddhist groups, a fact perhaps not unrelated to its apparent advocacy of a fusionist, 'Europeanized Buddhism.'[63]

As Joseph Kitagawa notes, in contrast to earlier periods in Japan's history, 'Japanese Buddhists today have developed a genuine kinship and respect for Buddhists in other lands.'[64] Recent decades have seen the formation of the Union of New Religious Organizations of Japan (established in 1951), representing over 100 groups,[65] and an annual All Japan Buddhist Conference, sponsored by the Japan Buddhist Federation, which facilitates 'mutual consultation and exchange of ideas among various denominational leaders.'[66] During the Shintō revival of the Meiji period (1868–1929), Buddhist groups in Japan formed a union to withstand persecution and promote the cause of Buddhism. Moreover, in the 1890s Buddhists joined with Christians and social liberals in forming the Teiyū Ethical Society to combat nationalism and religious sectarianism in Japan.[67]

Heinz Bechert identifies the Maha Bodhi Society, established in 1891, as 'the first international Buddhist organization.' It 'aimed to unite Buddhists of all countries and to make Bodh-Gāyā [the site of the Buddha's enlightenment] a centre of Buddhist religious devotion again.'[68] An early edition of the Society's journal, *Mahā Bodhi*, lists the Grand Lama of Tibet as the organization's patron, along with officers from Burma, Japan, and Ceylon, including the driving force of the Society, the celebrated Sinhalese reformer Anagārika Dharmapāla. The Society's stated objectives include a strong missionary motivation, 'to make known to all nations the sublime teachings of the BUDDHA, SAKYA MUNI,' and a social service agenda aimed at the poor and needy. Its perspective has been steadfastly pluralist from the beginning: 'The Society representing Buddhism in general, not any single aspect of it, shall preserve absolute neutrality with respect to the doctrines and dogmas taught by sections and sects among Buddhists.'[69] Significantly, the Maha Bodhi Society emerged out of the context of British/ Christian domination of Buddhism in nineteenth-century Ceylon, part of a larger reform movement (dubbed 'Protestant Buddhism' by Gananath Obeyesekere) that challenged the Protestant missionaries and was eventually spearheaded by the 'anti-missionary missionaries' of the Theosophical Society.[70]

Two international inter-Buddhist associations established in the mid-twentieth century merit mention here. The World Fellowship of Buddhists, established in 1950, arose out of the vision of its first president, Sinhalese scholar G. P. Malalasekera. This organization holds five 'aims and objects':

1. To promote among the members strict observance and practice of the teachings of the Buddha;
2. To secure unity, solidarity and brotherhood amongst Buddhists;
3. To propagate the sublime doctrine of the Buddha;

4. To organise and carry on social, educational and cultural activities and other humanitarian services;

5. To work for securing peace and harmony amongst men and happiness for all beings and to collaborate with other organizations working for the same ends.[71]

The World Buddhist Sangha Council, established in 1966, brought together monastics from various countries and two major branches of Buddhism. Note the pluralist sentiments in the Sangha Council's statement of purpose, as reported by Bechert: to 'unite all Buddhist monks in the world today, both Theravada and Mahayana, as one solid organization in spite of superficial minor differences and in order to develop their ethical, intellectual and spiritual standards and adapt themselves to changing social and economical conditions in the modern world.'[72]

Finally, it should be noted that *intra*-Buddhist associations share many of the motivations and purposes underlying *inter*-Buddhist associations. The Association of Soto Zen Buddhists, an umbrella organization of centers encompassing various Sōtō Zen sub-lineages, stresses propagation, education, and examination of Zen's place in American society.[73] Meditation-centered, predominantly American-convert umbrella organizations like Northwest Dharma Association in Seattle, Washington, Insight Meditation Community in the greater Washington, D.C., area, and Insight Meditation Network in Boulder, Colorado, facilitate interaction among like-minded practitioners. On the ethnic-Asian side, the Vietnamese American Unified Buddhist Congress (established in 1992) seeks to promote Buddhism in the United States and to address human rights violations against Buddhists in Vietnam.[74] Monks in the approximately 150 immigrant Theravāda temples in North America are represented by monastic Sangha associations like the Sri Lanka Sangha Council of North America, the Dhammayut Order in the United States of America (affiliated with the Dhammayuttika Nikaya of Thailand), and the Council of Thai Bhikkhus in the USA (affiliated with the Mahanikaya of Thailand). The last-named Council, established in 1976 and now representing the majority of North American Thai temples, includes in its purposes support for local Thai temples and 'the religious activities and missionary practices of Thai Bhikkhus [monks] in the U.S.A.,' and fostering of relations with 'other Buddhist and other religious organizations.'[75]

Inter-Buddhist Associations in Historical Perspective

The contemporary phenomenon of inter-Buddhist associations derives from particular social conditions and expresses itself in typical organizational patterns vis-à-vis the larger social context. The modern period has brought many historically isolated Buddhist traditions into closer contact and interaction with each other, either at the local level primarily through immigration trends or at the national and international levels through advances in travel and communication. Buddhist leaders sometimes naïvely claim uniqueness for the Buddhist plurality in their particular region,[76] and may slightly overstate the significance of contemporary interaction among various Buddhist groups, since ancient isolation of Buddhist traditions was never impervious. Even so, proximity and interaction obviously constitute necessary conditions for the formation of inter-Buddhist associations in the modern period.

But these conditions alone may not have sufficed to produce the type of inter-Buddhist associations featured in this essay, locally or otherwise. Another key factor appears to be the perception of Buddhism's minority status, including perceived threats or misrepresentations from the larger social context, whether that context be a metropolis or nation in the Christian West, or the Westernized (read: Christianized) modern world. This explains typical features of the contemporary inter-Buddhist association: the emphasis on solidarity and harmonious dialogue and fellowship among Buddhists; the cultivation of the Buddhist presence in an area; joint efforts in disseminating the Dharma; the pursuit of equitable relations with non-Buddhists, through interreligious dialogue and alliances as well as monitoring of public portrayals of Buddhism – all these can be understood from the perspective of social theory about minority-majority group relations.[77]

I find it particularly noteworthy that contemporary inter-Buddhist associations tend to adopt a pluralist approach in organizing Buddhists to address common concerns as a minority religious presence. In theory the other approaches mentioned during the course of this essay – fusion and assimilation – could be as successful as pluralism in forging disparate Buddhist groups into a unified body to confront a sometimes hostile non-Buddhist social context. Indeed, as we have seen, some North American Buddhists today call for either fusion or assimilation rather than pluralism, though perhaps as much out of personal predilection or philosophical principle as social strategy.

Premodern Buddhist history provides an instructive perspective here. One can make the case that, where disparate Buddhist groups have interacted throughout earlier Buddhism, assimilationist and fusionist sentiments have been invoked at least as much as pluralist sentiments, if not more so. For instance, the Indian emperor Ashoka (third century BCE) granted equal status and support to all religions in his realm, encouraging amicable interreligious relations. Himself partial to Buddhism, the historical Ashoka nevertheless does not appear to have been a partisan of any particular Buddhist group, wishing only that the respective monastic communities avoid internal dissention. In contrast to this portrait of religious pluralism, the Ashoka of later legend serves as the quintessential royal defender of Theravāda purity, setting the precedent for subsequent

State-Sangha relations in Theravāda lands through his monastic purge and sponsorship of the so-called Third Buddhist Council. According to tradition, the Pali canonical text called the Kathāvatthu stems from that council – translated 'Points of Controversy,' the Kathāvatthu establishes Theravādin orthodoxy by refuting the heterodoxies of other early Buddhist groups. As Charles Hallisey argues, the 'idea' of monastic councils that developed in Theravāda history (regardless of what comprised the actual 'events' themselves) functioned 'to establish the continuing validity of the Theravāda as a tradition'[78] – and, I would point out, by assimilationist tactics rather than through pluralist accommodation.[79]

As the three major branches of Buddhism – Theravāda, Mahāyāna, and Vajrayāna – took shape in later history, they interacted in certain noteworthy contexts. Several great monastery/university institutions developed in India and Central Asia between the Gupta and Muslim periods (ca. 300–1200 CE), the most famous at Nālandā in modern Bihar. As Noble Ross Reat explains, 'Buddhists representing the various schools co-existed peacefully' in these monastic universities, though 'in a constant state of scholarly debate.'[80] Nālandā required Mahāyāna philosophy as its core curriculum, and legend eventually linked the names of the greatest Mahāyāna luminaries (for example, Nāgārjuna and Vasubandhu) with this academy. Thus, even though the views of other Buddhist and even non-Buddhist traditions were studied at Nālandā, it seems inappropriate to label such an atmosphere 'pluralist' in the way that term is used in this essay. The contentiousness over – as opposed to appreciation for – the plurality of Buddhism marks the ancient approach in this case, in contrast to the modern inter-Buddhist association. A suitable label for the style of these ancient monastic universities might be 'marketplace assimilationism,' wherein the majority philosophical group willingly subjected its views to the test of the marketplace of ideas, confident of vindication through open debate. Interestingly, it appears that the university at Nālandā eventually adopted a more assertive assimilationism, as it came to be dominated by Tantric philosophy during its final centuries.[81]

Relations among the three monastic institutions in the capital of ancient Ceylon, Anurādhapura, featured an intriguing interplay of assimilationist and fusionist tendencies. The Mahāvihāra monastery of the orthodox Sthaviravāda school adopted a classically assimilationist stance toward the Abhayagiri Vihāra monastery, which split away from the Mahāvihāra in the first century BCE and became infused over the centuries with both Mahāyāna and Vajrayāna views. (The third monastery in Anurādhapura, the Jetavana, established in the fourth century CE, seems to have adopted a position somewhere between these two powerful institutions.) Once, with the aid of the king Mahāsena (r. 334–362 CE), an assertive monk at the Abhayagiri monastery made an unsuccessful attempt to convert the Mahāvihāra to Mahāyānism, during which the monks of the latter monastery were forced from the city for a period of nine years. When a later king, Silāmegha (r. 617–626 CE), asked the Mahāvihāra to join together with the Abhayagiri in performing a fundamental monastic ritual (the *uposatha* ceremony), the orthodox Mahāvihāra monks refused. Under threat of common danger during later centuries, for example, plague, economic strain, or minority status under foreign rule, the three monasteries cooperated to a greater degree, and even that bastion of Theravāda orthodoxy, the Mahāvihāra, at times adopted some non-Theravāda elements by virtue of its intercourse with the Abhayagiri Vihāra. Still, assimilationism won out in the end, as the twelfth-century king Parākramabāhu I, having thrown off foreign rule and seeking to emulate the Ashoka of ancient legend, 'abolished the Abhayagiri and Jetavana monasteries and decreed that their monks would have to return to the laity or seek reordination under the auspices of the Mahāvihāra. The issuance of this royal decree represented the final victory of Theravāda Buddhism in Sri Lanka.'[82]

A final example of premodern inter-Buddhist interaction comes from Japan, where a fanatic religious assimilationism accompanied larger social upheavals in some eras. In Anesaki's words, a 'militant spirit crept into religious circles' during the Kamakura period (1186–1333),[83] while religious leaders in the fifteenth and sixteenth centuries, the time of the so-called 'uprisings' of sects against one another, 'shared the warlike spirit and practice of the age and combined their religious ambition with the contest for power.'[84] The unification of Japan in the Tokugawa period (1600–1868) ended religious sectarian violence, but it could not impose a harmonious pluralism among the Buddhist sects, which engaged in 'interdenominational polemics...[that] took more the form of academic discussion than religious proselytizing.'[85]

For the most part in the historical situations just delineated, Buddhism occupied the status of majority religion in its larger social context, and inter-Buddhist relations tended to take either assimilationist or fusionist turns. In situations where Buddhism's status shifted away from an unambiguous majority position or came under serious threat, as during the historical Ashoka's liberal support of all religions or in some periods in medieval Ceylon, pluralist inter-Buddhist relations surfaced. Although contemporary inter-Buddhist associations may attribute their pluralist sentiments to Buddhism, the preceding discussion shows that pluralist interaction does not necessarily characterize Buddhist history. In the modern context of Buddhist minority status, pluralism has again surfaced as the alternative of choice for promoting solidarity and guaranteeing survival.

Certainly not all Buddhists in North American localities choose to interact with Buddhists of other ethnicities or traditions, but those that have succeeded in doing so have adopted pluralist over assimilationist or fusionist approaches. Intriguingly, this stands against predictions entertained in some quarters about the development of North American (indeed, Western) Buddhism as a whole. If inter-Buddhist associations point the way to the future (admittedly a large 'if'), then that future holds a pluralistically variegated North American Buddhism – perhaps 'Buddhisms' is a better term – rather than a fused or assimilated singular expression of Buddhism forged out of the discarded remnants of an earlier plurality of Buddhist expression.

References

Abe, Masao. 'On the Occasion of Buddha Day 1990: The Future Task of Buddhism.' *Pacific World*, n. s. 7 (Fall 1991): 96–99.

Adikaram, E. W. *Early History of Buddhism in Ceylon*. Colombo: M. D. Gunasena & Co., Ltd., 1946.

American Buddhist Congress. Biannual convocation booklet (17–19 November 1989).

Anesaki, Masaharu. *History of Japanese Religion*. Rutland, VT: Charles E. Tuttle Company, 1963.

'Articles of Incorporation.' Buddhist Council of Northern California (n.d.).

'Articles of Incorporation of Buddhist Council of the Midwest' (27 October 1987).

Babbin, Fred. 'The Buddhist Council of the Midwest: A Memoir.' *Bulletin* (Buddhist Temple of Chicago) 51, no. 11 (August 1996): 1–.

____. E-mail correspondence to author, 8 July 1997.

Baumann, Martin. 'Buddhism in the West: Phases, Orders and the Creation of an Integrative Buddhism.' *Internationales Asienforum* 27, nos. 3–4 (1996): 345–362.

____. 'Creating a European Path to Nirvāna: Historical and Contemporary Developments of Buddhism in Europe.' *Journal of Contemporary Religion* 10, no. 1 (1995): 55–70.

____. 'The Transplantation of Buddhism to Germany: Processive Modes and Strategies of Adaptation.' *Method and Theory in the Study of Religion* 6, no. 1 (1994): 35–61.

Bechert, Heinz. 'Buddhist Revival in East and West.' In Heinz Bechert and Richard Gombrich, eds., *The World of Buddhism: Buddhist Monks and Nuns in Society and Culture*, 273–285. New York: Facts On File, Inc., 1984.

Bloom, Alfred. E-mail correspondence to author, 23 August 1997.

Bond, George D. *The Buddhist Revival in Sri Lanka: Religious Tradition, Reinterpretation and Response*. Columbia, SC: University of South Carolina Press, 1988.

Brown, Robert McAfee. 'Ecumenical Movement.' In Mircea Eliade, ed., *Encyclopedia of Religion*, vol. 5: 17–27. New York: Macmillan, 1987.

'Buddhist-Catholic Dialogue on "Suffering".' *Dharma Vijaya [Los Angeles] Newsletter* (May 1983): 7.

Buddhist Council of the Midwest. 'Annual Report [to state of Illinois].' (27 September 1989).

____. 'Directory of Member Temples and Centers' (various years).

Buddhist Council of New York. Information sheet (n.d.).

Buddhist Sangha Council of Southern California. Brochure (November 1986).

'Bylaws of The Buddhist Council of the Midwest' (n.d.).

'College of Buddhist Studies Catalog 1994–1999.'
'Consensus on Commitment and Practice.' Buddhism Across Cultures Conference. Hsi Lai Temple, Hacienda Heights, CA (15 March 1997).
Croucher, Paul. *Buddhism in Australia 1848–1988.* New South Wales University Press, 1989.
Crow, Paul A., Jr. 'The Ecumenical Movement.' In Charles H. Lippy and Peter W. Williams, eds., *Encyclopedia of the American Religious Experience: Studies of Traditions and Movements,* vol. 2 : 977–993. New York: Charles Scribner's Sons, 1988.
Dart, John. 'Buddhists Plan to Revive Order of Nuns.' *Los Angeles Times,* 24 May 1997, sec. B, 5.
____. 'Generation Gap Seen among U.S. Buddhists.' *Los Angeles Times,* 2 December 1995, sec. B, 4–.
____. 'Vesak Festival Celebrates Life of Buddha.' *Los Angeles Times,* 5 May 1997, sec. B, 1–.
Dutt, Sukumar. *The Buddha and Five After-Centuries.* London: Luzac & Company Limited, 1957.
____. *Buddhist Monks and Monasteries of India: Their History and Their Contribution to Indian Culture.* London: George Allen and Unwin Ltd., 1962.
'An Early Journey: The Los Angeles Buddhist-Roman Catholic Dialogue' (February 1991).
Ellwood, Robert S. 'Buddhism in the West.' In Mircea Eliade, ed., *Encyclopedia of Religion,* vol. 2: 436–439. New York: Macmillan, 1987.
Fields, Rick. *How the Swans Came to the Lake: A Narrative History of Buddhism in America.* 3rd ed. Boston: Shambhala, 1992.
Finney, Henry C. 'American Zen's "Japan Connection": A Critical Case Study of Zen Buddhism's Diffusion to the West.' *Sociological Analysis* 52, no. 4 (1991): 379–396.
Gombrich, Richard F. *Theravāda Buddhism: A Social History from Ancient Benares to Modern Colombo.* New York: Routledge, 1988.
Gunawardana, R. A. L. H. *Robe and Plough: Monasticism and Economic Interest in Early Medieval Sri Lanka.* Tucson, AZ: University of Arizona Press, 1979.
Hallisey, Charles. 'Councils as Ideas and Events in the Theravāda.' *The Buddhist Forum* 2 (1991): 133–148.
Horinouchi, Isao. 'Americanized Buddhism: A Sociological Analysis of a Protestantized Japanese Religion.' Ph.D. diss., University of California, Davis, 1973.
<http://www.aloha.net/~albloom/haib/> Internet homepage of the Hawaii Association of International Buddhists.
Hunter, Louise H. *Buddhism in Hawaii: Its Impact on a Yankee Community.* Honolulu: University of Hawaii Press, 1971.
'Items of Interest.' *The Theosophic Messenger* 9, no. 11 (August 1908): 251.
Jamison, Frank R. 'Buddhism in Southwest Michigan: A Working Paper' (September 1994).
Journal of the Maha-Bodhi Society 6, no. 5 (September 1897).
Kashima, Tetsuden. *Buddhism in America: The Social Organization of an Ethnic Religious Institution.* Westport, CT: Greenwood Press, 1977.
Kitagawa, Joseph M. *Religion in Japanese History.* New York: Columbia University Press, 1966.
____. *On Understanding Japanese Religion.* Princeton, NJ: Princeton University Press, 1987.
Langlois, Rev. Kongo, Roshi, abbot of Zen Buddhist Temple of Chicago. Phone interview, 18 August 1997.

The Maha Bodhi Centenary Volume, 1891–1991.

McLellan, Janet. 'Buddhist Identities in Toronto: The Interplay of Local, National and Global Contexts.' Paper presented at Association for the Sociology of Religion annual meeting, New York, NY, August 1996.

____. Personal correspondence to author, March 1997.

Nattier, Jan. 'Buddhism Comes to Main Street.' *Wilson Quarterly* (Spring 1997): 72–80.

'North American Soto Zen Buddhism.' Mission statement (n.d.).

Numrich, Paul David. 'Americanization in Immigrant Theravada Buddhist Temples.' Ph.D. diss., Northwestern University, 1992.

____. *Old Wisdom in the New World: Americanization in Two Immigrant Theravada Buddhist Temples.* Knoxville, TN: University of Tennessee Press, 1996.

____. 'The Prospect of the *Sangha* in American Theravāda Buddhism.' In Charles S. Prebish and Kenneth K. Tanaka, eds., *Faces of Buddhism in America*. Berkeley: University of California Press, forthcoming.

____. 'Schism in the Sinhalese Buddhist Community of Los Angeles.' In Thomas Ryba, George Bond, and Leslie McTighe, eds., *Festschrift for Edmund Perry*. Evanston, IL: Northwestern University Press, forthcoming.

'Proposed Constitution and By-Laws of the Council of Buddhist Organizations' (17 December 1986).

Prothero, Stephen. E-mail correspondence to author, 20 August 1997.

Queen, Christopher S., ed. *Engaged Buddhism in the West*. Boston: Wisdom Publications, forthcoming.

Rahula, Walpola. *History of Buddhism in Ceylon*. Colombo: M. D. Gunasena & Co., Ltd., 1956.

Reat, Noble Ross. *Buddhism: A History*. Berkeley, CA: Asian Humanities Press, 1994.

'Record of the Proceedings of the Sixteenth General Conference of the World Fellowship of Buddhists' (1988).

Rhys Davids, T. W. 'Sects (Buddhist).' In James Hastings, ed., *Encyclopaedia of Religion and Ethics*, vol. 11: 307–309. New York: Charles Scribner's Sons, 1928.

'Sangha Council to Unify Buddhist Sects.' *Dharma Vijaya [Los Angeles] Newsletter* (September/August 1981): 4.

Schaefer, Richard T. *Racial and Ethnic Groups*. 5th ed. New York: HarperCollins, 1993.

'Statement of Consensus.' Conference on World Buddhism in North America. Zen Lotus Society, Ann Arbor, MI (10–17 July 1987).

'Tenth Anniversary, Vaisaka 1990.' Buddhist Sangha Council of Southern California. Pamphlet.

Texas Buddhist Council. 'Texas Buddhist Directory' (1995).

Three Treasures: Newsletter of the Buddhist Association of Southwest Michigan.

Tweed, Thomas A. *The American Encounter with Buddhism, 1844–1912: Victorian Culture and the Limits of Dissent*. Bloomington, IN: Indiana University Press, 1992.

U, Richard Paw. 'Americanization of Buddhism: The Need for Unity in Diversity.' *Newsletter* (Hawaii Association of International Buddhists) (Spring 1996), n.p.

____. 'The Dangers of Spiritual Colonialism in the Americanization of Buddhism.' *Newsletter* (Hawaii Association of International Buddhists) (Fall/Winter 1995), n.p.

Wagner, Venise. 'Buddhists Unite to Challenge Communists.' *Orange County Register* (13 December 1993), n.p.

Wakerman, Elyce. 'Alliance Seeks to Counter Religious Right.' in *Los Angeles Times*, 29 June 1996, sec. B: 4–.

Notes

1 My thanks to the following readers of an early draft of this essay, who should not thereby be held accountable for its final form: Fred Babbin, Charles Hallisey, Ron Kidd, N. Ross Reat, and Tricia Teater.

2 For a previous discussion of both the Buddhist Council of the Midwest and the larger phenomenon of inter-Buddhist organizations, see chapter 7 of my dissertation, 'Americanization in Immigrant Theravada Buddhist Temples,' Northwestern University, 1992.

3 Thomas A. Tweed, *The American Encounter with Buddhism, 1844–1912: Victorian Culture and the Limits of Dissent* (Bloomington, IN: Indiana University Press, 1992), 27, 44.

4 On Theosophy, the Parliament, and Open Court, see Rick Fields, *How the Swans Came to the Lake: A Narrative History of Buddhism in America*, 3rd ed. (Boston: Shambhala, 1992), chapters 6–8.

5 1997 'Directory of Member Temples and Centers,' Buddhist Council of the Midwest.

6 Rev. Kongo Langlois, Roshi, abbot of Zen Buddhist Temple of Chicago, phone interview, 18 August 1997.

7 On the Thai Buddhist community in Chicago, see my *Old Wisdom in the New World: Americanization in Two Immigrant Theravada Buddhist Temples* (Knoxville, TN: University of Tennessee Press, 1996).

8 'Proposed Constitution and By-Laws of the Council of Buddhist Organizations' (17 December 1986).

9 'Articles of Incorporation of Buddhist Council of the Midwest' (27 October 1987); 'Bylaws of The Buddhist Council of the Midwest' (n.d.).

10 Buddhist Council of the Midwest, 'Annual Report' (27 September 1989).

11 Wording taken from 1996 'Directory.'

12 1997 'Directory.'

13 Fred Babbin, 'The Buddhist Council of the Midwest: A Memoir,' *Bulletin* (Buddhist Temple of Chicago) 51, no. 11 (August 1996): 6.

14 BCM minutes, 13 January 1988.

15 BCM meeting, 23 April 1997; the letter was sent in May of 1997.

16 See the forthcoming book, *Engaged Buddhism in the West*, Christopher S. Queen, ed. (Boston: Wisdom Publications).

17 Fred Babbin, e-mail correspondence to author, 8 July 1997. At a recent BCM meeting Babbin distributed copies of Jan Nattier's essay, 'Buddhism Comes to Main Street' (*Wilson Quarterly* [Spring 1997]: 72–80), commending Nattier's observations about superior attitudes among 'Elite Buddhists' in America.

18 Robert S. Ellwood, 'Buddhism in the West,' in Mircea Eliade, ed., *Encyclopedia of Religion* (New York: Macmillan, 1987), vol. 2: 439. *Yāna* means 'vehicle,' as in *Mahāyāna*, 'Great Vehicle.'

19 Martin Baumann, 'Buddhism in the West: Phases, Orders and the Creation of an Intregrative Buddhism,' *Internationales Asienforum* 27, nos. 3–4 (1996): 345–362.

20 For example, Rick Fields, whose third edition of the popular *How the Swans Came to the Lake* is still informed by a fusionist vision despite his acknowledgement at one point (p. 370) of the pluralist reality of Buddhism in the United States.

21 BCM minutes, 17 June 1992, 26 August 1992. The position paper, 'Some Thoughts on American Buddhism – What Should It Be?' was submitted by Fred Babbin.

22 A significant, though unsuccessful, attempt in the 1930s in Hawaii is discussed below.
23 Janet McLellan, 'Buddhist Identities in Toronto' (paper presented at Association for the Sociology of Religion annual meeting, New York, NY, August 1996).
24 Richard T. Schaefer, *Racial and Ethnic Groups*, 5th ed. (New York: HarperCollins, 1993), 326.
25 The previous high in indigenous interest came around the turn of the twentieth century; see Tweed, *The American Encounter with Buddhism*. On institutional consolidation of indigenous Buddhism by the 1980s, see Fields, *How the Swans Came to the Lake*, chapter 16; Henry C. Finney, 'American Zen's "Japan Connection": A Critical Case Study of Zen Buddhism's Diffusion to the West,' *Sociological Analysis* 52, no. 4 (1991): 379–396.
26 Texas Buddhist Council, 'Texas Buddhist Directory' (1995).
27 'Articles of Incorporation,' art. 3, sec. E.3, E.4.
28 'College of Buddhist Studies Catalog 1994–1999.'
29 'Texas Buddhist Directory' (1995).
30 <http://www.aloha.net/~albloom/haib/>
31 Richard Paw U, 'The Dangers of Spiritual Colonialism in the Americanization of Buddhism,' *Newsletter* (Hawai'i Association of International Buddhists) (Fall/Winter 1995), n.p.
32 'Sangha Council to Unify Buddhist Sects,' *Dharma Vijaya [Los Angeles] Newsletter* (September/August, 1981): 4.
33 Masao Abe, 'On the Occasion of Buddha Day 1990: The Future Task of Buddhism,' *Pacific World*, n. s. 7 (Fall 1991): 99. According to one local source, Abe gave this same address at the Buddhist Council of the Midwest's 1993 International Visakha.
34 'Tenth Anniversary, Vaisaka 1990.'
35 'Americanization in Immigrant Theravada Buddhist Temples,' chapter 4, and *Old Wisdom in the New World*, chapter 2; for further detail on the conflict within the local immigrant Sri Lankan community, see my forthcoming essay, 'Schism in the Sinhalese Buddhist Community of Los Angeles,' in Thomas Ryba, George Bond, and Leslie McTighe, eds., *Festschrift for Edmund Perry* (Evanston, IL: Northwestern University Press).
36 Buddhist Sangha Council of Southern California brochure (November 1986).
37 'Tenth Anniversary, Vaisaka 1990.'
38 John Dart, 'Buddhists Plan to Revive Order of Nuns,' *Los Angeles Times*, 24 May 1997, sec. B, p. 5; see also my essay, 'The Prospect of the *Sangha* in American Theravāda Buddhism,' in Charles S. Prebish and Kenneth K. Tanaka, eds., *Faces of Buddhism in America* (University of California Press, forthcoming).
39 See 'Consensus on Commitment and Practice.' Although the Los Angeles conference was co-sponsored by the national American Buddhist Congress (see later in this essay), it appears to have been primarily a local affair, the connection between the two associations being their shared executive officer, Ven. Dr. Havanpola Ratanasara. On the 1987 Ann Arbor conference, see 'Statement of Consensus,' Conference on World Buddhism in North America.
40 Brochure (November 1986).
41 Buddhist Council of New York information sheet (n.d.).
42 'Buddhist-Catholic Dialogue on "Suffering",' *Dharma Vijaya [Los Angeles] Newsletter* (May 1983): 7; 'An Early Journey: The Los Angeles Buddhist-Roman Catholic Dialogue' (February 1991).
43 Elyce Wakerman, 'Alliance Seeks to Counter Religious Right,' *Los Angeles Times*, 29 June 1996, sec. B, pp. 4–.

44 'Texas Buddhist Directory' (1995).
45 Brochure (November 1986).
46 John Dart, 'Vesak Festival Celebrates Life of Buddha,' *Los Angeles Times*, 5 May 1997, sec. B, pp. 1–.
47 Richard Paw U, 'The Dangers of Spiritual Colonialism,' n.p.
48 E-mail correspondence to author, 25 July 1997.
49 Ibid.
50 'Texas Buddhist Directory' (1995).
51 Richard Paw U, 'Americanization of Buddhism: The Need for Unity in Diversity,' *Newsletter* (Hawai'i Association of International Buddhists) (Spring 1996), n.p. In an e-mail correspondence Alfred Bloom (23 August 1997) assured me that the Hawaii Association is 'definitely pluralist in approach.... We are not fusionist.'
52 Buddhist Council of New York information sheet (n.d.).
53 Frank R. Jamison, 'Buddhism in Southwest Michigan: A Working Paper' (September 1994).
54 *Three Treasures*.
55 Numrich, 'Americanization in Immigrant Theravada Buddhist Temples,' chapter 7.
56 Quoted in Tetsuden Kashima, *Buddhism in America: The Social Organization of an Ethnic Religious Institution* (Westport, CT: Greenwood Press, 1977), 55. The organization was the Buddhist Brotherhood of America.
57 On the situation in the mainland centers, see ibid., 54–55; on Buddhism in Hawai'i, see Isao Horinouchi, 'Americanized Buddhism: A Sociological Analysis of a Protestantized Japanese Religion,' Ph.D. diss., University of California, Davis, 1973; Louise H. Hunter, *Buddhism in Hawaii: Its Impact on a Yankee Community* (Honolulu: University of Hawaii Press, 1971). Stephen Prothero labels Hunt, Goldwater, and like-minded Western converts 'lumpers,' a suitable synonym for what I have called the 'fusionist' approach (e-mail correspondence to author, 20 August 1997). There is no historical or institutional connection between the current Hawaii Association of International Buddhists and previous efforts by Hunt and others.
58 McLellan, 'Buddhist Identities in Toronto'; also, personal correspondence to author, March 1997.
59 Paul Croucher, *Buddhism in Australia 1848–1988* (New South Wales University Press, 1989), 62–63, 104–105.
60 Martin Baumann, 'The Transplantation of Buddhism to Germany: Processive Modes and Strategies of Adaptation,' *Method and Theory in the Study of Religio* 6, no. 1 (1994): 49; and 'Creating a European Path to Nirvāna: Historical and Contemporary Developments of Buddhism in Europe,' *Journal of Contemporary Religion* 10, no. 1 (1995): 64.
61 See my 'Americanization in Immigrant Theravada Buddhist Temples,' chapter 7; also, John Dart, 'Generation Gap Seen among U.S. Buddhists,' *Los Angeles Time*, 2 December 1995, pt. B: 4–. Minutes reveal that the Buddhist Council of the Midwest has vacillated at times over its affiliation with the American Buddhist Congress.
62 Baumann, 'The Transplantation of Buddhism to Germany.' I do not know whether the Deutsche Buddhistische Union is related to a previous 'union' of German Buddhists formed in Leipzig around 1908, about which a brief notice appears in 'Items of Interest,' *The Theosophic Messenger* 9, no. 11 (August 1908): 251.
63 See Baumann, 'Creating a European Path to Nirvāna,' 65–67.

64 Joseph M. Kitagawa, *On Understanding Japanese Religion* (Princeton, NJ: Princeton University Press, 1987), 218.

65 Joseph M. Kitagawa, *Religion in Japanese History* (New York: Columbia University Press, 1966), 307.

66 Ibid., 293.

67 Masaharu Anesaki, *History of Japanese Religion* (Rutland, VT: Charles E. Tuttle Company, 1963), 335–336, 370.

68 Heinz Bechert, 'Buddhist Revival in East and West,' in Heinz Bechert and Richard Gombrich, eds., *The World of Buddhism: Buddhist Monks and Nuns in Society and Culture* (New York: Facts On File, Inc., 1984), 274.

69 *Journal of the Maha-Bodhi Society* 6, no. 5 (September 1897); capitals in original. Also, *The Maha Bodhi Centenary Volume, 1891–1991*, 308.

70 Richard F. Gombrich, *Theravāda Buddhism: A Social History from Ancient Benares to Modern Colombo* (New York: Routledge, 1988), 174. See also George D. Bond, *The Buddhist Revival in Sri Lanka: Religious Tradition, Reinterpretation and Response* (Columbia, SC: University of South Carolina Press, 1988), chapter 2.

71 'Record of the Proceedings of the Sixteenth General Conference of the World Fellowship of Buddhists' (1988).

72 Bechert, 'Buddhist Revival in East and West,' 285.

73 'North American Soto Zen Buddhism' (mission statement, n.d.).

74 Venise Wagner, 'Buddhists Unite to Challenge Communists,' in *Orange County Register* (13 December 1993), n.p.

75 See my 'Americanization in Immigrant Theravada Buddhist Temples,' chapter 7.

76 Abe (p. 96) opens his article with the claim that 'North California is a unique area in the world where almost all living forms of Buddhism are represented,' while the Buddhist Sangha Council of Southern California claims the same 'unique situation for Buddhism' in southern California's Los Angeles area ('An Early Journey,' p. 1). On the national level, the American Buddhist Congress has made the following dubious claim: 'The United States is unique in Buddhist history because it is enriched with all of the major Buddhist schools and ethnic traditions' (1989 biannual convocation booklet: 1).

77 Parenthetically, this also explains the similarities between the phenomenon of contemporary inter-Buddhist associations and the modern Christian ecumenical movement, the latter originating in the minority social situation of the foreign mission field where the divisions of Western denominationalism impeded the spread of the Gospel. In both Buddhist and Christian cases, inter-group interaction typically eschews serious dialogue about the details of a common doctrinal core. On the Christian ecumenical movement, see Robert McAfee Brown, 'Ecumenical Movement,' in Mircea Eliade, ed., *Encyclopedia of Religion* (New York: Macmillan, 1987), 5: 18; Paul A. Crow, Jr., 'The Ecumenical Movement,' in Charles H. Lippy and Peter W. Williams, eds., *Encyclopedia of the American Religious Experience: Studies of Traditions and Movements* (New York: Charles Scribner's Sons, 1988), 2: 984.

78 Charles Hallisey, 'Councils as Ideas and Events in the Theravāda,' *The Buddhist Forum* 2 (1991): 147.

79 On Ashoka, see Sukumar Dutt, *The Buddha and Five After-Centuries* (London: Luzac & Company Limited, 1957), chapter 11; also, Gombrich, *Theravāda Buddhism*, 127–136.

80 Noble Ross Reat, *Buddhism: A History* (Berkeley, CA: Asian Humanities Press, 1994), 72.

81 On the great monastic universities, see Sukumar Dutt, *Buddhist Monks and Monasteries of India: Their History and Their Contribution to Indian Culture* (London: George Allen and Unwin Ltd., 1962). I find it interesting that establishment of a Buddhist university 'on the lines of the ancient University of Nalanda' comprises one of the Maha Bodhi Society's objectives. I doubt that the Society distinguishes my three types of inter-Buddhist interaction. See *The Maha Bodhi Centenary Volume, 1891–1991*, 308.

82 Reat, *Buddhism: A History*, 92. See also E. W. Adikaram, *Early History of Buddhism in Ceylon* (Colombo: M. D. Gunasena & Co., Ltd., 1946); R. A. L. H. Gunawardana, *Robe and Plough: Monasticism and Economic Interest in Early Medieval Sri Lanka* (Tucson, AZ: University of Arizona Press, 1979); Walpola Rahula, *History of Buddhism in Ceylon* (Colombo: M. D. Gunasena & Co., Ltd., 1956).

83 Anesaki, *History of Japanese Religion*, 169.

84 Ibid., 229.

85 Ibid., 305. For more on Japanese sectarian strife, see Kitagawa, *Religion in Japanese History*; Reat, *Buddhism: A History*, chapter 10. Rhys Davids, writing in the early 20th century, would grant that only in Japan has Buddhism developed sectarianism 'in the European sense' of the term, though he construes the notion of 'sect' too narrowly in my opinion. See T. W. Rhys Davids, 'Sects (Buddhist),' in James Hastings, ed., *Encyclopaedia of Religion and Ethics* (New York: Charles Scribner's Sons, 1928), 11: 307–309.

CHAPTER NINE

The Pacific Buddha's Wild Practice: Gary Snyder's Environmental Ethic

Charles R. Strain

The Lay of the Land

Floating in a tiny boat
lightly on the water, rock with every ripple,

another skin that slides along the water
hung by sea and sky

green mountains turn to clouds
and slip slow by
. . . .
there is no place we are
but maybe here[1]

I approach this topic, this *topos* as I would a walk on a tundra – aware of being an interloper, sensing that I may be blundering across fragile networks of meaning. Poets and strange fauna are at home in a wild landscape where I struggle to find my bearings. Glimpsing the poet, do I pass on by or do I follow his trail all-so-warily?

Walking on walking,

　　　　　under foot　　　earth turns.

Streams and mountains never stay the same.[2]

In a recent article in *The Journal of Religion* Catherine Albanese argues against understanding environmental ethical debates as contesting visions within the framework of political liberalism. She simultaneously rejects as imprudent any exclusive option for either the 'harmonial ethic' of environmental holism or the liberal ethic of responsible management. Albanese appeals instead to Ralph Waldo Emerson as someone who devised a religious and syncretic model – to be sure, a model resting upon an internal, theoretical fault – which combined a harmonial sense of interdependence with a vigorous espousal of self-cultivation and self-reliant action.[3] '[T]hose environmentalists who have chosen to be single minded...,' Albanese concludes, 'have taken cosmological and ethical turns that are riddled with irony. If [Emerson] teaches anything, the lesson is that a moral middle ground may not be all bad.... The body of his work argues by its structural compound of unities and disunities that ethical confusion may be a source of creativity and hope.'[4]

There is enough here to make those committed to ethical reflection profoundly uneasy. Is there a form of religious hybridity whose creativity does not coarise with 'ethical confusion?' And does Albanese's typological duality adequately convey the lay of the land? Ian Harris says 'no' to the second question and has his doubts about the first. Focusing on the contributions of socially engaged Buddhism to environmental ethics, Harris offers a more nuanced, fourfold typology. His description of the first type, *eco-spirituality*, resembles Albanese's analysis of environmental holism. Eco-spirituality, Harris argues, is a 'developing global "virtual religion"' grounded in the insights of Deep Ecology and drawing freely from several religious traditions without adequately rooting itself in any of them.[5] But his discussion of a second type, *eco-justice*, shows the extent to which socially engaged Buddhists, like the Thai lay leader, Sulak Sivaraksa, have drawn inspiration not from political liberalism but from the more communitarian visions of Western liberation theologies. A third type, *eco-traditionalism*, attempts – unsuccessfully in Harris's estimation – to draw an environmental ethic from premodern Buddhist traditions.[6] Finally, *eco-apologetics* builds upon a romantic 'turn toward the East' among those who hold Christianity as at least partially responsible for Western civilization's despoilation of the environment. This model plays upon an uncritical assumption of the essential compatibility of Buddhist and environmental ethics.[7] Harris finds fault with the third and fourth type for their idealizing tendencies combined in the latter case with, perhaps, more than a dash of opportunism. The second type veers towards 'Protestant Buddhism,' a Buddhist variant modeled all-too-closely on liberal Christianity. But Harris saves his most trenchant criticism for the first type which, on the face of it, would seem to be most compatible with Buddhist teachings. Indeed, it is the eco-spirituality model's use of the Abhidharmic concept of dependent coarising (*pratitya samutpāda*) and Hua-yen teachings of interpenetration that Harris finds ethically problematic.[8]

> The intention here is to show that since all things are inter-related we should act in a spirit of reverence towards them all. However, the category of 'all things' includes insecticides, totalitarian regimes and nuclear weapons and the argument therefore possesses some rather

obvious problems. In short it suffers from a certain vacuity from the moral perspective.[9]

Harris ends his review of the fourfold typology with the hope that his analysis might aid 'in the *eventual* construction of an authentic Buddhist environmental ethic (Italics mine).'[10]

Harris's typology is eminently contestable. Flawed map though it may well be, I would rather take it for what it is – a provisional view of a *terra incognita* – and move beyond it. Gary Snyder's environmental ethic, I suggest, represents a fifth type, itself a variant of eco-spirituality and eco-justice. A particular orientation to enter what Snyder calls 'the practice of the wild' is the distinguishing characteristic of this fifth type. Poet. American Buddhist practitioner. Rural laborer. It may seem odd to look to Snyder for a breakthrough in ethical reflection and action. From Snyder's own point of view an artful rummaging in cultural woodlots, a deliberate ransacking of the mind's nooks and crannies is precisely what we need in order to learn how to survive.[11] This study itself is part of a larger effort to demonstrate the importance of socially engaged Buddhism not only for those reflecting ethically within the American Buddhist tradition but for social ethicists grounded in the religious traditions of the West.[12]

The Pacific Buddha

The hump-backed flute player
    walks all over.
    Sits on the boulders around the Great Basin
    his hump
    is a pack.

Hsüan Tsang
    went to India 629 AD
    returned to China 645
    with 657 sūtras, images, mandalas,
    and fifty relics –
    . . .
he carried
    'emptiness'
he carried
    'mind only'[13]

In poem after poem Snyder links, merges, juxtaposes sacred figures from either side of the Pacific. The hump-backed, flute-playing itinerant shaman, Kokop'ele, walks with the Buddhist pilgrim, Hsüan Tsang, the bearer of the *Heart Sūtra* to China. In the same poem the Paiute prophet, Wovoka, holds the universe in his empty hat. Or is it Krishna in a small dab of mud in his mouth? Or Vimalakīrti in his ten-foot-square hut? Or, perhaps, it is the White Mountains where the oldest living beings on earth – the bristlecone pine – dwell. 'All manner of beings/may swim in my sea/echoing up conch spiral corridors.'[14] '[T]radition is *not* really there,' Snyder argued in a 1979 interview 'unless you make it so.'

> I'm speaking from a lot of sources, from what I've learned. But it's like the air. It's free and there for all of us.... There's no cultural monopoly on any of this. What I have done is draw from what I perceive to be certain consistencies that led in the direction of a certain kind of health and sanity, of a certain kind of vision, *wherever I found them. And that's been deliberate.*[15]

Elsewhere Snyder explicitly affirms a fusion of 'Buddhism and Taoism,' 'animism and paganism,' 'ecosystem theory and environmental history' to form 'the twentieth-century syncretism of the "Turtle Island" view.'[16] Notice, however, that Snyder is not espousing a mishmash of traditions, a goulash. He praises Mahāyāna Buddhism for its decision, affirmed repeatedly, to remain open to multiple cultural influences yet steadfast in 'keeping the strictness and rightness of its own training method.'[17] The syncretism that Snyder espouses has an axis of intentionality that, we will see, operates primarily at the level of actual practice and secondarily at the level of theory.

I see the 'Pacific Buddha' exemplified in Snyder's work as formally analogous to Paul Gilroy's stunning description in *The Black Atlantic* of the African diaspora as a transformational presence within Western culture. Both the Black Atlantic and the Pacific Buddha are transnational, transcultural movements which are part of, yet deeply critical, of modernity. Rejecting essentialist doctrines and all concepts of a self-contained tradition, Gilroy argues that the Black Atlantic is a 'creole culture.' Against 'pseudo pluralists' whose positions assume a relativistic dispersal of meaning, Gilroy affirms the Black Atlantic as a 'fractal structure.' The polyphony and the 'montage technique' that create the Black Atlantic must not obscure its consistent intentionality. The Black Atlantic is a 'transvaluation of all values' of Western modernity.[18] If the Black Atlantic grows out of the terrors of slavery – re-visioned not as an *aberration* of, but as a defining characteristic of, the Western project – Snyder's work grows out of the conviction formed in his college years that he was part of a society 'that was destroying its own ground,' that not just Western capitalism but 'all of Western culture ... was off the track.'[19] Like the Black Atlantic, the Pacific Buddha is a creole culture, a fusion of multiple traditions, but, again like its counterpart, the Pacific Buddha is a form of practice more than a consistent teaching. As a practice, it too operates with a firm intentionality to perform a *jujitsu* upon the Western consciousness.[20]

The Romance of Dharma Gaia

To follow the secret path in company with a lover means both must have practiced the lonely yogas and wanderings, and then seek the center of the individual-body and group-body mandala; dedicating their two loving bodies to the whole network; the man evoking the Goddess in the girl on suitable occasions and worshiping her. She is his mudrā, prajñā, yoginī, or spell....

The Goddess 'Māyā' (measure/illusion) and 'Gone-beyond Wisdom' (Prajñāpāramitā, Mother of the Buddhas) are one. In her and holding her ... is the Adi-Buddha Dharmakāya...; *thus come*. The Dharma is this embrace; the energy of all being is this bliss....[21]

After spending most of the 1960s in Japan in formal Zen training under the tutelage of Sesso Oda Rōshi – interspersed with seasons working on an oil tanker – Snyder returned to the United States in the spring of 1969. Shortly thereafter he began to homestead with his family in the Sierra Nevada. *Earth House Hold* records those transitions and heady times. It would be a mistake to fracture Snyder's life into periods. Themes and ethical stances even when transcended continue a subterranean life. Essays like 'Buddhism and the Coming Revolution,' 'Why Tribe,' and 'Poetry and the Primitive' and selections like the one quoted above from the essay 'Dharma Queries' do, however, express a romantic, utopian version of eco-spirituality which, I believe, Snyder *has* largely transcended. Because Harris roundly criticizes this form of eco-spirituality as ethically vacuous, it is important to acknowledge this continuing strand in Snyder's theory and practice.

As the selection from 'Dharma Queries' indicates, Snyder in some of his earlier writings had a particular affinity for archetypal thinking and his archetypes were 'gender-tied.' Mythical expressions of interdependence and interpenetration conformed to these gender-tied archetypes. Two decades later, when confronted with his use of feminine imagery in particular, Snyder insisted upon both the utility *and* the danger of myths and archetypes.

We have to say that we need myth. And then you also have to say that you need to get to the end of myth. Myth can be understood as a kind of *provisional* ordering of the situation to get the territory at least clear enough so you can begin to work on it.... [M]ythology, images, can be used in more ways than one. We need to be able to discriminate between visions that liberate and visions that enslave....[22]

From his own perspective Snyder was, in part, agreeing with Harris's concerns. Simply yoking Buddhist concepts with visions of harmony with nature and bedecking that fusion with gender-tied archetypal imagery will not do. Paying attention to Snyder's qualification of his earlier romanticized and eroticized presentation of the human relationship with nature is not merely a way of charting Snyder's own development. The critique applies with equal force to contemporary ethical fusions such as Western Buddhists' appropriation of the 'Gaia Hypothesis.'[23] The editor of a classic Buddhist anthology on Buddhism and ecology, for example, opens his introduction by saying, 'The more time I spend sitting on my Zafu listening to what Peter Matthiessen calls the "ringing stillness of the universal mind," the more I feel the embrace of Gaia, or Mother Earth. It is an awareness of being cared for and nurtured, like being in a long, slow dance with the Goddess.'[24] Snyder, who as much as any other Buddhist thinker, fostered such a Gaia-consciousness through books like *Earth House Hold* recognizes its provisionality as a myth and its hypothetical character as science. He encourages us not to 'get too carried away with...archetypes' and to pay attention to the biological argument. Then he adds, 'But talking about the planet as Gaia *per se* will not do the planet a lot of good though. You still have to find a course of action, or program.'[25] Snyder's comment indicates that he eventually recognized the need to go beyond these simple correlations that in *Earth House Hold* he had happily proclaimed.

In the late 1960s Snyder's version of eco-justice was similarly utopian. In 'Buddhism and the Coming Revolution' he sees a simple fusion of Buddhist inner liberation with the goals of Western liberation movements. Such a fusion will enable Buddhists to transcend the ethical quietism of a 'totalistic' view in which 'the hawk, the swoop and the hare are one.' Against any quietism, he argues that '[t]he Bodhisattva lives by the sufferer's standard, and he must be effective in aiding those who suffer.'[26]

The comic apogee of this espousal of Buddhist utopianism comes in Snyder's 'Smokey the Bear Sutra.' Thinking that we needed a special 'Buddha to quell the fires of greed and war and to help us head off the biological holocaust that the twenty-first century may prove to be,' Snyder remodeled Smokey in the image of the warrior Bodhisattva Fudō Myō'ō.[27]

And if anyone is threatened by advertising, air pollution, or the police, they should chant SMOKEY THE BEAR'S WAR SPELL:

DROWN THEIR BUTTS
CRUSH THEIR BUTTS
DROWN THEIR BUTTS
CRUSH THEIR BUTTS

And SMOKEY THE BEAR will surely appear to put the enemy out with his vajra shovel.

Now those who recite this Sutra and then try to put it in practice will
    accumulate merit as countless as the sands of Arizona and Nevada,
Will help save the planet Earth from total oil slick,
Will enter the age of harmony of humans and nature,
Will win the tender love and caresses of men, women and beasts,

> Will always have ripe blackberries to eat and a sunny spot under a
> pine tree to sit at,
> AND IN THE END WILL WIN HIGHEST PERFECT ENLIGHTENMENT[28]

The trick, of course, was to put the *sūtra* in practice, and it is my contention that practice transforms Snyder's vision and creates an environmental ethic.

From Romance to Practice

> Our love is mixed with
> rocks and streams,
> a heartbeat, a breath, a gaze
>
> makes place in the dizzy eddy.
> Living this old clear way[29]

Perhaps the most important ethical decision that Snyder has made was to move with his family to the Sierra Nevada and to settle in the place that they called Kitkitdizze. From this decision arose both new forms of practice and an ethic of bioregionalism. Part of the shift – now a deeply engrained trait of the Pacific Buddha – was the recognition that monastic definitions of practice needed to be modified by lay Buddhist practitioners. 'Sitting ten hours a day means that somebody else is growing your food for you.... Somebody has to grow the tomatoes.'[30] Putting into play in new ways Mahāyāna teachings about the practice of everyday life, Snyder adapted his practice to the tasks at Kitkitdizze.

> Practice simply is one intensification of what is natural and around us
> all the time. Practice is to life as poetry is to spoken language.... One
> of the first practices that I learned is that when you're working with
> another person on a two-person crosscut saw, you never push, you
> only pull; my father taught me that when I was eight.... We all have
> to learn to change oil on time or we burn out our engines. We all have
> to learn how to cook.[31]

At this moment in the flow of his life, Snyder focused his practice on three dimensions of family, work, and place. All three entailed 'living more simply, living more responsibly,' living 'in the grain of things.'[32]

Family

The Family is the Practice Hall[33]

It would be a mistake to separate Snyder's ecological vision from the experience of raising his family at Kitkitdizze. In numerous places he has argued for a sacramental understanding of the ecosystem, a specifically Buddhist form of sacramental consciousness built on the Hua-yen image of Indra's Net, in which each node of the net is a jewel which reflects every other jewel.[34] Nowhere is this sense more deeply present than in his compassionate eros for the body of his family. In one poem that celebrates the birth of his first son, Kai, the boundaries between the moment of childbirth and a moment on board a tanker ship interpenetrate.

> What's your from-the-beginning face?
>> Kai.
>> born again
> To the Mother's hoarse bear-down
>> groan and dark red mask:
>> spiralling, glistening, blue-white, up
>
> And out from her
>>>> (dolphins leaping in threes
>>>> through blinding silver inter-
>>>> faces, Persian
>>>> Gulf tanker's, wave-slip
>>>> opening, boundless
>>>>> *whap*
>>> as they fall back,
>>> arcing
>>> into her –)
>
>>>> sea.[35]

If we do not merely perceive a 'sacramentalized ecosystem' but enact it, this practice begins with our own intertwined bodies. In 'The Bath,' Snyder washes a growing Kai by the light of a kerosene lantern, smelling the sweet scent of cedar and feeling the nip of cool night air at the door.

> He stands in warm water
> Soap all over the smooth of his thigh and stomach
>> 'Gary don't soap my hair!'
>> – his eye-sting fear –
>> the soapy hand feeling
>> through and around the globes and curves of his body
>> up in the crotch,
> And washing-tickling out the scrotum, little anus,
>> his penis curving up and getting hard
>> as I pull back skin and try to wash it
> Laughing and jumping, flinging arms around,
> I squat all naked too,
>>> *is this our body?*[36]

The antiphon *'is this our body... is this our body?'* becomes 'this is our body' as the family, clean from the bath, stretches 'out on the redwood benches hearts all beating/ Quiet to the simmer of the stove....'[37]

In 'What Happened Here Before' Snyder traces 300,000,000 years of ecological history in the Sierra Nevada – history that ebbs and flows while 'Turtle Island swims/in the ocean-sky swirl-void.' The poem ends with the family at work:

> my sons ask, who are we?
> drying apples picked from homestead trees
> drying berries, curing meat
> shooting arrows at a bale of straw
>
> military jets head northeast, roaring, every dawn.
> my sons ask, who are they?
>
> > WE SHALL SEE
> > WHO KNOWS
> > HOW TO BE
>
> Bluejay screeches from a pine[38]

Family practice and bluejay screeches cancel out the temporary roar of jets, just as the 300,000,000 years engulf a few millennia of civilization.

Work

> confidence, patience, good humor
> in the working of hands with the stone and grit of the world.[39]

Snyder grew up working on a farm. As a young man he worked seasonally as a logger; he shipped out on tankers.[40] Work – hard, physical work – is necessary to well-being.

> If there is any one thing that's unhealthy in America, it's that it is a whole civilization trying to get out of work.... There is a triple alienation when you try to avoid work: first, you're trying to get outside energy sources/resources to do it for you; second, you no longer know what your own body can do...; third, you lose the capacity to discover the unity of mind and body via your work.[41]

Snyder learned early how to work in an undivided way. Shortly after college, when he was just beginning to write poems, he had immersed himself in reading Milton. Working on a trail crew in Yosemite Park, he found himself tied up in knots building the trail and thinking about Milton. 'Finally, ... I said the hell with it, I'll just work. And instead of losing something I got something much greater. By just working, I found myself being, completely there, having the whole mountain inside of me, and finally having a whole language inside of me that became one with the rocks and with the trees.'[42] We will later see that work involves learning how to go with the grain of things. For Snyder work is always akin to wielding a crosscut saw with nature or the wild as the other partner.

Place

   – Coyote says 'You people should stay put here,
      learn your place,
         do good things. Me, I'm traveling on.'[43]

Snyder's bioregionalist ethic begins with not one but two categorical imperatives: 'First, don't move and second, find out what that teaches you.'[44] With his move by 1970 to the Sierra Nevada, Snyder took up the challenge of these imperatives. He sees bioregionalism not as a variant strain of an environmental ethic but as the communal ground necessary for the practice of environmentalism. Snyder is explicitly calling into question a Coyote environmentalism where one moves opportunistically from issue to issue, dashes from conference to conference, returns to some megapolis like San Francisco or Chicago where the velocity of change expels the detailed memory of place. In contrast, 'bioregionalism,' Snyder argues, 'calls for the commitment to this continent *place by place*, in terms of biogeographical regions and watersheds.'

> It calls us to see our country in terms of its landforms, plant life, weather patterns, and seasonal changes – its whole natural history before the net of political jurisdiction was cast over it. People are challenged to become 'reinhabitory' – that is, to become people who are learning to live and think 'as if' they were totally engaged with their place for the long future. This doesn't mean some return to a primitive lifestyle or utopian provincialism; it simply implies an engagement with community and a search for the sustainable sophisticated mix of economic practices that would enable people to live regionally and yet learn from and contribute to a planetary society.[45]

The particular Buddhist elements in this bioregionalist ethic are its emphasis on community, the *sangha,* as necessary for any transformation and on the practice of mindful concentration, *samadhi,* refocused as the kind of attention to the detailed variations of climate and soil, to what will flourish and what will not in this *place* that 'any true farmer' practices.[46] Snyder speculates that *samadhi,* in fact, predates farmers. The stillness of hunters, and the 'field-sensing' of gatherers laid the foundation for *zazen.* Bioregionalists require the same multidimensional field sensing as their

Neolithic forebears who memorized the landscape in all its details. 'You know that over there is milkweed from which come glue and string, over the hill beyond that is where the antelopes water.... That is a field sensing of the world. All of it partakes of the quality of *samadhi*.'[47] Snyder tells of having walked past a particularly 'gnarly canyon live oak' for twenty years and then finally attending to it. 'Or maybe it was ready to show itself to me,' he suspects. 'I felt its oldness, suchness, inwardness, oakness as if it were my own.' The two decades before were not wasted, he insists. Cutting brush, gathering firewood, watching for the mushroom's bulge, all were forms of practice for seeing the oak.[48]

Snyder also deliberately expands and alters the meaning of *sangha*. While praising certain Zen centers that have tenaciously clung to a place, Snyder finds fault with a purely 'intentional' community, a community gathered around an idea, a single purpose, or – in Buddhist terms – a community that only 'sits' together. Real community emerges when people realize that they are going to live in a place 'for a thousand years or more.'[49] Attention to issues becomes multilateral; schools, zoning regulations, the policies of the Forest Service draw local people across the boundaries that intentional communities erect. Environmentalists will organize to pass legislation in Washington to protect the environment which is good as far as it goes. But at the local level Snyder believes 'nobody else is watching but us.' Only a local community can keep the local Bureau of Land Management or Forest Service managers in check while simultaneously taking into account the importance of jobs for their neighbors. Conservationists can fight to preserve wilderness and then return home. With bioregionalists, Snyder insists, everything is at stake. They will fight like crazy for their homes, for the land, and for the long-term survival of the place where their children's children will live.[50]

Snyder's political image for the expanded *sangha* is a 'Village Council of All Beings.' Consider an ecosystem as 'a kind of mandala in which there are multiple relations. Each figure in the mandala – a little mouse or bird (or little god or demon figure) – has an important position and a role to play.'[51] A Village Council represents each of these beings. The equality of all members within the Council, however, is not formally adjudicated in terms of the rights of individuals, human or non-human. Snyder is realistic about the position of humans in the food chain. He has, for example, a great respect for hunting cultures which use every part of the slain animal 'right down to the sinew and hooves'; he shares with equanimity free-range chickens with bobcats, and, dwelling on largely non-arable land he acknowledges the economic value of carefully harvesting old-growth trees.[52]

The Village Council of All Beings is a communitarian model; it is also – in contrast to the presentation of this concept by other Buddhist ethicists – 'place specific.' The practice of reinhabitation assumes that humans have a place, must find a place in the wild. Having a place means using its resources wisely; it entails transgressing the lines of division separating wilderness preservation and natural resource management. In the Sierra Nevada it means clearing undergrowth, conducting bioregional inventories, banding migrant song birds, establishing the joint management of private and public lands. It requires developing a 'Three-Hundred-Year Kitkitdizze Plan.' Hubris? No. '[W]e are trying to learn the ground rules,' Snyder hopes, 'by which humans might live together with animals in an "inhabited wildlife corridor."'[53]

What guides this ethical practice? Anthropologists, like Victor Turner, have long called our attention to the role of 'root metaphors' in structuring social action or, more precisely, in constituting whole fields of morally freighted reflection and practice.[54] The metaphor of a 'Village Council of All Beings' provides a communitarian, that is, a non-formalistic understanding of species-equality. Snyder's appropriation of an ecological model, however, takes us beyond the 'village council' model of species-equality. Snyder's ethic sees each bioregion evolving toward a 'climax state' that couples 'maximum diversity and maximum stability in a natural system.' By contrast a monoculture is utterly fragile. Stability is directly proportional to diversity. 'If you have a field of nothing but grass, and grasshoppers land on it, that's the end of your grass.'[55] Drawing his ideas from ecological scientists, Ramon Margalef and Eugene and Herbert Odum, Snyder sees evolution pulled repeatedly towards climax states:

> [M]any species, old bones, lots of rotten leaves, complex energy pathways, woodpeckers living in swamps and covies harvesting tiny piles of grass.... In a climax situation a high percentage of the energy is derived not from grazing off the annual production of biomass, but from recycling of dead biomass, the duff on the forest floor, the trees that have fallen, the bodies of dead animals. Recycled. Detritus energy is liberated by fungi and lots of insects.'[56]

Clearly, this understanding of climax states accords with Snyder's Buddhist sense of interdependence. Just as clearly, the linkage between an ecological and a religious concept provides a path out of the swamps of moral vacuity. Insecticides, totalitarian regimes, and nuclear weapons *are* part of the whole but in the manner of rogue elements. It is possible for rogue elements to cut their swath – like grasshoppers – for whole millennia but it is hubris to believe that they or we will destroy life. 'In the larger scale, things *will* take care of themselves.' Far from severing the ethical nerve, this awareness undergirds one's commitment to the whole. To espouse a bioregionalist ethics is to have a sense of modesty about human actions; it is to be willing to talk in cycles of 40,000 years. Mostly it requires that we stay rooted in place, composting 'the leaf fall of day-to-day consciousness.'[57] Drying apples while jets roar overhead, Snyder says to his sons 'We shall see/who knows/how to be.'[58]

The Practice of the Wild

We remain alert so as not to get run down, but it turns out you only have to hop a few feet to one side and the whole huge machinery rolls by, not seeing you at all.[59]

a sheepskull forehead with its horn prongs
sitting on a boulder –
an offer of the flower of a
million years of nibbling forbs

to the emptiness of intelligence [60]

The practice of family life, of work, and of place gathers itself as the practice of the wild. Calling it a 'pivotal text,' one reviewer likens Snyder's 1990 collection of essays, *The Practice of the Wild*, to both *Walden* and the *Sand County Almanac*. It is the work of a 'postmodern man who escapes the clutches of the industrial growth paradigm.'[61] Imagine Odysseus clinging to the wooly fur of sheep as one-eyed, blind-eyed Cyclops gropes and grasps in vain. And be thankful for the sheep.

Sidestepping the industrial machinery, thinking with the empty mind of arctic sheep, Snyder performs *jujitsu* – itself an ancient practice – on Western consciousness. *Practice of the Wild* is the working out of a theme first announced in *Turtle Island*: 'Wildness is the state of complete awareness. That's why we need it.'[62] To uncover the meaning of 'the wild' is like tracking a gray fox – a rare glimpse followed by absence. The wild gets defined by what it is not – not tame, not cultivated, not civilized, not subordinate, not restrained. 'Turn it the other way,' Snyder insists. The wild *is* free, self-propagating, independent, self-authenticating. But it is especially 'wild systems' – an oxymoron for most of us – that attract Snyder's attention. The wild is, above all, self-organizing with its own 'long-range strategies.' It is the 'ordering of impermanence.'[63]

To think of the wild as other and as somewhere else is to miss the point. Natural resource management with its Cartesian stance grasps 'nature'; the wild wriggles free. *Wilderness* may be endangered and may need to be preserved by isolating it, insulating it. But the wild surrounds us: 'Exquisite complex beings in their energy webs inhabiting the fertile corners of the urban world in accord with the rules of wild systems, the visible hardy stalks and stems of vacant lots and railroads, the persistent raccoon squads, bacteria in the loam and in our yogurt.'[64]

Flipping his own practice of reinhabitation on its head, Snyder realizes that wild systems 'inhabit us.'[65] The jerk of your head at the drop of a cup behind you; the heart-in-your-throat at the ring of the phone past midnight, the quick smile, the ease of it, which you cannot *will* because the muscles that create it are controlled autonomically – all remind us that 'our bodies

155

are wild.' And so are our minds. To identify ourselves with the 'conscious agenda-planning ego' is to ignore most of what is going on. To locate the ethical self in the operations of that ego is to misunderstand *practice* utterly; to situate ethical reflection outside of practice is folly. Challenging the postmodernist understanding of language as construct, Snyder insists that it too is wild. 'We cannot as individuals or even as species take credit for this process. It came from someplace else: from the way clouds divide and mingle..., from the gleaming calligraphy of the ancient riverbeds ..., from the chuckles of grouse in ceanothus bushes.'[66] In classical Buddhist terms body, speech, and mind are wild. Practice as the realization of who we are, as realization of our Buddha Nature, is practice of the wild.

Practice of the Wild as Trans-species Erotics

The stream with its sounds is a long broad tongue
The looming mountain is a wide-awake body
Throughout the night song after song
How can I speak at dawn.[67]

The first step in the practice of the wild is to love it. For Snyder the Bodhisattva's vow to save all sentient beings entails a transcendence of the anthropocentrism of the moral imagination. Almost a cliche, yet no simple task. Snyder struggled for years with his *kōan*/vow or, more precisely, the vow 'stalked' him and, he says, 'finally pounced: I realized that I had vowed to let the sentient beings save *me*.'[68] The mutuality of this understanding of the Bodhisattva's vow is concretely experienced in what Snyder calls a 'trans-species erotics.'[69] If we think of practice merely as something *willed*, it is hard to imagine the 'practice' of eros. But listen for the ethical overtones in this love-poem entitled 'The Bear Mother.'

She veils herself
    to speak of eating salmon
  Teases me with
    'What do you know of my ways'
And kisses me through the mountain.

Through and under its layers, its
    gullies, its folds;
  Her mouth full of blueberries,
    We share.[70]

'Order in me, my love,' Augustine prays, hoping for the grace to constitute a moral life. Snyder could not agree more, only the ordering of love must be in accordance with wild systems and with the harsh mutuality – eating and being eaten – of those who share a bioregion. Are we back to the romanticized, gender-tied archetypes of Snyder's earlier work? I don't believe so. Keep in mind the *provisional* character of such core images as the Bear Mother. How then does this poem orient us to practice? Snyder has argued persistently that a sacramentalized consciousness is erotic. Our bodies are permeable; we intertwine.[71] In the context of Western dualism, Augustine showed the interpenetration of agape and eros. In the context of the Pacific Buddha's wild practice, Snyder expresses the intertwining of compassion and eros.

Practice of the Wild as the Etiquette of Freedom

Climbing Midnight Mountain sliding rock
find a sheep trail goes just right:
on the harder scree at the bases of faces,
follow it out, over ledges, find their hidden
sheltered beds.

Sweet rank smell makes the heart beat,
. . .
sheep dreaming place – [72]

Mutuality has its own rules, its own etiquette. 'An ethical life,' Snyder believes, 'is one that is mindful, mannerly and has style.' Kissing the Grizzly, her mouth full of blueberries, is certainly a trope of ethical style. When it comes to manners, Snyder goes on, the worst of moral flaws is a certain 'stinginess of thought which includes meanness in all its forms. Rudeness in thought or deed toward others, toward nature, reduces the chances of conviviality of interspecies communication, which are essential to physical and spiritual survival. . . .' Wastefulness and carelessness flow from the same spiritual stinginess. They are 'an ungracious unwillingness to complete the gift-exchange transaction.'[73] What we earlier saw as a field-sensing mindfulness appears to be the opposite of this stinginess of mind. Mindfulness is excrutiatingly difficult to practice. In 'Crash' Snyder recalls a motorcycle accident in Kyoto in which he knocked an old man off his bike: 'I saw my inattention;/ Tiny moment in the thread,/ Was where the whole world could have turned/ And gone another way.'[74]

So much for our stereotype of freedom. Freedom is best understood through the paradoxical title of one of the essays in *The Practice of the Wild* as 'on the path, off the trail.' Practice is *a* path and it is important that we be on *a* path. Master the day to day. Getting the children to the school bus, checking the oil in the car, wiping noses, and growing tomatoes put us on a path every bit as much as zazen. We are back to the triple practice of place, work, and family life. The path *'puts you out there,'* Snyder says, out there where surprises happen. Without a path we can never be off the trail.

'"Off the trail" is another name for the Way, and sauntering off the trail is the practice of the wild.'[75] Snyder is merely recycling the Taoist underpinnings of Zen awareness – the path we can follow is not *the* path. Knowing *when* to step off the trail, knowing *how* to do it with style, how to *saunter* off the trail, is key. Off the trail 'there is a "going" but no goer, no destination, only the whole field.'[76]

We can see the warning sign posted by the trail – there lies moral vacuity, ethical fogs and swamps. But being on the path and off the trail are, Snyder would say, not two. The children still need to get to the school bus on time. The meeting to plan the wildlife corridor still needs to be attended. On the other hand, all the rules, the path markers, carefully constructed out of the ethical debates among conservationists and deep ecologists, ecofeminists and evangelical stewards are simply *upaya*, skillful means. There is a wisdom of knowing the limits of these rules.

'Wild herbs, camas bulbs, quail, dye plants are away from the path.... The relentless complexity of the world is off to the side of the trail.'[77] Those wild herbs, more than likely, flourish within some ethically swampy terrain. The practice of the wild is not concerned with ethical or any other kind of purity. Going off the trail, we get muddy feet, dirty hands. Like Izanagi encountering in the underworld his beloved Izanami teeming with maggots, we encounter our own shame, fear, and abject behavior.[78] Practice of the wild goes on even in an ethical fog.

Conclusion: Streams and Mountains Never Stay the Same

A monk asked Dong-shan: 'Is there a practice for people to follow? Dong-shan answered: 'When you become a real person, there is such a practice.'[79]

Heading off the trail risks running in circles. Where are we? First, like Albanese's Emerson, Snyder refuses exclusive options in environmental debates. To be sure, he sees Deep Ecology as 'politically livelier, more courageous ... and more scientific' than human-centered resource management. From that understanding comes a necessary ethic of resistance, the hard work of battling at the local level against corporate interests and government officials with their glamorous projects, faulty assumptions and 'frivolous' statistics.[80] But Snyder is also wary of the 'Savers' who commodify nature by preserving it 'in a golden cage.'[81] People who reinhabit the land wish to learn from it how to *use* it well. They ask 'is there any way we can go *with* rather than against nature's tendency.'[82] The practice of the wild, like any authentic Buddhist ethic, follows a middle path. And this differentiates Snyder from Emerson. Practice *bridges* the fault lines of conflicting theories and transforms them into skillful means.

Second, I hope that I have shown that the practice of the wild represents a new, fifth type of Buddhist environmental ethic. A *bioregionalist* ethic is a less abstract version of the eco-justice model. There is also a toughness in Snyder's vision of the wild and in the daily practice of reinhabitation that I miss in what Albanese calls the 'harmonial ethic' or in the way those who follow the path of 'Dharma Gaia' construe the dependent coarising of Indra's Net. One does not really know a bioregion, let alone work in the grain of it, in a day, a decade, or even a generation.[83] And the wild is always messier than we would have wished. But Snyder's 'trans-species erotics' adds rich spice to the straight-laced model of 'Protestant Buddhism.'

Third, Snyder's practice of the wild is the means of transcending what Harris alleges to be the moral vacuity of the eco-spiritual model. There are, first of all, the daily moral challenges of family, place, and work. But, secondly, eco-spirituality becomes a practice that opens us to the suchness of a gnarled canyon oak, that enables us to see 'the wild in wild.' The ethical implications of this variation on eco-spirituality go well beyond an indiscriminate reverence for the whole. Quoting Dōgen, Snyder suggests, 'If you doubt mountains walking, you do not know your own walking.'[84] Clumsily paraphrasing, we can say: if you doubt the ordering of the wild, you cannot know how to order anything. Far from being ethically vacuous, the practice of the wild uses communitarian metaphors like that of a Village Council of All Beings and normative ecological concepts like 'climax states' as mediating terms for interpreting the self-organizing character of the wild and for actualizing traditional Buddhist precepts.[85]

Visions of the whole or of the truly good may be ethically problematic but they are not vacuous. Their primary function is to place the moral agent within a sustaining matrix so that it makes sense to be moral at all. Guiding norms are derived from mediating concepts. We saw in Snyder's early discussion of Buddhist quietism that locating the moral self in the standpoint of the sufferer was one way of tilting the vision of the whole in a certain direction. We could compare this 'tilting' to liberation theology's 'preferential option for the poor.' Concepts drawn from ecological science, like the concept of 'biodiversity' or that of 'climax states' or even the concept of an 'ecosystem,' mediate Buddhist doctrines of dependent coarising and interpenetration, giving them a normative slant. The notion of a climax state, in particular, helps us to distinguish those aspects of the whole which foster it and those which do not. But we also saw that these concepts and the root metaphors that underlie them are challenged by others and are historically relative. We can and must sort through these mediating terms dialectically. Snyder, however, turns us back to practice as the location for ongoing mediation. A Buddhist practice works with the fullest available knowledge without clinging to it as dogma. Practice, like intelligence, is as empty as a sheep's skull.

In the first precept for engaged Buddhists the Vietnamese monk, Thich Nhat Hanh, says: 'Do not be idolatrous about or bound to any doctrine, theory or ideology, even Buddhist ones. Buddhist systems of thought are guiding means; they are not absolute truth.'[86] There is a final way in which the Pacific Buddha's wild practice represents a new model. Snyder's understanding of the wild implies a transfiguration of classical Mahāyāna understandings of Buddha Nature. What does it mean to rethink Buddha Nature from the standpoint of the empty sheep skull sitting on an arctic ledge or from that of the bear lover/mother with berries in her mouth, that is, from the standpoint of the wild which inhabits us?[87]

At the heart of *The Practice of the Wild* is a meditation on Dōgen Kigen's 'Mountains and Water Sutra.' Dōgen's *sūtra*, like the Chinese landscapes with their mountains and streams, Snyder suggests, are images of the whole.[88]

> This, *thusness,* is the nature of the nature of nature, the wild in wild. So the blue mountains walk to the kitchen and back to the shop, to the desk, to the stove.... The blue mountains walk out to put another coin in the parking meter, and go on down to the 7-eleven. The blue mountains march out of the sea, shoulder the sky for awhile, and slip back into the waters.[89]

The practice of the wild is the practice of impermanence. It is not attached to the trope of order or to the trope of disorder. Both can be useful. Despite the language of 'climax states,' Snyder's practice, like Dōgen's before him, must attune itself to 'the blue mountains ... constantly walking.'[90] This practice acknowledges a multiplicity of meanings and purposes, many modes of being and perception. Within this multiplicity human intentionality and a human construal of reality have only a modest place. Again, Dōgen's words take on new life in the Sierra Nevada. 'All beings do not see mountains and waters in the same way. Some see water as wondrous blossoms.... Dragons see water as a palace or pavilion.... Humans see water as water.'[91] Perhaps because those who practice it are rooted in place, a bioregionalist ethic can go off the trail. Developing its own version of a field-sensing mindfulness, attuning itself to the wild in wild, it begins to see wondrous water palaces and walking mountains.

Walking on walking,
under foot   *earth turns*

Streams and mountains never stay the same.[92]

References

Albanese, Catherine. 'Having Nature All Ways: Liberal and Transcendental Perspectives on American Environmentalism.' *The Journal of Religion* 77 (January 1997): 20–43.

Badiner, Allan Hunt, ed. *Dharma Gaia: A Harvest of Essays in Buddhism and Ecology.* Berkeley: Parallax Press, 1990.

Dōgen, Kigen. 'Mountains and Water Sutra.' In *Moon in a Dewdrop: Writings of Zen Master Dogen*, edited by Kazuaki Tanahashi, 97–107. San Francisco: North Point Press, 1985.

Eppsteiner, Fred, ed. *The Path of Compassion: Writings on Socially Engaged Buddhism.* Berkeley: Parallax Press, 1988.

Fields, Rick. *How the Swans Came to the Lake: A Narrative History of Buddhism in America.* 3rd. ed. Boston: Shambhala Publications, 1992.

Gilroy, Paul. *The Black Atlantic: Modernity and Double Consciousness.* Cambridge, MA: Harvard University Press, 1993.

Halifax, Joan. 'The Third Body: Buddhism, Shamanism and Deep Ecology.' In *Dharma Gaia: A Harvest of Essays in Buddhism and Ecology*, edited by Allan Hunt Badiner, 20–38. Berkeley: Parallax Press, 1990.

Harris, Ian. 'Causation and "Telos": The Problem of Buddhist Environmental Ethics.' *Journal of Buddhist Ethics* 1 (1994): 45–56.

____. 'Getting to Grips with Buddhist Environmentalism: A Provisional Typology.' *Journal of Buddhist Ethics* 2 (1995): 173–90.

Jones, Ken. *The Social Face of Buddhism: An Approach to Political and Social Activism.* London: Wisdom Publications, 1989.

King, Sallie. *Buddha Nature.* Albany, NY: State University of New York Press, 1991.

McCann, Dennis P., and Charles R. Strain. *Polity and Praxis: A Program for American Practical Theology.* Minneapolis: Winston Press, 1985; reprint, Lanham, MD: University Press of America, 1990.

McClintock, James. *Nature's Kindred Spirits: Aldo Leopold, Joseph Wood Krutch, Edward Abbey, Annie Dillard and Gary Snyder.* Madison: University of Wisconsin Press, 1994.

MacIntyre, Alasdair. *After Virtue.* Notre Dame, IN: University of Notre Dame Press, 1981.

Martin, Julia. 'Coyote-Mind: An Interview with Gary Snyder.' *TriQuarterly* 79 (Fall 1990): 148–172.

Murphy, Patrick D. *Critical Essays on Gary Snyder.* Boston: G. K. Hall & Co., 1991.

____. *Understanding Gary Snyder.* Columbia, SC: University of South Carolina Press, 1992.

Nhat Hanh, Thich. *Interbeing: Fourteen Guidelines for Engaged Buddhism.* Rev. ed. Edited by Fred Eppsteiner. Berkeley: Parallax Press, 1993.

Nielsen, Dorothy. 'Prosopopeia and the Ethics of Ecological Advocacy in the Poetry of Denise Levertov and Gary Snyder.' *Contemporary Literature* 34 (Winter 1993): 691–713.

Oelschlaeger, Max. Review of *The Practice of the Wild*, by Gary Snyder. *Environmental Ethics* 14 (Summer 1992): 185–190.

Prebish, Charles. 'Ethics and Integration in American Buddhism.' *Journal of Buddhist Ethics* 2 (1995): 125–139.

Queen, Christopher S., and Sallie B. King, eds. *Engaged Buddhism: Buddhist Liberation Movements in Asia.* Albany, NY: State University of New York Press, 1996.

Schmithausen, Lambert. 'The Early Buddhist Tradition and Ecological Ethics.' *Journal of Buddhist Ethics* 4 (1997): 1–74.

Snyder, Gary. *Earth House Hold.* New York: New Directions, 1969.

____. *Mountains and Rivers without End.* Washington, D.C.: Counterpoint, 1996.

____. *No Nature: New and Selected Poems.* New York: Pantheon Books, 1992.

____. *A Place in Space: Ethics, Aesthetics and Watersheds.* Washington, D.C.: Counterpoint, 1995.

____. *The Practice of the Wild.* San Francisco: North Point Press, 1990.

____. *The Real Work: Interviews and Talks, 1964–1979.* Edited with an introduction by William Scott McLean. New York: New Directions, 1980.

____. *Regarding Wave.* New York: New Directions, 1970.

____. *Turtle Island.* New York: New Directions, 1974.

Strain, Charles R. 'Sapiential Eschatology and Social Transformation: Crossan's Jesus, Socially Engaged Buddhism and Liberation Theology.' In *Jesus and Faith: A Conversation on the Work of John Dominic Crossan,* edited by Jeffrey Carlson and Robert A. Ludwig, 115–31. Maryknoll, NY: Orbis Books, 1994.

____. 'Socially Engaged Buddhism's Contribution to the Transformation of Catholic Social Teachings on Human Rights.' In *Buddhism and Human Rights,* edited by Damien V. Keown, Charles S. Prebish, and Wayne R. Husted, 155–74. Richmond, England: Curzon Press, 1998.

Turner, Victor. *Drama, Fields and Metaphors: Symbolic Action in Human Society.* Ithaca, NY: Cornell University Press, 1974.

Worster, Donald. *Nature's Economy: a History of Ecological Ideas.* 2nd. ed. New York: Cambridge University Press, 1994.

Yamazato, Katsunori. 'How to Be in This Crisis: Gary Snyder's Cross-cultural Vision in *Turtle Island*.' In *Critical Essays on Gary Snyder,* edited by Patrick D. Murphy, 230–47. Boston: G. K. Hall & Co., 1991.

Notes

1 Gary Snyder, 'Afloat,' in *Mountains and Rivers without End* (Washington, D.C.: Counterpoint, 1996), 130–31 (hereafter cited as MRWE). An earlier version of this chapter was presented at the Religion and Ecology section of the American Academy of Religion, San Francisco, 1997.

2 'Endless Streams and Mountains,' MRWE, 9. Walking on walking, this chapter crosses numerous boundaries: the geographical boundaries of either side of the Pacific Rim; the visionary boundaries of poetry and ethics or of science and religion; and the ideological boundaries of ethical inquiries rooted in Buddhist, Native American, or Western religious traditions. I have found that Snyder's form of Buddhist practice, adapted to his life at Kitkitdizze, is the thread that keeps me from getting lost in this confusing terrain. In an earlier work with my colleague Dennis McCann, I provided a theoretical guidebook for sorting through the multiple elements of religious models for social engagement. See Dennis P. McCann and Charles R. Strain, *Polity and Praxis: A Program for an American Practical Theology* (Minneapolis: Winston Press, 1985; reprint, Lanham, MD: University Press of America, 1990). Here, I suggest that a guidebook is not the same as a guide. Let us see what we can learn by following a guide. The *locus classicus* for a contemporary Western understanding of practice is Alasdair MacIntyre's *After Virtue* (Notre Dame, IN: University of Notre Dame Press, 1981), 174–181. But I hope to demonstrate that Snyder takes us well beyond MacIntyre's schematic understanding of a practice. This chapter, then, focusing on Snyder's Buddhist practice is a contribution to the reconfiguration of *Western* social ethics.

A useful introduction to Snyder's life and his poetry is Patrick D. Murphy, *Understanding Gary Snyder* (Columbia, SC: University of South Carolina Press, 1992). For a critical examination of Snyder's thought from multiple standpoints, see Patrick D. Murphy, *Critical Essays on Gary Snyder* (Boston:

G.K. Hall & Co., 1991). For the 'crossfertilization' of multiple Buddhist sources in Snyder's thought, see Katsunori Yamazato, 'How to Be in This Crisis: Gary Snyder's Cross-cultural Vision in *Turtle Island*,' in Murphy, *Critical Essays*, 231–247. Rick Fields is typical of scholars who see Gary Snyder's contribution to American Buddhism occurring as part of the Beat Generation's dabblings and as part of the 1960s' countercultural explorations. While Fields acknowledges Snyder's persistent commitment to Buddhist practice over a much longer period of time, the emphasis on the 1950s and 60s, I suggest, risks overlooking Snyder's truly profound contributions. In fact, I will argue that the key shift in Snyder's life comes with his move to the Sierra Nevada in 1970 and this essay will largely concentrate on works published in the 1990s, though they obviously were the culmination of decades of meditation and poetic practice. See Rick Fields, *How the Swans Came to the Lake: A Narrative History of Buddhism in America*, 3rd ed. (Boston: Shambhala Publications, 1992), 212–223, 248–250, 256, 370.

3   Catherine Albanese, 'Having Nature All Ways: Liberal and Transcendental Perspectives on American Environmentalism,' *Journal of Religion* 77 (January 1997): 21–22, 32, 37–38.

4   Ibid., 43.

5   Ian Harris, 'Getting to Grips with Buddhist Environmentalism: a Provisional Typology,' *Journal of Buddhist Ethics* 2 (1995): 177–178.

6   Harris suggests that one exception to this general criticism is the work of Lambert Schmithausen. Harris, 180. See Lambert Schmithausen, 'The Early Buddhist Tradition and Ecological Ethics,' *Journal of Buddhist Ethics* 4 (1997): 1–74.

7   Harris, 177–181.

8   Ibid., 177–178.

9   Ibid., 177.

10 Harris, 184. Harris believes that an authentic Buddhist environmental ethic must come to grips with early Buddhism's 'radically pluralist ontology.' Harris, 178. Elsewhere he argues that an authentic Buddhist environmental ethic must cohere with the non-teleological understanding of causation in early Buddhism, a challenge that he finds daunting. See Ian Harris, 'Causation and "Telos": The Problem of Buddhist Environmental Ethics,' *Journal of Buddhist Ethics* 1 (1994): 45–56.

11 Gary Snyder, *The Real Work: Interviews and Talks, 1964–1979*, ed. with an introduction by William Scott McLean (New York: New Directions, 1980), 155–157 (hereafter cited as RW).

12 On socially engaged Buddhism, see, *inter alia*, Christopher S. Queen and Sallie B. King, *Engaged Buddhism: Buddhist Liberation Movements in Asia* (Albany, NY: State University of New York Press, 1996); Fred Eppsteiner, ed., *The Path of Compassion: Writings on Socially Engaged Buddhism* (Berkeley: Parallax Press, 1988); Ken Jones, *The Social Face of Buddhism: An Approach to Political and Social Activism* (London: Wisdom Publications, 1989); and Thich Nhat Hanh, *Interbeing: Fourteen Guidelines for Engaged Buddhism*, rev. ed., ed. Fred Eppsteiner (Berkeley: Parallax Press, 1993). On the impact of socially engaged Buddhism on Western social ethics, see Charles R. Strain, 'Sapiential Eschatology and Social Transformation: Crossan's Jesus, Socially Engaged Buddhism and Liberation Theology,' in *Jesus and Faith: A Conversation on the Work of John Dominic Crossan* (Maryknoll, NY: Orbis Books, 1994), 115–31; and 'Socially Engaged Buddhism's Contribution to the Transformation of Catholic Social Teachings on Human Rights,' in *Buddhism and Human Rights*,

155–174, ed. Damien V. Keown, Charles S. Prebish, and Wayne R. Husted (Richmond, England: Curzon Press, 1998).

13 'The Hump-backed Flute Player,' MRWE, 79.

14 Ibid., 80–81, 160–61; See 'The Mountain Spirit,' MRWE, 145–46, 173.

15 RW, 156 (italics mine). Charles Prebish reviews the ambiguities of adapting Buddhism to the American context in a recent article that evaluates, fifteen years after its publication, his own classic study of American Buddhism. He concludes that his worries about a tendency towards 'pathological eclecticism' were without ground. 'Ethics and Integration in American Buddhism,' *Journal of Buddhist Ethics* 2 (1995): 137. Snyder's rejoinder to critics indicates that he has been accused of such eclecticism. In particular, debate has swirled around his appropriation not of Buddhism but of the traditions of primal peoples. See Dorothy Nielsen, 'Prosopopoeia and the Ethics of Ecological Advocacy in Denise Levertov and Gary Snyder,' *Contemporary Literature* 34 (Winter 1993): 707–711. In part, Snyder simply glories in his eclecticism. Yet a closer look at this quote reveals the normative intent underlying the selective appropriation of multiple traditions.

16 Gary Snyder, *A Place in Space: Ethics, Aesthetics, and Watersheds* (Washington, D.C.: Counterpoint, 1995): 246 (hereafter cited as PS).

17 RW, 156.

18 Paul Gilroy, *The Black Atlantic: Modernity and Double Consciousness* (Cambridge, MA: Harvard University Press, 1993), 4–5, 36, 38–39, 73, 89.

19 RW, 94.

20 Ibid., 108–109. If Gilroy's claim that the Black Atlantic represents a distinctive form of syncretism that deconstructs the Western traditions that it enters and reconfigures them through such expressive cultural forms as music is as persuasive as I hold it to be, then we may well interpret Snyder as developing a form of syncretism in which deconstruction and reconfiguration is guided by a revised form of practice. I am suggesting that a close comparison of the Black Atlantic and the Pacific Buddha could catapult scholars into new ways of understanding religious and ethical syncretism.

21 Gary Snyder, *Earth House Hold* (New York: New Directions, 1969), 133–134 (hereafter cited as EHH).

22 Julia Martin, 'Coyote-Mind: An Interview with Gary Snyder,' *TriQuarterly* 79 (Fall 1990): 152.

23 On the development of the 'Gaia hypothesis' within the historical evolution of ecological theory, see Donald Worster, *Nature's Economy: A History of Ecological Ideas*, 2nd. ed. (New York: Cambridge University Press, 1994), 378–387. I am grateful to Charles Aaron Bobrow-Strain for references which enabled me to understand the scientific underpinnings of Snyder's thought and their historical context.

24 Allan Hunt Badiner, ed., *Dharma Gaia: A Harvest of Essays in Buddhism and Ecology* (Berkeley: Parallax Press, 1990), xiii. For an example of an uncritical correlation of the Gaia-hypothesis with Buddhist and Native American teachings that explicitly acknowledges a debt to Gary Snyder, see Joan Halifax, 'The Third Body: Buddhism, Shamanism and Deep Ecology,' in Badiner, 22–25.

25 Martin, 153–155.

26 EHH, 90–93.

27 PS, 29–30.

28 Ibid., 27–28.

29 'Cross Legg'd,' MRWE, 128

30 RW, 96.

31 Ibid., 134–135.
32 Ibid., 112.
33 Ibid., 106.
34 PS, 67.
35 Gary Snyder, 'Kai, Today,' *Regarding Wave* (New York: New Directions, 1970), 33.
36 Gary Snyder, 'The Bath,' *Turtle Island* (New York: New Directions, 1974), 12 (hereafter cited as TI).
37 Ibid., 13.
38 'What Happened Here Before,' TI, 80–81.
39 'An Offering for Tara,' MRWE, 107.
40 RW, 92–93.
41 Ibid., 103.
42 Ibid., 8.
43 'Old Woodrat's Stinky House,' MRWE, 121.
44 Martin, 170
45 PS, 246–247.
46 RW, 141.
47 Ibid., 107–108.
48 PS, 263.
49 RW, 117, 140–141; Martin, 159.
50 RW, 119–120.
51 PS, 76.
52 Ibid., 40, 66, 262.
53 Ibid., 7, 79, 260–262.
54 Victor Turner, *Drama, Fields and Metaphors: Symbolic Action in Human Society* (Ithaca, NY: Cornell University Press, 1974): 25–33 and *passim.*
55 PS, 137–38. '[O]ne must pick one's root metaphors carefully, for appropriateness and potential fruitfulness,' Turner insists. Turner, 25. For a more formal understanding of how religious and ethical reflection upon social engagement might select both metaphors and models to guide practice, see McCann and Strain. If we look at the poetic metaphors and the religious concepts which structure Snyder's thought and practice, it is also critical that we examine the ecological concepts with which they are correlated. These, too, have a history. The Odum brothers, for example, favored an understanding of ecological systems as governed by internal pushes toward order, constantly renewed. A more recent generation of ecological scientists have developed models which stress a world in chaos, constantly rocked by disturbances. In the newer view the 'equilibrium' of climax states virtually disappears. Likewise, there is no discernible progress towards a climax state. Each ecological system is a marriage of convenience that defends itself momentarily until overwhelmed by disturbance. But these theories too have been eclipsed by yet others which focus on complexity and discern 'shifting patterns in endless flux.' On the Odum brothers, see Worster, 362–73; on competing theories, see Worster, 388–420. See also James McClintock, *Nature's Kindred Spirits: Aldo Leopold, Joseph Wood Krutch, Edward Abbey, Annie Dillard and Gary Snyder* (Madison: University of Wisconsin Press, 1994), 115–118 and 158–159. In many ways there is a battle of tropes underlying this conflict of theories and Worster accuses various parties of the conflict of 'metaphoric excess.' Yet the ethicist need not despair. The same historical sorting and ethical evaluation of multiple metaphors and models in play in forming the Pacific Buddha can be applied, according to Worster, to the multiple competing theories of ecological science. See Worster, 392 and 425.

56 RW, 173.
57 RW, 124, 174; Martin, 161; PS, 127–128.
58 TI, 80–81.
59 Lew Welch as quoted in 'Night Highway 99,' MRWE, 11
60 'Arctic Midnight Twilight Cool North Breeze with Low Clouds Green Mountain Slopes, White Mountain Sheep,' MRWE, 93.
61 Max Oelschlager, review of *The Practice of the Wild* by Gary Snyder, *Environmental Ethics* 14 (Summer 1992): 185–186.
62 TI, 99; RW, 108–109.
63 Gary Snyder, *The Practice of the Wild* (San Francisco: North Point Press, 1990), 5, 8–11, 90 (hereafter cited as PW).
64 Ibid., 15, 181.
65 Ibid., 14.
66 Ibid., 16–17.
67 Ibid., 182.
68 PS, 210–211.
69 Su Tung-p'o's enlightenment poem as rendered in 'We Wash Our Bowls in This Water, MRWE, 138.
70 'The Bear Mother,' MRWE, 113.
71 'Cross Legg'd,' MRWE, 128–129.
72 'Arctic Midnight Twilight,' MRWE, 94.
73 PW, 21.
74 Gary Snyder, *No Nature: New and Selected Poems* (New York: Pantheon Books, 1992), 341.
75 PW, 15, 153–154.
76 Ibid., 151.
77 Ibid., 145.
78 Ibid., 110–111.
79 Ibid., 185.
80 Ibid., 95, 181.
81 PS, 238.
82 PW, 90.
83 Ibid., 39.
84 Ibid., 103.
85 Cf. PW, 181–183. I suspect that Harris might find this argument a bit too facile. See Harris, 'Getting to Grips,' 177–178. We know, for one thing, from almost two millennia of Natural Law reasoning in Western ethics that there can be no unproblematic grasp of Nature's way, of the wild's self-organizing. Snyder does not claim that there is. He is implicitly maintaining, however, that ethics – like language – comes from someplace else; it is not – *pace* all post- modernists – simply a construct. The practice of the wild, moving off into *terra incognita* presents us with a different order of intelligence on this topic.
86 Nhat Hanh, 17.
87 Compare Snyder's understanding of the 'the wild in wild' with Sallie B. King's classic treatment of the concept of Buddha Nature. *Buddha Nature* (Albany, NY: State University of New York, 1991).
88 PW, 97–115. Cf. Dōgen Kigen, 'Mountains and Water Sutra,' *Moon in a Dewdrop: The Writings of Zen Master Dogen*, ed. Kazuaki Tanahashi (San Francisco: North Point Press, 1985), 97–107. In 1996 Snyder published *Mountains and Rivers without End*, not a new collection of poems but an Indra's Net of interpenetrating poems that he had worked on for forty years. While the sources for Snyder's work are always multiple, the title intimates and

Snyder explicitly says that this distillation of a lifetime of poetic practice is in many respects the fruit of persistent reflection on Dōgen's *sūtra* and the Chinese landscape paintings. See MRWE, 153, 157. It is largely poems from *Mountains and Rivers without End* that have framed and structured my analysis. Attending to the Buddhist poet as a resource for ethical reflection, the reader must break apart the formal rigidities of an academic essay. Like the 'Oxherding Pictures,' Snyder's poems mirror the flow of a Chinese handscroll painting as it is carefully unwound. My prose commentary lags behind. 'Clearing the mind and sliding in/ to that created space,/ a web of waters streaming over rocks. ...' 'Endless Streams and Mountains,' MRWE, 5.

89 PW, 103.
90 Ibid., 98.
91 Dōgen as cited in PW, 107.
92 'Finding the Space in the Heart,' MRWE, 152.

CHAPTER TEN

The Internet as Window onto American Buddhism

Richard P. Hayes

It is a well-known principle of analytic psychology that when a person identifies very strongly with only the positive and praiseworthy aspects of the psyche, all those aspects of the psyche that do not match the persona that has been constructed for public consumption tend to be driven underground. From the subterranean shadow these rejected characteristics of the psyche continue to have an effect, although usually not in ways that the person fully acknowledges. After several years of following Buddhist discussion groups on the Internet, I have come to appreciate the many ways in which the use of electronic mail and news groups enables people to express their more shadowy thoughts and doubts – ideas to which they might hesitate to give free expression in the presence of a *lama* or a Zen master.

For those not yet familiar with the discussion groups that are available through various resources accessible by computer, let me first give a brief account of two kinds of discussion groups. The first type is called a news group. A news group is somewhat similar to an electronic bulletin board in that people post messages to a central location. All messages posted have brief titles indicating the subject. Anyone can connect to a particular news group and see a list of titles and their authors. The reader can then choose to read any of the messages that are posted. After reading a message, the reader may wish to post a reply. The reply then becomes another message that other readers can look at and perhaps reply to. Over the course of several days, a given news group is likely to have a dozen or so exchanges taking place on various topics. There are several news groups dedicated to topics related to Buddhism, including *talk.religion.buddhism*; *alt.religion. buddhism.tibetan*; and *uk.religion.buddhist*. As the titles suggest, the news groups are dedicated to broad topics, the broadest being open to discussion of any topic within Buddhism and the two narrower ones to Tibetan Buddhism and Buddhism in the United Kingdom. Contributors and readers to all three news groups come from all around the world, but the majority on the 'alt' and 'talk' groups are from the United States, while the majority on the 'uk' groups are naturally from the United Kingdom.

The second kind of electronic discussion group is one that distributes messages to subscribers from a central location through electronic mail. On this kind of electronic forum, any e-mail message sent to the address of the forum will automatically be distributed to every subscriber to that forum. E-mail discussion groups may be either moderated or unmoderated. When a group is moderated, every message sent to the address of the electronic forum is first sent to the moderator, who then decides whether to forward the message to the list of subscribers. The e-mail discussion group that I have read for the longest time (six years as of 1997) is called Forum on Indian and Buddhist Studies (*BUDDHIST@VM1.MCGILL.CA*), an unmoderated list that was founded in Japan but is now physically located at McGill University in Canada. This list has consistently had between two hundred and three hundred subscribers at any given time, of which about 65 percent are from the United States and Canada. Few subscribers are academics and most of the regular contributors are Buddhists of various kinds, although some are non-Buddhists who have an interest in Buddhist ideas. Another e-mail discussion group that I read regularly is one that I helped to found in 1992 and have been moderating for most of the time during the past three years. This is called Buddhist Academic Discussion Forum (*buddha-l@ulkyvm.louisville.edu*). As the formal name implies, 'BUDDHA-L' (as it is commonly known) was originally meant to be a forum in which academic specialists in Buddhist studies could discuss their concerns as teachers and researchers. As the group has evolved, however, it has become broader than that, having become a place where practitioners and academics exchange ideas, opinions, and information about all aspects of Buddhism. Of the nearly seven hundred subscribers, nearly 70 percent are from the United States, Canada, and Mexico.

Themes from the Shadows

In a private e-mail message to me in January 1997, a regular reader of the list BUDDHA-L wrote why she appreciated having access to such a list. 'For the first time,' she said, 'I have found a community of intelligent, thoughtful people to share my love of Buddhist practise and debate–scholars and layfolk alike.' The Internet, she went on to explain, provides a place where Buddhist practitioners can raise questions of the sort that they might feel reluctant to address to their own spiritual leaders or to fellow practitioners, for fear of seeming overly skeptical or insincere or ignorant. In what follows, I shall recapitulate commonly occurring themes on two e-mail discussion groups that deal with Buddhism, namely BUDDHA-L and BUDDHIST. I shall treat the topics under four headings: questions of authority, doctrine, practice, and cultural identity.

Questions of Authority

It hardly needs to be said that the issue of religious authority has been a complex one in the West, particularly since the time of the Protestant Reformation. Since the dawn of the European Enlightenment, Westerners have become increasingly protective of their individuality, including their rights as individuals to think for themselves and to arrive at their own conclusions without being constrained by religious or political authorities. It is no accident, then, that one of the classical texts that has most caught the attention of Westerners is the Buddha's celebrated advice to the Kālāmas (Anguttara Nikāya I:189) not to accept any conclusions on the basis of hearsay, expertise, or respect for one's guru, but rather to suspend judgement about what is healthy, admirable, and beneficial until one knows these things for oneself. During the six years that I have been following discussions on the Internet, my impression is that I have seen this text cited more than any other. People frequently confess that they were first attracted to Buddhism by the spirit of this text, only to discover that there is much in Buddhist life that is disappointing to one expecting the openness that the advice to the Kālāmas seems to promise. One of the first discussions I recall seeing on the Buddhist list was a rather heated debate on an issue I have seen discussed many times since: Is it necessary to have a teacher to practice Buddhism effectively? What has interested me most about this debate is not the fact that it takes place, for it seems a reasonable enough question; rather, what has often surprised me is the emotional intensity with which members on both sides of the issue state their cases. Apparently, it is as threatening to those who follow *gurus* to think that it might be possible to make progress without a *guru* as it is for more isolated people to think that they are missing something essential by not having a *guru*. One fairly representative message is this excerpt that appeared in 1992:

> I wouldn't be surprised if there is quite a number of people out there who are basically followers of the dharma but whose feelings about it are as unsettled as mine, who are frustrated about its contemporary expressions, discontent, somewhat enlightened but also quite con- fused. I am dissatisfied with most of the contemporary forms of Buddhism. In my view, they all drag along too much cultural baggage, too much of an outdated worldview, too much uncritical acceptance of time-honored convention and dogma, too much submission to authoritarian views. There is an urgent need for something new to arise, something which preserves the basic insights of Buddhism but marries them with the rational, skeptical, scientific, self-reliant and individualistic worldview prevalent in the West at this time.
>
> For example, I think it is futile to try to export Eastern Buddhism lock, stock and barrel, as Tibetan and Zen Buddhists are prone to do,

i.e. to try to force-graft these self-contained systems onto our Western culture. In my mind, this only leads to a schizophrenic existence on the part of those who follow these systems. Just think of Western followers of Tibetan Buddhist schools which place great emphasis on guru yoga, e.g. the Kagyu and Nyingma schools. They are being asked to become like children before their all-wise, never-erring teacher; yet we also expect them to be independent, self-reliant, critical-thinking members of a very complex society. The same applies to Zen: what I have seen in visits to Zen centers in the U.S. is almost 100% Japanese-culture Zen, even in centers run by first-generation American Zen teachers. Maybe it takes second-generation American Zen teachers to loosen up on this obsession with preserving the original down to the last trivial detail. Charlotte Joko Beck seems to have moved away a bit from the original, probably with no loss of vitality in the teaching.[1]

For some people, I suspect, the discovery that Buddhism in practice has authority figures may be enough to dampen their initial enthusiasm, if not extinguish it altogether. For those who survive the initial shock of learning that there are standards of authority in Buddhism and who resign themselves to being influenced by them, the next serious problem that arises is just how one goes about deciding which kind of authority is most beneficial to submit to. Here, quite a range of opinions are manifested on the Internet. Some regular contributors clearly have made a personal commitment to a particular teacher or school and seem to regard other schools as having less to offer; one can expect a certain amount of sectarian polemics, although most of it seems to be good-natured playfulness rather than bigotry. Other contributors obviously feel more comfortable with an ecumenical approach and consistently take pains to point out that the different schools of Buddhism are merely different ways of expressing the same basic message.

Another observation that can be made about the collective attitude on types of authority is that a good many Internet users regard academic expertise with suspicion. The study of classical texts in their original languages, although admired by many, is seen by many others as evidence that the scholar has little or no direct experiential familiarity with Buddhist contemplative practices and therefore probably has developed few of the virtues that arise only out of firsthand experience with reality. A fairly typical example of what I am referring to is the following message, written in response to something I had written:

It would seem that Richard is at it again. As usual he seems to be determined to abuse Western logic to beat all the magic out of something he does not appear to understand. Does it really take that much to shake him out of his sleep and fog of doubt that he only experiences clearly when he is under unusual stress? Burn your books, Richard, and you might catch a glimpse of what the world is really like – full of magic and wonderful experiences everywhere. Forget the logic, it is a trap for the unwary, wipe the book dust from your eyes, look and feel. When you find the truth you'll know it, I assure you.[2]

Judging from conversations I have had with my academic colleagues in Christian and Jewish studies, these suspicions of academia are very widespread within North American religious circles, where it is often taken for granted (with some justification) that secular education is based upon a hostility to, or at least a suspicion of, religious piety. Religious anti-intellectualism seems to be a general feature of North American culture that many people from that culture, including intellectuals themselves, carry into whatever they do, including the practices of both scholarship and Buddhism.

Questions of Doctrine

Regardless of the type of authority to which Buddhists who use the Internet turn, the questions they raise are consistently similar. One of the most frequently debated issues in Western Buddhism has been the matter of whether it is necessary to believe in rebirth and what it means within the context of Buddhism. One can find people along the entire spectrum of possible answers to this question, often stating their positions with great conviction and force, not always with much sympathy for those who take a different stance. Over the years I have seen this issue debated many times, but I have never been able to detect any obvious patterns in what kind of person is most likely to take which position. In other words, I have not detected a correlation between how one answers this question and one's level of education or Buddhist sectarian affiliation. It seems to be very much a matter of individual taste.

The issue of how literally one should take Jātaka tales and other Buddhist texts that speak of rebirth is merely one instance of a deeper uncertainty that seems to haunt the minds of Western Buddhists. That is the uncertainty of what exactly is understood by the concept of right view, the first item on the Noble Eightfold Path. From what I have seen on the Internet, Westerners have a deeply ingrained habit of thinking of right view as a Buddhist equivalent of the Christian emphasis on creed. Even those who have learned that right view has little to do with adhering to officially approved doctrine still have a tendency to revert to thinking of right view mostly in creedal terms. The following excerpts from an item posted to a news group illustrate this tendency to link right view with creed. The item was in response to a report that Stephen Batchelor had questioned the value for Western Buddhists of the doctrine of rebirth:

I must go on to say that if you believe in being responsible for your own actions, that is KARMA, it will be logical to follow that you should also believe in REBIRTH, because rebirth cannot take place without the necessary karma created by your deeds. These 2 concepts go hand in hand and you must either accept them both or reject them together. Again, there is no in-between.

We cannot have 'Buddhists' who go about refuting karma and rebirth, because that is equivalent to having 'Buddhists' who don't believe the teachings of the Buddha! How absurd would that be!

Therefore I implore all Buddhists out there: Distance yourself from those who would undermine Buddhism, and never abandon the Triple Gems.[3]

The Internet, like many other aspects of human life, provides opportunities to observe the phenomenon of overcompensation. Thus, on the various Buddhist discussion groups, one can see an intense focus by some on matters of creed and doctrine and an equally intense antipathy by others to expressions of doctrinal enthusiasm. On the Buddhist lists, this overreaction most often takes the form of a solemn reminder that the way things are is ultimately beyond discursive thought and therefore beyond articulation. The following passage is fairly representative of this kind of attitude.

if i were to voice the kinds of questions that are being raised here to my former master, i would get a few slaps of the stick, and be told to stop wasting my time.

i'm not saying that this is the correct response to such questions; i'm only saying that in certain religious contexts (and as this is a religious forum...), such questions would not be entertained, as they are too 'academic.'

i suppose that's the paradox of having a 'forum on indian and buddhist studies.' several strands of buddhism (and one may say religion in general) is precisely NOT about studying (or rather, a life devoted to studying for its own sake). they are about praxis, and any knowledge gleaned from it is strictly secondary.[4]

Questions of Practice

All these questions of orthodoxy naturally tie in eventually to questions of orthopraxis. However one decides the complex issue of authority and doctrine, the most difficult issues for many American Buddhist converts are those related to the correct way to practice the religion. The question of what kind of practice one ought to do is of course intimately connected with the question of what goal one is hoping to achieve through it. The question of goals is arguably a doctrinal matter, for it is a question of how much it is reasonable to expect to accomplish. This topic comes up repeatedly for discussion on the Internet as people ask and try to respond to questions such as these: Is the aim of a Buddhist to become an omniscient Buddha, and if so, how much does one have to know to be able to claim to know everything? Is the aim of a Buddhist to become completely free of all vices and unwholesome propensities no matter how subtle they may be? If so, then is this goal feasible? Or is the goal of Buddhism to learn not to have any more goals? As can be expected, the answers to these questions vary considerably, and it is difficult to predict what kind of position will be taken by what kind of person.

Regardless of what one sees as the goals, or absence thereof, of Buddhist practice, there seems to be general agreement to the proposition that it is a good idea to observe some precepts along the way. This question of precepts is one of the most vexed among American Buddhists using the Internet. Just as Western converts to Buddhism usually have a difficult time breaking the habit of looking for creeds to affirm, they also have a difficult time overcoming a preoccupation with finding laws to obey. When most North Americans look to Asian Buddhists for guidance in this matter, however, they often experience disappointment. They discover that Buddhist guidelines are very general and vague and that Buddhists are encouraged to act in ways that do not seek the disapproval of the mainstream culture. When Asian teachers report their understanding of the details of Buddhist precepts, they naturally report what their own cultures approve and disapprove. Most Asian societies are more restrictive and behaviorally conservative than North American society is at present, perhaps especially in the area of sexuality. Many members of the American Buddhist community have expressed dismay upon finding, for example, that many Asian Buddhist teachers express disapproval of extramarital sex and of homosexuality. To Buddhists whose first fascination with Buddhism has been in part based on a perception of Buddhism as less rigid and more permissive on moral issues than Catholicism and conservative Protestantism, Asian Buddhist attitudes on many moral issues are hardly good news. The matter becomes worse as Americans discover that the conduct of Buddhist teachers does not always match the moral strictness that is being taught.

A behavioral issue that has been debated more often than that of sexuality has been the question of diet, and especially whether it is incumbent on a Buddhist to be vegetarian. This question gets a full airing several times a year; more often than not, the tone of the discussion is both defensive and offensive. Dietary preferences are clearly one of the ways in which people have always defined their individuality and their group allegiances, and discussions on the topic are rarely dispassionate, as the following message shows:

174

When I talk about the Vedic sacrifice in class, I usually find that students cannot understand how people could ever have condoned the sacrifice of animals. To help them get some handle on the situation, I remind them that approximately 750,000 cows are killed in the USA every day. And then I tell them all about Thanksgiving Day. Today is Thanksgiving Day in the United States of America. On this day, Americans (as citizens of the USA sometimes call themselves, apparently forgetting that there are twenty-one other countries on the American continents) give thanks by sacrificing and consuming several million turkeys and pumpkin pies.

The question naturally arises: what are Americans giving thanks for, and whom are they thanking? In the time of the Puritans, Thanksgiving Day was set aside as a time when Christians could give thanks for the fact that they could eat the plentiful food provided to them by the labour of savages and pagans. At the same time, the Puritans gave thanks that they themselves were not savages and pagans. Today, however, since Americans no longer have this to be thankful for, they celebrate to give thanks for the fact that they are not turkeys.

Buddhists in classical India abhorred the sacrifice of goats. By way of contrast, Buddhists in modern America have learned that it is not cool to abhor anything, since that would be dualistic. In order not to appear dualistic or judgmental about anything (except dualists), American Buddhists accept (or at least pretend to accept) everything (except dualists). The annual slaughter of turkeys does not bother them, because they see being bothered by anything as an obstacle to universal compassion.[5]

One of the debates on the Internet that I personally found the most interesting had little to do with food or sex. This was a long debate on the Gulf War. What I found surprising in general during that war was how little public criticism there was of the military tactics being used by U.S. and British forces against Iraq. In particular I found it surprising that little criticism of the war came from United States Buddhists – there was more, I think, from Buddhists in Canada. Perhaps because I had taken it for granted that Buddhists would tend more towards pacifism, I was disappointed to see how many Western Buddhists, particularly from the United States, argued on Buddhist principles that warfare is sometimes necessary and unavoidable and that the Iraqi incursion into Kuwait was one such occasion. On the other hand, the very fact that I was so disappointed in Buddhists from the United States at this time helped me to see that I was doing precisely what I so often warn others against doing, namely, making my own personal preoccupations – in this case, my commitment to nonviolence and pacifism – into a universal standard by which to judge the moral integrity of other Buddhists.

Questions of Personal Identity

In the previous section I observed that dietary preferences are connected to issues of personal identity. People define their own personal boundaries by making choices on a wide range of issues, food being merely one of them, and then defending their personal territory with sometimes unexpected degrees of ferocity. In Western society, one of the areas in which people have considerable freedom to make choices is that of personal religion. Religion therefore becomes one of the elements in the carefully delineated and fervently guarded domain of one's ego. At the same time, precisely because religion is a matter of personal choice, people are usually expected, even if only by themselves, to give some principled account for why they have made the choices they have made. It is, in other words, considered reasonable to ask oneself why one decided to become a Buddhist rather than following some other religion or no religion at all.

Many of the communications posted on such e-mail discussion groups as BUDDHIST and BUDDHA-L are the result of people asking themselves and each other what it means for a person of Western cultural background to take up the practice of a religion that has developed primarily in Asia. The impression I have is that this question becomes more difficult to answer as an individual's knowledge of Buddhism increases. The more a person learns about the complex interrelationships between symbols, myths, presuppositions, explicit doctrines, and practices within Buddhism, the more one becomes aware of how little one really understands about what is involved in being a Buddhist. It may become more apparent what is *not* involved than what *is* involved. For example, it becomes apparent rather soon that a Westerner's task in becoming a Buddhist does not involve remaking oneself as a Tibetan, Korean, or Japanese person. Instead, it involves remaking oneself as a different kind of Western person. The problem, however, is that it is not always obvious which features of one's former Western self can be kept and which must be discarded. Moreover, if one bears in mind that many Western people who turn to Buddhism are to some extent alienated from the system of values that have made them who they are, then it is easy to see that for many Western Buddhists, it is not at all clear which features of themselves they would like to keep and which they would like to discard.

Working out even provisional solutions to all these problems of self-discovery requires asking questions of the sort that many people are shy to address to traditional Dharma teachers, or perhaps to anyone face-to-face. Electronic media provide a way of addressing issues and seeking the opinions of other people without actually having to meet those other people. A remarkable feature of the Internet is that people can discuss personal problems in some depth with people they would not even recognize if they saw them on the street. Few other media offer such a combination of intimacy, immediacy, and anonymity.

Where Are We Headed?

In this final section I would like to offer some reflections on where my observations of the Internet indicate that we academics who share an interest in American Buddhism ought to be headed. Although many observations could be made, I will restrict myself to making but one point. I have been struck many times at how little most new Buddhists know about the history of Buddhism, whether of its institutional or its intellectual history. Therefore, I would urge that we have a duty not only to study American Buddhists but also to inform them. There is no doubt in my mind that any efforts we might make in this direction would be appreciated – anti-academic sentiments notwithstanding. Recently, I received a private message from a man in Oklahoma who said he had been reading several e-mail discussion groups on Buddhism for three years. He had been practicing Buddhism for seventeen years, during which time he had moved from Zen to Tibetan Buddhism to Theravāda, all without leaving Oklahoma. After offering a long account of his various encounters with Buddhism, he wrote about his discovery of various Buddhist discussion groups on the Internet.

> I read the ZENDO list for a couple of years, wherein the most important thing I learned was that far too many Westerners (myself particularly included) were 'attached' to a sugary bliss peace concept of Buddhism. It took only a couple of days of reading BUDDHA-L/BUDDHIST to realize just how astoundingly uninformed or misinformed I was regarding a wide range of basic issues.

After chronicling the various ways in which reading the lists had helped broaden his appreciation of Buddhism, the gentleman from Oklahoma ended his long message by saying something that, while addressed to me personally, could have been addressed to every academic who bothers to make the fruits of his or her studies and reflections accessible to people who have less opportunity to study. He said:

> I only hope that in a hundred years, when some poor sod is trying to write yet another history of Western Buddhism, he or she digs down to see the impact your lists has made.

I doubt very much that this particular wish will come true, but I would add to it a wish of my own. If someone in one hundred years does dig down to see what impact we scholars have collectively had in the formation of American Buddhism, I hope they will be able to see that we have done our best to bring it out of the shadows.

Getting Plugged In

Subscribing to one of the e-mail discussion groups is easy for anyone who has access to an e-mail account. One need only send a one-line message to the address of the automated server for the list. The server for BUDDHA-L, for example, is *LISTSERV@ULKYVM.LOUISVILLE.EDU*. The message to get oneself onto the subscription list is simply: SUB BUDDHA-L John Henry (substitute your own name for 'John Henry'). The address for the BUDDHIST server is *LISTSERV@VM1.MCGILL.CA*. The syntax of the command is the same; substitute BUDDHIST for BUDDHA-L. Once subscribed to BUDDHA-L, you may send a command to the list server to send you a file explaining in detail how to search the archived files of all the messages posted during the past twelve months. The command to get that file is: GET BUDDHA-L FAQ.

If you have software for browsing the Internet, such as Netscape, or a web browser included in one of the commercial servers, such as America On Line (AOL) or Compuserve, you can point your browser to *http://www.dejanews.com*. This web site provides a means of searching through a large data base in which past messages to news groups are stored. By using key words to search through the data base, one can get a list of messages written on particular topics. Searching on a word such as 'Buddhism' will turn up over five thousand messages from different news groups, while typing in 'Buddhism and vegetarianism' will turn up fewer than twenty messages in which both the word 'Buddhism' and 'vegetarianism' have occurred. Once a basic list of messages is obtained, one can then view the messages, reply to them, send a query to their author, find a list of all other messages by that same author, find other messages on the same topic, and so forth.

One further possibility for those with web browsers is to point your browser to *www.io.com/~cin*. This is the address of a home page called the Buddhist Resource File. Following the instructions there will enable one to gain access to hundreds of on-line resources, such as e-mail forums, bibliographies, dictionaries, collections of electronic texts, home pages, and archives dedicated to a wide range of topics within Buddhism.

Anyone planning to do research on those members of the North American Buddhist community who communicate with one another through news groups on the Internet is likely find a gold mine of raw data just waiting to be refined and shaped into fascinating books, articles, and conference presentations.

Notes

1 Jochen Kleinshmict, 'Dissatisfaction with Expression of Dharma in the West,' on Forum on Indian and Buddhist Studies (then at BUDDHIST@JPNTUVM0.BITNET), May 28, 1992.

2 Karel Hladky, 'Thinking about Experience,' on Forum on Indian and Buddhist Studies (BUDDHIST@JPNTUVM0.BITNET), November 11, 1992.
3 Wayne Woo, 'The Need to Keep Buddhism Whole,' on news group talk.religion.buddhism, October 9, 1997.
4 Randy K. Otaka, 'On the Effects of Meditation,' on Forum on Indian and Buddhist Studies (then at BUDDHIST@VM1.MCGILL.CA), January 16, 1997.
5 Richard Hayes, 'Giving Thanks,' on Forum on Indian and Buddhist Studies (then at BUDDHIST@VM1.MCGILL.CA), November 25, 1993.

Part Four

The Scholar's Place in American Buddhist Studies

CHAPTER ELEVEN

The Academic Study of Buddhism in America: A Silent *Sangha*

Charles Prebish

Virtually everyone who begins an academic career in Buddhist Studies eventually pours through Étienne Lamotte's exciting volume *Histoire de Bouddhisme Indien des origines à l'ère Saka*, either in the original French or in Sara Webb-Boin's English translation.[1] That Lamotte was a Catholic priest seems not to have impaired either his understanding of, or respect for, the Buddhist tradition, although he did worry a bit from time to time about the reaction of the Vatican to his work. Edward Conze once remarked: 'When I last saw him [Lamotte], he had risen to the rank of Monseigneur and worried about how his "Histoire" had been received at the Vatican. "*Mon professeur*, do you think they will regard the book as *hérétique*?" They obviously did not.'[2] Although there have been only a few scholarly studies chronicling the academic investigation of Buddhism by Western researchers, and fewer still of the academic discipline known as Buddhist Studies, until quite recently, the issue of the religious affiliation of the researcher has not been part of the mix. Almost exclusively, the founding mothers and founding fathers of Buddhist Studies in the West have had personal religious commitments entirely separate from Buddhism.

As a novice graduate student in the Buddhist Studies program at the University of Wisconsin in the fall of 1967, I heard a story from the senior students about the recent visit of Edward Conze, the world's foremost scholar of that complicated form of Mahāyāna literature known as *prajñāpāramitā*. The narrative had nothing whatsoever to do with Professor Conze's great scholarly passion. Instead, it concerned a question, playfully put to the scholar during a seminar session: 'Dr. Conze, do *you* actually meditate?' Conze's simple reply: 'Yes.' But the student pressed on: 'Ever *get* anywhere?' The brusque response: 'First trance state.' The dialogue abruptly ceased and the issue was never broached again. Upon hearing that story as a naïve fledgling Buddhologist, I was utterly and absolutely astounded to learn that *any scholar* of Buddhism actually *did* anything Buddhist. Now, more than thirty years later, it is rather ordinary for individuals teaching Buddhist Studies in universities throughout the world to be 'scholar-practitioners,' involved in the practice of rituals associated with various Buddhist traditions and sects. The back cover of Georges Dreyfus's new book *Recognizing Reality: Dharmakīrti's Philosophy and Its Tibetan Interpretations*, for example, mentions his academic affiliation *and* the fact that he earned the monastic Geshe degree following fifteen years of study in Tibetan Buddhist monasteries in India.[3] Nonetheless, it is not always easy for these academics to reveal their religious orientation in an environment that is not uniformly supportive of such choices. Thus, this paper will serve the dual purpose of describing not only the *development* of the academic study of Buddhism in America but also some of the ways in which that development has affected the personal lives of those scholars who have made formal religious commitments to the Buddhist tradition.

European Antecedents

Curators of the Buddha: The Study of Buddhism under Colonialism,[4] a volume of scholarly essays edited by Donald Lopez, Jr., has attracted much attention. It was the topic of a panel at the 1995 annual meeting of the American Academy of Religion and the subject of a review article, 'Buddhist Studies in the Post-Colonial Age,' by Jan Nattier.[5] The book is a careful exercise in self-reflection, and Nattier is correct when she begins her article by observing, 'This is a provocative book in many senses of the word. By exploring not just the ideas but the attitudes conveyed in the writings of several founding fathers of Buddhist Studies in the West ... *Curators of the Buddha* will provoke its readers into seeing these figures in a new light.'[6] The book is not the first attempt to contextualize and comment upon the discipline of Buddhist Studies in the West, however.

Although there was very little reliable information in the West pertaining to Buddhism prior to the nineteenth century, Henri de Lubac's *La Rencontre du bouddhisme et l'occident*,[7] published in 1952, is especially useful in summarizing this early literature. Of course one can find such landmark works as Simon de la Loubère's *Du Royaume de Siam*,[8] published in 1691, but it was not until the early nineteenth century, with the appearance of Michel François Ozeray's *Recherches sur Buddhou*[9] (1817), that the picture began to brighten. Soon, the pioneering efforts of Henry Thomas Colebrooke, Brian Houghton Hodgson, Alexander Csoma de Körös, and Eugène Burnouf, followed by their intellectual heirs, brought the reliable study of Buddhism to Europe.

Despite the fact that the primary focus of the present volume is on North America rather than Europe, it is nonetheless imperative to sample the flavor of the Buddhist Studies that caught the fancy of the intellectual forebears of the American scholars of Buddhism. To a large extent, this interest in Buddhism was philological, converging on the increasing availability of Sanskrit and Pali manuscripts that were appearing on the European continent. Perhaps the most thorough examination of this development is Russell Webb's 'Pali Buddhist Studies in the West,'[10] serialized in the now defunct *Pali Buddhist Review*, which systematically reviews the developments of Pali and Buddhist Studies in virtually all European countries, as well as Canada and the United States. Webb continues this work, having updated these early studies, in 'Contemporary European Scholarship on Buddhism,'[11] published in 1989. But the interested scholar should also examine William Peiris's *The Western Contribution to Buddhism*,[12] which contains much historical detail and interesting character sketches of the early scholars of Buddhism. Jan W. de Jong's *A Brief History of Buddhist Studies in Europe and America*[13] also offers valuable information, although America is virtually absent from the volume, despite its title.

Several distinctions appear obvious from an examination of these sources. First, geographic associations seem to identify at least two 'schools' of Buddhology: the Anglo-German and the Franco-Belgian. The former (and older) was led by Thomas W. Rhys Davids and Hermann Oldenberg, while the latter included primarily Louis de La Vallée Poussin, Jean Przyluski, Sylvain Lévi, Paul Demiéville, and Étienne Lamotte. To these schools, Edward Conze, quite reasonably, adds a third: the Leningrad school,[14] including Stcherbatsky, Rosenberg, and Obermiller. The Anglo-German school almost exclusively emphasized the Pali literary tradition, while the Franco-Belgian school utilized the Sanskritic materials, along with their corresponding translations and commentaries in Chinese and Tibetan. The Leningrad school is clearly closer to the Franco-Belgian school than the Anglo-German. These are general classifications, but they nonetheless capture the style of the traditions as they have been maintained over the last century.

Early Buddhist Studies in America

Thomas Tweed's *The American Encounter with Buddhism 1844–1912: Victorian Culture and the Limits of Dissent*[15] is a wonderful and complete introduction to the early pioneers of the American Buddhist movement. For those unwilling to wade through more than two hundred pages of Tweed's meticulous prose, a pleasant narrative can be found in Rick Fields's chapter on 'The Restless Pioneers' in his *How the Swans Came to the Lake*.[16] Unfortunately, there are no such books or chapters documenting the development of the discipline of Buddhist Studies in America,[17] and the existence of such work remains a *desideratum*. Here we can only begin to sketch a very short overview of Buddhist Studies in America.

Although some might consider Eugène Burnouf the founding father of Buddhist Studies as a discipline,[18] the beginnings of Buddhist Studies in the

United States seems inextricably bound to three primary individuals: Paul Carus, Henry Clarke Warren, and Charles Rockwell Lanman. Carus arrived in America in the 1880s with a Ph.D. from Tübingen, eventually becoming the editor of *Open Court* journal and later of Open Court Publishing Company. His career and relationship to American Buddhist Studies are chronicled in an interesting new article by Martin Verhoeven, 'Americanizing the Buddha: The Perils and Promise of Acculturation.'[19] Although he wrote more than a dozen books of his own, including the still widely read *The Gospel of Buddha* (1894), Carus is probably best known for bringing D. T. Suzuki to America and employing him at Open Court for many years.

Henry Clarke Warren and Charles Rockwell Lanman were more scholarly in their approach than Carus, and worked diligently to establish the Buddhist literary tradition in America. Lanman had studied Sanskrit under William Dwight Whitney, earning his doctorate in 1875 before moving on to Johns Hopkins, and eventually becoming Professor of Sanskrit at Harvard University in 1880. Warren had studied Sanskrit with Lanman at Johns Hopkins, and followed his learned master back to Harvard, where the two struck up an alliance that culminated in the creation of a new publication series known as 'The Harvard Oriental Series.' Hendrik Kern's edition of the *Jātakamālā*, or collection of Buddhist birth stories, was the first edition, with Warren's famous *Buddhism in Translations* becoming the third volume in 1896.

Following Warren's death in 1899, and with Lanman moving on to other studies in the Indic tradition, the development of Buddhist Studies was carried on by others. One of these early trailblazers was Eugene Watson Burlingame, who had studied with Lanman at Harvard before shifting to Yale, where he worked industriously on a variety of Pali texts. By 1921 he had published a three-volume translation of the *Dhammapada* commentary in the Harvard Oriental Series. Burlingame was followed by W. Y. Evans-Wentz, a 1907 Stanford graduate, who studied extensively in Europe, and is best known for his collaborative compiling of the translations of his teacher, Kazi Dawa-Sandup. By the time of Evans-Wentz's death in 1965, a new group of Buddhological scholars had developed on the American scene, including such committed scholars as Winston King, Richard Gard, and Kenneth K. S. Ch'en.

Despite the work of these early educators, it was not until after 1960 that Buddhist Studies began to emerge as a significant discipline in the American university system and publishing industry. During the Vietnam War years and immediately thereafter, Buddhist Studies was to enjoy a boom, largely through the efforts of such leading professors as Richard Hugh Robinson of the University of Wisconsin, Masatoshi Nagatomi of Harvard University, and Alex Wayman of Columbia University. No doubt there were many reasons for the increased development of Buddhist Studies, not the least of which were the increase in area studies programs in American universities; growing government interest in things Asian; the immense social anomie that permeated American culture in the 1960s; and the growing dissatisfaction with (and perhaps rejection of) traditional religion. During the 1960s, a formal graduate program was instituted at the University of Wisconsin, offering both an M.A. and a Ph.D. in Buddhist Studies. Interdisciplinary programs emphasizing the study of Buddhism were soon available at Berkeley and Columbia as well. As other programs arose, such as the program at the Center for the Study of World Religions at Harvard University, and the history of religions program at the University of Chicago, it became possible to gain sophisticated training in all aspects of the Buddhist tradition, and in all Buddhist canonical languages as well. As a result, a new generation of young Buddhologists was born, appearing rapidly on the campuses of many American universities, and rivaling their overseas peers in both training and insight.

This picture of expanding American Buddhology is perhaps not so rosy as one might think, its rapid growth notwithstanding. As interest grew, funding for graduate education did not keep pace, and would-be Buddhologists no longer had the luxury of being able to spend six or more *fully-funded* years in preparation for the Ph.D. As a result, the breadth and scope of their training was compromised, resulting in greater specialization. The consequence was that very few new Buddhologists were appearing with the complete philological training and geographical comprehensiveness of their teachers. Thus, it became usual to find individuals focusing on *one tradition*, such as Indian or Tibetan or Chinese or Japanese Buddhism, but rarely *all* of the traditions. And if the distinctions that characterize the Anglo-German, Franco-Belgian, and Leningrad schools, mentioned above, are accurate, the 'American' school is equally divided within itself.

Current Buddhist Studies

More than fifteen years ago, I titled a review article on recent Buddhist literature 'Buddhist Studies American Style: A Shot in the Dark,' explaining at the outset that the conjured image of Inspector Clouseau 'falling through banisters, walking into walls, crashing out of windows, and somehow miraculously getting the job done with the assistance of his loyal Oriental servant,'[20] was not an accidental choice on my part; that Buddhist Studies in America was just as erratic as poor Clouseau.

Lately, as noted above, Buddhist Studies in America has begun to engage in the useful process of self-reflection, and the results of that inquiry are fruitful and inspiring. Following David Seyfort Ruegg's insightful 'Some Observations on the Present and Future of Buddhist Studies,'[21] the *Journal of the International Association of Buddhist Studies* devoted an entire issue (Winter 1995) to the topic entitled 'On Method,' providing the occasion for scholars to reflect on various aspects of the discipline. José Cabezón summarizes the critical question:

> Although the academic study of Buddhism is much older than the International Association of Buddhist Studies and the journal to which it gave rise, the founding of the latter, which represents a significant – perhaps pivotal – step in the institutionalization of the field, is something that occurred less than twenty years ago. Nonetheless, whether a true discipline or not – whether or not Buddhist Studies has already achieved disciplinary status, whether it is proto-disciplinary or superdisciplinary – there is an apparent integrity to Buddhist Studies that at the very least calls for an analysis of the field in holistic terms.[22]

One must be aware, too, that there is a vast chasm between Buddhist Studies and other disciplinary studies in religion, such as Christian Studies. In the same forum, Luis Gómez notes:

> The difference between Christian and Buddhist Studies is perhaps in part explained by the fact that Buddhist Studies continues to be a Western enterprise about a non-Western cultural product, a discourse about Buddhism taking place in a non-Buddhist context for a non-Buddhist audience of super-specialists, whose intellectual work persists in isolation from the mainstream of Western literature, art, and philosophy, and occasionally even from the mainstream of contemporary Buddhist doctrinal reflection. The audience to which Christian Studies speaks shares with the Judeo-Christian tradition a more or less common language. It is possible, if not natural, for members of the audience to accept the conceit that they belong to the tradition and the tradition belongs to them.... Furthermore, whereas Christianity and Christian Studies as we know them are the fruit of a continuous interaction with Western secularism, rationalism, and the modern and postmodern Western self, most of our Buddhist materials and many of our Asian informants belong to a very different cultural tradition. The methods and expectations of our scholarship and our audiences have been shaped by a cultural history very different from that of Buddhist traditions.[23]

The homogeneity that a 'common pattern of institutional support provides' is simply lacking in Buddhist Studies, as Buddhologists invariably find their academic homes in Religious Studies departments, area studies centers, language institutes, and even schools of theology, as Cabezón points out.[24] Thus, when he goes on to identify Buddhist Studies as a 'hodge-podge,' signalling its *heterogeneity*, this is no surprise. Nor should it be when he proclaims, 'Now that the cat is out of the bag, what will guarantee the stability and longevity of the discipline is not the *insistence on homogeneity*, which in any case can now only be achieved through force, but instead by *embracing heterogeneity.*'[25]

To this point, what has also been ostensibly lacking in the discussion is a consideration of that portion of the community of North American Buddhologists which falls into a category that is most properly labelled 'scholar-practitioner.' Of the 106 respondents to the survey whose results will be reported below, *at least* 25 percent are openly Buddhist (although religious affiliation was *not* one of the items queried). It is my best estimate that *at least* another 25 percent remain silent about their Buddhist practice, for reasons which will become apparent. In many respects, these 'silent Buddhists' are known to each other, but not to the larger community. During my early years at Pennsylvania State University, my Buddhist Studies predecessor, Garma Chen-chi Chang, often invited me into his home for morning discussion. On these days he frequently met me in completely informal attire and made green tea for us to share as we sat on the floor of his living room. Never did this discussion ever address my progress in my new position in the religious studies department. Never did this discussion ever address my research progress or predicaments. Instead, it always concerned my own Buddhist practice, and the utterly compassionate advice of an older, and wiser, longstanding practitioner. My colleague worried not at all about my professional growth, which he assumed would develop properly, but about my spiritual health in a new and challenging environment. It was a discussion we shared with each other and never with non-Buddhists. Later, I learned why. In 1972, after a short research trip to Riverside, California, to work briefly with Professor Francis (Dōjun) Cook, a fine scholar and a serious Zen practitioner who was contributing several chapters to my forthcoming book *Buddhism: A Modern Perspective*, and who was more at ease with his personal commitment to Buddhism than any Westerner I had ever met, I finally summoned the strength to declare to one of my Penn State colleagues that I was indeed Buddhist. His immediate response, knowing my Jewish heritage, was to say, 'Oh, now you've become *Buddhish.*' It wasn't a joke, and I always wondered if it colored his future estimates of my scholarship.

In 'The Ghost at the Table: On the Study of Buddhism and the Study of Religion,' Malcolm David Eckel writes in his conclusion:

> It is not just students who are attracted to religious studies because they 'want to know what it is to be human and humane, and intuit that religion deals with such things.' There are at least a few scholars of Buddhism who feel the same way. For me the biggest unsettled question in the study of Buddhism is not whether Buddhism is religious or even whether the study of Buddhism is religious; it is whether scholars in this field can find a voice that does justice to their own religious concerns and can demonstrate to the academy why their kind of knowledge is worth having.[26]

Later in this paper we shall examine with much specificity *how* the academic study of Buddhism in America now proceeds, but even the question of *where* to study Buddhism has been gaining greater, and continued, attention, and not only in scholarly sources. In a recent issue of *Tricycle: The Buddhist Review*, Duncan Ryūken Williams, an ordained Sōtō Zen priest and Ph.D. candidate at Harvard University, compiled a short list of institutions which offer graduate study in Buddhism. Although Williams's listing includes the expected sorts of categories ('Most Comprehensive Programs,' 'Institutions with Strength in Indo-Tibetan Buddhist Studies,' and so forth), he also includes a category called 'Practitioner-Friendly Institutions.' About these he says,

> [T]here are a number of degree programs that encourage or support Buddhist practice and scholarship among students. These 'practi-tioner-friendly' programs generally offer one of three things: the ability to pursue a degree in the context of Buddhist priestly training, courses in the practice of Buddhism that complement academic study, or an emphasis on Buddhism from a normative point of view.[27]

Williams comes right to the edge of the scholar-practitioner pond when he notes, 'At most universities, faculty members in Buddhist studies tend to be far fewer in number than their Christian or Jewish counterparts,'[28] but he chooses not to jump into the issue. Cabezón and Gómez elect to take the leap, both dramatically and insightfully. In advancing his comprehensive discussion of the discipline of Buddhist Studies, Cabezón suggests:

> One of the best entries into the identification of the variant kinds of scholarship is not through their sympathetic depiction, but through their caricature in stereotypes. These stereotypes are associated with specific racial/ethnic, national, religious and gender characteristics. Like all stereotypes, they are falsehoods: racist, sexist, and generally exhibiting the type of intolerance to which we as human beings are unfortunately heir. But exist they do.[29]

While Cabezón lists nine specific stereotypes, each of which is interesting in its own right, it is the first of those that informs this enterprise:

> Critical distance from the object of intellectual analysis is necessary. Buddhists, by virtue of their religious commitment, lack such critical distance from Buddhism. Hence, Buddhists are *never* good buddhol-ogists. Or, alternatively, those who take any aspect of Buddhist doctrine seriously (whether pro or con) are scientifically suspect by virtue of allowing their individual beliefs to affect their scholarship. Good scholarship is neutral as regards questions of truth. Hence, evaluative/ normative scholarship falls outside the purview of Buddhist Studies.[30]

Without undervaluing the critical goals implicit in all Buddhological scholarship, Gómez adds yet another dimension to the conversation, arguably the most critical. He says:

> Contemporary Buddhists, wherever they might be, are also an audience for our scholarship.... They can be a source (however maligned and deprived of authority they may sometimes appear) because, inevitably, they speak to us and make demands on us.... But in our field the object is also a voice that speaks to us and hears us. It is present not only as object but as a set of voices that demands something from us. In fact our 'object' has had a biographic presence in all of our lives – *especially on those of us who can remember moments in our life narratives in which we have 'felt Buddhist' or 'have been Buddhists' or have 'practiced,' as the contemporary English expression has it*. I would venture more, even for those who at one time or another have seen in some fragment of Buddhist tradition a particle of inspiration or an atom of insight, Buddhism is an object that makes claims on their lives. For those who have failed even to experience this last form of interaction with the object, there must have been at least moments of minimal encounters with seeking students or, after a dry and erudite lecture, one of those emotional questions from the audience that makes all scholars nervous.[31]

Of course the above places the contemporary Buddhologist squarely between the proverbial rock and hard place. If one acknowledges a personal commitment to the tradition being studied, the suspicion Cabezón cites so clearly is immediately voiced; but if one remains silent, how can the demands Gómez outlines be fairly confronted? These are issues not confronted by the American scholar of Judaism or Christianity, and they are a powerful impetus for the silence among Buddhologists alluded to in the paper title.

The Academic Study of Buddhism in America: A Current Analysis

This paper has made references to the perceptive reflections on the field of Buddhist Studies by Cabezón, Conze, de Jong, Gómez, Lopez, Peiris, and Ruegg, among others. What each of the above studies has lacked is a statistical component, and of course the need for data that a survey might provide is not, as I have indicated elsewhere,[32] without current precedent.

In the winter 1991 issue of the *Journal of the American Academy of Religion*, former editor Ray L. Hart was afforded 112 pages to present the results of a survey entitled 'Religious and Theological Studies in American Higher Education: A Pilot Study.'[33] Thirty-five pages of his 'report' were devoted to a presentation of the statistical evidence gleaned from a questionnaire distributed to 678 faculty members at 11 types of institutions;

the rest of the space was devoted to Hart's interpretive narrative. Interestingly, he devotes an entire section of that narrative to a consideration of the key questions: 'What is the relation between the *study* of religion and theology and the *practice* of religion?' and 'What should the relation be?' Perhaps as expected, he could find only one statement on which all faculty everywhere agree: 'One who practices religion needs to study it.'[34] This of course begs the larger question, and Hart tries to clarify the three obvious positions he elicited:[35]

1. The first view is that the study of religion and the practice of religion are two integral 'terms'; each has its 'site' and the two are not internally related.
2. The second view is that 'the relation is completely open.'
3. The third view will by now be obvious: the study of religion presupposes practice, and is undertaken to prepare for and enhance practice.

Hart's useful findings have already been widely utilized in the discipline, clearly reflecting the perceived importance of self-definition and self-recognition within the broad profession of Religious Studies.

Curiously, Hart's findings were nearly chronologically coincident with a five-year administrative review of the Buddhism Section of the American Academy of Religion (AAR), arguably the largest academic arena for Buddhologists in North America (if not the entire world). AAR's external evaluator for that review, Malcolm David Eckel of Boston University, noted in his December 1991 report:

> The most important achievement of the Buddhism Group and Section at the AAR in the last 10 years has been to create a safe and reliable forum for Buddhist scholars who represent a wide variety of approaches, disciplines, and geographical orientations to exchange views and build bonds of cooperation and understanding that create an active and imaginative scholarly community.[36]

In a later article,[37] Eckel reveals that in the five years between 1986 and 1991, the attendance at the Buddhism Section's annual business meeting grew from 60 to 140, and the mailing list expanded from 106 to 600!

With interest piqued by the data included in Hart's report and the suppositions inherent in Eckel's, in October 1992, I set out to gather materials from the North American community of Buddhologists that would afford this community data similar to Hart's upon which to conduct a second level of self-reflection. It was clear from the outset that the 600-member mailing list mentioned above contained, in addition to so-called Buddhologists, a large number of scholars of other Asian religions, many non-specialist comparativists, and a profusion of 'others.' After careful sorting and synthesis, a list of 125 scholars whose primary teaching and research work fell within the discipline of Buddhist Studies was compiled, and these individuals were sent requests soliciting both data and narrative statements about the discipline. Following two additional requests, and with a rather surprising response rate of 69.6 percent (compared with Hart's 64 percent), the received material was collated. The preliminary results were presented in a paper at the 1993 AAR annual meeting in Washington, D.C., and published in the fledgling electronic journal *Gassho*, with the full results appearing slightly later in *Religion*,[38] jointly published in England and the United States.

For this current paper, a second survey was conducted, beginning in fall 1995. In the intervening years, the list was updated, revised, and refined, reflecting the arrival of new scholars into the Buddhological community, the death of others, and shifting interests. Thus, the initial list of requests in the new survey numbered 140, with 106 responses received (or 75.7 percent). On an individual level, the results collected provide an ample look at the demographics of Buddhist Studies in America. With regard to individual training, I am able to document the gender, educational background, language facility, and the like for those polled. Institutionally, I have tracked the respective academic rank of the respondents, the type of university in which they teach, and the specific department that employs each. I have collected data on memberships in professional organizations, editorships held, geographical area(s) of specialization, grants and fellowships received, professional papers presented, honors awarded, and various categories of publications (including books, refereed articles, and book reviews). From the narratives included with many of the responses, I have been able to determine a sense of the sample's collective perception of those issues deemed critical to the continuing development and advancement of the discipline. It was also possible to compile information on universities with extensive resources for the study of Buddhism. As such, the remainder of this paper provides the documentation for the most recent, and most productive, generation of Buddhologists in America.

Individual Results

Regarding basic demographics, in Hart's survey, 85.4 percent of the respondents were male, 14.4 percent female, with .2 percent not answering (p. 796). In my latest sample, 83 percent were male, 17 percent female, representing a small increase in percentage of females from my previous investigation (which was 85.1 percent male, 14.9 percent female). Hart's survey revealed 90 percent of the respondents with one or more doctoral degrees; 9 percent with no doctoral degree; and 1 percent expecting the doctoral degree (p. 800). In my sample, 99.1 percent (105 of 106) had a Ph.D/Th.D. This was quite consistent with my previous survey, which revealed a 98.8 percent rate for doctoral degrees. However, my sample seems to suggest a slightly younger discipline overall than several years ago: my earlier sample yielded 1975.9 as the average year for the granting of the terminal degree, whereas the newer sample shows 1980.0 as the average year. The earliest doctoral degree recorded was 1948 and the most recent 1996. In decades, the breakdown yields:

Decade Ph.D/Th.D Granted	Number of Respondents
1990s	21
1980s	45
1970s	25
1960s	12
1950s	1
1940s	1

The majority of the respondents in my studies earned their doctorates at the following universities:

University	1993 Survey	1995 Survey
University of Chicago	8	14
University of Wisconsin	10	12
Harvard University	10	10
Columbia University	5	10
Yale University	6	7
University of Virginia	7	7
Stanford University	–	6
University of California (Berkeley)	4	5
Princeton University	3	4
Temple University	5	4
Northwestern University	3	3
University of Michigan	–	3
University of Washington	–	2
Tokyo University	–	2

In my 1993 survey, 44.9 percent of those responding taught in various public institutions, while 55.1 percent were employed by private institutions. The 1995 sample closely mirrors that result, with 44.4 percent of those responding teaching in various public institutions, 52.8 percent employed by private institutions, and 2.8 percent employed in other professional settings. Regarding rank, the following results were obtained:

Rank	1993 Survey	1995 Survey
Emeritus	–	2.8%
Full Professor	36.0%	33.0%
Associate Professor	31.4%	33.0%
Assistant Professor	22.1%	22.7%
Lecturer	–	3.8%
Other	10.5%	4.7%

In the 1993 survey, the emeritus rank was combined with Lecturer, Adjunct Professor, Dean, and Acting Dean. In 1995, a separate category for Emeritus is listed.

In terms of specialization, any comparison between samples would be incongruous because, for the 1993 sample, only one primary specialization was recorded, while in the 1995 sample, it became clear that in many cases, multiple specializations were emphasized. As such, in 1993, 37.0 percent of the sample reported specializing in Japan/East Asia, while 29.6 percent reported India/South Asia, 23.5 percent Tibet/Inner Asia, 6.2 percent China/East Asia, 2.5 percent Korea/East Asia, and 1.2 percent indicated other choices. Bearing in mind that multiple listings were allowed in the 1995 sample, yielding a total in excess of 100 percent, the survey showed:

Area	Number of Respondents	Percent
Japan/East Asia	39	36.8
India/South Asia	37	34.9
Tibet/Inner Asia	22	20.8
China/East Asia	16	15.1
Korea/East Asia	2	1.9
Other Areas	3	2.8

Language facility seems to be rather consistent with area specialization, taking into account that many scholars develop a multiplicity of language skills, and that Sanskrit appears to be the consistent foundation language from which other studies in Buddhism proceed:

Language	Number of Respondents
Sanskrit	59
Japanese	49
Pali/Prakrit	43
Chinese	37
Tibetan	33
Korean	2

Other languages cited include Hindi, Sinhalese, Nepali, Thai, Mongolian, Sogdian, and Vietnamese.

With regard to membership in professional and learned societies, Hart's study produced extremely surprising results, considering the nature of his sample.[39] Of the seven most populated professional organizations, *four* had traditionally Asian constituencies: the Association for Asian Studies (2nd; 22 percent); the American Oriental Society (4th; 17 percent); the International Association of Buddhist Studies (tied for 6th; 8 percent); and the Society for Asian and Comparative Philosophy (tied for 6th; 8 percent). Not unexpectedly, the American Academy of Religion topped the list with 67 percent, while the Society of Biblical Literature was third with 19 percent. In the Buddhist Studies sample, a wide variety of professional societies was noted. Presented below is a comparison of the 1993 and 1995 results:

Organization	1993 Response Percent (No.)	1995 Response Percent (No.)
American Academy of Religion	75.9% (66)	87.7% (93)
Association for Asian Studies	57.5% (50)	57.8% (61)
International Association of Buddhist Studies	43.7% (38)	47.2% (50)
Society for Buddhist-Christian Studies	19.5% (17)	20.8% (22)
Society for Asian and Comp. Philosophy	17.2% (15)	15.1% (16)
American Oriental Society	16.1% (14)	12.3% (13)
Society for the Study of Japanese Religions	10.3% (9)	11.3% (12)
Society for the Study of Chinese Religions	8.0% (7)	11.3% (12)
Society for Tantric Studies	–	9.4% (10)
International Association of Shin Buddhist Studies	6.9% (6)	8.5% (9)
Pali Text Society	6.9% (6)	4.7% (5)

Other societies garnering multiple mention by the respondents, in decreasing order, include the Buddhist Peace Fellowship, the Tibet Society, the International Association for the History of Religion, the T'ang Studies Society, and the International Association of Tibetan Studies. As expected, most respondents reported multiple, and often many, memberships.

Many respondents in the most recent Buddhist Studies sample reported significant offices and administrative positions in the above societies. These include:

American Academy of Religion
> **Office:**
>> President (1)
>> Board of Directors (1)

> **Chair/Co-Chair:**
>> Buddhism Group/Section (5)
>> Japanese Religions Group (3)
>> Comparative Studies in Religion Section (3)
>> Tantric Studies Seminar (2)
>> Asian Religions/History of Religion Section (2)
>> Electronic Publications Committee (2)
>> Publications Committee (2)
>> Himalayan & Tibetan Religions Consultation (1)
>> Program Committee (1)
>> Religion & Ecology Group (1)

Steering Committee:
Buddhism Group/Section (9)
Japanese Religions Group (5)
Ritual Studies Group (3)
Himalayan & Tibetan Religions Consultation (3)
Tantric Studies Seminar (2)
Korean Religions Group (2)
Religion and Ecology Group (1)
Mysticism Group (1)
East Asian Religions Consultation (1)
Asian Religions/History of Religion Section (1)
Comparative Study in Hinduism & Judaism Consultation (1)

Association for Asian Studies
Buddhist Studies Steering Committee (4)
Board of Directors (2)
Program Committee (1)
Korean Studies Chair (1)
South Asia Council (1)
Northeast Asia Council (1)

International Association of Buddhist Studies
Board of Directors (4)
General Secretary (2)
Secretary (1)
Associate Secretary (1)
Treasurer (1)

Society for Buddhist-Christian Studies
Board of Directors (5)
President (2)
Vice-President (2)
Secretary (1)

Society for the Study of Japanese Religions
President (3)

Society for the Study of Chinese Religions
President (1)
Secretary-Treasurer (1)
Board of Directors (1)

International Association of Shin Buddhist Studies
Vice-President (3)
Steering Committee (2)
Board of Directors (1)

In addition, respondents reported one Executive Director and five Board of Directors positions with the Kuroda Institute and at least one reported position in the Pali Text Society, American Oriental Society, Tibet Society, Mongolian Society, Society for Asian and Comparative Philosophy, and the Buddhist Peace Fellowship.

The sample has shown a remarkably high level of activity in presenting scholarly papers at the annual meetings of the professional societies listed above. Additionally, those sampled have been very active in presenting scholarly papers (not simply 'lectures') in other professional settings, such as international conferences, regional professional meetings, and thematic conferences sponsored by various institutions. Adjusting the results to reflect those who did not respond with information on this item, the findings show:

Papers at Annual Meeting	4.4 per respondent
Other Scholarly Papers	12.2 per respondent

Thus, the average respondent has made 16.6 professional presentations during their academic career. That this figure is slightly lower than the 19.8 figure reported in the 1993 sample reflects the earlier supposition that the 1995 sample is slightly junior to the previous group of respondents.

The Buddhist Studies sample presented a high magnitude of success in grant and fellowship acquisition, both during graduate training and after the granting of the Ph.D. degree. Again adjusting for those who did not respond with information in this category of inquiry, the sample reported 2.2 grants per respondent at the graduate school level. This included such items as National Defense Education Act Fellowships, Fulbright awards, and the like, but not assistantships of any kind. With Ph.D. in hand, the sample then reported:

Grant/Fellowship Agency	1993 Sample (No. of Awards)	1995 Sample (No. of Awards)
National Endowment for the Humanities	57	73
Fulbright	35	24
American Council of Learned Societies	14	24
Japan Foundation	13	17
Social Science Research Council	8	8
American Academy of Religion	–	5
Lilly Foundation	–	4
Pew Charitable Trusts	–	4

In addition, grants from the Ford Foundation, Mellon Foundation, Danforth Foundation, and Rockefeller Foundation were cited, along with hundreds of grants internally administered by the various faculty members' host institutions. National and international grants yielded 2.1 awards per respondent, while internal university grants totaled 2.4 awards per respondent. As such, the sample reports a total of 6.7 awards per respondent across the scope of their activity in the discipline.

Just as the Buddhist Studies sample presented highly active involvement in professional societies and significant success in grant and fellowship acquisition, it also demonstrated a high degree of accomplishment in securing meaningful editorial positions with leading academic presses and journals. No less than 6 individuals are editors for book series with university presses, while another 10 sit on university press editorial boards. Presses represented in this group include Oxford University Press, Indiana University Press, University of California Press, University of Michigan Press, Princeton University Press, University of Virginia Press, and the State University of New York Press. Additionally, 19 respondents edit book series for commercial/trade publishers, while another 7 are editorial board members. Some of the presses cited in this category include Snow Lion, Shambhala, Motilal Banarsidass, Curzon Press, Wadsworth, Buddhica Britannica, the Kuroda Institute Series (published by the University of Hawaii Press), and the AAR Monograph and AAR Texts and Translations Series (both published by Scholars Press).

Many respondents report major editorial positions with journals, including:

Editor-in-Chief/Co-Editor (14)
Buddhist-Christian Studies
Buddhist and Tibetan Studies
Critical Review of Books in Religion
History of Religions
Indo-Judaic Studies
Japanese Journal of Religious Studies
Journal of Buddhist Ethics
Journal of Buddhist Literature
Journal of the International
   Association of Buddhist Studies
Korean Culture
Pacific World

Associate/Assistant Editor (9)
Critical Review of Books in
   Religion
The Eastern Buddhist
History of Religions
Journal of Asian Studies
Journal of Ecumenical Studies
Journal of Indian Philosophy
Journal of the International
   Association of Buddhist Studies
Journal of Religious Ethics

As well, 9 individuals hold or have held Book Review Editorships at *Buddhist-Christian Studies, Journal of Chinese Philosophy, Pacific World, Philosophy East and West,* and *Religious Studies Review.* Another 2 have held Guest Editor positions at *Cahiers d'Extrême-Asie* and *Journal of Religious Ethics.* Finally, 45 respondents cited positions on the editorial boards of many of the journals listed above, as well as the *Chung-Hwa Buddhist Studies Journal, Garuda, Gender and World Religion, Journal of Asian Philosophy, Journal of the American Academy of Religion, Journal of Chinese Religions, Journal of Comparative Sociology and Religion, Journal of Feminist Studies in Religion, Numen, Soundings, Studies in Central and East Asian Religion, T'ang Studies,* and *The Tibet Journal.*

Although it has never been clear how to report scholarly publication data with precision, Ray Hart's study utilizes three categories: (1) Books, (2) Articles, Essays, Chapters, and (3) Book Reviews. Hart is only concerned with the immediately past five-year period. In other words, Hart presents no career publication data, a statistic which may well be more revealing than his five-year information. Thus, in this study, I have confined myself to presenting *only* career data. The categories are at once problematic in that Hart does not distinguish between refereed and non-refereed publications, a distinction now made in virtually all colleges and universities. Equally, Hart makes no distinction between books authored and books edited, another distinction that is part of the politically correct protocol of the American system of higher education.

In an attempt to address the exigencies of that system, I have sought to refine Hart's categories somewhat in favor of presenting more meaningful statistics. In so doing, I have separated the book category into two sub-categories: (a) Books Authored/Co-Authored and (b) Books Edited/Co-Edited. I have also pared Hart's Articles, Essays, Chapters category into Refereed Articles and Chapters (taking the stand, not shared in all university evaluations, that chapters are indeed refereed, often bringing to bear a higher standard than many refereed journals). In my schema, the following career results can be reported:

Category of Publication	1993 Sample Average (No.)	1995 Sample Average (No.)
Books Authored/Co-Authored	2.4 (209)	2.3 (239)
Books Edited/Co-Edited	1.7 (148)	1.1 (116)
Refereed Articles & Refereed Chapters	16.8 (1462)[40]	6.5 (689)
Book Reviews	12.7 (1105)	12.9 (962)[41]

Allowing adjustment of the sample to reflect career duration, the two sets of results are remarkably similar. Further, by refining the data collection in the 1995 sample, it was possible to determine that 126 of the 355 books reported were published with university presses. Allowing for multiple authorship/editorship, it was possible to name and rank those book publishers most often utilized as publication avenues for Buddhist Studies. As such, we can offer the following ranked list:[42]

University Presses	Trade/Commercial Presses
1. State University of New York Press	1. Snow Lion
2. University of Hawaii Press	2. Prentice-Hall
3. Princeton University Press	3. E.J. Brill (tie)
4. University of California Press	3. Motilal Banarsidass (tie)

5. Oxford University Press
6. University of Chicago Press
7. Columbia University Press
8. Cambridge University Press
9. Penn State University Press (tie)
9. University of S. Carolina Press (tie)

5. Tungta (tie)
5. Wisdom Publications (tie)
7. Shambhala (tie)
7. Greenwood Press (tie)
7. Orbis (tie)
7. Asian Humanities Press (tie)

It is also possible to determine a ranked list of refereed journals most often utilized as a publication outlet by the overall sample. This list includes:[43]

1. *History of Religions*
2. *Buddhist-Christian Studies*
3. *Journal of the International Association of Buddhist Studies*
4. *Philosophy East and West*
5. *The Eastern Buddhist*
6. *Journal of the American Academy of Religion*
7. *Japanese Journal of Religious Studies*
8. *Journal of the American Oriental Society*
9. *Pacific World*
10. *Tibet Journal*
11. *Numen* (tie)
11. *Journal of Indian Philosophy* (tie)
13. *The Journal of Asian Studies* (tie)
13. *Religion* (tie)
13. *Monumenta Nipponica* (tie)
13. *Journal of Religious Studies* (tie)
13. *Studia Missionalia* (tie)
13. *Journal of Chinese Philosophy* (tie)

Institutional Results

On the surface, it would appear that tracking institutional programs in Buddhist Studies should be quite easy. One might simply turn first to those universities, listed earlier, which produced the largest numbers of doctoral degrees among the 106 respondents to the individual portion of the survey. By cross-referencing with the latest *Directory of Departments and Programs of Religious Studies in North America* (edited by David G. Truemper), and with the appropriate portion of the World Wide Web pages maintained by these major universities, the results ought to be readily apparent. One could then add to the tracking process by following *where* the recipients of these doctoral degrees are currently employed. To some extent, that was how I compiled my 1993 results, although the World Wide Web was far less useful at that time.

In 1993, I reported that only two North American universities had more than three full-time faculty members whose work falls within the discipline of Buddhology: the University of Virginia and the University of Chicago. Additionally, I reported that Harvard University, Columbia University, the University of Michigan, Princeton University, and McMaster University had three full-time Buddhist Studies faculty members as well; a much larger list of universities with two Buddhist Studies faculty was cited.

However, like all disciplines, Buddhist Studies is continually changing, primarily as a result of faculty relocation, altered interests, retirement, and new hires from the continually increasing number of newly minted scholars entering the field. José Cabezón accurately points out:

> For about a decade or so, buddhologists in North America have found employment in increasing numbers in departments of religious studies and schools of theology. Often this has meant that we have had to expand our pedagogical repertoire beyond courses in Buddhist Studies to accommodate the curricular need of these institutions.[44]

After surveying a number of issues having impact on Buddhist Studies, Cabezón goes on to conclude:

> All of these factors have contributed to what we might call the diversification of the buddhologist: a movement away from classical Buddhist Studies based on the philological study of written texts, and toward the investigation of more general, comparative and often theoretical issues that have implications (and audiences) outside of Buddhist Studies. Some colleagues have resigned themselves to this situation: a set of circumstances that must be tolerated for the sake of gainful employment. Others – and I count myself in this camp – have found the pressure to greater diversification intellectually stimulating, affording an opportunity to enter into broader conversations where Buddhist texts are one, but not the only, voice.[45]

Thus it is no longer completely clear what constitutes a full-time Buddhologist, and when one factors in the movement in the opposite direction – scholars from other disciplines incorporating Buddhist materials into their work – the entire issue of listing the number of full-time Buddhologists in any unit becomes quite murky.

One such attempt to at least begin the task of surveying institutions has been undertaken by Duncan Williams of Harvard University and cited above. Williams devises a number of classificatory categories for the accredited degree-granting institutions he surveys:[46]

Practitioner-Friendly Institutions
California Institute of Integral Studies
Graduate Theological Union
Hsi Lai University
Institute of Buddhist Studies
Naropa Institute

Most Comprehensive Programs
Harvard University
Indiana University
University of Chicago
University of Hawaii at Manoa
University of Michigan
University of Virginia

Institutions with Strength in East Asian Buddhist Studies
Princeton University
Stanford University
University of Arizona
University of California at Los Angeles
University of California at Santa Barbara
University of Pennsylvania
Yale University

Institutions with Strength in Indo-Tibetan Buddhist Studies
Harvard University
University of Michigan
University of Virginia
University of Washington

Institutions with Strength in Southeast Asian Buddhist Studies
Harvard University
University of Chicago

Other Noteworthy Programs
Columbia University
University of California at Berkeley
University of Texas at Austin
University of Wisconsin

These results reflect precisely the kind of dilemma suggested by Cabezón: what to include and what not to include, and who counts where? For example, the University of Wisconsin, which is one of only two universities in the United States to offer a Ph.D. in Buddhist Studies, is omitted from Williams's 'Most Comprehensive Programs' list and cited only as a 'Noteworthy Program.' In fact, the University of Wisconsin continues to list a complete and comprehensive curriculum in Buddhist Studies in spite of the fact that faculty members Williams listed will soon be retired. Williams chooses not to list outstanding undergraduate institutions that offers Buddhist Studies, such as Carleton, Williams, Smith, and Amherst. Finally, Williams defines the term 'America,' to mean the 'United States.' Yet a number of Canadian universities boast strong Buddhist Studies faculties. McMaster University, for example, has a faculty that includes Phyllis Granoff, Graeme MacQueen, Koichi Shinohara, and Yun-hua Jan, *emeritus*. The University of Calgary could easily have been included as well (with Leslie Kawamura, A. W. Barber, X. J. Yang, and regular visiting appointments through the Numata Chair in Buddhist Studies). This review highlights the fact that identifying and classifying the Buddhist Studies academic landscape is significantly more difficult than first meets the eye.

Despite the fact that there is no easy way to synthesize faculty size with the comprehensiveness of any given Buddhist Studies curriculum, current materials in my possession at least enable me to provide a listing that attempts to harmonize the two factors above and thus augments, and hopefully enhances, that of Duncan Williams. As such, the following listing proceeds from the institution with the most complete program in Buddhist Studies downward (and includes all faculty who make a substantial contribution to that program).

Harvard University
Charles Hallisey
Helen Hardacre
Christopher Queen
Oktor Skjaervo
Stanley Tambiah
Leonard van der Kuijp

Indiana University
Stephen Bokenkamp
Robert Campany
John McRae
Jan Nattier
Eliot Sperling
Michael Walter

Princeton University
Martin Collcutt
Gananath Obeyesekere
Soho Machida
Jacqueline Stone
Stephen Teiser

University of Hawaii
Helen Baroni
David Chappell
David Kalupahana
Steve Odin
Graham Parkes
George Tanabe
Willa Tanabe
Oung Thwin

University of Wisconsin
Gudrun Buhnemann
Minoru Kiyota
Geshe Sopa
Gautam Vajracharya
Tongchai Winchakul
André Wink

University of Virginia
David Germano
Paul Groner
Jeffrey Hopkins
Karen Lang
H. L. Seneviratne

University of Chicago
Steven Collins
Paul Griffiths
Matthew Kapstein
Frank Reynolds

University of Washington
Collett Cox
Ter Ellingson
Charles Keyes
Richard Salomon

McMaster University
Phyllis Granoff
Graeme MacQueen
Koichi Shinohara

University of Michigan
Luis Gómez
Donald Lopez
Robert Sharf

University of Colorado
Robert Lester
Reginald Ray
Eric Reinders

University of Calgary
A. W. Barber
Leslie Kawamura
X. J Yang

In addition to the above, a number of other North American universities and colleges have at least two faculty members whose work falls primarily into the discipline of Buddhist Studies: Carleton College (Roger Jackson, Mark Unno), Columbia University (Ryuichi Abe and Robert Thurman), Florida State University (Tessa Bartholomeusz, Daniel Lusthaus), McGill University (Richard Hayes, Arvind Sharma), Smith College (Jamie Hubbard, Taitetsu Unno), State University of New York at Stony Brook (Sung Taek Cho, Sung Bae Park), University of California at Berkeley (Padmanabh Jaini, Lewis Lancaster), University of California at Los Angeles (Robert Buswell, William Bodiford), and the University of Saskatchewan (James Mullens, Braj Sinha).

Conclusions

In the years between 1972 and 1978, while I was doing fieldwork for my book *American Buddhism*, I visited more American Buddhist groups than I can now remember and, although such educational enterprises as Nyingma Institute (founded in 1973) and Naropa Institute (founded in 1974) were still young and sparse on the American Buddhist landscape, there was scarcely a group I visited that didn't aggressively emphasize the relationship between, and need for, *both* study and practice. In an experiential age, with religious antinomianism of virtually all kinds rampant, this insistence on study along with practice startled me.

Stories reflecting the study/practice dichotomy are abundant in both the primary and secondary literature on the subject. Walpola Rahula's *History of Buddhism in Ceylon* provides a good summary of the issue.[47] During the first century BCE, in the midst of potential foreign invasion and a severe famine, Sri Lankan monks feared that the Buddhist Tripitaka, preserved only in oral tradition, might be lost. Thus the scriptures were committed to writing for the first time. Nonetheless, in the aftermath of the entire dilemma, a new question arose: What is the basis of the 'Teaching' (i.e., *Sāsana*)-learning or practice? A clear difference of opinion resulted in the development of two groups: the Dhammakathikas, who claimed that learning was the basis of the *Sāsana*, and the Pamsukūlikas, who argued for practice as the basis. The Dhammakathikas apparently won out, as attested to by several commentarial statements quoted by Rahula.[48]

The two vocations described above came to be known as *gantha-dhura*, or the 'vocation of books,' and *vipassanā-dhura*, or the vocation of meditation, with the *former* being regarded as the superior training (because surely meditation would not be possible if the teachings were lost). Rahula points out that *gantha-dhura* originally referred *only* to the learning and teaching of the Tripitaka, but in time, came to refer also to 'languages, grammar, history, logic, medicine, and other fields of study.'[49] Moreover, not the least characteristic of these two divisions was that the *vipassanā-dhura* monks began to live in the forest, where they could best pursue their vocation undisturbed, while the *gantha-dhura* monks began to dwell in villages and towns. As such, the *gantha-dhura* monks began to play a significant role in Buddhist education. Peter Harvey, for example, notes,

> The *Sangha* has also been active in education. In the lands of Southern and Northern Buddhism, monasteries were the major, or sole, source of education until modern times. This is reflected in the fact that the most common Burmese term for a monastery, *kyaung*, means 'school.'[50]

Rahula says as much, quoting R. K. Mookerji's *Ancient Indian Education*:

> The history of the Buddhist system of education is practically that of the Buddhist Order or Sangha.... The Buddhist world did not offer any educational opportunities apart from or independently of its monasteries. All education, sacred as well as secular, was in the hands of the monks.[51]

In view of the above, it would probably not be going too far in referring to the *gantha-dhura* monks as 'scholar-monks.' It is these so-called 'scholar-monks' that would largely fulfill the role of 'settled monastic renunciant,' in Reginald Ray's creative three-tiered model for Buddhist practitioners (contrasted with the 'forest renunciant' and 'layperson').[52]

Why is this distinction so important? It is significant for at least two reasons. First, and most obviously, it reveals why the tradition of study in Buddhism, so long minimized in popular and scholarly investigations of the American Buddhist tradition, has had such an impact on that same tradition and why it has resulted in the rapid development of American Buddhist schools and institutes of higher learning in the latter quarter of this century. Furthermore, it explains why the American Buddhist movement has encouraged a high level of 'Buddhist literacy' among its practitioners. However, it also highlights the fact that the American Buddhist movement has been almost exclusively a *lay* movement. While many leaders of various American Buddhist groups may have had formal monastic training (irrespective of whether they continue to lead monastic lifestyles), the vast majority of their disciples have not. Thus, the educational model on which American Buddhists pattern their behavior is contrary to the traditional Asian Buddhist archetype. It is, in fact, the *converse* of the traditional model. As such, at least with regard to Buddhist study and education, there is a leadership gap in the American Buddhist community, one largely not filled by an American *sangha* of 'scholar-monks.'

What has been the response to the educational leadership gap on the part of American Buddhist communities? I think the explanation has been twofold. On the one hand, there is a movement in some American Buddhist communities to identify those individuals *within the community itself* who are best suited, and best trained, to serve the educational needs of the community and to confer appropriate authority in these individuals in a formal way. Recently, Sakyong Mipham Rinpoche, son of Chögyam Trungpa and now head of the Shambhala International community, declared nine community members 'Acharyas,' an Indian Buddhist designation for a respected teacher. These nine individuals, one of whom holds the Ph.D. degree from the University of Chicago with specialization in Buddhism, were authorized to take on enhanced teaching and leadership roles in their community and beyond. In the words of one of the nine:

> We all felt a commitment to deepen the understanding in the West of Kagyu, Nyingma, and Shambhala traditions. There was also a common feeling that we could take a lead in looking outward beyond our community to engage in creative and open-minded dialogue with other spiritual traditions, and to explore the many forms of contemporary and traditional wisdom.[53]

While there are a few communities where monks or nuns are in residence and the traditional Asian model is maintained, such as Hsi Lai Temple, most American Buddhist communities are bound by necessity to follow the procedure utilized by Shambhala International. Unlike many Asian countries where 'Buddhist Studies finds consistent institutional support from religious circles,'[54] American scholars are not likely to benefit from enterprises which enhance the opportunities of their Asian counterparts, such as Ryūkoku University in Japan.[55] There is, however, another alternative, where the American Buddhological scholar-practitioner is vital in the ongoing development of the American Buddhist tradition.

Above, it was noted that in Asia the monastic renunciants were almost exclusively responsible for the religious education of the lay-*sangha*. On the other hand, virtually everyone who writes on American Buddhism sees it almost exclusively as a lay movement, devoid of a *significant* monastic component. Emma Layman, one of the earliest researchers in the field, says as much: 'In general, American Buddhists are expected to lead their lives within the lay community rather than in a monastic setting....'[56] Later, Rick Fields echoes the same sentiment: 'Generalization of any kind seems to dissolve in the face of such cultural and religious diversity. And yet it does seem safe to suggest that lay practice is the real heart and koan of American Buddhism.'[57] In the absence of the traditional 'scholar-monks' so prevalent in Asia, it may well be that the 'scholar-practitioners' of today's American Buddhism will fulfill the role of 'quasi-monastics,' or at least treasure-troves of Buddhist literacy and information, functioning as guides through whom one's understanding of the Dharma may be sharpened. In this way, individual practice might once again be balanced with individual study so that Buddhist study deepens one's practice, while Buddhist practice informs one's study. Obviously, such a suggestion spawns two further questions: (1) Are there sufficient scholar-practitioners currently active in American Buddhism to make such an impact? and (2) Are they actually making that impact?

With regard to the former question, much of the information reported above is necessarily anecdotal. By simply making mental notes at the various conferences attended by American Buddhologists, based on discussions of individual practice, one can develop a roster of scholar-practitioners who are openly Buddhist; and while such a roster is not publishable in a survey which guarantees anonymity, the number is quite clearly *at least* 25 percent. I first became aware of ways in which personal study and practice interpenetrated during my initial summer at Naropa Institute in 1974, when at least one individual showed me the arrangement of his academic study and personal shrine, side by side in the same room. And it was not unusual for Buddhologists to teach their academic classes immediately preceding or following a shared session of meditation practice. When the American Academy of Religion last held its annual meeting in Kansas City, I attended a dinner with seven other academic Buddhologists, all of whom were Buddhists. One of my favorite memories of Calgary, where I held the Numata Chair of Buddhist Studies in the fall of 1993, revolves around my first visit to the home of Professor A. W. Barber. Not only was his hospitality superb, but his Buddhist shrine was elegant, *and it was the first thing he showed me in his home*. To be sure, the descriptions that might be offered are very plentiful. My best estimate is that another factor of *at least* 25 percent is almost certainly Buddhist, but very careful not to make public expressions of its religiosity, for fear of professional reprisal, keenly felt or perceived.

The second question is perhaps not so difficult to assess as the first. As one surveys the vast corpus of literature that surrounds the academic programs sponsored by numerous American Buddhist groups, the names of academic scholars of Buddhism have begun to dominate the roster of invited presenters, and these individuals are almost exclusively Buddhists. At a recent conference on Buddhism in America, held in Boston in January 1997, one practitioner playfully confided that he wondered if such occasions as this might be thought of as a 'Pro Tour for Buddhologists,' as he clamored off to hear Professor Robert Thurman deliver a Keynote Address titled 'Toward American Buddhism.' In other words, many American Buddhist masters have come to acknowledge and incorporate the professional contributions of these American Buddhist scholar-practitioners into the religious life of their communities, recognizing the unique and vital role they fulfill.

This is a new and emerging phenomenon as well. In 1977, I attended a well-planned and carefully executed conference at Syracuse University, devoted to the ambitious theme of 'The Flowering of Buddhism in America.' Despite the academic-sounding titles of many of the presentations, nearly all of the papers were prepared by non-academic practitioners. Seventeen years later, when the Institute of Buddhist Studies in Berkeley, California, sponsored a semester-long symposium called 'Buddhisms in America: An Expanding Frontier,' every single participant had impressive academic credentials, and more than two-thirds of the nearly twenty presenters were Buddhist practitioners.

Ray Hart concludes in his investigation of religious and theological studies in American higher education that the data 'cannot be reported in a form that is statistically meaningful.'[58] I would argue, instead, that the data in my surveys are meaningful in evaluating the productivity of Buddhist Studies scholars and in beginning to demonstrate how the discipline defines itself. In collating the data in my surveys, and evaluating the narrative statements submitted, two clear sentiments emerged. The first, which was quite obvious, reflected the number of colleagues who came to the study of Buddhism, and to academe, as a result of their practice of Buddhism as a religious tradition; or those who cultivated a commitment to the personal practice of Buddhism as a result of their academic endeavors. For many in this first group, this has created a powerful tension between scholarship and religious commitment, between Buddhology and personal faith. The second sentiment seemed to signal a shift away from Buddhist texts and philosophy (the Buddhist 'theology' which some of us have been accused of propagating) toward an investigation of Buddhism's contextual relationship with culture. Or, as José Cabezón puts it:

> There is today a call for the increased investigation of alternative semiotic forms – oral and vernacular traditions, epigraphy, ritual, patterns of social and institutional evolution, gender, lay and folk traditions, arts archaeology and architecture.... The critique is really a call for greater balance and holism within the field; it is not only a

demand that equal recognition be given to new areas of research, but a call for an integrated and mutually interpenetrating research program aimed at the understanding of Buddhism as a multi-faceted entity.[59]

At the outset of this paper, reference was made to the recently published volume *Curators of the Buddha: The Study of Buddhism under Colonialism*, along with a number of comments about the book from a review article by Jan Nattier. To be sure, Nattier is correct when she outlines some of the issues overlooked in the volume: a consideration of the difference in outlook and methodology between specialists in Tibetan Buddhism and those of Chinese Buddhism, variations in the training and perspective between Buddhist Studies scholars trained in Religious Studies departments and those who were trained in area studies programs, those who have had a personal dialogue with a Buddhist community and those who have not, and a consideration of the 'rifts' in North American Buddhist Studies.[60] Yet, after praising Lopez for his frankness and willingness, as an American Buddhologist, to discuss his own encounter with Buddhism, she concludes by saying,

If there are difficulties here, they are not with the keen and self-critical eye with which Lopez reflects on his own experience as a student of Buddhism but with the degree to which he generalizes from that experience to characterize prevailing attitudes in the Buddhist Studies field at large.[61]

Whether these generalizations are correct or not remains to be seen. At least the question has now moved beyond Father Lamotte's concern with being *hérétique*.

References

Cabezón, José. 'Buddhist Studies as a Discipline and the Role of Theory.' *Journal of the International Association of Buddhist Studies* 18, no. 2 (Winter 1995): 231–268.

Conze, Edward. 'Recent Progress in Buddhist Studies.' In *Thirty Years of Buddhist Studies*. Oxford: Bruno Cassirer, 1967.

de Jong, J. W. *A Brief History of Buddhist Studies in Europe and America*. Bibliotheca Indo-Buddhica, no. 33. 2nd rev. ed. Delhi: Sri Satguru, 1987.

Eckel, Malcolm David. 'The Ghost at the Table: On the Study of Buddhism and the Study of Religion.' *Journal of the American Academy of Religion* 62, no. 4 (Winter 1994): 1085–1110.

Gómez, Luis. 'Unspoken Paradigms: Meanderings through the Metaphors of a Field.' *Journal of the International Association of Buddhist Studies* 18, no. 2 (Winter 1995): 183–230.

Lopez, Donald S., Jr., ed. *Curators of the Buddha*. Chicago: University of Chicago Press, 1995.

Nattier, Jan. 'Buddhist Studies in the Post-Colonial Age.' *Journal of the American Academy of Religion*, 65, 2 (Summer 1997); 469–85.

Peiris, William. *The Western Contribution to Buddhism*. Delhi: Motilal Banarsidass, 1973.

Prebish, Charles. 'The Academic Study of Buddhism in the United States: A Current Analysis.' *Religion* 24 (1994): 271–278.

Webb, Russell. 'Contemporary European Scholarship on Buddhism.' In Tadeusz Skorupski, ed. *The Buddhist Heritage*, 247–76. Buddhica Britannica, vol. 1. Tring: The Institute for Buddhist Studies, 1989.

____. 'Pali Buddhist Studies in the West.' *Pali Buddhist Review* 1, no. 3 (1976): 169–180; 2, no. 1 (1977): 55–62; 2, no. 2 (1977): 114–122; 2, no. 3 (1977): 162–167; 3, no. 1 (1978): 35–36; 3, no. 2 (1978): 84–87; 3, no. 3 (1978): 146–153; 4, no. 1–2 (1979): 28–31; 4, no. 4 (1979): 86–90; 5, no. 1–2 (1980): 39–41; 5, no. 3 (1980): 89–92.

Williams, Duncan Ryūken. 'Where to Study?' *Tricycle: The Buddhist Review* 6, no. 3 (Spring 1997): 68–69, 115–117.

Notes

1 Both Lamotte's original volume and Sara Webb-Boin's translation were published by the Institut Orientaliste of the Université de Louvain, in 1958 and 1988, respectively.

2 Edward Conze, *The Memoirs of a Modern Gnostic*, pt. 2 (Sherborne, England: The Samizdat Publishing Company, 1979), 43.

3 See Georges B. J. Dreyfus, *Recognizing Reality: Dharmakīrti's Philosophy and Its Tibetan Interpretations* (Albany, NY: State University of New York Press, 1997). It is interesting to note that Dreyfus lists his Geshe Lharampa degree (earned in 1985) on his *curriculum vitae* along with his M.A. (1987) and Ph.D. (1991) from the University of Virginia.

4 See Donald S. Lopez, Jr., ed., *Curators of the Buddha: The Study of Buddhism under Colonialism* (Chicago: University of Chicago Press, 1995).

5 Jan Nattier, 'Buddhist Studies in the Post-Colonial Age,' *Journal of the American Academy of Religion*, 65, 2 (Summer 1997); 469–85.

6 Ibid., 469.

7 Henri de Lubac, *La Rencontre de bouddhisme et de l'occident* (Paris: Aubier, 1952).

8 See Simon de la Loubère, *Du Royaume de Siam* (Paris, 1952).

9 See Michel François Ozeray, *Recherches sur Buddhou* (Paris, 1817).

10 See Russell Webb, 'Pali Buddhist Studies in the West,' *Pali Buddhist Review* 1, no. 3 (1976): 169–80; 2, no. 1 (1977): 55–62; 2, no. 2 (1977): 114–22; 2, no. 3 (1977): 162–67; 3, no. 1 (1978): 35–36; 3, no. 2 (1978): 84–87; 3, no. 3 (1978): 146–53; 4, no. 1–2 (1979): 28–31; 4, no. 4 (1979): 86–90; 5, no. 1–2 (1980): 39–41; 5, no. 3 (1980): 89–92.

11 Russell Webb, 'Contemporary European Scholarship on Buddhism,' in Tadeusz Skorupski, ed., *The Buddhist Heritage*, vol. 1 of *Buddhica Britannica* (Tring: The Institute of Buddhist Studies, 1989): 247–76.

12 See William Peiris, *The Western Contribution to Buddhism* (Delhi: Motilal Banarsidass, 1973).

13 Jan W. de Jong's *A Brief History of Buddhist Studies in Europe and America*, 2nd revised and enlarged ed. (Delhi: Sri Satguru Publications, 1987), originally appeared as two articles in *The Eastern Buddhist*. The first carried the same title as the eventual book and appeared in n.s. 7 (1974); the second was titled

'Recent Buddhist Studies in Europe and America 1973–83' and appeared in n.s. 17 (1984). It is curious that of the roughly 400 individuals listed in the Index under 'Names of Scholars,' less than 5 percent are primarily associated with North America. Like nearly all of de Jong's publications, this one bristles with his trenchant editorializing and brutal evaluations. In the foreword, he mentions Guy Welbon's engaging *The Buddhist Nirvāna and Its Western Interpreters* (Chicago: University of Chicago Press, 1968), based on Welbon's doctoral dissertation at the University of Chicago, concluding that 'The usefulness of his book is diminished by the fact that the author was not sufficiently equipped for this difficult task' (p. 2), and citing the reference to his even more acerbic review in the *Journal of Indian Philosophy.*

14 Edward Conze, 'Recent Progress in Buddhist Studies,' *The Middle Way* 34 (1959): 6–14; 34 (1960): 144–50; 35 (1960): 93–98, 110. This was later included in *Thirty Years of Buddhist Studies: Selected Essays by Edward Conze* (Columbia, SC: University of South Carolina Press, 1968), 1–32. Conze maintains the terminology utilized by C. Regamey.

15 See Thomas A. Tweed, *The American Encounter with Buddhism 1844–1912: Victorian Culture and the Limits of Dissent* (Bloomington: Indiana University Press, 1992).

16 See Rick Fields, *How the Swans Came to the Lake: A Narrative History of Buddhism in America*, 3rd ed., revised and updated (Boston: Shambhala Publications, 1992), 54–69.

17 I am not the only one to make this point. José Cabezón, in 'Buddhist Studies as a Discipline and the Role of Theory,' *Journal of the International Association of Buddhist Studies* 18, no. 2 (Winter 1995), says as much: 'No comprehensive history of Buddhist Studies as a discipline exists' (p. 236, n. 8).

18 See, for example, Luis Gómez, 'Unspoken Paradigms: Meanderings through the Metaphors of a Field,' *Journal of the International Association of Buddhist Studies* 18, no. 2 (Winter 1995): 193, n. 8.

19 In Charles S. Prebish and Kenneth K. Tanaka, eds., *The Faces of Buddhism in America* (Berkeley: University of California Press, 1998).

20 See Charles S. Prebish, 'Buddhist Studies American Style: A Shot in the Dark,' *Religious Studies Review* 9, no. 4 (October 1983): 323–30.

21 In *Journal of the International Association of Buddhist Studies* 15, no. 1 (Summer 1992).

22 Cabezón, 'Buddhist Studies as a Discipline,' 236.

23 Gómez, 'Unspoken Paradigms,' 190.

24 See Cabezón, 'Buddhist Studies as a Discipline,' 236–38. The quoted phrase is Cabezón's as well.

25 Ibid., 236, 240.

26 [26] In *Journal of the American Academy of Religion* 62, no. 4 (Winter 1994): 1107–08.

27 Duncan Ryūken Williams, 'Where to Study?' *Tricycle: The Buddhist Review* 6, no. 3 (Spring 1997): 68.

28 Ibid.

29 Cabezón, 'Buddhist Studies as a Discipline,' 243.

30 Ibid. To his credit, Cabezón cites Jacques May's alternative view in 'Études Bouddhiques: Domaine, Disciplines, Perspectives,' *Études de Lettres* (Lausanne), ser. 3, 6, no. 4 (1973): 18.

31 Gómez, 'Unspoken Paradigms,' 214–15. The italics are mine.

32 See Charles S. Prebish, 'The Academic Study of Buddhism in America: A Current Analysis,' *Religion* 24 (1994): 271–78.

33 See Ray L. Hart, 'Religious and Theological Studies in American Higher Education: A Pilot Study,' *Journal of the American Academy of Religion* 59, no. 4 (Winter 1991): 715–827.

34 Hart, 'Religious and Theological Studies,' 779.

35 Ibid., 780–81.

36 Malcolm David Eckel, 'Review and Evaluation of the Buddhism Section of the American Academy of Religion,' 1991, 2.

37 Eckel, 'The Ghost at the Table,' 1088.

38 The *Gassho* article, 'The Academic Study of Buddhism in America: A Current Analysis,' appeared in vol.e 1, no. 2 (January-February 1994), while the *Religion* article, 'The Academic Study of Buddhism in the United States: A Current Analysis,' appeared in vol. 24 (1994): 271–78.

39 Hart, 'Religious and Theological Studies,' 809.

40 This category was not separated in the first survey, but redesigned in the second.

41 Only 72 respondents listed book reviews, and this is reflected in the statistical average.

42 To some extent, with regard to trade/commercial publishers, the personal favorites of a number of prolific authors. As such, the citations for Prentice-Hall and Tungta reflect the publications of Robert Ellwood and Charles Fu, respectively. Other university presses mentioned include Indiana University Press, University of Virginia Press, Stanford University Press, and the University of Michigan Press. Other trade publishers mentioned frequently include Allen and Unwin, Harper and Row, M. D. Gunasena, Peter Lang, St. Martin's Press, Curzon Press, HarperCollins, Beacon, Wadsworth, Scholars Press, Anima, Eerdmans, Munshiram Manoharlal, Mellen Press, Westminster, and Mouton.

43 In at least two cases, journals cited reflect the personal favorites of two prolific scholars: *Journal of Chinese Philosophy* (for Charles Fu) and *Studia Missionalia* (for Alex Wayman). Other journals receiving a significant numbers of citations include: *Cahiers d'Extrême-Asie, Religious Studies Review, Journal of Indian and Buddhist Studies, Journal of the Pali Text Society, Journal of Feminist Studies of Religion, Indo-Iranian Journal, Journal of Buddhist Ethics, Journal of Religious Ethics, Buddhist Studies Review*, and *Korean Culture*.

44 Cabezón, 'Buddhist Studies as a Discipline,' 255.

45 Ibid., 255–56.

46 Williams, 'Where to Study?'

47 See Walpola Rahula, *History of Buddhism in Celyon*, 2nd ed. (Colombo: M. D. Gunasena, 1966), 157–63.

48 Ibid., 158–59: 'Even if there be a hundred thousand bhikkhus practicing *vipassanā* (meditation), there will be no realization of the Noble Path if there is no learning (doctrine, *pariyatti*)' (from the Commentary on the *Anguttara Nikāya*). Commentaries from the *Dīgha Nikāya, Majjhima Nikāya*, and *Vibhanga* echo the same sentiment.

49 Ibid., 161.

50 Peter Harvey, *An Introduction to Buddhism: Teachings, History and Practices* (Cambridge: Cambridge University Press, 1990), 242.

51 Rahula, *History of Buddhism in Ceylon*, 287.

52 See Reginald Ray, *Buddhist Saints in India: A Study in Buddhist Values and Orientations* (New York: Oxford University Press, 1994), 433–47.

53 Jeremy Hayward, 'Acharyas Define Teaching Role,' *Shambhala Sun* 5, no. 4 (March 1997), 'Shambhala News Section,' 1.

54 Cabezón, 'Buddhist Studies as a Discipline,' 237.

55 See, for example, Daniel Metraux, *The History and Theology of Soka Gakkai: A Japanese New Religion* (Lewiston, NY: The Edwin Mellen Press, 1988), 126–28.
56 Emma McCloy Layman, *Buddhism in America* (Chicago: Nelson-Hall, 1976), 18.
57 Fields, *How the Swans Came to the Lake*, 371.
58 Hart, 'Religious and Theological Studies,' 763.
59 Cabezón, 'Buddhist Studies as a Discipline,' 262–63.
60 Nattier, 'Buddhist Studies in the Post-Colonial Age,' 484.
61 Ibid., 480.

CHAPTER TWELVE

Buddhist Studies at Naropa: Sectarian or Academic?

Robert E. Goss

A Naropa education initiates a lifelong process of creative personal development that extends beyond the college experience. Learning is a rigorous and joyful journey at the Naropa Institute. As a member of our community, you train wholeheartedly in your fields of study, gaining knowledge from a perspective that fosters precision, gentleness, and spontaneity. This approach is called 'contemplative education,' and is based on a deep respect for tradition and the intelligence within each person.[1]

The Buddha's message spread throughout Asia, transmitted from teachers to students. Asian Buddhisms were formed by a variety of Buddhist pedagogies, often monastic and sometimes lay, which emerged from a variety of lineages and interacted with a variety of Asian cultures and educational forms in South and Southeast Asia, Central and Inner Asia, and East Asia. And now Buddhist pedagogies have emerged in the American cultural context, with numerous Dharma centers and educational programs, although most American Buddhist educational centers have not pursued the pedagogical strategy of becoming accredited academic institutions.[2]

In a *Tricycle* article, Duncan Williams makes a distinction between practitioner-friendly institutions and academic-based studies of Buddhism in religion or Asian language departments. Williams observes, 'These practitioner-friendly programs generally offer three things: the ability to pursue a degree in the context of Buddhist priestly training, courses in the practice of Buddhism that complement academic study, or emphasis on the study of Buddhism from a normative point of view.'[3] He lists Naropa Institute along with the California Institute of Integral Studies, Graduate Theological Institute, and the Institute of Buddhist Studies as the practitioner-friendly Buddhist programs.[4] Buddhist Studies programs in research universities are accorded an academic status not conferred on practitioner-friendly degree programs because of the latter's advocacy of practice and sectarian values. But are these programs less academic because of their stress on practice along with the academic study of Buddhism? Are there any American institutions that are comparable to practitioner-friendly academic institutions?

The Naropa Institute is a pioneer educational institution describing itself as a 'Buddhist inspired, nonsectarian liberal arts college with undergraduate and graduate programs.' It has used the model of American higher education as a pedagogical strategy to transmit Buddhist values and practices. Naropa's program differs from Buddhist studies in U.S. research universities by its particular educational philosophy that unites meditative practice with academic discipline. It differs from Buddhist meditation centers by developing accredited educational programs that blend a liberal arts curriculum with contemplative practice and by confering degrees.

The Naropa Institute is named after the famous eleventh-century *yogin* who was abbot of Nālanda, the monastic university in North India. Naropa (1016–1100), realizing that he understood 'only the words and not the meaning,'[5] abandoned his academic position after years of intellectual studies, according to his biography. He recognized that knowledge divorced from meditative practice was not the way to achieve wisdom and understanding of the world. Naropa became an itinerant *yogin* who transmitted his contemplative practice to the Kagyu lineage in Tibet. In the entrance hall of Naropa's main building there is a painting of the Indian ascetic sitting cross-legged on a tiger skin mat in the Himalayas and holding a scroll with the words *prajñāgarbha* (womb of transcendental wisdom). The scroll painting typifies the Institute's pedagogical approach of balancing academic studies with traditional Buddhist contemplative practices.

This chapter will examine the Americanization of Buddhist education at the Naropa Institute, its mission, pedagogical strategies, and educational programs.[6] The title of the chapter poses the question of whether Naropa's educational programs are sectarian or academic. I will contextualize the question with parallels from American church-related colleges and universities and by drawing upon the larger contemporary debate of the place of religion in higher education. Then, it may become clear how a Buddhist-inspired educational model may make its own contribution to the complex relationship of religion to American higher education.

Naropa Institute

The 1960s and 1970s were a fertile time for Buddhism in America. Zen masters were attracting numerous students. The Beat poets expressed Buddhist notions and themes in their poems. And numerous new students were attracted to Buddhism through meditation retreats and inter-religious dialogue.[7] In the midst of such activities, Naropa was founded in 1975 by Chögyam Trungpa Rinpoche as a summer institute which featured Allen Ginsberg, Anne Waldman, John Cage, Gregory Bateson, Ram Dass, Herbert Guenther, and Agehananda Bharati. There were courses on meditation, *T'ai chi*, *thangka* painting, tea ceremony, Tibetan and Sanskrit, Mādhyamika philosophy, physics, and psychology. There were nightly readings of poetry, performances, debates, colloquiums, and informal round table discussions.[8] Naropa Institute expected two hundred students, yet two thousand students came to Boulder for what writer Rick Fields described as a 'summer Woodstock of Consciousness.'[9] Two years later the school became a year-round institute in Boulder offering a contemplative education curriculum which grounded academic studies in spiritual practice. Nearly twenty-three years later, Naropa has evolved into a Buddhist-inspired school with fully accredited degree programs on the undergraduate and graduate levels, an internationally renowned summer writing program, and on-going continuing education programs. Naropa is the first accredited American Buddhist-inspired college, but it claims to be nonsectarian and open to all who want a liberal arts education with a contemplative slant. There have been other attempts to found Buddhist colleges, but these have been modest in scale and have not survived over time.

Chögyam Trungpa and His Teaching Lineages

There is no way to speak about the mission and vision of the Naropa Institute without speaking about its founder, Chögyam Trungpa. He provided the inspiration that continues today to be an active presence for many of the faculty and students. Trungpa, the eleventh Tulku of Surmang Monastery and an important teacher in the Kagyu lineage, was sixteen years old when the Chinese invaded Tibet in 1959. He asked his teacher, Jamgon Kongtrul, whether he should flee to India or stay in Tibet. Jamgon Kongtrul answered, 'The law of *karma* cannot change; each one must face his allotted destiny; each must follow the guidance of his own inner conscience.'[10] This seemed to be a pivotal event in the life of Trungpa, and he followed his inner voice to embark upon his own, unconventional odyssey to Europe and America. Trungpa refused to conform to stereotypical ideas of what a Tibetan *lama* should be. He studied at Oxford, renounced the trappings of monastic life, and founded the Samye-Ling meditation center in Scotland in 1967.

In 1970, Trungpa received a visa to enter the United States, where he began to found *dharma* centers in many urban areas. In 1973, he established the Vajradhatu, a nationwide organization to consolidate the religious activities of the *dharma* centers. The Vajradhatu educational program became the conduit for Trungpa's Kagyu practice lineage. During these years, Trungpa was said to have heavily abused alcohol and drugs and to have had numerous sexual affairs, and his unconventional lifestyle provided challenges and scandals for some Western Buddhists with preconceived notions of holiness.

Chögyam Trungpa introduced a new non-Buddhist lineage of Shambhala training into his educational curriculum. The Shambhala training arises from a treasure text (*gter-ma*) revealed to him in a vision.[11] Along with the Nyingma sect, the Kagyu have had a long tradition of treasure texts recorded and discovered centuries later or revealed in visions or dreams. Trungpa received the text in a dream and wrote the root verses down. He later elaborated upon the root verses with a commentary that became the basis for the five levels of Shambhala training.

Geoffrey Samuel, Reginald Ray, and Judith Simmer-Brown have traced the Shambhala lineage back to the nineteenth-century Rimed movement in eastern Tibet.[12] The Rimed movement attempted to open Buddhist practices to the indigenous elements within Tibetan culture – popular traditions, Bön, Taoist, and even Neo-Confucian traditions. The term *rimed* (*ris med*) is frequently translated as 'eclectic,' but the Tibetanist David Seyford Ruegg has argued that this rendering is inadequate: 'In fact,' Ruegg asserts,' this *rimed* movement was not exactly eclectic but universalistic (and encyclopedic), *rimed* (*pa*) (the antonymn of *risu ch'ed-pa*) meaning unbounded, all-embracing, unlimited, and also impartial.'[13] The students of Trungpa at Naropa construe *rimed* as 'nonsectarian.'

The Rimed movement helped to break down some sectarian rivalry among the Nyingma, Kagyu, and Bön traditions – representing a synthesis quite different from the Gelug sect which follows the synthesis of the path proposed by Tsong Khapa (1357–1419).[14] Both the Gelug and Rimed traditions contain shamanic and monastic emphases, but the Rimed tradition stressed the shamanic and *tantric* dimensions to a far greater extent.[15] The Rimed tradition was not simply an academic movement but was also a popular ecumenical movement that made valuable teachings, free of sectarian rivalry, available. Rimed *lamas* were often less committed to their particular formal practice lineages and sectarian rivalry, for they were willing to cross lineage lines to receive teachings from the most famous teachers.

Chögyam Trungpa's Shambhala treasure teachings rework the millenarian Shambhala myth to represent the ideal of a secular enlightenment.[16] According to the *KalacakraTantra*, Shambhala is a harmonious society, governed by a lineage of enlightened rulers. At a future date, Shambhala will send a peaceful army to save the world from destruction and establish an enlightened society.

Chögyam Trungpa's Shambhala teachings promote a path of social action that de-escalates the politics of domination with gentleness, love, and sanity. They are founded on a basic supposition that there is a basic human wisdom in religious traditions and human culture which can be developed to solve the world's crises. The Shambhala training program fulfilled his long-held dream of making contemplative practice accessible to those who were not interested in formally studying Buddhism. Trungpa taught many of his students, now faculty at Naropa, to pursue a spiritual path within the world and to incorporate the secular world as part of that sacred path. Shambhala training is an ecumenical path that harnesses shamanic methods of envisioning the ordinary world as sacred and yoking natural energies for personal and social transformation.[17] It teaches a path of sacred warrior-ship that develops awareness of basic goodness, gentleness, fearlessness, non-aggression, letting go, authentic action, leadership skills, and genuine love of the sacred world to create an enlightened society. Trungpa's Shambhala teachings incorporate calligraphy, flower arrangement, poetry, theater, dance, fine arts, and martial arts to develop these innate human qualities of sacred warriorship. His fundamental vision of Shambhala training is to bring 'art to everyday life,' to integrate the sacred and the secular, and to transform the world into an enlightened society.

When Naropa describes itself as a Buddhist-inspired, 'nonsectarian' liberal arts college, nonsectarian translates the Tibetan *rimed*. Nonsectarian does not, however, mean 'secular' as it is commonly used in higher education. Nonsectarian is perhaps understood as ecumenical openness to contemplative practices and arts of the world religious traditions that foster precision, gentleness, and spontaneity. Naropa's 1995 self-study opens with a quote from Trungpa, expressing the Shambhala vision as the core of its institutional vision of education:

> When human beings lose their connection to nature, heaven and earth, then they do not know how to nurture their environment, or how to rule their world – which is saying the same thing. Human beings destroy their ecology, at the same time, destroy one another. From the perspective, healing our society goes hand in hand with healing our personal, elemental connection with the phenomenal world.[18]

Trungpa's Shambhala teachings incorporate the sacred wisdom of other religious traditions to integrate contemplative practices with the liberal arts to heal the self and the world.

Institutional Development

From that first summer institute in 1974, Chögyam Trungpa was interested in contemplative practices and traditions that extended beyond the Buddhist canon. He founded the Nalanda Foundation, an umbrella educational organization linking the first Naropa Summer Institute to meditation and teaching centers in more than one hundred cities. In these early years, Naropa and the Vajradhatu Society were intertwined, and in subsequent years the two institutions evolved differently.

Institutionally, there have been several milestones in Naropa's development. By 1977, the Institute initiated a self-study for candidacy status with the North Central Association (NCA), the regional accrediting body. The NCA Review Board approved the visiting team's recommendation that candidacy status be granted. Biennial visits from NCA teams continued until 1986, raising program concerns, admission requirements, and annual reports. The complex world of American higher education exerted a pressure upon Naropa to seek academic legitimacy, and the accreditation process pressed for education standardization, processes, and policies. In 1988, the Commission on Institutes of Higher Education upheld the NCA's recommendation and granted Naropa Institute accreditation.

In the mid 1980s, Lucien Wulsin was asked by Barbara Dilley, then President of Naropa, to become Chair of the Board of the Directors of Naropa. Wulsin, a graduate of Harvard College, a lawyer, entrepreneur, and banker, brought institutional direction and experience to Naropa. One of the first things that Wulsin effected was the de-institutionalization of Naropa from the Vajradhatu Society. This schism was not unique. Many of the oldest Protestant colleges were once denominationally affiliated, and it took over one hundred years for many Protestant colleges to disaffiliate from their founding denominations, even as they still tried to maintain some values of the founding denominational Christian vision in their commitment to liberal arts education. Similar de-institutionalization of higher education institutions from Catholic religious orders took place in the late 1960s and in the 1970s. Webster University, where I teach, was the first Catholic college in the United States to pioneer de-institutionalization from the Sisters of Loretto. There were many Catholics who felt that the Sisters of Loretto sold out Webster University, then Webster College, to secularism. Similarly, there were lots of people in the Vajradhatu who felt that Naropa had sold out its original religious heritage for a secular, mainstream education.

Naropa and the Vajradhatu Society evolved in independent directions. Trungpa encouraged Naropa to pursue affiliation with the North Central Association for institutional accreditation, and the drive towards accreditation contributed to the institute's separation from the Vajradhatu Society. On the other hand, the Vajradhatu's main center moved to Halifax, Canada, and the school effectively pursued an ecumenical mission separate from the Vajradhatu Society. The death of Chögyam Trungpa further troubled many of the core faculty, who feared the dilution of the religious heritage at the institute and the original vision of its founder. Trungpa's memory has, however, continued to provide guidance and inspiration for Naropa's educational vision: 'There are fewer and fewer people who knew Trungpa or his vast vision about Naropa,' says Judith Simmer-Brown. 'I know that his blessings are present in what we're doing.'[19]

Such a separation from the Vajradhatu Society was necessary for the natural development of Naropa as an institution and of its liberal arts curriculum. It allowed for a shift from a Buddhist to a more heterogeneous administrative staff and faculty, yet de-institutionalization set up creative tensions within Naropa – tensions between maintaining its Buddhist heritage and developing a professional academic community. Requisite needs for a professional, administrative, and academic staff could not be readily met within the Buddhist community. The accreditation process further challenged Naropa to develop the administrative functions of an American university with all the institutional procedures and policies that pertain thereto.

Finally, another parallel that needs noting was the search for a president in 1991. Naropa's Board of Trustees conducted a national search. After interviewing nine candidates, most of whom were not Buddhist, the Board of Trustees decided to hire John Cobb, a graduate of Harvard College and Yale Law School and a member of the Buddhist community. Many Jesuit colleges and universities, for example, continue to limit presidential searches to Jesuits if only because of their institutional heritage and connections to its donor base. Similarly, the selection of John Cobb underscores Naropa's Buddhist heritage and vision of education. He is committed to preserving Naropa's vision of integrating education and spirituality: 'we are conscious of the need for renewal and revival and an expression of unification in education.'[20] Aware of its contemplative vision, President Cobb has factored strategic planning and capital fund-raising for facility expansion to accommodate the steady growth of full-time and part-time students.

Faculty

The Naropa Institute has over thirty full-time faculty serving on the core faculty and, because of its practitioner/teacher orientation, it employs a large pool of adjunct faculty. There are twelve faculty who have been with Naropa for sixteen years or longer. Full-time faculty salaries are comparatively still on the low side, and Naropa has depended upon the faculty commitment to the vision of contemplative education. Additional faculty income may come from teaching additional courses, supervising interns and independent studies, reading theses and manuscripts. Full-time teaching consists of eighteen credit hours per year. Faculty, like those at other institutions, are required to provide service to the department, academic advising, participate in faculty and departmental meetings, and practice a contemplative discipline. They are expected to remain current in their disciplines and scholarship as well as provide community service beyond Naropa. There are independent networks of faculty and staff that meet informally each week or once a month, and these networks allow for informal faculty connectedness and sharing.

Unlike most U.S. colleges and universities, Naropa has no tenure system of faculty promotion. For the first four years, a faculty member undergoes a 'core candidacy.' In the first two years faculty are reviewed annually to give them regular feedback. They are eligible for promotion from core candidate to Assistant Professor at the end of the third year. Core rank progresses to Associate II and then to full Professor. During the fourth year, a peer-review board of three – a faculty member from the same department, one from another department, and the third from administrative staff – is convened to evaluate the candidate for promotion to the core faculty. Faculty promotion is determined on a point system based on the number of years teaching, self-evaluations, and peer evaluations. Self-evaluation, instructor and course evaluations, course syllabi, professional involvement, and institutional service are used for faculty evaluation by a peer-review board. The review board makes recommendation to the Vice-President for Academic Affairs, who, in turn, makes recommendations to the President for final approval. Spence McWilliams, Vice-President of Academic Affairs, describes the Naropa process of promotion and retention as 'much gentler' than the tenure process in other institutions where he has worked. Effective from the summer of 1997, Naropa has implemented a new faculty design, with sabbatical raises.

Educational Programs

Naropa Institute is a transfer college, requiring undergraduate students to have completed thirty credit hours or the equivalent of their freshman year prior to admission. Students entering with less than sixty semester credit hours are required to fulfill the general education requirements: 1) Naropa Seminar, consisting of short courses on wisdom, values, and spiritual disciplines; 2) Cognitive Studies, offered by the Department of Psychology; 3) Coming to Voice, designed to develop students' communication skills; and 4) Great Works, a study of literature as applied to the art of living.[21] These foundational courses give students the opportunity to integrate a liberal arts education with contemplative vision and practice. Naropa offers bachelor degrees in contemplative psychology, interarts (dance, music, theater), visual arts, creative writing and literature, environmental studies, early childhood education, traditional Asian arts (*t'ai chi chuan*, *aikido*, and *yoga*), comparative religion, and interdisciplinary studies. In comparison to many colleges, Naropa's liberal arts offerings are limited.

Graduate degree programs are offered on the masters level in Buddhist studies, creative writing and poetics, gerontology, engaged Buddhism, contemplative psychotherapy, somatic psychology, and transpersonal counseling psychology. Naropa has developed experiential learning in residential community settings in Nepal and Bali, and it is now developing a program in Bhutan.[22] These study-abroad programs provide students from

Naropa and other academic institutions the opportunity to experience contemplative education within traditional cultural settings with local faculty and artisans.

The Jack Kerouac School of Disembodied Poetics founded by Allen Ginsberg and Anne Waldman has been an integral part of Naropa degree programs and the Summer Institute. It has developed an internationally renowned writing program attracting numerous students, visiting scholars, poets, fiction writers, artists, and religious teachers. The poets of the Kerouac school have pioneered a style of poetics that is often rebellious and blends Buddhism with a postmodern perspective.[23]

Some Current Programs

Naropa's unique educational vision can be illustrated by considering four of its M.A. programs. The M.A. in Buddhist Studies builds on its undergraduate program in Religious Studies. It offers three areas of concentration: contemplative arts, languages, and engaged Buddhism.[24] All three tracks share a core curriculum: 1) five courses in the history, culture, and institutions of the various Buddhist traditions; 2) four courses in reading Buddhist texts; 3) Buddhist meditation practicums; and 4) living Buddhist teachers and masters. The contemplative track requires not only the study of Buddhist meditation but also the contemplative practices of other religious traditions. The language track is limited to the Buddhist canonical languages of Sanskrit and Classical Tibetan.[25]

The Engaged Buddhism track involves the study of classical Buddhist philosophy, meditation, and ritual as well as the study of social change, alternative communities, institutions, values, social work, and activism. The Engaged Buddhism program is comparable to the pastoral programs of Christian divinity schools; it includes training in pastoral counseling, CPE (Clinical Pastoral Education), chaplain internships in hospitals, prisons, hospices, and homeless shelters. Students develop skills in community organizing, leadership, and conflict resolution.

The M.A. in Contemplative Psychology blends Buddhist psychology and mindfulness/awareness meditation with Western humanistic psychology. The program includes a course on Buddhist *abhidharma*, or systematization of psychology. At the heart of the program is a ten-week *maitri* (friendliness) retreat in a scenic setting. It is an intensive residential, community retreat that integrates meditation and study. Students are introduced to the Mahāyāna meditative practices to cultivate awareness and compassion. A distinctive feature is the '*maitri* space awareness,' which involves five rooms, with distinctive colors and lights. Each room is designed to evoke a basic emotional state of relating to oneself and others. This *maitri* program provides an experiential ground for understanding confused states of mind and developing compassion for others. It also develops a learning community that intends to provide student support and feedback. Like many other M.A. programs in psychotherapy, the Naropa program requires students internships in community agencies and mental health facilities.

The M.A. in Environmental Leadership combines the study of ecosystems and human systems with the path of personal and social transformation. Four interdisciplinary core courses are required: 1) Transforming Systems: Deep Ecology and General Systems Theory; 2) Evolution of Ecological Thinking and the Human/Nature Contract; 3) Creating Cultures at Home with Nature; and 4) Leadership: The Art and Ethic of Getting Things Done. During the academic year, a number of visiting guests lead four-day intensives on particular topics. Thai Buddhist social activist, Sulak Sivaraksa, has been a regular guest for the Environmental Leadership and Engaged Buddhism programs. The uniqueness of the environmental program is its attempt to bring contemplative awareness to study and practice in the field.

The M.F.A. in Writing and Poetics grew out of the Jack Kerouac School of Disembodied Poetics. The curriculum is designed for students who wish to pursue creative writing within a contemplative environment. The full program consists of two summer institutes and three semesters of courses and a final semester in which candidates prepare the creative manuscript and a critical thesis. *Bombay Gin,* Naropa's literary magazine, is edited by M.F.A. students. What is unique about this writing program is not only the contemplative practice but also its project outreach. The project outreach places M.F.A. students in prisons, schools, homeless shelters, retirement homes, and hospitals. Students instruct and inspire these communities in imaginative exercises of language and poetics, and they learn social awareness and creative engagement from their placements. Final semester students may apply for a semester-long residency at Zen Mountain Monastery outside of Woodstock, New York, where they can work on their manuscripts in a contemplative environment or where they can train in editing and publishing at the Monastery's Dharma Communications Center.

Additional Educational Programs

In addition to its undergraduate and graduate programs, Naropa offers Continuing Education programs and a Summer Institute. The purpose of Continuing Education at Naropa is to bring contemplative studies to a wider community than those engaged in degree programs and to serve those who are interested in creating a life-long learning community. Initially, local members of the Boulder community were invited to attend Naropa courses on a non-credit basis. As Naropa degree programs rapidly grew, courses became more unavailable to non-degree students. This gave rise to a separate continuing education program with its own courses during the academic year, and in the fall of 1994, Naropa established Continuing Education as a separate entity. Continuing Education is accomplished under the format of lectures, workshops, courses, and special events. Programs are offered in world wisdom traditions; arts and creativity; community, environment, and culture; health, healing, and psychology; and journeys. The world wisdom traditions program includes meditation and contemplative practices from the great world religions, including shamanic cultures and spiritual models of social action. Arts and creativity include visual and performing arts, while other courses are offered in environmental activism, popular psychology, and alternative health. Continuing Education not only provides additional revenue for the institution but draws new students into the Institute's degree programs.

Like Continuing Education, Naropa's Summer Institute attracts new candidates for the full-time degree programs. Many students who attend the Summer Institute receive a taste of the Naropa environment and find themselves applying to one of its programs. The Summer Institute preserves vestiges of that original 'Summer of Woodstock Consciousness,' with faculty performances, informal discussions, workshops, and receptions. The Summer Institute consists of the Summer Writing Program, special events, and conferences. The Summer Program in Writing and Poetics is a month-long convocation of students, poets, scholars, writers, Buddhist and non-Buddhist teachers, and musicians. It brings practitioners of the visual and performing arts together with poets and fiction writers. In May 1997 Naropa held the Spirituality in Education Conference, which featured such outside speakers as the Dalai Lama, Huston Smith, Joan Halifax, Jeremy Hayward, Parker Palmer, Ron Miller, and others. The Spirituality in Education Conference examined the place of spirituality within contemporary education, covering such broad topics as the ground of learning, pluralism and identity, educational communities, and tradition and innovation. An innovative aspect of this conference was an internet seminar, 'Exploring the Role of the Internet in Spiritual and Contemplative Learning,' as well as a number of online discussion groups on the talks of the various conference speakers. Some of the Summer Institute's events have included a Tribute to the Life and Artistic Work of Kenneth Patchen, a Body and Soul Conference (featuring Ram Dass and Maya Angelou), and the Sixth Annual Somatic Psychology Symposium, whose theme was Trauma and Development. The Naropa Summer Institute has also made an active contribution to the Buddhist-Christian dialogue by hosting seven conferences on Buddhist and Christian meditation since 1981.

Two additional purposes for the summer programing are community outreach and degree-program recruitment. The summer programs attract a number of professional educators who want to learn and experience the Naropa style of education. Summer advertising generates many requests for information about Naropa's academic programs. In its self-study, Naropa assessed the institutional value of the summer programs: 'These programs enhance the year-round curricula by bringing fresh insights into curriculum areas, providing the context for exploring experimental approaches in education, aiding in investigating new programs of study, and recruiting new year-round faculty.'[26]

Contemplative Education

In 1994, the Board of Trustees adopted the following mission statement which elaborates on Naropa's vision of contemplative education:

- to offer educational programs that cultivate awareness of the present moment through intellectual, artistic, and meditative disciplines;
- to foster a learning community that uncovers wisdom and heart;
- to cultivate openness and communication, sharpen critical intellect;
- to exemplify the principles of the Naropa Institute's Buddhist educational heritage:
- to encourage the integration of world wisdom traditions with modern culture; and
- to offer nonsectarian community open to all.[27]

Naropa claims to be a learning community characterized by its particular emphasis on contemplative education and its focus on transforming society. Contemplative education includes cultivating awareness of the present moment, striving for excellence in all disciplines, joining personal experience with what is learned, applying wisdom from many world traditions to contemporary socio-cultural challenges, and forming a nonsectarian, inclusive community.

Contemplative education involves more than academic content by including practice. However, such contemplative education cannot be said to preclude intellectual rigor and discipline. Several graduate students from Naropa's M.A. in Buddhist Studies are now in doctoral programs in Buddhist studies at the University of Chicago, the University of Virginia, and Harvard University. Students become members of a practice-oriented, academic community, studying in particular fields of discipline while learning from a contemplative perspective that fosters academic precision, gentleness, and spontaneity.

Contemplative education also includes numerous meditative practices that promote equanimity, mindfulness, and letting go. One Tuesday each semester, there are no classes. This day is reserved as a 'practice day' when students, faculty, and administrative staff engage in some form of meditation practice, whether it is sitting practice, T'ai chi, Hasidic prayer, Christian contemplation, journal keeping, or *yoga*. Much of the meditation taught at Naropa has its foundation in traditional Buddhist practices. Some degree programs and individual classes require students to be involved in meditative practice, while some faculty begin their classes with a few moments of meditative silence. Naropa has a Meditation Practice Coordinator (MPC) who is available to lead and instruct students in meditation practice. The Meditation Practice Coordinator has the responsibility for connecting students with a meditation instructor. Eighty-five percent of students surveyed have found this relationship to be 'beneficial.' There are no additional charges for meditation instruction at Naropa. As the curriculum has grown and included more meditation-based classes, there has been a need to hire meditation instructors as teaching assistants. The MPC has included local religious organizations as well as non-Buddhist traditions in a referral-base for students. Just as many universities and colleges have chapels, Naropa has a permanent meditation hall large enough to accommodate up to fifty or sixty practitioners, and several other halls can accomodate three hundred practitioners.

Each semester Religious Studies includes a practice week when classes are suspended for meditational practice, instruction, and creative workshops. I happened to visit Naropa Institute during such a practice week. Dr. Reginald Ray gave instructions on mindfulness and. led some three hundred students, staff, and faculty in sitting practice. That afternoon, I listened to a faculty panel from the visual arts, the interarts, and the writing program discuss how mindfulness fine-tuned their performance, creativity, and their attentiveness. Contemplative learning infuses mindfulness, insight, and friendliness into the curriculum. It sets up an environment where students come to know themselves and learn to deal with their confusion and emotional problems. Students are then mentored in integrative meditative practices to rebuild their lives with gentleness, spaciousness, and love.

In a recruitment brochure, Naropa expresses its educational mission: 'The goals of contemplative education are to deepen students' knowledge of themselves and their place in the contemporary world, to develop and strengthen personal discipline within a specific field of study, and to nurture a desire to contribute to the world with understanding and compassion.'[28]

New Program Development

Programs at Naropa have historically developed because of the pioneering spirit of its founder and faculty. In 1974, Trungpa asked Anne Waldman and Allen Ginsberg to start a poetry school: the Jack Kerouac School of Disembodied Poetics was born. Many programs have had such beginnings at Naropa Institute. The creative vision of the faculty led to the evolution of the various undergraduate and graduate programs. Several faculty members and administrators have likened various departments to start-up businesses. Some programs, such as gerontology, have developed partnerships with long-term care facilities in Boulder, while the Engaged Buddhism program has helped staff the Boulder County Hospice.

There has been a shift from individual faculty and departmental initiatives to more comprehensive institutional planning. This has corresponded with the evolution of long-term planning, market analysis, and institutional resource management. The Board of Trustees adopted a staggered schedule for the development of new programs and required that each new program pay for itself. All new program proposals require an exhaustive two-year review by the Curriculum Committee, Faculty Executive Committee, Administrative Council, and President's Council before submission to the Board of Trustees for approval. These policies have enabled Naropa to begin to grapple with the budgetary costs of growth and to strengthen its foundational programs before new programs are added.

Campus Facilities

Naropa's campus facilities are located on 3.7 acres in downtown Boulder. The rapid growth of programs and the student body in the 1990s has necessitated planning for future campus expansion. Because the Institute leases classroom space off campus, there is an ongoing search for alternative sites as well as a capital campaign to support this expansion. I expect that off-site facilities will be located during the interim, and a larger classroom building is in the planning stage.

The Naropa Institute Library is small in comparison to the libraries of major research universities, but it has some jewels for researchers. Its tape archive houses some seven thousand unique items not found anywhere else in the world. The archive houses several hundred videotapes of Chögyam Trungpa giving teachings from 1974 until his death. Naropa maintains one of the largest audiotape collections of poetry readings, workshops, and panel discussions in the United States. Nearly every poetry reading at Naropa has been taped since the founding of the Jack Kerouac School of Disembodied Poetics. The tape archive will certainly attract scholarly attention in the future as Naropa turns its attention to the acculturation of Tibetan Buddhism in the American context.

The Performing Arts Center, described as the 'heartbeat' of Naropa, produces sixty performance events per year.[29] Its theater program gives students hands-on experience in performance, theater design, production skills, and space and equipment management. During the Summer Institute, faculty in theater studies, music, and dance offer performances for enrolled students. Performances include dance, music, poetry readings, experimental theater, and lot of interarts work which joins dance with calligraphy, music and poetry, as well as martial arts and theater. The Performing Arts Center also hosts some of the best meditation teachers when they come to Boulder to give teachings.

Students

Who goes to Naropa? Students are a heterogenous population. Of the 800 or so full-time students, 25 percent are undergraduates. Five percent of the student body are international students, and 60 percent of the students are from outside Colorado. Forty-two percent of the students are between 20 and 29 years old; 31 percent are between 30 and 39; 22 percent are between 40 and 49; and 5 percent are over 50. The ratio of female to male students has remained constant, around 2:1.38. Thirty percent of full-time students are practicing Buddhists, while the non-Buddhist students practice some form of contemplative arts.

The majority of non-Buddhist students who matriculate into Naropa's degree programs come to experience the creative climate of the Summer Institute, find value in contemplative education, or want a communal learning experience. In my visit to Naropa, I had several opportunities to speak informally with undergraduate and graduate students. Buddhist students come to Naropa to deepen their Buddhist studies and practices while non-Buddhist students found contemplative practices helpful to their future careers in mental health, hospice, or long-term care facilities for the elderly. What all the students I interviewed liked about Naropa was that it was a personal learning community where faculty and students engage in mutual education and where faculty are available to students.

A minimum of five hours of meditation per week is required of all degree candidates at the Institute. Meditation courses include the academic study of traditional meditation texts, discussions, and exams. For M.A. students, papers are required to demonstrate mastery of issues related to meditation. Final grades are calculated on a pass/fail basis for meditative practice; letter grades are given for academic work.

Sectarian or Academic?

A recent flood of books from neoconservative and mainline Christian scholars has considered the progressive marginalization of religion in American higher education.[30] The books describe the marginalization of Christianity and the loss of Christian identity at colleges and universities, resulting in a materialistic, secular culture. During the eighteenth and nineteenth centuries, hundreds of colleges were founded by Protestant mainline and evangelical denominations and by Roman Catholics. Many American Protestant denominations founded colleges to promote denominational loyalties and values while serving the public interest by advancing a nonsectarian public philosophy. Higher education was considered an essential ingredient for public service in a Christian society. Daniel Coit Gilman, the founder of Johns Hopkins University, said: 'the ultimate end of all educational and scientific effort, as well as of all legislation and statesmanship is identical with that at which Christianity aims, "Peace on earth, good-will to men."'[31] Protestant Christian education translated Christian values into a nonsectarian philosophy of public service.

At the turn of the nineteenth century, liberal Protestantism morally justified the professionalization and specialization of higher education with a 'social gospel' of public service. Liberal Protestantism contributed to the marginalization of religion in higher education by moving away from its sectarian roots toward nonsectarian education and by its commitment to public education and public life. Neoconservative scholar George Marsden has noted that as liberal Protestant theology located salvation in social advance and public life, it removed any distinction between church and state. This fusion affected twentieth-century universities and colleges, which became loosely connected to their denominational heritage and promoted a 'liberal Protestantism without Protestantism.'[32] Cultural and religious pluralism further pushed traditional Protestant Christian educational concerns to the periphery of universities.

Many Christian neoconservative critics of higher education now want to go back to a golden age when colleges were places where students engaged each other intellectually and grew spiritually. For George Marsden, sectarianism is good in higher education, offering a distinctive theology and a specific understanding of morality that promotes loyalty to a specific Christian tradition.[33] Marsden's educational vision opposes nonsectarianism, cultural and religious pluralism within a Christian college or university.[34] Marsden would exclude all those who did not share his particular Christian religious worldview from admission to the sectarian academy.

Catholic colleges and universities found themselves caught between Rome's suspicion of an American heresy and the need to legitimize themselves through accreditation agencies. They attempted to maintain a distinctive Catholic identity while pursuing models of American higher education. From the 1920s to 1950s, Catholic higher education claimed a public role in trying to bring Catholic values to the United States.[35] In the late 1950s, Catholics found themselves assimilating into the larger cultural models of secular education. Many Catholic higher education institutions have followed the earlier lead of denominational Protestant colleges and universities, either preserving theology departments to maintain their religious heritage or transforming theology departments into religious studies.

Despite the inclusion of many religion departments and a few divinity schools, religion has moved from the center to the periphery of university life in Protestant and Catholic educational institutions over the past one hundred years. By the 1970s, the rationale for religion departments shifted from a view of religion as one of the humanities with a moral purpose to religion as a social science. Growing cultural pluralism gave rise to the strengthening and founding of the history of religions programs. The term 'nonsectarian' has become a codeword for the academic disengagement of the study of religion from religious values. In the *Bulletin for the Council of the Societies for the Study of Religion*, Brian E. Malley calls for engaged religious studies to break out of monastic patterns of scholarship that have evolved in the last few decades.[36] Malley believes that religious studies has disengaged itself from value-advocacy questions as it attempted to define space for itself within the late-twentieth-century university.

In an interview Judith Simmer-Brown, a professor and founder of the Engaged Buddhism program at the Naropa Institute, addressed the issue of sectarian versus academic study in Naropa's contemplative education curriculum:

> In general, sectarian Buddhism is not the agenda, but an under-standing of an enlightened society is very much the agenda. Within the Buddhist studies program, I am concerned that people learn about Buddhist history. I don't care whether people are Buddhist, but I really do care whether they practice some meditation and that they come to know something about who they are. So that is our general approach. And the other part is bringing the practice of meditation to your scholarship. Meditation is not an excuse that you can't do a proper paper; every paper needs to have the personal and the scholarly mixed together. There has to be some juice! You can't do a paper just as an exercise for an assignment. There has to be something there.[37]

For Naropa, meditative practice negates neither academic study nor scholarship; it exemplifies a traditional Buddhist approach to pedagogy which joins personal experience with what is learned in study.

The contemporary disengagement between religion and higher education has resulted in an absence of moral values and meaning in modern thinking. Rabbi Zalman Schacter-Shalomi, Chair of World Wisdoms at Naropa, addresses the spiritual aridity in higher education and the uniqueness of a Naropa education:

> The liberal arts and humanities are neglected in fiscal appropriations and what once were universities are now more and more becoming mere politechnical, training factories for techies. How special is this school! How unusual is Naropa! Here you receive transpersonal education par excellence. Classes open with meditation. Values are embedded in the curriculum. Transformational spirituality has the tools, the skillful means to help us change.[38]

Rabbi Schacter-Shalomi echoes the concerns of George Marsden and other Christian neoconservatives who are alarmed at the loss of spiritual values in higher education. He articulates a Naropa vision of education that refuses to turn out students lacking in compassion and social values. Many of our universities have vast resources of knowledge for research and professional specialization but have lost the religious vision of engaging and transforming society.

For Naropa, nonsectarian does not translate to nonspiritual but to an engaged spiritual pluralism and practice. Like some neoconservative Christian perspectives of higher education, Naropa understands that spiritual practice provides a core vision for the liberal arts and that spiritual values need to be embedded within the curriculum. Unlike the neoconservative Christian solution of sectarian education, it does not eschew cultural pluralism but embraces religious and cultural pluralism within a contemplative education model. Its *rimed* heritage keeps open its sectarian Buddhist vision to cultural and religious pluralism, the liberal and the fine arts. Naropa is consciously seeking to build bridges between the sacred and the secular in American education, fostering an educational vision of the liberal arts that once again connects contemplative practice to morality and public service. Naropa offers a particular educational vision that a spiritual dimension can be central to its curriculum and its pedagogies.

The Spirituality in Education Conference at Naropa brought participants with an educational vision that counters the current trends in higher education and is congruent with the goals of contemplative education.[39] The online conference listed recommended readings which provide holistic models for education.[40] These readings imagine a holistic vision of education based on an epistemological paradigm that unites reflection and practice for social engagement. Unlike some Christian neoconservatives, these authors do not segregate religious pluralism from the curriculum but promote religious pluralism and engage secular studies.

At the Spirituality in Education Conference, anthropologist and Buddhist practitioner Joan Halifax compared education to an initiation process with three phases: severance, threshold, and return. Ideally, students separate themselves from the familiar, enter into the threshold where boundaries of self are tested and broken, and return to the world with a spirit of engagement. Halifax envisions a model of education that is redemptive of the individual and the community:

> We have to ask of our educational system, What does it mean to develop an ethic of love, of compassion? How can we educate people so they return to the community with their love and compassion renewed? How can we open our young to the unknown? Our education in this time needs to be fundamentally about redemption. It must teach us how to offer ourselves selflessly for the well-being of others. We need to revision education in the West in the twenty-first century as a way to enter the unknown, bear witness to joy and suffering, and heal ourselves and the world.[41]

Naropa, likewise, envisions education as a means to learn about oneself and the world while developing contemplative practice and an ethic of compassion. Recently, Mark Schwehn has argued that college and university campuses need to become learning communities shaped by virtues rooted in particular religious beliefs, such as humility, faith, self-sacrifice, and charity, while former Southern Methodist University President Merrimon Cuninggim argues that church-related schools can believe in the academic values of truth, freedom, justice, and kinship.[42] The Naropa Institute represents a particular Buddhist vision of higher education, and some American educators may be ready to recognize its particular philosophy of education.

In 1995 the Naropa Institutional Self-Study Report articulated its educational goal: 'The goal of the Institute is to provide an environment of gentleness and discipline in which to cultivate discoverers and innovators who will actively work in the world for the benefit of others.'[43] Naropa challenges the spiritual aridness of academic institutions and even of departments of religious studies that focus on research and forget the transformational value of spiritual praxis. Naropa promotes a pedagogy of spiritual and social transformation much like divinity schools. Universities established divinity schools as educational means of retaining their original religious heritage, bringing religion into connection with the humanities, and training clergy for the American culture. Currently, many divinity schools are engaging the diversity of religious and cultural worldviews in the U.S. in the late twentieth century. Unlike divinity schools, Naropa does not prepare clergy (Buddhist monastics) but lay Buddhists and non-Buddhists for engaging these diverse worldviews.[44]

Naropa offers a degree program that prepares students with engaged Buddhist principles and practices to encounter and challenge rapid global secularization, economic development, rampant materialism, and social and environmental problems. Engaged education, Naropa style, involves bringing together Buddhists of all persuasions and students of many other contemplative traditions into a learning community to educate themselves to respond to global, political, and environmental problems. Naropa engages American culture, addressing its social problems, and its educational philosophy recognizes that social transformation of structures entails inner, or contemplative, work. Social change and personal change are inseparable, and Naropa's contemplative educational programs aim to unite theory and practice for personal and social transformation.

The current debate on the place of religion and spiritual vision within higher education often looks back to a golden age of Protestant hegemony in American culture and public life. In the late twentieth century, the U.S. has become far more religiously diverse and culturally pluralistic. Naropa may certainly contribute to the debate but not by promoting a Buddhist sectarian model of education as proposed by Christian neoconservatives.

The Institute offers an alternative educational model, originally inspired by Buddhist principles, that advocates reason, self-understanding, and social service while recognizing a secular world with cultural and religious pluralism as a locus for spiritual engagement. It does not seek a sectarian solution of withdrawal from cultural pluralism but a nonsectarian solution of educational engagement with the world inspired by its Buddhist vision of education and its *rimed* vision of cultural pluralism. Only time will tell how Naropa's vision of restoring the sacred as the seat of the liberal arts will influence American higher education. Will it follow the American route of the church-related schools? Or will it maintain its distinctive contemplative heritage, commitment to cultural pluralism, and social engagement within American higher education?

Bibliography

Batchelor, Stephen. *The Awakening of the West.* Berkeley: Parallax Press, 1994.

Bernbaum, Edwin. *The Way to Shambhala.* New York: Anchor, 1980.

Cuninggim, Merrimon.*Uneasy Partners: The College and the Church.* Nashville: Abingdon Press, 1994.

Davis, Susan E. 'East Meets West and Sparks.' *Yoga Journal* 121 (April 1995): 76ff.

Fields, Rick. *How the Swans Came to the Lake.* 3rd rev. ed. Boston: Shambhala, 1992.

____. 'Mindstreaming.' *Yoga Journal* 121 (April 1995): 4.

Hayward, Jeremy. *Sacred World: A Guide to Shambhala Warriorship in Daily Life.* New York: Bantam Books, 1995.

Gleason, Philip. *Contending with Modernity: Catholic Higher Education in the Twentieth Century.* New York: Oxford University Press, 1995

Malley, Brian E. 'Toward an Engaged Religious Studies.' *Bulletin: The Council of Societies for the Study of Religion* 26, no. 1 (February 1997): 11–12.

Mardsen, George M. *The Soul of the American University: From Protestant Establishment to Established Nonbelief.* New York: Oxford University Press, 1994.

Marsden, George M., and Bradley Longfield, eds. *The Secularization of the Academy.* New York: Oxford University Press, 1992.

Palmer, Parker J. *To Know as We Are Known.* New York: HarperCollins, 1993.

Ray, Reginald. *Buddhist Saints in India.* New York: Oxford University Press, 1995.

Ruegg, D. Seyfort. 'A Tibetan Odyssey: A Review Article.' *Journal of the Royal Asiatic Society* 2 (1989): 304–311.

Sack, Daniel. 'Struggling for the Soul of the American University: Studies on Religion and Higher Education.' *Religious Studies Review* 23, no. 1 (January 1997): 35–39.

Samuel, Geoffrey. *Civilized Shamans: Buddhism in Tibetan Societies.* Washington, D.C.: Smithsonian Institute, 1993.

Schwehn, Mark R. *Exiles from Eden: Religion and the Academic Vocation in America.* New York: Oxford University Press, 1993.

Sloan, Douglas. *Faith and Knowledge: Mainline Protestant and American Education.* Louisville: Westminister/John Knox Press, 1994.

Schacter-Shalomi, Zalman. Graduation Address, Naropa Institute, June 1996. Unpublished.

Trungpa, Chögyam. *Born in Tibet*. Boston: Shambhala, 1997.
____. *Shambhala: The Sacred Path of the Warrior*. Boston: Shambhala, 1984.
Waldman, Anne, and Andrew Schelling. *Disembodied Poetics*. Santa Fe, NM: University of New Mexico Press, 1995.
Walker, Susan, ed. *Speaking in Silence: Christians and Buddhists on the Contemplative Way*. Mahwah, NJ: Paulist Press, 1987.
Williams, Duncan Ryūken. 'Where To Study?' *Tricycle* 6, no. 3 (Spring 1997): 68–69, 115–17.

Notes

1 From an interview with Roger Dorris, faculty for the Engaged Buddhism Program at Naropa, March 10, 1997.

2 Dharma and retreat centers have been the major conduit for the transmission of Buddhist teachings. See Rick Fields, *How the Swans Came to America*, 3rd rev. ed. (Boston: Shambhala, 1992), 225ff.

3 Duncan Ryūken Williams, 'Where To Study?' *Tricycle* 6, no. 3 (Spring 1997): 68–69, 115–117.

4 Ibid., 69. Williams fails to mention the practitioner-friendly Dharma Realm Buddhist University in Talmadge, California, which offers an M.A. in Buddhist Studies.

5 Herbert Guenther, *The Life and Teaching of Naropa* (Boston: Shambhala, 1986), 24–25.

6 On a research grant from Webster University, Dennis Klass and I had the opportunity to visit Boulder for research on Buddhism and the grieving process. I had the opportunity to visit Naropa and interview faculty, department chairs, administrators, and students. Naropa also provided me with all recruitment materials, catalogues, and its own institutional self-study for this examination.

7 I made a Zen retreat under Sasaki Rōshi at the Trappist monastery in Spencer, Massachusetts. A number of Trappists monks had been practicing *zazen* for several years.

8 Fields, *How the Swans Came to the Lake*, 316–318.

9 Rick Fields, 'Mindstreaming,' *Yoga Journal* 121 (April 1995): 4.

10 Chögyam Trungpa, *Born in Tibet* (Boston: Shambhala, 1977), 115.

11 Chögyam Trungpa, *Shambhala: The Sacred Path of the Warrior* (Boston: Shambhala, 1984). See also Jeremy Hayward, *Sacred World: A Guide to Shambhala Warriorship in Daily Life* (New York: Bantam Books, 1995). On treasure texts, see Janet R. Gyatso, 'Drawn from the Tibetan Treasury: The gTerma Literature,' in *Tibetan Literature: Studies in Genre*, ed. José Ignacio Cabezòn and Roger R. Jackson (Ithaca, NY: Snow Lion, 1996), 146–169.

12 Geoffrey Samuel, *Civilized Shamans: Buddhism in Tibetan Societies* (Washington, D.C.: Smithsonian Institute, 1993), 346–349, 537–543. In personal conversation, both Judith Simmer-Brown and Reginald Ray traced Trungpa to the Rimed movement in nineteenth-century Eastern Tibet. The Vajradhatu does likewise; see 'Shambhala Vision' on the Vajradhatu web page, <http://www.shambhala.org/int/vision.html>.

13 D. Seyfort Ruegg, 'A Tibetan Odyssey: A Review Article,' *Journal of the Royal Asiatic Society* 2 (1989): 310.

14 See Samuel, *Civilized Shamans*, 546–551.

15 Ibid., 344–349.

16 See Edwin Bernbaum, *The Way to Shambhala* (New York: Anchor, 1980).

17 I believe the *rimed* heritage of Naropa is best comprehended not as nonsectarian

but as ecumenical or interfaith. From the very beginning, Naropa has maintained an interfaith perspective. It consciously includes interfaith contemplative practices and traditions in its curriculum.

18 The Naropa Institute, *Institutional Self-Study Report*, March 1995, 3.
19 Susan E. Davis, 'East Meets West and Sparks,' *Yoga Journal* 121 (April 1995): 88.
20 1996 *Peterson's*.
21 The Naropa Institute, *Institutional Self-Study Report*, 17.
22 Naropa's study abroad programs are similar to Antioch College's semester in Bodhgaya. It is in the process of developing a program in Bhutan.
23 See, for example, Anne Waldman and Andrew Schelling, *Disembodied Poetics* (Santa Fe, NM: University of New Mexico Press, 1995).
24 See the fruits of some of the individual talks and interfaith dialogue published in Susan Walker, ed., *Speaking in Silence: Christians and Buddhists on the Contemplative Way* (Mahwah, NJ: Paulist Press, 1987).
25 Rockwell's classical Tibetan grammar book is one of the most student-friendly Tibetan grammar texts. John Rockwell, Jr., *A Primer for Classical Literary Tibetan*, 2nd ed. (Barnet, VT: Samadhi Booksore, 1991).
26 The Naropa Institute, *Institutional Self-Study Report*, 121.
27 Ibid., 25.
28 1996 *Peterson's*.
29 The Naropa Institute, *Institutional Self-Study Report*, 128.
30 For a summary of the issues, see Daniel Sack, 'Struggling for the Soul of the American University: Studies on Religion and Higher Education,' *Religious Studies Review* 23, no. 1 (January 1997): 35–39. Also see Douglas Sloan, *Faith and Knowledge: Mainline Protestant and American Education* (Louisville: Westminister/John Knox Press, 1994); Mark R. Schwehn, *Exiles from Eden: Religion and the Academic Vocation in America* (New York: Oxford University Press, 1993); Philip Gleason, *Contending with Modernity: Catholic Higher Education in the Twentieth Century* (New York: Oxford University Press, 1995): George M. Mardsen, *The Soul of the American University: From Protestant Establishment to Established Nonbelief* (New York: Oxford University Press, 1994); George M. Marsden and Bradley J. Longfield, eds., *The Secularization of the Academy* (New York: Oxford University Press, 1992).
31 Quoted in George M. Marsden, 'The Soul of the American University: A Historical Overview,' in Marsden and Longfield, eds., *The Secularization of the Academ*, 17.
32 Mardsen, *The Soul of the American University*, 408–428.
33 Ibid., 61.
34 Cuninggim argues that there still is a place for religion in higher education without restricting it to a church sectarianism. See Cuninggim's criticism of Marsden: Merrimom Cunninggim, *Uneasy Partners: The College and the Church* (Nashville: Abingdon Press, 1994), 71–72.
35 See Gleason, *Contending with Modernity*.
36 Brian E. Malley, 'Toward an Engaged Religious Studies,' *Bulletin: The Council of Societies for the Study of Religion* 26, no. 1 (February 1997): 11–12.
37 Interview with Judith Simmer-Brown, March 14, 1997.
38 Rabbi Zalman Schacter-Shalomi, 'Graduation Address', Naropa Institute, June 1996 (unpublished).
39 The diverse faculty members included Joan Halifax, Rachel Naomi Remen, Diana Chapman Walsh, John Taylor Gatto, Parker J. Palmer, Ron Miller, Vincent Harding, Tenzin Gyatso, Jeremy Hayward, David Orr, Zalman

Schacter-Shalomi, Huston Smith, Judith Simmer-Brown. The papers will be edited and published in a later volume.

40 Some of the recommended readings were: Phillip Snow Gang, *Rethinking Education* (Brookfield, VT: Dagaz Press, 1989); Phillip Snow Gang, Lynn Nina Meyerhoff, and Dorothy J. Maver, *Conscious Education: The Bridge to Freedom* (Grafton, VT: Daghaz Press, 1992); Ron Miller, *What are Schools For? Holistic Education in American Culture* (Brandon, VT: Holisitic Education Press, 1992); James Moffet, *The Universal Schoolhouse: Spiritual Awakening Through Education* (San Francisco: Jossey-Bass Publishers, 1994); Parker J. Palmer, *To Know as We Are Known* (New York: HarperCollins, 1993); David E. Purpel, *The Moral and Spiritual Crisis in Education: A Curriculum for Justice and Compassion in Education* (New York: Bergin & Garvey Publishers, 1989). All from Spirituality in Education Online, <http://csf.Colorado.edu/internet/townsend-carena.html>.

41 Spirituality in Education Online, <http://csf.Colorado.edu/sine/sat/halifax2.html>.

42 Schwehn. *Exiles from Eden*, 44–67. Cuninggim, *Uneasy Partners*, 93–99.

43 The Naropa Institute, *Institutional Self-Study Report*, 8.

44 See Conrad Cherry, *Hurrying toward Zion: Universities, Divinity Schools, and American Protestantism* (Bloomington, IN: Indiana University Press, 1995).

CHAPTER THIRTEEN

Buddhist Worlds in the U.S.A.: A Survey of the Territory

Richard Hughes Seager

I had never really considered writing a textbook on anything until about a year ago, when an editor from Columbia University Press called with a proposal for a book on Buddhism in America. I was first put off by his being with the Reference Division, which suggested producing concise entries on Buddhist people and places in the United States. I was only slightly more interested to find he was after a textbook, which suggested to me an historical treatment of philosophy, something unattractive to me from a creative point of view and well beyond my competency. 'I am not sure I am the person to write a textbook on American Buddhism,' I said cautiously. I had been developing a project on sacred space in New York state and was leery about having that work derailed. 'Aren't you the Richard Hughes Seager who wrote on the Columbian Exposition and the World's Parliament?' he asked.

Having written on the 1893 World's Parliament of Religions did not mean I thought of myself as a someone who might work on Buddhism in America. On the contrary. The Parliament represented to me the long, often painful distances I had traveled from my original love for Asian religions. I first entered graduate studies as a friend of all things Asian, but quickly plunged into Buddhism and Hinduism. I was not a practitioner of any religion, but a sixties humanist. During those years, I never practiced as did many of my friends and academic peers and friends. But I remained enthralled with Asian religions, particularly those of India, and began to study Sanskrit and to collect multivolume *purāṇas* and hard-bound *sūtras* and to cultivate a taste for *tantric* art.

Eventually I moved from the comparative field into Harvard's new 'Modern West' program for doctoral training, becoming its first 'modern westernist.' I chose a North American concentration because the focus of my Asian interests had shifted. I had become more interested in the way Asian religions operate in the popular imagination of people in the West, specifically in the United States, than in the Asian traditions themselves. I aspired to study that vast and complex arena casually referred to as the history of the East/West encounter.

Given the program at the time, however, I found myself with little time to think about the early Jesuits in China and Japan or Annie Besant's Theosophy because 'Modern West' was then more or less defined at Harvard by Protestantism. The contours of the field began with Martin Luther, ran through the English Puritans to Jonathan Edwards, and concluded with the Niebuhr brothers. As a kind of ethnic and religious reaction formation, I became fascinated instead with the modern Marian revival in France, Voltaire and the rites of the French Revolution, and the continental avant-garde. I became deeply enmeshed in the history of the many Western struggles over the soul of modernity. I rediscovered both my Protestant and Catholic roots and reveled for a time in my birthright claim on Roman Christian antiquity.

The Modern West, whether Anglophile or Francophile, was then an interpretive milieu in which Edward Said's Orientalist thesis was on the cutting edge, and its influence lured me away from my romance with Hinduism and Buddhism. I redescribed my eastward turn as a compensatory move, a psychoanalytically read ethnic and erotic displacement. I came to think that all the murky personal stuff that drew me into the world of the *purāṇas*, *sūtras*, and *tantras* in the first place would someday go into my 'big' book.

In the meantime, the Parliament was suggested to me by my adviser as a natural extension of my original interests. But I soon found I could not separate the Parliament as a moment in the East/West encounter (which is the only reason comparativists remember it) from its importance as a highly political event in American Protestant, Catholic, and Jewish history. My biggest dissertation headache was to find a way to sweep the entire panorama of religious forces present at the assembly into a single overriding thesis. For many months, I wrestled with ideas about the Parliament as alienated consciousness on a global scale (which it may have been) or as the global apotheosis of the eighteenth-century Enlightenment (which I am quite certain it was). But I could not figure out how to argue those two theses simultaneously.

I finally lit upon something closer to home – the Parliament as an expression of an elite system of cultural, theological, and religious values in Gilded Age America. This shifted the emphasis to more familiar ground – to interpretive angles related to immigration and assimilation and to dominance, submission, and resistance in religion. I thought about a global melting-pot, the Pax Britannica morphing into a Pax Americana, and commerce-driven processes of modernization and globalization at work in a turn-of-the-century ecumene. I steeped myself in the nuanced meanings that inform ideas about Christians and non-Christians, gentiles and heathens, civilized and barbarians, and non-ethnics and ethnics in

American society. Given that the Parliament was held at Chicago's World's Columbian Exposition, I thought a great deal about the meaning of Greek revival and Beaux Arts architecture and about the aesthetic expression of civil values in iconography and ritual. For years, I wondered more about the meaning of Doric columns than about Buddhism in America.

My work on the 1893 Parliament eventually drew me into the planning of its 1993 centennial. This had the fortunate effect of creating an alternative lens through which to reflect on the original event, by placing me in the midst of contemporary inter-religious dialogue and encounter rooted, not in texts, but in face-to-face relations.

From the Four Noble Truths to Richard Gere

I warmed to the prospect of doing the book when it became apparent that Columbia was after neither a classic reference book nor a dry textbook, but a smart, interpretive guide to American Buddhism for general readers. The book was to be one in a series devoted to different religio-ethnic groupings – Evangelical Protestantism, Black Religions, Catholicism, Orthodox Christians, Judaism, the Sikhs, the Hindus, the Moslems, and Buddhism. The series was to address a real or perceived 'crisis' in teaching American religion, which had resulted from the triumph of pluralistic sensibilities. Americanists, it was said, are abandoning mainstream Protestantism as a normative model in favor of a 'representative topics' approach to American religion. From a marketing point of view, the optimal situation was to create texts to aid Americanists in teaching Judaism, Buddhism, and Evangelical Protestantism, for instance, in a one-semester class devoted to representative developments in American religion. Comparativists might also use one of these books for an American unit on a great tradition such as Hinduism, Judaism, Christianity, Buddhism, or Islam.

Columbia suggested no uniform template for each book in the series, but broad guidelines were established to foster rough compatibility. The religious dimension was to be in the foreground, with generous attention to scripture and other texts that serve to define, illuminate, motivate, and inspire. It was suggested that each one begin with the consideration of a ritual that in some way epitomized the community in question. But each volume was also to include social historical concerns, demographics, biographical sketches of prominent leaders and rank-and-file participants, and attention to substantive issues facing communities. The material in question was to be presented with an even hand. Controversy was to be approached with moderation, personal interpretive agendas kept to a minimum. A decent budget was available for illustrations.

I took on the project for a variety of reasons. It appealed to the generalist in me, which had come to the fore as a result of teaching at a liberal arts college, where the entire academic task becomes recast for undergraduates.

Having recently completed some work on a CD-ROM project on American religion for a general audience, I had come to find synthesizing complex material to be an intellectual challenge.[1] It also appealed to the social animal in me because research would require chats with many different Buddhists across the country.

The decisive factor in my undertaking the project, however, was the editor's caveat that the book was to be conceived and written for a target audience of undergraduates and general readers, not scholars, who might find the volume to be of interest only incidentally. This made the proposition both doable and entertaining because I know what many undergraduates want – Richard Gere, Tina Turner, the Beastie Boys, the Dalai Lama, Jack Kerouac, and 'way cool' metaphysics. And I also know I can deliver what they need – the life of the Buddha, a basic philosophical vocabulary, a brief introduction to Buddhist Asia and the East/West encounter, and sustained attention to concrete developments in America's many Buddhist communities.

A Wide Variety But a Spotty Bibliography

The full scope of the project dawned on me only when I undertook an exploratory research trip to the west and southwest. Nothing I had read prepared me for the extraordinary range of Buddhisms currently setting down roots in the U.S. – new immigrants and old 'WASP' Buddhists; traditionalists and radical innovators; psychotherapists and shamanic New Agers. This list goes on. The interpretive vertigo induced by these site visits was amplified by logging onto the 'Cyber-sangha' when I returned home. The discovery of high quality, if highly uneven, resources at my disposal was a revelation – descriptions of tea ceremonies in the Diamond Sangha, autobiographies of Thai forest monks, *dharma* talks by Maezumi Rōshi. One can download the histories, biographies, and program notes of *dharma* centers worldwide, although these yield truly comprehensive views of only a few communities.

I soon found the interpretive challenge posed by these extensive primary materials to be compounded by the spotty coverage of American Buddhism in the scholarly bibliography. There has been a boom in Buddhist publishing over the last decade, but the extraordinary array of good books put out by U.S. Buddhist presses are mostly primary texts. They display the vigor of American Buddhism and will undoubtedly present future historians with solid evidence that the 'Zen boom' of the 1950s flourished into a highly variegated movement. But few, if any, of these many books give an historian much in the line of scholarly interpretation. The slim American Buddhist bibliography already in existence includes a number of highly valuable books, but these are written out of different disciplines with varied interpretive agendas. They rarely make reference to interpretations in the broader field of American religious history. A number focus on 'New Age' eclecticism or 'new religions,' but these interpretive lines contribute little to understanding current issues in the American Buddhist community.

A look at some of the standard texts on American Buddhism gives a sense of this mixed bag of scholarly activity. The study of Buddhism in America began in 1974, with the publication of the two-volume *Buddhist Churches in America*, a denominational account of the Shin Buddhism of three generations of Japanese American immigrants.[2] In the same year, Robert Ellwood published *The Eagle and the Rising Sun*, which provided an introduction to post-war Buddhist movements in Japan and their impact in America.[3] A look at a fuller range of forms of Buddhism became available in 1976 with Emma McCloy Layman's *Buddhism in America* and three years later with Charles Prebish's *American Buddhism*.[4] Layman wrote in a journalistic, anecdotal vein, while Prebish, a Buddhologist, gave a more systematic introduction to institutions, centers, and practices of different kinds of Buddhism. He positioned much of his interpretive discussion with reference to the 'consciousness explosion' of the 1960s, which did so much to give shape to the beat-hip strand in American Buddhist history. Both books, though snapshots of the 1970s, remain of value in a field that lacks a basic chronology of the many developments in American Buddhism over the last several decades.

At about the same time, scholarship on Shin Buddhism advanced significantly with the publication of Tetsuden Kashima's *Buddhism in America: The Social Organization of an Ethnic Religious Institution*.[5] It remains an outstanding piece of interpretive work that has received little sustained attention in the broader field of American religious history. Kashima handles a wide range of issues familiar to Americanists who deal with Jewish and Catholic history, such as the wedding of religion and ethnicity and the complex, often problematic, relations between immigrants and the American mainstream. Additional work focusing on very different aspects of American Buddhism has been published only recently. Jane Hurst looks at Sōka Gakkai in the U.S., a movement most familiar to scholars through the work of those who have studied it in Britain.[6] Paul Numrich's *Old Wisdom in the New World* is the best in a very slim field that addresses religion in today's Buddhist immigrant community.[7] To my knowledge, there is no historical or interpretive work on either the Vipassana movement or on the many different Vajrayāna communities.

For a variety of reasons, Rick Fields's *When the Swans Came to the Lake* is in a class of its own.[8] It is more an affectionate chronicle than a critical history, but it gave sixties converts to Buddhism their own American Buddhist lineage or, perhaps more correctly, a sense of their own indigenous spiritual history. A major reason for the appeal of *Swans* is the sweeping scope of its narrative. Fields built his account on a sequence of developments in American religious history, some of which had been familiar only to specialists – the Buddhism of Henry Steel Olcott and Helena Blavatsky, the warm reception for the Buddhist delegation at the World's Parliament, and the eastward turn of a handful of Boston brahmins. He linked these to new information about pioneering Japanese Buddhist leaders who came to the U.S. between 1900 and 1950 and to material on the Beats. But Fields gave *Swans* and the spiritual history it describes authority by claiming Emerson, Whitman, and Thoreau as 'restless pioneers' for an Asian American spiritual lineage, which was to turn into a Buddhist torrent only in the wake of the 1960s.[9]

Fields's work also encouraged Americanists to open up American Buddhist topics to more critical modes of inquiry. With a plot grounded in native figures from the Transcendentalists to Olcott, Philangi Dasa, Paul Carus, Dwight Goddard, and the Beats, Fields's lineage called to mind other liberal religious traditions well-known in American religious history. J. Stillson Judah called a cluster of developments, which includes Christian Science and New Thought, the 'metaphysical movements,' whose origins he traced to late Puritanism.[10] Sydney Ahlstorm named a related phenomena 'harmonial religion,' which is a broad and eclectic stream of spiritual philosophy that runs from the antebellum period into the many New Age movements.[11] The most influential of these currents is a churchly form of religious liberalism that William R. Hutchison described as the 'modernist impulse' in American Protestant theology.[12] Hutchison traced this impulse from the early Unitarians, through the golden age of Gilded Age liberalism, to the immanentist theologies that began to emerge on the threshold of the 1960s.[13]

With their lineage placed alongside these other streams of American liberal religion, the Buddhists in *Swans* became more accessible to American religious historiography, which is a point of departure for two recent books on American Buddhist history by Americanists. They both probed in different ways the intellectual, religious, cultural, and ethnic boundaries between Buddhism and the religion of the American Protestant mainstream, which in the American field has always been considered the ultimate arbiter of religious values, at least until quite recently.

Thomas A. Tweed examined the emergence of a discussion about Victorian-era Buddhism, which arose when a small cluster of Americans (Tweed suggests at most several thousand) explored its religious worldview as a vehicle for religious dissent.[14] He found that Buddhist advocates and critics alike used typically mainstream religious values such as theism, spiritual individualism, optimism, and activism as their criteria for judgment as to whether Buddhism was suited to a larger role in the American religious enterprise. Tweed found some Victorians willing to forego theism and individualism in order to embrace Buddhism, but many more could not reconcile its contemplative dimensions with optimism, activism, and the ideal of self-reliance. My work on the Parliament approached a similar question but in a very different setting – the exuberant celebrations at Chicago's World's Columbian Exposition and World's Parliament of Religions.[15] I found the expansive universalism of Christian liberals to play an important role by creating a heady sense of religious consensus on the assembly floor. But this consensus was more illusion than fact. Liberal theological universalism was predicated on Christian triumphalism, racist and ethnocentric evolutionary theories, and imperial pretensions. At the same time, this buoyant theology was of such an amorphous shape and so devoid of specific content that it was easily appropriated by the Asian delegates to win the affections of their American audience.

Stephen Prothero reached farther afield to examine critically American religious liberalism at work in an indigenous Buddhist locale, by exploring Henry Olcott's life and work as a Buddhist Theosophist in south Asia.[16] Prothero concluded that Olcott's Theosophical and educational work was a great success, but his life was also a cautionary tale about American liberalism when it came to Buddhist Asia. Prothero argued that Olcott's brand of idealist and reform-minded Buddhism was an example of 'creolization,' by which he meant that Olcott's religious thought, while cast in a Buddhist vocabulary, had a grammatical structure which was thoroughly Protestant and American. Certain of validity of his Protestant/Buddhist hybrid, Olcott could draw the conclusion that, contrary to his original expectations, there was not a single true Buddhist in Sri Lanka. Not surprisingly, this brought him into direct conflict with Anagarika Dharmapala, his one-time protégé, and other Buddhist leaders of the Sinhalese revival.

These two accounts suggest the interpretive opportunities that are possible when Buddhist material and American religious historiographic concerns are brought into play. Their conclusions about the character and limits of American religious liberalism might help to shed critical light on debates about the Americanization of Buddhism heard in the community today. More to the point, they also help to set *Swans'* greatest weakness in high relief. In creating an indigenous lineage from mainstream American materials, Fields structured a narrative history that operates much like traditional *heilsgeschichte*. In this case, Zen practitioners, and to a lesser extent converts within the Vipassana and Tibetan Buddhist communities, appear as the natural heirs to a long and authentic American spiritual history. This is to a large extent a pious fiction, even if one that gives *Swans* its considerable charm and energy. More importantly, it effectively gives precedence to Buddhism over Hinduism and other assorted traditions that are heir to this same alternative stream. It also marginalizes other forms of American Buddhism such as the Shin tradition, which appears in *Swans* only in an ancillary way, and Sōka Gakkai, which is virtually absent, even in its subsequent revised editions. Nor is substantive attention given to

Buddhism in contemporary Asian immigrant communities, which is an understandable oversight given that few commentators noted until quite recently how Asian immigration was changing the Buddhist scene.

Despite these shortcoming, Fields's book deserves, and is likely to retain, its status as a classic chronicle of American Buddhist history. But this does not alter the fact that the bibliography on American Buddhism is as yet inadequate to the task of a comprehensive study of the full range of U.S. Buddhist communities.

Buddhist Worlds in the U.S.A.

The challenge is to write an engaging, synoptic, but necessarily selective account of American Buddhism as a religious, social, ethnic, and cultural phenomena, in which its different communities are discussed in a common interpretive gauge and with an even hand. A first section of the book will treat the life and teaching of the Buddha and those developments in Asian Buddhist history of particular importance to American Buddhism, including attention to modernizing movements in the nineteenth and twentieth centuries. A second section will be a critical look at selected events in the East/West encounter over the last few centuries, to emphasize the complexity of religious encounters among representatives of different civilizations. A concluding section will be devoted to contemporary developments such as race, ethnicity, and gender issues; Buddhism and the arts; the emergence of socially engaged Buddhism; Buddhist/Christian dialogue; and Buddhist ecumenical movements.

The core of the book is in six chapters of about twenty-five pages each in a section with the working title 'Buddhist Worlds in the U.S.A.' Due to the uneven quality of bibliographic materials and to the unique character of each community, every chapter will be an almost stand-alone essay on a particular Buddhist tradition and its American 'instantiation.' Even so, common elements are to be shared by each. The bulk of each essay will be devoted to explicitly religious material – sacred spaces and rituals, outstanding American leaders, their ideas in representative texts, and their activities. But throughout the entire section I am developing a broad immigration and Americanization thesis to structure the overall discussion. Buddhism will be characterized as an imported but not a 'new' American religion. It has been brought into the United States where the religiously normative and functionally dominant religion has been the Judeo-Christian tradition in general and Protestant Christianity more specifically. For a century, Buddhism has been and still is being carried to the United States through myriad channels by different kinds of people for many different reasons. Once here, it put down – and continues to put down – roots and to adjust to a highly secularized and commercialized society in a wide variety of ways, all of them part of a complex, multi-vocal, yet-to-be fully accomplished process of Americanization. A seventh chapter in this section will be devoted to American Buddhist miscellany, which will provide an opportunity for a consideration of expressions of Buddhism that elude traditional categorization.

The following are sketches of interpretive strategies for each chapter, together with citations that indicate the kind of secondary and primary material that are readily available.

Jōdo Shinshū and the Japanese Immigrant Experience

The Buddhist Churches of America (BCA), representing the Jōdo Shinshū (one of the Japanese Pure Land lineages), is the first tradition under consideration for a variety of reasons. This is one area of American Buddhist history in which an institutional focus easily defines the subject matter, and a sufficiently sophisticated and fairly compact body of scholarly historical work already exists.[17] The history of the Buddhist Churches also sets dynamic issues of immigration at the center stage. BCA history is an Asian and Buddhist variant of classical processes of the Americanization of a religious tradition closely associated with an immigrant ethnic group, the complexity of which is familiar to Americanists from the experiences of American Catholics and Jews. BCA scholarship includes well-articulated discussions about important perennial issues related to religion and immigration – language issues; the ebb and flow of overseas influences; the problems of the second, third, and fourth generations; intermarriage; and the use of cultural and religious forms such as *taiko*, Japanese folk drumming, as means to bolster ethnic identity.

At the same time, the BCA experience is unique insofar as its Japanese membership faced anti-Asian sentiments and experienced the internment camps, developments which are widely noted to have had a withering effect on the community. They have, nevertheless, been Asian Buddhist pioneers in a country in which public religious discourse has long focused on the religious mission of a Christian or Judeo-Christian nation. As a result of its unique history, BCA also has an oblique relationship with other forms of American Buddhism. It does not significantly factor into the current Buddhist vogue. As is the case with many Catholics and Jews,[18] challenges that currently face the BCA membership have less to do with setting down religious roots than with adjusting to their arrival in the professional-managerial class and the erosion of ethnic identity.

Zen and the Buddhist Mainstream

Zen is the most widely known and influential form of Buddhism in the United States. For purposes of argument, it can be called the American Buddhist mainstream. The processes of its Americanization are related to the transmission of the *dharma* by Japanese teachers, who often came to the U.S. as immigrants and missionaries to teach modernist forms of Buddhism to American students. We are currently witnessing an important moment in the Americanization of Zen, as the students of these earlier teachers have become the leaders of the community and are producing a second and occasionally a third generation of American Zen students. The early history of American Zen has been told by Rick Fields and does not bear extensive repeating. The 1950s Zen boom and the early interest of the Beats will already have been dealt with as a topic in East/West history. This shifts the weight of the historical discussion from the earlier Senzaki/ Sokei-an generation and such figures as Alan Watts and D. T. Suzuki onto Eidō Tai Shimano, Maezumi Rōshi, and Suzuki Rōshi, their students, and their students' students. Some attention needs to be given to the Korean Zen of Seung Sahn's Kwan Um school[19] and to the less well-known figure Samu Sunim, who has established temples in Ann Arbor, Toronto, and Chicago.

Despite the work of Fields and others, there is no single, synoptic account of the formation and growth of the different Zen lineages.[20] My current thinking is to approach the topic by sketching in figures and institutions such as Robert and Ann Aitken and the Diamond Sangha, Joshū Sasaki Rōshi and his network of Rinzai centers in California and the southwest, and the achievements of Eidō Shimano and Philip Kapleau in New York. This is an attempt at some degree of comprehensiveness. The focus, however, will be on the San Francisco Zen Center and Zen Center of Los Angeles,[21] two major centers with a considerable reach, which became linked to other U.S. Sōtō groups in 1997 in an experimental institution called Kaikō Center of North American Sōtō Zen Buddhism.[22] I will, however, pay special attention to the White Plum Sangha, which is composed of the students of Maezumi Rōshi, for a variety of reasons. There is good and accessible information about him and his more prominent students – Bernard Tetsugen Glassman, John Daidō Loori, Charlotte Joko Beck, Dennis Genpō Merzel, and others. The *dharma* they teach and the kind of work they do give a concrete sense of the different modalities in the Americanization of Zen Buddhism and the breadth and diversity of activity within the Zen community.[23]

The Tibetan Diaspora and the Vajrayāna Milieu

The complex metaphysical worldview, mythologies, and liturgical practices of Vajrayāna Buddhism are on the line in a high stakes game of geo-religious politics, pop culture, and Americanization to a far greater degree than any other form of Buddhism in the United States. The Americanization of Tibetan Buddhism, while apparently quite successful, is also proceeding very unevenly. Political issues surrounding the Tibetan diaspora and the charismatic figure of the Dalai Lama have propelled Tibetan Buddhism toward the American mainstream, while, at the same time, a range of strategies from the preservation of traditions to their self-conscious adaptation to American norms have emerged within different communities. There is little difficulty in assembling material for a discussion of political issues – the Chinese invasion, Tibetan resettlement here and abroad, and pertinent religious questions, be they related to the Dalai Lama's tours in America or the controversy surrounding the Panchen Lama.[24] Developing a discussion on growth and change within the Tibetan Buddhist religious communities over the past thirty years is much trickier. Despite its rich publishing record in the last two decades and its apparent flourishing in the United States, Tibetan Buddhism has little secondary literature that charts, much less interprets, the often baffling relations among the many Tibetan Buddhist teachers, institutions, and lineages.

One can, however, develop a valuable discussion with reference to a range of adaptive strategies found within the American Vajrayāna community. Tarthang Tulku, an early Tibetan leader in the U.S., combined philosophical reinterpretation with the preservation of tradition in the Nyingma Institute and its associated activities.[25] Surya Das, a well-regarded American convert, student of Nyoshul Khenpo, and Dzogchen practitioner and teacher, is exploring a more thorough-going Americanization through the Dzogchen Foundation in Cambridge. His new book, *Awakening the Buddha Within*, is an excellent example of the recasting of tradition in an American idiom.[26] A highly illustrative contrast between two types of adaptive strategies is found in the centers associated with the Kagyu lineage. The first is not an explicit Americanization strategy at all, but an effort to maintain a pristine Tibetan monastic compound, Karma Triyana Dharmachakra (KTD), as the North American seat of the Gwalya Karmapa, head of the Kagyu order, whose seventeenth incarnation has been at the center of a uniquely Tibetan '*tulku* controversy.'[27] Under the direction of Khenpo Karthar, KTD has also become the flagship for some twenty-five traditional practice centers and a three-year retreat center in the United States.[28] In contrast, the life and legacy of Chögyam Trungpa represent more self-conscious attempts to adapt the Tibetan *dharma* to the West. Major steps in Trungpa's work are well known from the establishment of Samye Linge in the U.K. and Tail of the Tiger in Vermont to the move to Colorado and the founding of Naropa Institute, Shambhala training, and the Cape Breton community.[29] His death and the subsequent controversies in the Shambhala community are also widely understood to have been among the events that furthered Americanizing tendencies.[30] Trungpa-related developments, such as the growth of the Naropa Institute, the development of Rocky Mountain Shambhala Center, and the emergence of teachers like Pema Chödron represent highly creative adaptations of Vajrayāna in America.[31]

248

The Parallel Worlds of American Theravāda

In his work on the Americanization of Theravāda Buddhism in the immigrant community, Paul Numrich discusses what he calls 'the parallelism thesis' – the fact that immigrants and converts tend to form two congregations within a single temple, which amiably co-exist with one another and interact to a limited degree but make little sustained contact. He suggests further that this parallelism mirrors a larger development on a national scale, whose existence may have long terms effects on its process of Americanization.[32]

The idea of parallel worlds is a useful metaphor for structuring a discussion of the various forms of Buddhism with Theravāda roots currently flourishing in the U.S. Numrich's book provides ample information to discuss one of these worlds, that of post-1965 Thai and Sri Lankan immigrants in American cities. His account of the shaping force of traditional sectarianism and ethnicity and the challenges facing monastics as they adapt to the American landscape is of a piece with the kind of scholarship familiar from earlier immigrants' histories. The other worlds of American Theravāda Buddhism have no comparable secondary scholarship, but they are richly documented in readily available primary material. The historical and religious layers to this world are, moreover, fairly easy to discern. The foundation rests on those Americans who, since the 1960s, have traveled to Asian countries with strong Theravāda traditions to study and practice Buddhism, often with monks in forest monasteries.[33] One traditional form of Theravāda Buddhism is found in the transplantation of this forest tradition to the United States in such places as the Abhayagiri Buddhist Monastery in northern California and Metta Forest Monastery outside San Diego.[34] A second, more intentionally adaptive form is the Vipassana meditation movement closely associated with Jack Kornfield, Sharon Salzberg, and Joseph Goldstein, which is most notably institutionalized in the Insight Meditation Society (IMS) in Barre, Massachusetts, where a wide range of Theravāda teachers find a home.[35] The farther reaches of this movement are to be found in the stress reduction techniques of Jon Kabat-Zinn, who fosters a kind of post-Buddhist Vipassana meditation under the auspices of educational innovation and behavioral medicine.[36]

Nichiren Shōshū and Sōka Gakkai

Like Zen, Vajrayāna, and Theravāda-related developments, one other major form of convert Buddhism in America, Nichiren Buddhism, most particularly Sōka Gakkai, is intimately linked to the spiritual ferment associated with the 1960s. Americanization was from the outset an explicit ideal of the movement. Under the leadership of George Williams, Sōka

Gakkai identified itself with American patriotism and the success myth, which helped to create a religious style that developed within its own horizon in a way quite different than Zen. Somewhat distanced from the more alienated and psychedelic elements in the largely white and middle-class counter-culture, Sōka Gakkai, unlike other forms of convert Buddhism, has had a powerful appeal for many Latinos and African Americans. Daisaku Ikeda, now the leader of what is called Sōka Gakkai International, set in motion liberalizing reforms in 1990, which have had a wide-reaching effect on the movement in this country. In 1992, long-standing tensions between the Nichiren Shoshu Temple priesthood and Sōka Gakkai came to a head in a definitive parting of the way between the two groups. Since that time, Sōka Gakkai (now Sōka Gakkai U.S.A.), which was an already highly Americanized lay community, moved further in that direction by encouraging lay initiatives to fill the gap created by the loss of its traditional institutions, rituals, and clergy. It may well be that Sōka Gakkai is now at the forefront of the Americanization of Buddhism and, given the reported size of its membership, may yet make a claim as to being the defining movement in American Buddhism.

The literature on Nichiren Shoshu and Sōka Gakkai is adequate, especially for the period prior to the schism.[37] There are a number of Nichiren Shoshu Web sites that extensively present various facets of orthodox doctrine and practice.[38] These are mirrored by Sōka Gakkai sites, the content of which seems to reflect the streamlined religiosity of this self-avowed humanist Buddhist movement.[39] The ideas of Daisaku Ikeda, the chief architect of SGI humanism, are well documented and readily accessible.[40] There are also a number of Web sites that reflect the intense anger and hostility caused by the Nichiren/Sōka Gakkai split, which, although conspicuously biased, provide insight into both the ritual, succession, and philosophical issues at stake in the schism and the allegations of misconduct by Ikeda.[41]

Other Immigrant Buddhisms

The interpretive literature on other Buddhist immigrant groups is spotty and does not add up to a coherent field. As a result, this chapter will of necessity be a collage of complex, only partially comprehended, instances of the persistence and adaptation of ethnic Buddhist traditions in the Chinese, Vietnamese, Cambodian, and Korean Buddhist communities. One consistent tack will be to highlight perennial developments among immigrants, such as those addressed in Numrich's *Old Wisdom* and in the more well-developed fields of Catholic and Jewish immigration history, while noting at the same time the emergence of an increasingly self-conscious Asian American or Asian-Pacific minority community.[42] This may also be the place to introduce a discussion of Thich Nhat Hanh, who as both a prominent leader among convert Buddhists and a well-known figure among the Vietnamese, is a powerful, if all too rare, link between the Asian and Caucasian Buddhist communities.

The uninformed nature of the debate surrounding the Democratic National Committee, 'Asian money,' John Huang, and Hsi Lai Temple in Hacienda Heights, California, underscores how Buddhism among Chinese Americans, the oldest Asian community in the United States, suffers from inadequate scholarship. A number of Web sites provide substantial data on several different kinds of Chinese Buddhist movements on the West Coast, such as the Fo Kuang Shan Association, the True Buddha School, and the Tzu-Chi Foundation.[43] Organizations based in the East include the Buddhist Association of the United States and Ch'an Meditation Society.[44] Limited secondary materials exist, although some unpublished works and research from the Harvard Pluralism Project will help to remedy this.[45] Ethnic studies, such as the literature on Monterey Park, California, provide background information on the creation of secondary institutions and the formation of ethnic identities but rarely examine the role of religion in the creation of community.[46] Less is available on the more recently arriving Asian American Buddhist communities.[47] Glimpses of the on-going processes of Americanization, however, can be found in Web sites and in magazines and newspapers. For example, the Los Angeles metropolitan area press has recently given much attention to controversies over temple building and home temples. These new additions to the Los Angeles basin have raised legal, aesthetic, civic, and moral issues, all of which are rooted in zoning regulations. This kind of grassroots controversy, referenced to related relevant scholarly work, is highly illustrative of the concrete meaning of Americanization.[48]

American Buddhist Miscellany

A good deal of the vibrancy of American Buddhism at this date is found in a variety of expressions that elude categorization. Some of these expressions might be typified as creative forms of New World eclecticism, as in the work of Joan Halifax, who combines Buddhist practice with expertise in shamanism and anthropology in her work on death and dying.[49] Other expressions are better described as Buddhist and Buddhist-like images, sensibilities, and ideas that free-float in the culture but surface in both ridiculous and sublime forms in films, cartoons, and advertising.[50] Still others are activities that are historically related to Buddhism, but often operate in the U.S. independent of the religious aspects of the tradition. One such activity is training in the Asian martial arts, which, quite aside from programs offered in dharma centers, has an immense following in this country. John Donohue, in *Warrior Dreams and Forge of the Spirit*, gives fine interpretations of the form and meaning of the martial arts in America, but there seems to be no hard data on whether the far-flung martial arts network serves as a path for *karateka* and other arts aficionados to formal practice within one or another Buddhist community.[51] The Cyber-sangha phenomena is also a factor to be reckoned with when attempting to describe ways in which Buddhism is penetrating the broader ranges of American culture.[52] Some of the Buddhism to be found on the Web is 'authentic,' some highly personalized and unquestionably idiosyncratic, but it is all witness to the fact that Buddhism follows many paths into American society.

A Concluding Consideration: The First Propagation

The task of surveying the landscape of late-twentieth-century Buddhism in the United States is daunting, but it is made easier by acknowledging the fact that the forms it is taking are far too rich and multifarious to allow for an exhaustive treatment. Selectivity is required, as is an overall interpretive schema. There is, moreover, an epic quality to the story of the movement of the *dharma* from Asia to the United States, which is heightened by the fact that, in the context of universal history, American Buddhism has come into being only very recently. As an historian who once aspired, quite impossibly and with much grandiosity, to study the entire sweep of the history of the East/West encounter, I have a keen sense of how the transplantation of a religious tradition is an epochal and epoch-long undertaking. It is far more than an international exchange of ideas, sentiments, convictions, and practices. It is a long process of encounter and dialogue, an entire series of calls and responses, between and among representatives of discrete civilizations. That Buddhism has come to the U.S. carried on the wings of exile, immigration, global pop culture, and commerce has certainly speeded up the transmission process. But it is not clear that this has made the task of creating an authentic, but uniquely indigenous, *dharma* with deep and enduring roots any easier.

In the course of refreshing my memory about the history of Buddhism in Asia, I found myself looking at China, Japan, and Tibet to find precedents that might serve as models that could inform the current Buddhist scene in America. But the modern world, with its new political orders, sciences and technologies, marketplace economies, and Edge Cities, is separated by a material, spiritual, and imaginative chasm from first-century China, sixth-century Japan, and seventh-century Tibet to a degree that it is pointless to look hard for specific cases.

But still, given the modest American Buddhist timeline, I found myself returning to the idea of 'a first propagation,' a metaphor drawn from early Tibetan Buddhist history. The first American Buddhists were unquestionably Chinese and Japanese and they deserve credit as true pioneers, but having spent long decades either excluded from mainstream society or preoccupied within immigrant communities, their impact was not deeply felt in the broader reaches of American society. 1893 is the early and convenient date used by commentators to point to the emergence of an enthusiasm for Buddhism in the United States. It marks the public successes of the Asian Buddhist missionaries at the World's Parliament of Religions and the taking of refuge by C. T. Strauss, who is accounted to be America's first convert Buddhist. But only after the middle of the twentieth century did anything happen that resembles a substantial movement towards Buddhism, first in the Zen boomlet of the 1950s and then in the real Buddhist boom that ignited in the late 1960s and 1970s. In the meantime, a new mass immigration of Asian Buddhists from Sri Lanka, China, Thailand, Cambodia, Laos, Burma, Taiwan, Korea, and Vietnam had begun.

All this is to say that, in the larger frame of things, it is probably best not to confuse the maturing of a first generation of convert Buddhists with the maturing of an American Buddhism. This first generation labored long and hard to plant the *dharma* and to construct vibrant institutions and had, in the process (if the stories they tell are any indication at all), a good bit of fun. Among them are some of America's Hsüang-tsangs, Eisais, and Padmasambhavas. But the first propagation metaphor is a reminder that we are now witnessing only the immediate aftermath of the first, large-scale fluorescence of Buddhism in America. The rapid turning of the wheel of *dharma* in the last three decades churned up great clouds of New World dust, much of which still remains suspended in air. It is too early to make a call on what American Buddhism is. And historical precedents in Asia suggest that there is a great deal more yet to come.

References

Activity Committee in Association of Sōtō Zen Buddhists. *Buddha's Seeds Taking Firm Roots in North American* Soil. Los Angeles: Association of Sōtō Zen Buddhists, 1997.
Aitken, Robert. *Taking the Path of Zen*. San Francisco: North Point Press, 1982.
Alhstrom, Sydney. *A Religious History of the American People*. New Haven: Yale University Press, 1972.
Beck, Charlotte Joko. *Everyday Zen: Love and Work*. San Francisco: Harper and Row, 1989.
____. *Nothing Special: Living Zen*. San Francisco: Harper San Francisco, 1993.
Boucher, Sandy. 'In Love with the Dharma.' *MS Magazine* (May-June 1991): 80–81.
Browning, James Clyde. 'Tarthang Tulku and the Quest for an American Buddhism.' Ph.D. diss., Baylor University, 1986.
Breyer, Chloe Anne. 'Religious Liberty in Law and Practice: Vietnamese Home Temples and the First Amendment.' *Journal of Church and State* 35 (Spring 1993): 368–401.
Bstan-dzin-rgya-mtsho, Dalai Lama XIV. *My Land and My People*. New York: Potala, 1977.
____. *Freedom in Exile: The Autobiography of the Dalai Lama*. New York: HarperCollins, 1990.

Buddhist Churches of America. *Buddhist Churches of America*. 2 vols. Chicago: Nobart Publishers, 1974.

Butler, Katy. 'Encountering the Shadow in Buddhist America.' *Common Boundary* (May-June 1990): 14–22.

Butterfield, Stephen. *The Double Mirror: A Skeptical Journey into Buddhist Tantra*. Berkeley: North Atlantic Books, 1994.

Causton, Richard. *The Buddha in Daily Life: An Introduction to the Buddhism of Nichiren Daishonin*. London: Rider Books, 1995.

Chödron, Pema. *Start Where You Are: A Guide to Compassionate Living*. Boston: Shambhala Publications, 1994.

Das, Lama Surya. *Awakening the Buddha Within: Eight Steps to Enlightenment*. New York: Broadway Books, 1997.

Dolan, Jay P. *The American Catholic Experience*. New York: Doubleday and Company, 1985.

Donohue, John J. *The Forge of the Spirit: Structure, Motion, and Meaning in the Japanese Martial Traditions*. New York: Garland Publishers, 1991.

____. *Warrior Dreams: The Martial Arts and the American Imagination*. Westport, CT: Bergin and Garvey, 1994.

Eck, Diana, and the Harvard Pluralism Project. *On Common Ground: World Religions in America*. CD-ROM. New York: Columbia University Press, 1997.

Ellwood, Robert. *The Eagle and the Rising Sun: Americans and the New Religions of Japan*. Philadelphia: Westminster Press, 1974.

Fields, Rick. *How the Swans Came to the Lake: A Narrative History of Buddhism in America*, 3rd ed., rev. and updated. Boulder, CO: Shambhala Publications, 1992.

____. *Taking Refuge in L.A.: Life in a Vietnamese Buddhist Temple*. New York: Aperture Foundation, 1987.

Fong, Timothy P. *The First Suburban Chinatown: The Remaking of Monterey Park*. Philadelphia: Temple University Press, 1994.

Glassman, Bernard, and Rick Fields. *Instruction to the Cook: A Zen Master's Lessons in Living a Life That Matters*. New York: Bell Tower, 1996.

Goodman, Michael Harris. *The Last Dalai Lama*. London: Sidgwick & Jackson, 1986.

Halifax, Joan, ed. *Shamanic Voices: A Survey of Visionary Narratives*. New York: E.P. Dutton, 1979.

____. *The Fruitful Darkness: Reconnecting with the Body of the Earth*. San Francisco: Harper San Francisco, 1993.

Hertzberg, Arthur. *The Jews in America: Four Centuries of an Uneasy Relationship*. New York: Simon and Shuster, 1989.

Horton, John. *The Politics of Diversity: Immigration, Resistance, and Change in Monterey Park, California*. Philadelphia: Temple University Press, 1995.

Hurst, Jane D. *Nichiren Shoshu Buddhism and the Soka Gakkai in America: The Ethos of a New Religious Movement*. New York: Garland Publishers, 1992.

Hutchison, William R., ed. *American Protestant Thought in the Liberal Era*. Lanham, MD: University Press of America, 1968.

____. *The Modernist Impulse in American Protestantism*. Cambridge, MA: Harvard University Press, 1976.

Ikeda, Daisaku. *Unlocking the Mysteries of Birth and Death: Buddhism in the Contemporary World*. London: Warner Books, 1988.

____. *A New Humanism: The University Addresses of Daisaku Ikeda*. New York and Tokyo: Weatherhill Inc., 1996.

Judah, J. Stillson. *The History and Philosophy of the Metaphysical Movements in America*. Philadelphia: Westminster Press 1967.

Kabat-Zinn, Jon. *Full Catastrophe Living: Using the Wisdom of Your Body and Mind to Face Stress, Pain, and Illness.* New York: Delacorte Press, 1990.

____. *Wherever You Go, There You Are : Mindfulness Meditation in Everyday Life.* New York: Hyperion, 1994.

Kashima, Tetsuden. *Buddhism in America: The Social Organization of an Ethnic Religious Institution.* Westport, CT: Greenwood Press, 1977.

____. 'The Buddhist Churches of America: Challenges for Changes in the 21st Century Article.' *Pacific World*, n.s. 6 (1990): 28–40.

Kornfield, Jack. *Living Dharma: Teachings of Twelve Buddhist Masters.* 1977. Boston: Shambhala Publications, 1996.

Layman, Emma McCloy. *Buddhism in America.* Chicago: Nelson Hall, 1976.

Lee, Robert. 'Imagined Communities: Asian-America in the 1990s.' *Journal of American-East Asian Relations* 3 (1994): 181–191.

Lee, Rose Hum. *The Chinese in the United States.* Hong Kong: Hong Kong University Press, 1960.

Lin, Irene. 'Journey to the Far West: Chinese Buddhism in America.' *Amerasia Journal* 22 (1996): 107–132.

Loori, John Daido. *The Eight Gates Of Zen: Spiritual Training in a American Zen Monastery.* Mt. Tremper, NY: Dharma Communications, 1992.

____. *The Heart Of Being: Moral and Ethical Teachings of Zen Buddhism.* Boston: Charles E. Tuttle, 1996.

____. *Now I Know You: A Video Tribute to Taizan Maezumi Roshi.* Produced by John Daido Loori. 56 min. Dharma Communications, 1996. Videocassette.

____. *Watching the Rock Grow: The History of Zen Mountain Monastery.* Produced by John Daido Loori. 64 min. Dharma Communications, 1990. Videocassette.

MacKenzie, Vicki. *Reborn in the West: The Reincarnation Masters.* New York: Marlowe & Company, 1996.

McLellan, Janet. 'Religion and Ethnicity: The Role of Buddhism in Maintaining Ethnic Identity among Tibetans in Lindsay, Ontario.' *Canadian Ethnic Studies* 19 (1987): 63–76.

Maezumi, Taizan. *On Zen Practice II: Body, Breath and Mind.* Los Angeles: Zen Center of Los Angeles, 1977.

Maezumi, Taizan, and Bernard Glassman. *The Hazy Moon of Enlightenment.* Los Angeles: Zen Center of Los Angeles, 1978.

Merzel, Dennis Genpo. *Beyond Sanity and Madness: The Way of Zen Master Dogen.* Boston: Charles E. Tuttle Co., 1994.

____. *The Eye Never Sleeps.* Boston: Shambhala Publications., 1991.

Nordstrom, Louis, ed. *Namu Dai Bosa: A Transmission of Zen Buddhism to America.* New York: Zen Studies Center, 1976.

Numrich, Paul. *Old Wisdom in the New World: Americanization in Two Immigrant Theravada Buddhist Temples.* Knoxville, TN: University of Tennessee Press, 1996.

Pitkow, Marlene. 'A Temple for Tourists in New York Chinatown.' *Journal of American Culture* 10 (1987): 107–114.

Prebish, Charles S. *American Buddhism.* North Scituate, MA: Duxbury Press, 1979.

Preston, David L. *The Social Organization of Zen Practice: Constructing Transcultural Reality.* Cambridge: Cambridge University Press, 1988.

Prothero, Stephen R. 'Introduction,' *Big Sky Mind: Buddhism and the Beat Generation*, ed. Carole Tonkinson. New York: Riverhead, 1995.

____. *The White Buddhist: The Asian Odyssey of Henry Steel Olcott.* Bloomington: Indiana University Press, 1996.

Rutledge, Paul James. 'The Role of Religion in Ethnic Self-Identity: The Vietnamese in Oklahoma City, 1975–1982.' Ph.D. diss., University of Oklahoma, 1982.

Robert H. Sharf, 'Sanbōkyōdan: Zen and the Way of the New Religions.' *Japanese Journal of Religious Studies* 22, no. 3–4 (Fall 1995): 417–458.

____. 'Harada-Yasutani School of Zen Buddhism' [on-line] (April 20, 1997) URL http://coombs.anu.edu.au/WWWVLPages/BuddhPages/ HaradaYasutani.html

Seager, Richard Hughes, ed. *Dawn of Religious Pluralism: Voices from the World's Parliament of Religions.* La Salle, IL: Open Court Press, 1993.

____. *The World's Parliament of Religions: The East/West Encounter, Chicago, 1893.* Bloomington: Indiana University Press, 1995.

Shainberg, Lawrence. *Ambivalent Zen: A Memoir.* New York: Pantheon, 1995.

Storlie, Erik Fraser. *Nothing on My Mind: An Intimate Account of American Zen.* Boston: Shambhala Publications, 1996.

Tanaka, Kenneth. *Ocean: An Introduction to Jodo-Shinshu Buddhism in America* Berkeley: WisdomOcean Publications, 1997.

Taylor, J. L. *Forest Monks and the Nation-State: An Anthropological and Historical Study in Northeastern Thailand.* Singapore: Institute of Southeast Asian Studies, 1993.

Trungpa, Chögyam. *Cutting through Spiritual Materialism.* Edited by John Baker and Marvin Casper. Berkeley: Shambhala Publications, 1973.

____. *Crazy Wisdom.* Edited by Sherab Chödzin. Boston : Shambhala Publications, 1991.

____. *Meditation in Action.* Berkeley: Shambhala Publications, 1969.

____. *Shambhala: The Sacred Path of the Warrior.* Edited by Carolyn Rose Gimian. Boulder, CO: Shambhala Publications, 1984.

Tuck, Donald R. *Buddhist Churches of America: Jodo Shinshu.* Lewiston, NY: Edwin Mellen Press, 1987.

Tweed, Thomas A. *The American Encounter with Buddhism, 1844–1912: Victorian Culture and the Limits of Dissent.* Bloomington: Indiana University Press, 1992.

Tworkov, Helen. *Zen in America: Profiles of Five Teachers.* San Francisco: North Point Press, 1989.

Van Esterik, Penny. *Taking Refuge: Lao Buddhists in North America.* Tempe, AZ: Arizona State University, 1992.

Wilson, Bryan, and Karel Dobbelaere. *A Time to Chant: The Soka Gakkai Buddhists in Britain.* Oxford: Clarendon Press, 1994.

Yu, Eui-Young. 'The Growth of Korean Buddhism in the United States, with Special Reference to Southern California.' *Pacific World: Journal of the Institute of Buddhist Studies,* n.s., 4 (1988): 82–93.

Zaleski, Jeff. *The Soul of Cyber Space: How Technology Is Changing Our Spiritual Lives.* New York: HarperCollins Publishers, 1997.

Notes

1 During some recent work for *On Common Ground,* a CD-ROM project on American religion by Diana Eck and the Pluralism Project at Harvard, I had come to find synthesizing complex material for a general audience to be an intellectual challenge. Diana L. Eck, *On Common Ground: World Religions in America,* Macintosh version, CD-Rom (New York: Columbia University Press, 1997)

2 Buddhist Churches of America, *Buddhist Churches of America,* 2 vols. (Chicago: Nobart Publishers, 1974).

3 Robert Ellwood, *The Eagle and the Rising Sun: Americans and the New Religions of Japan* (Philadelphia: Westminster Press, 1974).

4 Emma McCloy Layman, *Buddhism in America* (Chicago: Nelson Hall, 1976); Charles S. Prebish, *American Buddhism* (North Scituate, MA: Duxbury Press, 1979).

5 Tetsuden Kashima, *Buddhism in America: The Social Organization of an Ethnic Religious Institution* (Westport, CT: Greenwood Press, 1977).

6 Jane D. Hurst, *Nichiren Shoshu Buddhism and the Soka Gakkai in America: The Ethos of a New Religious Movement* (New York: Garland Publishers Inc., 1992).

7 Paul Numrich, *Old Wisdom in the New World: Americanization in Two Immigrant Theravada Buddhist Temples* (Knoxville: University of Tennessee Press, 1996): 63–79.

8 Rick Fields, *How the Swans Came to the Lake: A Narrative History of Buddhism in America* (Boulder: Shambhala, 1981).

9 For a more critical look at the relations between the Transcendentalists and Beats, see Stephen Prothero, Introduction to *Big Sky Mind: Buddhism and the Beat Generation*, edited by Carole Tonkinson (New York: Riverhead, 1995), 1–20.

10 J. Stillson Judah, *The History and Philosophy of the Metaphysical Movements in America* (Philadelphia: Westminster Press 1967).

11 Sydney Alhstrom, *A Religious History of the American People* (New Haven: Yale University Press, 1972), 483–490, 1019–54. Ahlstrom's treatment of Asian religions in the U.S. is representative of the way in which American religious historians approached them until quite recently.

12 William R. Hutchison, *The Modernist Impulse in American Protestantism* (Cambridge, MA: Harvard University Press, 1976).

13 William R. Hutchison, ed., *American Protestant Thought in the Liberal Era* (Lanham, MD: University Press of America, 1968).

14 Thomas A. Tweed, *The American Encounter with Buddhism, 1844–1912: Victorian Culture and the Limits of Dissent* (Bloomington: Indiana University Press, 1992).

15 Richard Hughes Seager, *The World's Parliament of Religions: The East/West Encounter, Chicago, 1893* (Bloomington: Indiana University Press, 1995). See also Seager, ed., *Dawn of Religious Pluralism: Voices from the World's Parliament of Religions* (Lasalle, IL: Open Court Press, 1993).

16 Stephen R. Prothero, *The White Buddhist: The Asian Odyssey of Henry Steel Olcott* (Bloomington: Indiana University Press, 1996), 7–9, 176–77.

17 For basic historical and religious material, see *Buddhist Churches of America*; Tetsuden Kashima, *Buddhism in America* (Westport, CT: Greenwood Press, 1977); and Donald R. Tuck, *Buddhist Churches of America: Jodo Shinshu* (Lewiston, NY: Edwin Mellen Press, 1987). For a more intimate treatment of religious ideas and issues, see Kenneth Tanaka, *Ocean: An Introduction to Jodo-Shinshu Buddhism in America* (Berkeley: WisdomOcean Publications, 1997). For challenges facing the BCA, see Tetsuden Kashima, 'The Buddhist Churches of America: Challenges for Changes in the 21st Century,' *Pacific World*, n.s., 6 (1990): 28–40. Excellent Web resources for Shin Buddhism, including current information on the activities of individual BCA churches and temples in the United States, can be found at 'LinksPitaka, Jōdo Shinshū [on-line] (20 April 1997) URL http://www.ville-ge.ch/musinfo/ethg/ducor/shinshu.htm.

18 The literature related to Jews and Catholics and questions of their assimilation and identity is voluminous and highly political. For brief, standard accounts

that may help to bring out comparisons with the contemporary experience of Japanese in the BCA see, Arthur Hertzberg, *The Jews in America: Four Centuries of an Uneasy Relationship* (New York: Simon and Schuster, 1989), 377–388 ;and Jay P. Dolan, *The American Catholic Experience* (New York: Doubleday and Company, 1985), 421–454.

19 Access to Kwan Um centers nationwide is found at 'Kwan Um School of Zen' [on-line] (21 April 1997) URL http://www.kwanumzen.com/.

20 Robert Aitken, *Taking the Path of Zen* (San Francisco: North Point Press, 1982); Louis Nordstrom, ed., *Namu Dai Bosa: A Transmission of Zen Buddhism to America* (New York: Zen Studies Center, 1976); Robert H. Sharf, 'Sanbōkyōdan: Zen and the Way of the New Religions,' *Japanese Journal of Religious Studies* 22, no. 3–4 (Fall 1995): 417–458; and 'Harada-Yasutani School of Zen Buddhism' [on-line] (20 April 1997) URL http://coombs.anu. edu.au/WWWVLPages/BuddhPages/ HaradaYasutani.html. A more intimate look at prominent teachers is found in Helen Tworkov, *Zen in America: Profiles of Five Teachers* (San Francisco: North Point Press, 1989). Relevant memoirs about experiences within the American Zen community are found in Lawrence Shainberg, *Ambivalent Zen: A Memoir* (New York: Pantheon, 1995), and Erik Fraser Storlie, *Nothing on My Mind: An Intimate Account of American Zen* (Boston: Shambhala Publications, 1996).

21 San Francisco Zen Center and its affiliates are at 'San Francisco Zen Center' [on-line] (21 April 1997) URL http://www.zendo.com/~sfzc/ index.html and at 'Related Zen Groups' [on-line] (21 April 1997) URL http://www.zendo.com/ ~sfzc/relgroup.html. The Zen Center of Los Angeles is found at 'Zen Center of Los Angeles' [on-line] (21 April 1997) URL http://www.zencenter.com/. The most extensive Web site among Maezumi Rōshi successors is at 'Zen Mountain Monastery' [on-line] (21 April, 1997) URL http://www1.mhv.net/~dharmacom/.

22 Activity Committee in Association of Sōtō Zen Buddhists, *Buddha's Seeds Taking Firm Roots in North American Soil* (Los Angeles: Association of Sōtō Zen Buddhists, 1997).

23 The White Plum *sangha* is a group of teachers whose work is fairly well documented. For a sociological study of the Zen Center of Los Angeles, see David L. Preston, *The Social Organization of Zen Practice: Constructing Transcultural Reality* (Cambridge: Cambridge University Press, 1988). In addition to many incidental pieces on the Web, books by *sangha* figures include Taizan Maezumi and Bernard Glassman, *The Hazy Moon of Enlightenment* (Los Angeles: Zen Center of Los Angeles, 1978) and *On Zen Practice II: Body, Breath and Mind* (Los Angeles: Zen Center of Los Angeles, 1977); Bernard Glassman and Rick Fields, *Instruction to the Cook: A Zen Master's Lessons in Living a Life That Matters* (New York: Bell Tower, 1996); John Daido Loori, *The Eight Gates of Zen: Spiritual Training in a American Zen Monastery* (Mt. Tremper, NY: Dharma Communications, 1992) and*The Heart Of Being: Moral And Ethical Teachings of Zen Buddhism* (Boston: Charles E. Tuttle, 1996); Charlotte Joko Beck, *Everyday Zen: Love and Work* (San Francisco: Harper and Row, 1989) and *Nothing Special: Living Zen* (San Francisco: Harper San Francisco, 1993); Dennis Genpo Merzel, *The Eye Never Sleeps* (Boston: Shambhala Publications, 1991) and *Beyond Sanity and Madness: The Way Of Zen Master Dogen* (Boston: Charles E. Tuttle Co., 1994). See also two excellent video sources, *Watching the Rock Grow: The History of Zen Mountain Monastery*, exec. prod. John Daido Loori, 64 min., Dharma Communications, 1990, videocassette, and *Now I Know You: A Video Tribute to Taizan Maezumi Roshi*, exec. prod. John Daido Loori, 56 min., Dharma Communications, 1996, videocassette.

24 Bstan-dzin-rgya-mtsho, Dalai Lama XIV, *My Land and My People* (New York: Potala, 1977); Bstan-dzin-rgya-mtsho, Dalai Lama XIV, *Freedom in Exile: the Autobiography of the Dalai Lama* (New York: HarperCollins, 1990). Michael Harris Goodman, *The Last Dalai Lama* (London: Sidgwick & Jackson, 1986). 'Free Tibet' [on-line] (22 April 1997) URL http://www.manymedia.com/tibet/ index.html#centralindex.

25 'Nyingma Centers' [on-line] (27 April 1997) URL http://www.nyingma.org/; James Clyde Browning, 'Tarthang Tulku and the Quest for an American Buddhism' (Ph.D. diss., Baylor University, 1986). See also 'Opening the Odiyan Mandala' [on-line] (8 September 1997) URL http://www.nyingma.org/odiyan/ odiyan.html.

26 'Dzogchen Foundation' [on-line] (28 April 1997) URL http://www.dzogchen.org/; Lama Surya Das, *Awakening the Buddha Within: Eight Steps to Enlightenment* (New York: Broadway Books, 1997).

27 The best site that treats both Karma Triyana Dharmachakra and the seventeenth Karmapa is found at 'Ocean of Mercy' [on-line] (28 April 1997) URL http://www.brainlink.com/~karma/home.html. The most comprehensive site for the opposing Kagyu camp is at 'Karma Kagyu Buddhist Network' [on-line] (29 April 1997) URL http://www.kkbn.com/. For a descriptive account of the phenomena of *tulkus* being identified in the West, see Vicki MacKenzie, *Reborn in the West: The Reincarnation Masters* (New York: Marlowe & Company, 1996).

28 The site that most thoroughly documents KTD activities is at 'Karma Triyana Dharmachakra: the North American Seat of the Seventeenth Gwalya Karmapa' [on-line] (8 September 1997) URL http://www.kagyu.org/.

29 Chögyam Trungpa, *Meditation in Action* (Berkeley: Shambhala Publications, 1969); *Cutting through Spiritual Materialism* (Berkeley: Shambhala Publications, 1973); *Crazy Wisdom* (Boston: Shambhala Publications, 1991); *Shambhala: the Sacred Path of the Warrior* (Boulder, CO: Shambhala Publications, 1984). The Shambhala gateway is at 'Welcome to Shambhala' [on-line] (27 April 1997) URL http://www.shambhala.org/.

30 Katy Butler, 'Encountering the Shadow in Buddhist America,' *Common Boundary* (May-June 1990): 14–22; Sandy Boucher, 'In Love with the Dharma,' *MS Magazine* (May-June 1991): 80–81.

31 Chödron's adaptive spirit is seen in her presentation of *lojong* teaching and *tonglon* practice in an American vein in Pema Chödron, *Start Where You Are: A Guide to Compassionate Living* (Boston: Shambhala Publications, 1994). For a memoir about life and practice within the Shambhala community, see Stephen Butterfield, *The Double Mirror: A Skeptical Journey into Buddhist Tantra* (Berkeley: North Atlantic Books, 1994).

32 Numrich, *Old Wisdom in the New World*, 63–79.

33 'Theravada Text Archives: The Thai Forest Tradition' [on-line] (27 April 1997) URL http://world.std.com/~metta/ftp/thai.html; Jack Kornfield, *Living Dharma: Teachings of Twelve Buddhist Masters* (1977; Boston: Shambhala Publications, 1996); and J. L. Taylor, *Forest Monks and the Nation-State: An Anthropological and Historical Study in Northeastern Thailand* (Singapore: Institute of Southeast Asian Studies, 1993).

34 'Abhayagiri Buddhist Monastery' [on-line] (27 April 1997) URL http:// www.dharmanet.org/Abhayagiri/index.html; 'Metta Forest Monastery' [on-line] (27 April 1997) URL http://users.deltanet.com/~gmsmith/watmetta.html; 'Ajaan Geoff'[on-line] (27 April 1997) URL http://users.deltanet.com/ ~gmsmith/ TG.page.html.

35 'Insight Meditation Society Homepage' [on-line] (27 April 1997) URL http://www.dharma.org/ims.htm.

36 Jon Kabat-Zinn, *Full Catastrophe Living: Using the Wisdom of Your Body and Mind to Face Stress, Pain, and Illness* (New York: Delacorte Press, 1990), and *Wherever You Go, There You Are: Mindfulness Meditation in Everyday Life* (New York: Hyperion, 1994).

37 Theological and liturgical concerns are well covered in Richard Causton, *The Buddha in Daily Life: An Introduction to the Buddhism of Nichiren Daishonin* (London: Rider Books, 1995). Good if indirect light is shed on the American situation, particularly in the epilogue on the schism, in Bryan Wilson and Karel Dobbelaere, *A Time to Chant: The Soka Gakkai Buddhists in Britain* (Oxford: Clarendon Press, 1994). The most up-to-date account of Sōka Gakkai in the U.S. is found in Jane D. Hurst, *Nichiren Shoshu Buddhism and the Soka Gakkai in America: The Ethos of a New Religious Movement* (New York: Garland Publications, 1992).

38 A gateway to the major orthodox Nichiren Shōshū sites is at 'Nichiren Web Sites' [on-line] (27 April 1997) URL http://vanbc.wimsey.com/ ~glenz/nichsite.html.

39 'SGI-USA' [on-line] (27 April 1997) URL http://sgi-usa.org/.

40 For an introduction to the public face of Ikeda's Buddhist humanism, see Daisaku Ikeda, *A New Humanism: The University Addresses of Daisaku Ikeda* (New York and Tokyo: Weatherhill, 1996). For a more philosophical and doctrinal view, see Daisaku Ikeda, *Unlocking the Mysteries of Birth and Death: Buddhism in the Contemporary World* (London: Warner Books, 1988).

41 'The Clearing House Archive' [on-line] (27 April 1997) URL http://coyote.accessnv.com/tamonten/ and 'Deviations of the Soka Gakkai' [on-line] (27 April 1997) URL http://ww2.netnitco.net/users/ jqpublic/deviations.html. These sites are targeted at Sōka Gakkai, which seems to have remained aloof from the fray in public, at least on the Web.

42 Among the best of the many Asian American Web sites that give access to voluntary organizations, cultural (but not religious) institutions, on-line magazines, and student groups is 'The Asian American Cybernauts Page' [on-line] (28 April 1997) URL http://netasia.com/~ebihara/ wataru_aacyber.html. A useful review of three current, often-cited books on the Asian American movement is Robert Lee, 'Imagined Communities: Asian-America in the 1990s,' *Journal of American-East Asian Relations* 3 (1994): 181–91.

43 The best gateway to Fo Kuang Shan sites, including Hsi Lai temple, is at 'Fo Kuang Shan' [on-line] (28 April 1997) URL http://www.ibps.org/ index.htm. U.S. and international True Buddha School sites can be accessed at 'True Buddha School Net' [on-line] (29 April 1997) URL http://206.171.254.193/. Information regarding the North American work of the Tzu-Chi Foundation is found at 'Buddhist Compassion Relief Tzu-Chi Foundation' [on-line] (29 April 1997) URL http://www.tzuchi.org/ and at 'Tzu-Chi Institute for Complementary and Alternative Health Care' [on-line] (29 April 1997) URL http://www.icam.healthcare.ubc.ca/ home/ICAMHome.htm.

44 'Buddhist Association of the United States (BAUS)' [on-line] (28 April 1997) URL http://www.baus.org/; 'Ch'an Meditation Society' [on-line] (28 April 1997) URL http://www.chan1.org/.

45 Published works include Rose Hum Lee, *The Chinese in the United States* (Hong Kong: Hong Kong University Press, 1960); Marlene Pitkow, 'A Temple for Tourists in New York Chinatown,' *Journal of American Culture* 10 (1987): 107–114; Irene Lin, 'Journey to the Far West: Chinese Buddhism in America' *Amerasia Journal* 22 (1996): 107–132. Unpublished (and far more substantial

work) developed for the Harvard Pluralism Project include Wen-ji Qin, 'Chinese Buddhism in New York and Boston' (Summer 1992), and Stuart Chandler, 'Building a Pure Land on Earth through Humanistic Buddhism,' (n.d.) and 'A Directory of Chinese Buddhist Organizations in the United States' (February 1993). Chandler's 'Buddhist Chinese American or American Chinese Buddhist: Issues of Identity and the Practice of Chinese Forms of Buddhism in America' is forthcoming in *Faces of Buddhism in America*, ed. Kenneth Tanaka and Charles Prebish (Berkeley: University of California Press, 1998).

46 John Horton, *The Politics of Diversity: Immigration, Resistance, and Change in Monterey Park, California* (Philadelphia: Temple University Press, 1995); Timothy P. Fong, *The First Suburban Chinatown: The Remaking of Monterey Park* (Philadelphia: Temple University Press, 1994).

47 Studies that address the current immigration and include Buddhist-related material are Penny Van Esterik, *Taking Refuge: Lao Buddhists in North America* (Tempe, AZ: Arizona State University, 1992); Janet McLellan, 'Religion and Ethnicity: The Role of Buddhism in Maintaining Ethnic Identity among Tibetans in Lindsay, Ontario,' *Canadian Ethnic Studies* 19 (1987): 63–76; Paul James Rutledge, 'The Role of Religion in Ethnic Self-Identity: The Vietnamese in Oklahoma City, 1975–1982' (Ph.D. diss., University of Oklahoma, 1982). In a more religious studies vein see Eui-Young Yu, 'The Growth of Korean Buddhism in the United States, with Special Reference to Southern California,' *Pacific World: Journal of the Institute of Buddhist Studies*, n.s., 4 (1988): 82–93. For a moving, impressionist account, see Rick Fields, *Taking Refuge in L.A.: Life in a Vietnamese Buddhist Temple* (New York: Aperture Foundation, 1987).

48 'Home Temples Trouble Neighbors and Governments,' *Los Angeles Times*, October 7, 1996; 'A Civics Lesson: Buddhists Told to Surrender,' *Los Angeles Times*, March 9, 1997; Chloe Anne Breyer, 'Religious Liberty in Law and Practice: Vietnamese Home Temples and the First Amendment,' *Journal of Church and State* 35 (Spring 1993): 368–401.

49 Joan Halifax, ed., *Shamanic Voices: A Survey of Visionary Narratives* (New York: E. P. Dutton, 1979) and *The Fruitful Darkness: Reconnecting with the Body of the Earth* (San Francisco: Harper San Francisco, 1993).

50 Prothero surveys some of this territory in a tongue-in-cheek essay in Salon Magazine. Stephen Prothero, 'Buddha Chic,' *Salon Magazine* [on-line] (14 September 1997) URL http://www.salonmagazine.com/may97/ news/ news2970524.html.

51 John J. Donohue, *The Forge of the Spirit: Structure, Motion, and Meaning in the Japanese Martial Traditions* (New York: Garland Publishers, 1991) and *Warrior Dreams: The Martial Arts and the American Imagination* (Westport, CT: Bergin and Garvey, 1994). For a comprehensive gateway to martial arts sources on the Web, see 'Martial Art Sources on the Internet' [on-line] (8 September 1997) URL http://www.dote.hu/ %7Eaikido/cimek2.html.

52 Much might be said about Buddhism on the Web, but for a recently published account of religion and technology which includes a chapter on Buddhism, see Jeff Zaleski, *The Soul of Cyber Space: How Technology is Changing Our Spiritual Lives* (New York: HarperCollins Publishers, 1997).

APPENDIX A

Dissertations and Theses on American Buddhism

compiled by Duncan Ryūken Williams

One way to document the development of a field of study is to track doctoral dissertations awarded in that particular field. In the 1970s, as graduate programs in Buddhist studies, American religious history, sociology, anthropology, psychology, and American literature began to award Ph.D.'s for dissertations that dealt with various aspects of American Buddhism, its study began to gain prominence. Today, as the essays in this volume attest, scholars at major universities with diverse methodological backgrounds have begun to research seriously the phenomenon of American Buddhism.

This appendix attempts to list comprehensively not only doctoral dissertations but M.A. and B.A. theses as well. Please feel free to contact Duncan Williams to report any omissions.

1937
Takahashi, Kyojiro. 'A Social Study of the Japanese Shinto and Buddhism in Los Angeles.' M.A. thesis, University of Southern California.

1947
Spencer, Robert. 'Japanese Buddhism in the United States: A Study in Acculturation.' Ph.D. diss., University of California, Berkeley.

1951
Rust, William. 'The Shin Sect of Buddhism in America: Its Antecedents, Beliefs, and Present Condition.' Ph.D. diss., University of Southern California.

1970
Hibbert, Thomas. 'Three Zen Institutions: An Ethnographic Study.' Senior thesis, Reed College.

1971
Wise, David. 'Dharma West: A Social-Psychological Inquiry into Zen in San Francisco.' Ph.D. diss., University of California, Berkeley.

1972
Kalbacher, Catherine. 'Zen in America.' Ph.D. diss., University of California, Berkeley.

1973

Horinouchi, Isao. 'Americanized Buddhism: A Sociological Analysis of a Protestantized Japanese Religion.' Ph.D. diss., University of California, Davis.

Okada, Richard. 'Zen and the Poetry of Gary Snyder.' Ph.D. diss., University of Wisconsin.

1975

Fujitani, Pat. 'History of Buddhist Women in Hawaii: Shinshu Experience.' Senior thesis, University of Hawaii.

Kashima, Tetsuden. 'The Social Organization of the Buddhist Churches of America: Continuity and Social Change.' Ph.D. diss., University of California, San Diego.

Wilkinson, Stephan. 'Nichiren Shoshu Sokagakkai in America: An Analysis of Ultimate Concerns between 1960 and 1965.' Ph.D. diss., University of Iowa.

1976

Snow, David. 'The Nichiren Shoshu Buddhist Movement in America: A Sociological Examination of Its Value Orientation, Recruitment Efforts and Spread.' Ph.D. diss., University of California, Los Angeles.

1977

Holtzapple, Vicki. 'Soka Gakkai in Midwestern America: A Case Study of a Transpositional Movement.' Ph.D. diss., Washington University.

1978

O'Donnell, Richard. 'Alan Watts: Zen, Language, and Philosophy.' M.A. thesis, California State University, Long Beach.

1979

Kim, Young Hwan. 'Buddhism and Its Implications for American Physical Education.' Ph.D. diss., Kent State University.

1980

Heifetz, Julie. 'The Role of the Clergy at the Vietnamese Buddhist Temple in Los Angeles as Culture Brokers in Vietnamese Refugee Resettlement.' M.A. thesis, University of Houston.

Hurst, Jane. 'The Nichiren Shoshū Sokagakkai in America: The Ethos of a New Religious Movement.' Ph.D. diss., Temple University.

Krane, Loren. 'Personality and Socio-Political Activism in an American Buddhist Group: The Insight Meditation Society.' Ph.D. diss., California School of Professional Psychology.

Le, Daniel Dinh. 'Vietnamese Refugees' Perceptions and Methods for Coping with Mental Illnesses.' Ph.D. diss., United States International University.

O'Neil, Frances. 'A Theoretical Analysis of Zen Buddhist Principles in Education and Two Cases of Their Implementation in America.' Ph.D. diss., University of Connecticut.

Young, Gloria. 'The New Transcendentalism in Post-Industrial Society: Life Styles and the Search for Meaning in the New Age.' Ph.D. diss., University of Texas, Austin.

1981

Ling, Paul. 'The Intensive Buddhist Meditation Retreat and the Self: Psychological and Theravadin Considerations.' Ph.D. diss., Boston University.

Pickett, Rebecca. 'Gary Snyder and the Mythological Present.' Ph.D. diss., University of Nebraska, Lincoln.

Vryheid, Robert. 'An American Buddhist Monastery: Sociocultural Aspects of Soto Zen Training.' Ph.D. diss., University of Oregon.

1982

Routledge, Paul. 'The Role of Religion in Ethnic Identity: The Vietnamese of Oklahoma City, 1975–1982.' Ph.D. diss., University of Oklahoma.

1984

Modlin, Robin. 'Principles and Practices of Thirty-One American Buddhist Families.' M.A. thesis, California Institute of Integral Studies.

Parks, Yoko. 'Chanting Is Efficacious: Changes in the Organization and Beliefs of the American Sokagakkai.' Ph.D. diss., University of Pennsylvania.

1985

De Santis, James. 'Effects of Intensive Zen Buddhist Meditation Retreat on Rogerian Consequence as Real-Self/Ideal-Self Disparity on the California Q-Sort.' Ph.D. diss., California School of Professional Psychology.

Nguyen, Son Xuan. 'Evangelization of Vietnamese Buddhist Refugees.' Ph.D. diss., Claremont School of Theology.

Powell, Melvin, Jr. 'Nichiren Shoshu Soka Gakkai of America in Tucson, Arizona: Portrait of an Imported Religion.' M.A. thesis, University of Arizona.

1986

Browning, James. 'Tarthang Tulku and the Quest for an American Buddhism.' Ph.D. diss., Baylor University.

Fulton, Paul. 'The Psychological Ethnography of Anatta: Self and Selves in American Vipassana Buddhism.' Ph.D. diss., Harvard University.

Imamura, Ryo. 'A Comparative Study of Temple and Non-Temple Buddhist Ministers of the Jodo Shin Sect Using Jungian Psychological Types.' Ph.D. diss., University of San Francisco.

Kraus, James. 'Gary Snyder's Biopoetics: A Study of the Poet as Ecologist.' Ph.D. diss., University of Hawaii.

Wells, Katheryn. 'The Form and Function of Dance in the Fifth SGI World Peace Youth Culture Festival.' M.A. thesis, University of Hawaii.

1987

Black, John. 'Zen Practice in Transformation: A Case Study of the Cambridge Buddhist Association.' Senior thesis, Harvard University.

Blackburn, Anne. 'The Evolution of Sinhalese Buddhist Identity.' Senior thesis, Swarthmore College.

Yamazato, Katsunori. 'Seeking a Fulcrum: Gary Snyder and Japan (1956–1975).' Ph.D. diss., University of California, Davis.

1989

Hack, Sheryl. 'Collective Identity and Sacred Space: A Study of Seven Zen Communities in Northern California.' M.A. thesis, University of Delaware.

Schuler, Robert. 'Journeys Toward the Original Mind: The Longer Poems of Gary Snyder.' Ph.D. diss., University of Minnesota.

Tweed, Thomas. 'The American Encounter with Buddhism, 1844–1912: Response to Buddhism, Dissent and Consent, and Victorian Religious Culture.' Ph.D. diss., Stanford University.

Zuckerman, Daniel. 'Theravada Buddhism, Psychotherapy, and American Buddhism.' Senior thesis, Harvard University.

1990

Dreifuss, Alan. 'A Phenomenological Inquiry of Six Psychotherapists Who Practice Buddhist Meditation.' Ph.D. diss., California Institute of Integral Studies.

Prothero, Stephan. 'Henry Steel Olcott (1832–1907) and the Construction of "Protestant Buddhism"' Ph.D. diss., Harvard University.
Wu, Yushan. 'From Hippieism to Zen Buddhism: Counterculture Ideology and Social Change in America.' M.A. thesis, Boston College, 1990.

1991

Hinz, William. 'Alan Watts' Theological Anthrolopogy and Its Implications for Religious Education.' M.A. thesis, McGill University.
Williams, Duncan. 'The Interface of Buddhism and Environmentalism in North America.' Senior thesis, Reed College.

1992

Breyer, Chloe. 'Religious Liberty in Law and Practice: Vietnamese Home Temples in California and the First Amendment.' Senior thesis, Harvard University.
Lawson, Jonathan. 'The Religious Process of Wild Renewal: Buddhism, Wilderness Ethics, and Poetics in the Work of Gary Snyder.' Senior thesis, Guilford College.
Lin, Jyan-Lung. 'Gary Snyder's Poetry: A Study of the Formation and Transformation of His Enlightened Vision.' Ph.D. diss., Michigan State University.
Numrich, Paul. 'Americanization in Immigrant Theravada Buddhist Temples.' Ph.D. diss., Northwestern University.

1993

Gottschall, Claudia. '"Unspeakable Visions": Beat Consciousness and Its Textual Representation.' Ph.D. diss., University of Oregon.
Langford, Donald. 'The Primacy of Place in Gary Snyder's Ecological Vision.' Ph.D. diss., Ohio State University.
McGonigle, Marianne. 'Elements of Buddhism in the Works of Mark Tobey and Agnes Martin.' M.A. thesis, Texas Woman's University.
McLellan, Janet. 'Many Petals of the Lotus: Redefinitions of Buddhist Identity in Toronto.' Ph.D. diss., York University.
Murray, Anne. 'Jewels in the Net: Women Bringing Relation into the Light of American Buddhist Practice.' Senior thesis, Harvard University.
Eldershaw, Lynn. 'Refugees in the Dharma: A Study of Revitalization in the Buddhist Church of Halifax.' M.A. thesis, Acadia University.

1994

Bedard, Stephane. 'Traduire la Parole de Sagesse Orientale: Oralité et Signifiance dans l'Oeuvre de Chögyam Trungpa.' Ph.D. diss., Université Laval.
Fish, Mark. 'A Staged Revolution: The Influence of Zen Buddhism on the Living Theatre in the 1950s and 1960s.' Senior thesis, Harvard University.
Gayle, Robin. 'An Interaction between Western Psychotherapeutic Methodology and Eastern Buddhist Spirituality.' Ph.D. diss., California Institute of Integral Studies.
Oxman, Daniel. 'Principal Meditative Projects in Theravada Buddhist Thought and Their Psycho-Therapeutic Implications as Experienced in the California Bay Area.' Ph.D. diss., California Institute of Integral Studies.
Schiller, Lauren. 'Buddhism in Contemporary America.' M.A. thesis, Southern Connecticut State University.
Soucy, Alexander. 'Gender and Division of Labour in a Vietnamese-Canadian Buddhist Pagoda.' M.A. thesis, Concordia University.
Vowels, Yvonne. 'Toward a Third Wave Feminist Revolution: Feminists, Buddhists, and 12 Step Practitioners Encountering Difference.' Ph.D. diss., Graduate Theological Union.

1995

Goad, Angela. 'The Zen Truth in J. D. Salinger: "It's Very Hard to Meditate and Live a Spiritual Life in America"' M.A. thesis, Northeast Missouri State University.

Nelson, Mark. 'Quieting the Mind, Manifesting Mind: The Zen Buddhist Roots of John Cage's Early Chance-Determined and Indetermined Compositions.' Ph.D. diss., Princeton University.

Taylor, Marsha. 'How Buddhist Vietnamese Parents Make Decisions for Their Adolescent Children Who Attend Tara High School: A Case Study (Georgia).' Ph.D. diss., Georgia State University.

1996

Grabiel, Susan. 'The Hsi Lai Buddhist Temple: A New Locus for the Lotus, from Secular Space to Sacred Place.' M.A. thesis, California State University, Fullerton.

Sterling, Sean. 'Affective Change Following a Ten Day Vipassana Meditation Retreat.' Ph.D. diss., California School of Professional Psychology.

Waterman, Jorie. 'Buddhist Tradition and Innovation in the Life and Teaching of Thich Nhat Hanh.' Senior thesis, Harvard University.

Wizer, Michael. 'A Descriptive Study of the Stress Reduction and Relaxation Program at the University of Massachusetts Medical Center.' Ph.D. diss., Indiana University of Pennsylvania.

Yamauchi, Jeffrey. 'The Greening of American Zen: An Historical Overview and a Specific Application.' M.A. thesis, Prescott College.

1997

Metcalf, Franz. 'Why Do Americans Practice Zen Buddhism?' Ph.D. diss., University of Chicago.

Storseth, Terri. 'On the Road with the Monkey: The Transmission of Zen Buddhism in Two Contemporary American Novels.' Ph.D. diss., University of Washington.

Verhoeven, Martin. '"Americanizing the Buddha": The World's Parliament of Religions, Paul Carus, and the Making of Modern Buddhism.' Ph.D. diss., University of Wisconsin.

APPENDIX B

North American Dissertations and Theses on Topics Related to Buddhism

compiled by Duncan Ryūken Williams

This appendix attempts a comprehensive list of Ph.D. dissertations, as well as M.A. and B.A. theses, written at North American universities on topics related to Buddhism. Please feel free to contact Duncan Williams to report any omissions.

1892
Handley, John. 'Buddhism versus Brahmanism.' Ph.D. diss., New York University.
McCreedy, Robert. 'Buddhism.' Ph.D. diss., New York University.
Morita, Kumato. 'Lotze's Conception of the Soul Compared with That of Buddhism.' Ph.D. diss., Yale University.

1893
Parker, Lindsay. 'Gautama Buddha and Jesus Christ as Moral Teachers.' Ph.D. diss., New York University.

1894
MacClymont, D. T. 'Buddhism and Christianity.' Ph.D. diss., New York University.

1908
Moore, Justin. 'Sayings of Buddha, the "Iti-Vuttaka," A Pali Work of the Buddhist Canon.' Ph.D. diss., Columbia University.

1909
Kelley, Elias. 'The Ethics of Buddhism in Theory and Practice.' Ph.D. diss., Boston University.

1910
Burlingame, Eugene. 'Buddhaghosa's "Dhammapada" Commentary.' Ph.D. diss., University of Pennsylvania.

1913
Yabe, Kiyoshi. 'The Teaching of Buddha in Regard to the Family Relations.' M.A. thesis, University of Chicago.

1917
Works, Una. 'The Kingdom of God Ideal of Jesus and the Nirvana Ideal of Buddha: A Comparison.' M.A. thesis, University of Chicago.

1922
Kudara, Toryu. 'The Influence of the "Namu Amida Butsu" in Japan.' M.A. thesis, Columbia University.

1926

Knox, Harry. 'The Missionary Methods of Buddhism.' M.A. thesis, University of Chicago.

1927

Mortensen, Ralph. 'The Awakening of Faith in the Mahayana.' Ph.D. diss., Hartford Seminary.

1929

Kawakami, Kenso. 'The Social Background of the Development of Jodo Buddhism.' Ph.D. diss., University of Chicago.

Phelps, Dryden. 'A Study of the Origin and Early Development of Ch'an Buddhism Based on Documents in the Ch'in Ting Ku Chin T'u Shu Chi Ch'eng and Sources Primarily Related to Bodhidharma.' Ph.D. diss., University of California, Berkeley.

1930

Hilburn, Samuel. 'The Social History of the Rise of Amida Buddhism in Japan.' Ph.D. diss., University of Chicago.

Nakarai, Toyozo. 'A Study of the Impact of Buddhism upon Japanese Life as Revealed in the Odes of the Kokin-shu.' Ph.D. diss., University of Michigan.

1931

Rogers, Jesse. 'The Challenge of Buddhism.' Ph.D. diss., Southern Baptist Theological Seminary.

1932

Landon, Kenneth. 'The Development of Siamese Buddhism.' M.A. thesis, University of Chicago.

Ogura, Kosei. 'A Sociological Study of the Buddhist Churches in North America, With a Case Study of Gardena, California, Congregation.' M.A. thesis, University of Southern California.

Ware, J. R. 'Wei Shou on Buddhism.' Ph.D. diss., Harvard University.

1934

Gaut, Lilah. 'The Influence of Certain Buddhist Symbols on Chinese Textiles and Other Art Objects.' M.A. thesis, University of Chicago.

Natori, Junichi. 'A Study of Loyalty as Found in Shinto, Confucianism, and Japanese Buddhism' Th.D. diss., Boston University.

Rawlings, Eleanor. 'A Study of Avalokitesvara.' M.A. thesis, University of Chicago.

1937

Shacklock, Floyd. 'The Amida Sects in Japanese Buddhism.' Ph.D. diss., Hartford Seminary.

Takahashi, Kyojiro. 'A Social Study of the Japanese Shinto and Buddhism in Los Angeles.' M.A. thesis, University of Southern California.

1938

Nelson, Andrew. 'The Origin, History and Present Status of the Temples of Japan.' Ph.D. diss., University of Washington.

1939

Reischauer, Edwin. 'Ennin's Diary of his Travels in T'ang China, 838–847.' Ph.D. diss., Harvard University.

1940

Wells, Kenneth. 'Thai Buddhism, Its Rites and Activities.' Ph.D. diss., Columbia University.

1941
Munsterberg, Hugo. 'Buddhist Bronzes of the Six Dynasties Period.' Ph.D. diss., Harvard University.

1944
Chou, Yi-liang. 'Tantrism in China.' Ph.D. diss., Harvard University.
Soper, Alexander. 'The Evolution of Buddhist Architecture in Japan.' Ph.D. diss., Princeton University.

1946
Ch'en, Kenneth. 'A Study of the Svagata Story in the Divyavadana in Its Sanskrit, Pali, Tibetan, and Chinese Versions.' Ph.D. diss., Harvard University.

1947
Spencer, Robert. 'Japanese Buddhism in the United States: A Sudy in Acculturation.' Ph.D. diss., University of California, Berkeley.

1948
Wright, Arthur. 'Fo-t'u-teng: A Biography.' Ph.D. diss., Harvard University.
Yampolsky, Philip. 'The Essentials of Salvation: A Translation of the First Two Divisions of the Ōjō yōshū by Genshin.' M.A. thesis, Columbia University.

1950
Gard, Richard. 'An Introduction to the Study of Madhyamika Buddhism, with Special Consideration of Its Historical, Textual, and Philosophical Problems' Claremont Graduate School.
Harris, Lindell. 'The Doctrine of Salvation in Japanese Buddhism.' Ph.D. diss., Southwestern Baptist Theological Seminary.
Murayama, Milton. 'A Comparison of Wang Yang-ming and Zen Buddhism.' M.A. thesis, Columbia University.
Slater, Robert H. L. 'Paradox and Nirvana: A Study of Religious Ultimates with Specific Reference to Burmese Buddhism.' Ph.D. diss., Columbia University.

1951
Davidson, Joseph. 'The Lotus Sutra in Chinese Art to the Year One Thousand.' Ph.D. diss., Yale University.
Kitagawa, Joseph. 'Kōbō Daishi and Shingon Buddhism.' Ph.D. diss., University of Chicago.
Rust, William. 'The Shin Sect of Buddhism in America: Its Antecedents, Beliefs, and Present Condition.' Ph.D. diss., University of Southern California.

1952
Alper, Chester. 'Buddhism, Brahmanism, Hinduism, and Herman Hesse.' Senior thesis, Harvard University.
Murray, John. 'Edwin Arnold's Buddhism.' Ph.D. diss., University of Florida.

1956
Anderson, Ronald. 'Nishi Honganji and Japanese Buddhist Nationalism, 1862–1945.' Ph.D. diss., University of California, Berkeley.

1957
Callaway, Tucker. 'A Comparison of the Christian Doctrine of Salvation with That of Some of the Major Sects of Japanese Buddhism.' Ph.D. diss., Princeton Theological Seminary.
Nagatomi, Masatoshi. 'A Study of Dharmakirti's Pramānavārttika: An English Translation and Annotation of the Pramānavārttika, Book 1.' Ph.D. diss., Harvard University.

1958

Fong, Wen. 'Five Hundred Lohans at the Daitokuji' Ph.D. diss., Princeton University.

1959

Lee, Sang Kun. 'Jesus Christ as Revealed in the Gospel of John Compared with Buddha in Mahayanism' Th.D. diss., Dallas Theological Seminary.

Wayman, Alex. 'Analysis of the Sravakabhumi Manuscript.' Ph.D. diss., University of California, Berkeley.

1959

Bushkoff, Sheila. 'The Buddha Figure in Mathuran Art.' M.A. thesis, University of Chicago.

Hurvitz, Leon. 'Chih-i (538–597): An Introduction to the Life and Ideas of a Chinese Buddhist Monk.' Ph.D. diss., Columbia University.

1960

Becker, Ernest. 'Zen Buddhism, Brainwashing, and Psychotherapy: A Theoretical Study in Induced Regression and Cultural Values.' Ph.D. diss., Syracuse University.

Bush, Richard. 'Foundations of Ethics in the Sacred Scriptures of Ancient Hinduism and Early Buddhism.' Ph.D. diss., University of Chicago.

Casey, David. 'Aspects of the Sunyata-Absolute of Nagarjuna of Second Century A.D. Andhra.' Ph.D. diss., Harvard University.

Mammarella, Raymond. 'Contemporary Education and the Spirit of Zen.' Ph.D. diss., Columbia University.

1962

Ames, Michael. 'Religious Syncretism in Buddhist Ceylon.' Ph.D. diss., Harvard University.

Chuck, James. 'Zen Buddhism and Paul Tillich: A Comparison of Their Views on Man's Predicament and the Means of Its Resolution.' Ph.D. diss., Pacific School of Religion.

Maupin, Edward. 'An Exploratory Study of Individual Differences in Response to a Zen Meditation Exercise.' Ph.D. diss., University of Michigan.

Wilson, Joe. 'Some Principles in Buddhist Expansion.' Ph.D. diss., Southern Baptist Theological Seminary.

1963

Bloom, Alfred. 'Shinran: His Life and Thought.' Ph.D. diss., Harvard University.

Colbath, James. 'The Japanese Noh Drama and Its Relation to Zen Buddhism.' Ph.D. diss., Case Western Reserve University.

Murase, Mieko. 'The Tenjin Engi Scrolls: A Study of their Genealogical Relationship.' Ph.D. diss., Columbia University.

Poklen, Jeffrey. 'Two Sculptures and an Essay: The Relationship between Zen Buddhism and Art.' M.A. thesis, Cornell University.

1964

Dohanian, Diran. 'The Mahāyāna Buddhist Sculpture of Ceylon.' Ph.D. diss., Harvard University.

Orloff, Alicia. 'The Influence of Buddhist Negation on the Concept of Divinity: Indian Background of Honji Suijaku.' Ph.D. diss., Claremont Graduate School.

Pandey, Nand. 'The Influence of Hindu and Buddhist Thought on Aldous Huxley.' Ph.D. diss., Stanford University.

Streng, Frederick. 'Nargarjuna's Use of "Emptiness", as a Religious Expression: A Study in Religious Epistemology.' Ph.D. diss., University of Chicago.

Welbon, Guy. 'Europe and Nirvana: Studies in Europe's Discovery of Buddhism.' Ph.D. diss., University of Chicago.

1965

Earhart, H. Byron. 'A Religious Study of the Mount Haguro Sect of *Shugendō*: An Example of Japanese Mountain Religion.' Ph.D. diss., University of Chicago.

Hesselgrave, David. 'A Propagation Profile of Soka Gakkai.' Ph.D. diss., University of Minnesota.

Miyuki, Mokusen. 'An Analysis of Buddhist Influence on the Formation of the Sung Concept of Li-Ch'i.' Ph.D. diss., Claremont Graduate School.

Yampolsky, Philip. '"Platform Sutra of the Sixth Patriarch": Annotated Translation with an Introduction and Text.' Ph.D. diss., Columbia University.

1966

Begley, Wayne. 'The Chronology of Mahayana Buddhist Architecture and Painting at Ajanta.' Ph.D. diss., University of Pennsylvania.

Duvall, Mary. 'Man's Concept of his Religous Fulfillment: A Cross-Cultural Study of Teihard de Chardin and Classical Buddhist, Hindu, and Confucian Thought.' Ph.D. diss., Fordham University.

Kim, Hee-jin. 'The Life and Thought of Dogen.' Ph.D. diss., Claremont Graduate School.

Weinstein, Stanley. 'The Kanjin Kakumushō.' Ph.D. diss., Harvard University.

1967

De Silva, Padmasiri. 'A Study of Motivational Theory in Early Buddhism with Reference to the Psychology of Freud.' Ph.D. diss., University of Hawaii.

Gomez, Luis. 'Selected Verses from the Gandavyuha: Text, Critical Apparatus and Translation.' Ph.D. diss., Yale University.

Rosemont, Henry. 'Logic, Language, and Zen.' Ph.D. diss., University of Washington.

Seneviratne, H. L. 'Rebellion in the Kandyan Kingdom.' M.A. thesis, University of Rochester.

Swearer, Donald. 'Knowledge as Salvation: A Study in Early Buddhism.' Ph.D. diss., Princeton University.

Tapingkae, Amnuay. 'Eternity and Enlightenment: A Comparative Study of the Educational Philosophies of American Idealism and Theravada Buddhism.' Ph.D. diss., University of Washington.

1968

Ingram, Paul. 'Pure Land Buddhism in Japan: A Study of the Doctrine of Faith in the Teachings of Honen and Shinran.' Ph.D. diss., Claremont Graduate School.

Lancaster, Lewis. 'An Analysis of the Astasahasrika-Prajnaparamita-Sutra from the Chinese Translations.' Ph.D. diss., University of Wisconsin.

Lane, Skelton. 'Social Movements and Social Change: The Soka Gakkai of Japan.' Ph.D. diss., Claremont Graduate School.

1969

Dornish, Margaret. 'Joshu's Bridge: D. T. Suzuki's Message and Wisdom, The Early Years, 1897–1927.' Ph.D. diss., Claremont Graduate School.

DeMartino, Richard. 'The Zen Understanding of Man.' Ph.D. diss., Temple University.

Hall, Arnold. 'The Concept of Political Reform in Buddhist Literature.' Ph.D. diss., Claremont Graduate School.

Ichikawa, Akira. 'Some Political and Social Implications of Buddhism: Thought and Practice.' Ph.D. diss., University of Minnesota.

Lamont, Hamilton. 'The Debate on Karma between Tai Kuie and Chou Hsu-chih: An Annotated Translation and Introduction.' Senior thesis, Harvard University.

Morrell, Robert. '*Shasekishū* of Mujū (1226–1312).' Ph.D. diss., Stanford University.

Seo, Kyung-Bo. 'A Study of Korean Zen Buddhism Approached through the "Chodangjip".' Ph.D. diss., Temple University.

Zelliot, Eleanor. 'Dr. Ambedkar and the Mahar Movement.' Ph.D. diss., University of Pennsylvania.

1970

Amore, Roy. 'The Concept and Practice of Doing Merit in Early Theravada Buddhism.' Ph.D. diss., Columbia University.

Anacker, Stefan. 'Vasubandhu, Three Aspects: A Study of a Buddhist Philosopher.' Ph.D. diss., University of Wisconsin.

Boyd, James. 'Satan and Mara: Comparative Study of the Symbols of Evil in Early Greek Christian and Early Indian Buddhist Traditions.' Ph.D. diss., North-western University.

Dale, Kenneth. 'An Investigation of the Factors Responsible for the Impact of *Hoza* of Rissho Kosei-kai as a Means of Religious Propagation in Contemporary Japan.' Ph.D. diss., Union Theological Seminarry.

Dilworth, David. 'Nishida Kitarō (1870–1945) : The Development of His Thought.' Ph.D. diss., Columbia University.

Hibbert, Thomas. 'Three Zen Institutions: An Ethnographic Study.' Senior thesis, Reed College.

Hung, Tran Thanh. 'Buddhism and Politics in Southeast Asia.' Ph.D. diss., Claremont Graduate School.

Lesh, Terry. 'The Relationship between Zen Meditation and the Development of Accurate Emphathy.' Ph.D. diss., University of Oregon.

Matsunaga, Daigan. 'A Critical Analysis of the Buddhist Concept of Hell.' Ph.D. diss., Claremont Graduate School.

Palmer, Arthur. 'Buddhist Politics: Japan's Clean Government Party.' Ph.D. diss., Claremont Graduate School.

Paul, Sherry Ortner. 'Food for Thought: A Key Symbol in Sherpa Culture.' Ph.D. diss., University of Chicago.

Pilgrim, Richard. 'The Japanese Nō Drama as a Religious Event.' Ph.D. diss., University of Chicago.

Toganoo, Shozui. 'The Symbol-System of Shingon Buddhism.' Ph.D. diss., Claremont Graduate School.

Ury, Marian. '*Genkō shakusho*, Japan's First Comprehensive History of Buddhism, with Introduction and Notes.' Ph.D. diss., University of California, Berkeley.

1971

Andrews, Allan. 'The Nembutsu Teachings of Genshin's *Ōjōyōshū* and Their Significance for Japanese Religion.' Ph.D. diss., Claremont Graduate School.

Bingham, Irwin. 'Communication and the Tao: A Study of the Communication Theory Implicit in the Taoist and Buddhist Traditions of China.' Ph.D. diss., Southern Illinois University.

Lethcoe, Nancy. 'The Bodhisattva-Structure in Kumarajiva's "Astasahasrika-Prajnaparamita-Sutra".' Ph.D. diss., University of Wisconsin.

McDermott, James. 'Developments in the Early Buddhist Concept of Kamma/Karma.' Ph.D. diss., Princeton University.

Prebish, Charles. 'The Sanskrit Pratimoksa Sutras of the Mahasamghikas and Mulasarvastivadins: Texts, Translations, and an Introductory Exposition.' Ph.D. diss., University of Wisconsin.

Pruden, Leo. 'The *Risshū-kōyō*: An Annotated Translation.' Ph.D. diss., Harvard University.

Reynolds, Frank. 'Buddhism and Sacral Kingship: A Study in the History of Thai Religion.' Ph.D. diss., University of Chicago.

Rhie, Marilyn. 'A Study of the Historical Literary Evidence and Stylistic Chronological Dating of the Buddhist Images in the Main Hall of the Fo-kuang Monastery at Wu-t'ai Shan.' Ph.D. diss., University of Chicago.

Stephenson, Alan. 'Prolegomenon to Buddhist Social Ethics.' Ph.D. diss., Claremont Graduate School.

Swanger, Eugene. 'The World Fellowship of Buddhists, 1950 to 1966 C.E.: Unitive and Divergency Factors in a Buddhist Quest for Unity.' Ph.D. diss., University of Iowa.

Wise, David. 'Dharma West: A Social-Psychological Inquiry into Zen in San Francisco.' Ph.D. diss., University of California, Berkeley.

1972

Berzin, Alexander. 'Lam.rim.nam.ngag: A Standard Intermediate Level Textbook of the Graded Course to Enlightenment: Selected Materials from the Indo-Tibetan "Mahayana" Buddhist Textual and Oral Traditions.' Ph.D. diss., Harvard University.

Bond, George. 'The Problem of Interpretation in Theravada Buddhism and Christianity.' Ph.D. diss., Northwestern University.

Carter, John. 'Dhamma: Western Academic and Sinhalese Buddhist Interpretations, A Study of a Religious Concept.' Ph.D. diss., Harvard University.

Cooper, Robert. 'Silent as Light: A Christian-Zen Inquiry.' Ph.D. diss., Vanderbilt University.

Davisson, Charles. 'The Record of Discourses of Lin-chi: A Partial Translation with an Introduction and Notes.' Senior thesis, Harvard University.

Daye, Douglas. 'Metalogical Studies in Sixth-Century Buddhist Proto-Metalogic from the Sanskrit and Chinese Texts of the Nyayapravesa: Or Unpacking Ordinary Sanskrit.' Ph.D. diss., University of Wisconsin.

Falk, Nancy. 'The Study of Cult with Special Reference to the Cult of the Buddha's Relics in Ancient South Asia.' Ph.D. diss., University of Chicago.

Hoftiezer, Robert. 'Zen as Educational Praxis: A Study of the Educational Characteristics of the Practice of Zen Buddhism.' Ph.D. diss., State University of New York, Buffalo.

Jha, Ram. 'The Vedantic and the Buddhist Concept of Reality as Interpreted by Samkara and Nagarjuna.' Ph.D. diss., California Institute of Integral Studies.

Johnston, Gilbert. 'Kiyozawa Manshi's Buddhist Faith and Its Relation to Modern Japanese Society.' Ph.D. diss., Harvard University.

Kalbacher, Catherine. 'Zen in America.' Ph.D. diss., University of California, Berkeley.

Kobayashi, Maizie. 'The Educational Implications of Existentialism and Buddhism.' Ph.D. diss., Ohia State University.

Lee, Lena. 'Korean Buddhist Sculpture of the United Silla Dynasty (A.D. 668–935).' Ph.D. diss., Harvard University.

Pandey, Lakshuman. 'Buddhist Conception of Omniscience.' Ph.D. diss., McMaster University.

Pedersen, Priscilla. 'Shidō Munan in Zen Tradition.' M.A. thesis, Columbia University.

Rickert, Richard. 'Aesthetic Interpreting and Describing: Their Functions in Regard to the "Transinterpretive" Art of Kafka and of Zen.' Ph.D. diss., University of North Carolina.

Rogers, Minor. 'Rennyo Shōnin 1415–1499: A Transformation in Shin Buddhist Piety.' Ph.D. diss., Harvard University.

Solomon, Ira. 'Rennyo and the Rise of Honganji in Muromachi Japan.' Ph.D. diss., Columbia University.

Thurman, Robert. 'Golden Speech: A Portrait of Sumati Kīrti – Presenting English translations of the Eloquence-essences, The Smaller and the Greater (Cpts. I-III).' Ph.D. diss., Harvard University.

Van Horn, Jack. 'Devotionalism in Early Buddhism' Columbia University.

Van Tuyl, Charles. 'An Analysis of Chapter Twenty-Eight of the "Hundred Thousand Songs" of Mila-raspa, A Buddhist Poet and Saint of Tibet.' Ph.D. diss., Indiana University.

Villacorta, Wilfredo. 'Theravada Buddhism as a Value Standard of Attitudes toward International Law: Ceylon and Thailand.' Ph.D. diss., Catholic University of America.

Wargo, Robert. 'The Logic of Basho and the Concept of Nothingness in the Philosophy of Nishida Kitarō.' Ph.D. diss., University of Michigan.

1973

Corless, Roger. 'T'an-luan's Commentary on the Pure Land Discourse: An Annotated Translation and Soteriological Analysis of the *Wang-sheng-lun chu*.' Ph.D. diss., University of Wisconsin.

Cowger, Ernest. 'The Effects of Meditation (Zazen) upon Selected Dimensions of Personal Development.' Ph.D. diss., University of Georgia.

Frye, Stanley. 'The Sutra of Forty-Two Sections.' Ph.D. diss., Indiana University.

Greenblatt, Kristin. 'Yun-ch'i Chu-hung: The Career of a Ming Buddhist Monk.' Ph.D. diss., Columbia University.

Hoa, Le Van. 'Correlates of the Politically Radical-Conservative Attitudes among Buddhist Clergyman Leaders in South Vietnam.' Ph.D. diss., University of Kentucky.

Horinouchi, Isao. 'Americanized Buddhism: A Sociological Analysis of a Protestantized Japanese Religion.' Ph.D. diss., University of California, Davis.

Kemper, Steven. 'The Social Order of the Sinhalese Buddhist *Sangha*.' Ph.D. diss., University of Chicago.

Kim, Jong-Won. 'Daisetz T. Suzuki and Paul J. Tillich: A Comparative Study of Their Thoughts on Ethics in Relation to Being.' Ph.D. diss., Graduate Theological Union.

LaFleur, William. 'Saigyō the Priest and His Poetry of Reclusion: A Buddhist Valorization of Nature in Twelfth-Century Japan.' Ph.D. diss., University of Chicago.

McCallum, Donald. 'The Evolution of the Buddha and Bodhisattva Figures in Japanese Sculpture of the Ninth and Tenth Centuries.' Ph.D. diss., New York University.

Okada, Richard. 'Zen and the Poetry of Gary Snyder.' Ph.D. diss., University of Wisconsin.

Pan, Cedric. 'Nietzsche's Philosophy in Buddhist Perspectives.' Ph.D. diss., Southern Illinois University.

Pas, Julian. 'Shan-Tao's Commentary on the Amitayur-Buddhanusmrti-Sutra.' Ph.D. diss., McMaster University.

Ray, Reginald. '"Mandala" Symbolism in Tantric Buddhism.' Ph.D. diss., University of Chicago.

Reynolds, Craig. 'The Buddhist Monkhood in Nineteenth-Century Thailand.' Ph.D. diss., Cornell University.

Sanford, James. 'Ikkyū Sōjun: A Zen Monk of Fifteenth-Century Japan.' Ph.D. diss., Harvard University.

Seneviratne, Heraliwala. 'The Natural History of a Buddhist Liturgy, Being a Study in the Nature and Transformation of Kandyan Sinhalese Metropolitan Ritual.' Ph.D. diss., University of Rochester.

Shapiro, Dean. 'The Effects of a "Zen Meditation-Behavioral Self-Management" Training Package in Treating Methadone Addiction: A Formative Study.' Ph.D. diss., Stanford University.

Shigefuji, Shinei. 'Nembutsu in Shinran and His Teachers: A Comparison.' Ph.D. diss., Northwestern University.

Smathers, Frank. 'Loving Bedfellows: Whitman and Zen.' M.A. thesis, Florida Atlantic University.

Sumanashanta, Medagampala. 'A Comparison of Buddhist and Christian Perfection.' Ph.D. diss., Northwestern University.

Underwood, Frederic. 'Buddhist Insight: The Nature and Function of Panna in the Pali Nikayas.' Ph.D. diss., Columbia University.

Yu, Chai-Shin. 'A Comparative Study of the Founder's Availability, the Community, and the Discipline in Early Buddhism and in Early Christianity.' Ph.D. diss., McMaster University.

1974

Jacobs, Michael. 'Bhikku Buddhadasa: A Thai Buddhist and the Psycho-Social Dialectic of Cultural Evolution and Transformation through Religious Reformation.' M.A. thesis, American University.

Ko, Sung-won. 'Dada and Buddhist Thought: Takahashi Shinkichi as a Dada Poet Compared to Tristan Tzara.' Ph.D. diss., New York University.

Lee, Byong. 'An Analytical Study of Sacred Buddhist Chant of Korea.' Ph.D. diss., University of Washington.

Matthews, Victor. 'The Concept of Craving in Early Buddhism.' Ph.D. diss., McMaster University.

Paul, Diana. 'A Prolegomena to the "Srimaladevi Sutra" and the Tathagatagarbha Theory: The Role of Women in Buddhism.' Ph.D. diss., University of Wisconsin.

Pruess, James. 'Veneration and Merit-Seeking at Sacred Places: Buddhist Pilgrimage in Contemporary Thailand.' Ph.D. diss., University of Washington.

Ruppenthal, Stephan. 'The Transmission of Buddhism in the Poetry of Han Shan.' Ph.D. diss., University of California, Berkeley.

Tanabe, George, Jr. 'Myōe Shōnin: Tradition and Reform in Early Kamakura Buddhism.' M.A. thesis, Columbia University.

Thomas, James. 'The Self between East and West: Concepts of Self in Mead, Jung, and Mahayana Buddhism.' Ph.D. diss., Claremont Graduate School.

Wey, Nancy. 'Mu-ch'i and Zen Painting.' Ph.D. diss., University of Chicago.

1975

Aronson, Harvey. 'Love, Compassion, Sympathetic Joy and Equanimity in Theravada Buddhism.' Ph.D. diss., University of Wisconsin.

Bodman, Richard. 'Literary Theory in Sui and T'ang: A Study and Translation of Kūkai's *Bunkyō hifuron*.' Ph.D. diss., Cornell University.

Broughton, Jeffrey. 'Kuei-feng Tsung-mi: The Convergence of Ch'an and the Teachings.' Ph.D. diss., Columbia University.

Brown, Robert. 'The Institutional Disappearence of Buddhism from Northern India.' Senior thesis, Harvard University.

Carson, Linda. 'Zen Meditation in the Elderly.' Ph.D. diss., University of Nevada.

Cleary, Thomas. 'Sayings and Doings of Pai-chang Huai-hai: Ch'an Master of Great Wisdom.' Ph.D. diss., Harvard University.

Damon, Jan. 'Ritual Visualization in Hindu and Buddhist Tantrism.' M.A. thesis, California Institute of Integral Studies.

Evans, Richard. 'The Name as Symbol in the New Testament and the Writings of Shinran.' Ph.D. diss., Northwestern University.

Fujitani, Pat. 'History of Buddhist Women in Hawaii: Shinshu Experience.' Senior thesis, University of Hawaii.

Gjertson, Donald. 'A Study and Translation of the "Ming-pao Chi": A T'ang Dynasty Collection of Buddhist Tales.' Ph.D. diss., Stanford University.

Graham, Thomas. 'The Reconstruction of Popular Buddhism in Medieval China: Using Selected "Pien-wen" from Tun-Huang.' Ph.D. diss., University of Iowa.

Gupta, Bina. 'The Conception of the Self in Hume and Buddhism.' Ph.D. diss., Southern Illinois University.

Han, Ki-Bum. 'Zen and the Bible: A Study of D. T. Suzuki's Dialogues with Christianity.' Ph.D. diss., Temple University.

Jastram, Judy. 'Three Chapters from the "Gandavyuha Sutra": A Critical Edition of the Sanskrit and Tibetan Texts of the Youth Sudhana's Visits to the Bhiksus Meghasri, Sagramegha, and Supratisthita, with English Translation and Commentary.' Ph.D. diss., University of California, Berkeley.

Kashima, Tetsuden. 'The Social Organization of the Buddhist Churches of America: Continuity and Social Change.' Ph.D. diss., University of California, San Diego.

Kasulis, Thomas. 'Action Performs Man: The Meaning of the Person in Japanese Zen Buddhism.' Ph.D. diss., Yale University.

Lai, Whalen. 'The Awakening of Faith in Mahayana: A Study of the Unfolding Sinitic Mahayana Motifs.' Ph.D. diss., Harvard University.

Ludwig, Theodore. 'Religio-Aesthetic Experience in the Japanese Medieval Arts with Reference to the Way of Tea.' Ph.D. diss., University of Chicago.

McClung, Larry. 'The "Vessantara Jataka": Paradigm for a Buddhist Utopian Ideal.' Ph.D. diss., Princeton University.

Newell, William. 'An Interpretation of Religious Consciousness as Seen in Early Mahayana Buddhism' Th.M. thesis, Harvard University.

Piyananda, Dickwela. 'The Concept of Mind in Early Buddhism.' Ph.D. diss., Catholic University of America.

Robinson, Jones. 'The Eight-Four Siddhas (Caturasiti-siddha-pravrtti).' Ph.D. diss., University of Wisconsin.

Sasaguchi, Rei. 'The Image of the Contemplating Bodhisattva in Chinese Buddhist Sculpture of the Sixth Century.' Ph.D. diss., Harvard University.

Schwartz, Karl. 'The Pongyi-Tsaya/Padre-Maestro Complex: Epistemology and Pedagogy in Buddhist Burma and the Catholic Philippines.' Ph.D. diss., University of Wisconsin.

Shimizu, Yoshiaki. 'Problems of Moku'an Rei'en (?1323-1345).' Ph.D. diss., Princeton University.

Wilkinson, Stephan. 'Nichiren Shoshu Sokagakkai in America: An Analysis of Ultimate Concerns between 1960 and 1965.' Ph.D. diss., University of Iowa.

Yoo, Edward. 'Educational Ideology in Buddhism: Special Application to South Korean Education.' Ph.D. diss., Vanderbilt University.

1976

Bamroongruksa, Wira. 'The Transitional Model: A Synthesis of Western Assumptions and Buddhist Philosophical Concepts for Educational Planning in Thailand.' Ph.D. diss., University of Oregon.

Berling, Judith. 'The Uniting of the Ways: The Syncretic Thought of Lin Chao-en (1517–1598).' Ph.D. diss., Columbia University.

Best, Jonathan. 'Buddhism in Paekche: A Cultural Approach to Early Korean History and Sculpture.' Ph.D. diss., Harvard University.

Birnbaum, Donald Raoul. 'The Lapiz Lazuli Radiance Buddha, Master of Healing: A Study in Iconography and Meaning.' Ph.D. diss., Columbia University.

Burr, Ronald. 'Zen, Ontology, and Human Action.' Ph.D. diss., University of California, Santa Barbara.

Chapple, David. 'Tao-Ch'o (562–645): A Pioneer of Chinese Pure Land Buddhism.' Ph.D. diss., Yale University.

Collcutt, Martin. 'The Zen Monastic Institution in Medieval Japan.' Ph.D. diss., Harvard University.

Donner, Neal. 'The Great Cessation and Insight: An Annotated Translation of the First Two Rolls of the Sui Dynasty Meditation Text, The Mo-ho chih-kuan.' Ph.D. diss., University of British Columbia.

Dowling, Thomas. 'Vasubandhu on the "Avijnapati-Rupa": A Study in Fifth-Century Abhidharma Buddhism.' Ph.D. diss., Columbia University.

Finch, Roger. 'The Sri-parivarta (Chapters XVI and XVII) from Sinqu Sali's Uighur Translation of I-tsing's Version of the Suvarnaprabhasottama-sutra.' Ph.D. diss., Harvard University.

Fittipaldi, Silvio. 'The Encounter between Roman Catholicism and Zen Buddhism from a Roman Catholic Point of View.' Ph.D. diss., Temple University.

Gimello, Robert. 'Chih-yen (602–668) and the Foundations of Hua-Yen Buddhism.' Ph.D. diss., Columbia University.

Guth, Christine. 'Early Shinto Sculpture: The Hachiman Triad of the Tōji and Yakushi-ji.' Ph.D. diss., Harvard University.

Guthrie, Stewart. 'A Japanese "New Religion": Risshō Kōsei kai in a Japanese Farming Village.' Ph.D. diss., Yale University.

Hixon, Alexander. 'Mahayana Buddhist Influence on the Gauda School of Advaya Vedanta: An Analysis of the "Gaudapadakarika".' Ph.D. diss., Columbia University.

Holmes, Ivar. 'Chāndi Mendut: Its Form, Meaning, and Antecedents.' Senior thesis, Harvard University.

Hoover, Judith. 'Hindu and Buddhist Mysticism: The Still Point in the Turning Worlds of T. S. Eliot and Octavio Paz.' Ph.D. diss., University of Illinois, Urbana-Champaigne.

Kawamura, Leslie. 'Vinitadeva's Contribution to the Buddhist Mentalistic Trend.' Ph.D. diss., University of Saskatchewan.

Kirschner, Sam. 'Zen Meditators: A Clinical Study.' Ph.D. diss., Adelphi University.

Klimburg-Salter, Deborah. 'Buddhist Painting of the Hindu Kush.' Ph.D. diss., Harvard University.

Kodera,Takashi James. 'Dogen's Formative Years in China: An Historical and Annotated Translation of the *Hōkyō-ki*.' Ph.D. diss., Columbia University.

Lishka, Dennis. 'Buddhist Wisdom and Its Expression as Art: The Dharma of the Zen Master Takuan.' Ph.D. diss., University of Wisconsin.

Mair, Victor. 'Popular Narratives from Tun-huang.' Ph.D. diss., Harvard University.

McGuire, Francis. 'Practical Mysticism: The Psychosocial Dynamics of Change in the Mystical Traditions, Christianity and Zen Buddhism.' Ph.D. diss., Graduate Theological Union.

Matsumoto, Moritaka. 'Chang Sheng-wen's Long Roll of Buddhist Images: A Reconstruction and Iconology.' Ph.D. diss., Princeton University.

Müller, Wilhelm. 'Shingon-Mysticism: Subhākarasimha and I-Hsing's Commentary to the Mahavairocana-sūtra, Chapter One, An Annotated Translation.' Ph.D. diss., University of California, Los Angeles.

Oh, Kang-Nam. 'A Study of Chinese Hua-Yen Buddhism with Specific Reference to the "Dharamadhatus" ("Fa-chieh") Doctrine.' Ph.D. diss., McMaster University.

Rodd, Laurel. 'Nichiren (1222–1282): An Intellectual Biography Based on His Letters and Essays.' M.A. thesis, Arizona State University.

Schuster, Nancy. 'The "Ugrapariprccha," the "Maharatnakuta sutra," and Early Mahayana Buddhism.' Ph.D. diss., University of Toronto.

Sharrin, Ronald. 'Some Steps toward a Conceptual Framework for Therapy Based on Buddhism.' Ph.D. diss., California School of Professional Psychology, Los Angeles.

Sherburne, Richard. 'A Study of Atisa's Commentary on His Lamp of the Enlightenment Path.' Ph.D. diss., University of Washington.

Siderits, Mark. 'The Formlessness of the Good: Toward a Buddhist Theory of Value.' Ph.D. diss., Yale University.

Sinha, Braj. 'Problem of Time and Temporality in Samkhya-Yoga and Abhidharma Buddhism' McMaster University.

Sircar, Rina. 'Psycho-Ethical Aspects of Buddhism.' Ph.D. diss., California Institute of Integral Studies.

Smith, Otis. 'Zen No Mind: An Interpretation in a Contemporary Idiom of Zen in Theory and Practice.' Ph.D. diss., University of Wisconsin

Snow, David. 'The Nichiren Shoshu Buddhist Movement in America: A Sociological Examination of Its Value Orientation, Recruitment Efforts and Spread.' Ph.D. diss., University of California, Los Angeles.

Storlie, Erik. 'Grace and Works, Enlightenment and Practice: Paradox and Poetry in John Cotton, Jonathan Edwards, and Dogen Zenji.' Ph.D. diss., University of Minnesota.

Utz, David. 'An Unpublished Sogdian Version of the Mahayana Mahaparinirvana-sutra in the German Turfan Collection.' Ph.D. diss., Harvard University.

Whitehead, James. 'The Sinicization of Buddhism: A Study of the "Vimalakirti-nirdesa Sutra" and Its Interpretation in China from the Third through the Sixth Century.' Ph.D. diss., Harvard University.

Yoo, Chul Ok. 'Nishida Kitaro's Concept of Absolute Nothingness in Its Relationship to Japanese Culture.' Ph.D. diss., Boston University.

Zwilling, Leonard. 'Dharmakīrti on Apoha.' Ph.D. diss., University of Wisconsin.

1977

Baker, Stuart. 'An Analytical Approach to Early Buddhist Thought.' M.A. thesis, California Institute of Integral Studies.

Chantharasakul, Apa. 'A Comparative Study of Existentialism and Theravada Buddhism as Educational Philosophies.' Ph.D. diss., University of Northern Colorado.

Clifford, Terrence. 'Diamond Healing: The Buddhist Medicine and Medical Psychiatry of Tibet.' Ph.D. diss., Union for Experimenting Colleges and Universities.

Dawes, Charles. 'The Path of Spiritual Progress in Theravada Buddhism.' Ph.D. diss., California Institute of Integral Studies.

Delaney, William. 'Sociocultural Aspects of Aging in Buddhist Northern Thailand.' Ph.D. diss., University of Illinois, Urbana-Champaigne.

Fader, Larry. 'Philosophically Significant Western Understandings of D. T. Suzuki's Interpretations of Zen and Their Influence on Occidental Culture, Examined Critically in Relation to Suzuki's Thought in his English-Language Writings.' Ph.D. diss., Temple University.

Foard, James. 'Ippen Shōnin and Popular Buddhism in Kamakura Japan.' Ph.D. diss., Stanford University.

Freedman, Michael. 'The Characterization of Ananda in the "Pali Canon" of the Theravada: A Hagiographic Study.' Ph.D. diss., McMaster University.

Hellner, Timothy. 'Two Kinds of Thinking: As Represented in the Buddhist Tradition and the Writings of Heidegger.' M.A. thesis, University of Louisville.

Holt, John. 'Bhikkhu Discipline: Salvation and Community in the Vinayapitaka.' Ph.D. diss., University of Chicago.

Holtzapple, Vicki. 'Soka Gakkai in Midwestern America: A Case Study of a Transpositional Movement.' Ph.D. diss., Washington University.

Keel, Hee-Sung. 'Chinul: The Founder of Korean Sön (Zen) Tradition.' Ph.D. diss., Harvard University.

Kloetzli, Walter. 'The Teaching of Light: Toward a Mahayanist Cosmology and Its Placement in Buddhist, Indian and Extra-Indian Perspectives.' Ph.D. diss., University of Chicago.

Kong, Roberta. 'The Influence of Buddhist Philosophy on the Neo-Confucianism of Ch'eng Hao and Ch'eng I.' Ph.D. diss., State University of New York, Albany

Kornfield, Jack. 'The Psychology of Mindfulness Meditation.' Ph.D. diss., Saybrook Institute.

Kramphaibul, Pronthip. 'The "Bot": Buddhist Architecture in Thailand.' M.A. thesis, California State University, Long Beach.

McMullin, Neil. 'Oda Nobunaga and the Buddhist Institutions.' Ph.D. diss., University of British Columbia.

Moles, Edward. 'Zen Meditation: A Study of Regression in Service of the Ego.' Ph.D. diss., California School of Professional Psychology.

Mori, Koichi. 'Study of Makiguchi Tsunesaburō: The Founder of Soka Gakkai' Th.D. diss., Graduate Theological Union.

Nagai, Evelyn. 'Iconographic Innovations in Kuchean Buddhist Art.' Ph.D. diss., University of California, Berkeley.

O'Donoghue, Patrick. 'Nichiren in Modern Buddhism: A Study in Catechetical Adaptation in Japan's Soka Gakkai Leadership.' Ph.D. diss., Catholic University of America.

Parker, Kenneth. 'The Life and Writings of Takuan Zenji (1573-1645).' Ph.D. diss., University of Pennsylvania.

Rittenberg, William. 'Buad Naag: The Structure and Performance of a Thai Buddhist Ordination Ceremony.' Ph.D. diss., University of California, Los Angeles.

Strong, John. 'Making Merit in the "Asokavadana": A Study of Buddhist Acts of Offering in the Post-Parinirvana Age.' Ph.D. diss., University of Chicago.

Teshima, Jacob. 'Zen Buddhism and Hasidism: A Comparative Study.' Ph.D. diss., Jewish Theological Seminary of America.

Tyler, Royall. 'Suzuki Shōsan (1577–1655): A Fighting Man of Zen.' Ph.D. diss., Columbia University.

Wetzler, Peter. 'Yoshishige no Yasutane: Lineage, Learning, Office, and Amida's Pure Land.' Ph.D. diss., University of California, Berkeley.

Zack, Stephen. 'Buddhist Education under Prince Wachirayan Warorot.' Ph.D. diss., Cornell University.

Zeuschuer, Robert. 'An Analysis of the Philosophical Criticisms of Northern Ch'an Buddhism.' Ph.D. diss., University of Hawaii.

1978

Augustine, Morris. 'The Buddhist Notion of Faith.' Ph.D. diss., Graduate Theological Union.

Barrett, Timothy. 'Buddhism, Taoism, and Confucianism in the Thought of Li Ao.' Ph.D. diss., Yale University.

Browning, Ronald. 'Psychotherapeutic Change East and West: Buddhist Psychological Paradigm of Change with Reference to Pychoanalysis.' Ph.D. diss., California School of Professional Psychology.

Davis, David. 'The Kaga Ikkō-ikki, 1473-1580.' Ph.D. diss., University of Chicago.

Domiter, Paul. 'Zen Meditation, Exceptancy, and their Relative Contributions to Changes in Perceptual Flexibility.' Ph.D. diss., University of Miami.

Glass, Joel. 'Selected Buddhist Educational Texts of Tibet: Translation and Explication.' Ph.D. diss., University of Kentucky.

Harmon, Roger. 'Buddhism and Action: The Thammathuut ('Ambassador of Dharma') Program in Thailand.' Ph.D. diss., University of Washington.

Kim, Samuel. 'The Korean Monk-Soldiers in the Imjin Wars: An Analysis of Buddhist Resistance to the Hideyoshi Invasion, 1592–1598.' Ph.D. diss., Columbia University.

Krebs, Harry. 'The Religious Thought of Nishitani Keiji.' Ph.D. diss., Temple University.

LePain, Marc. 'The Parable of the Lost Heir: A Story of the Mahāyāna Journey to Buddhahood.' Ph.D. diss., Fordham University.

Levering, Miriam. 'Ch'an Enlightenment for Laymen: Ta-hui and the New Religious Culture of the Sung.' Ph.D. diss., Harvard University.

McKeon, Joseph. 'Faith in Early Buddhist Teachings.' Ph.D. diss., Fordham University.

MacQueen, Graeme. 'A Study of the Srāmānyaphala Sūtra.' Ph.D. diss., Harvard University.

Macy, Joanna. 'Interdependence: Mutual Causality in Early Buddhist Teachings and General Systems Theory.' Ph.D. diss., Syracuse University.

Métraux, Daniel. 'The Religious and Social Philosophy of the Sōkagakkai.' Ph.D. diss., Columbia University.

Nishimura, Anne. 'The Daitokuji Triptych: A Southern Sung Prototype in Japanese Painting.' Senior thesis, Harvard University.

O'Connor, Richard. 'Urbanism and Religion: Community, Hierarchy and Sanctity in Urban Thai Buddhist Temples.' Ph.D. diss., Cornell University.

O'Donnell, Richard. 'Alan Watts: Zen, Language, and Philosophy.' M.A. thesis, California State University, Long Beach.

Pokaeo, Soree. 'Comprehension of the Buddhist Two Planes of Knowledge as a Conceptual Scheme for the Practice of Counseling' Ed.D. diss., Northern Illinois University.

Prangpatanpon, Sakda. 'A Buddhist Philosophy of Education: With Implications for Education in Thailand.' Ph.D. diss., Boston College.

Roccasalvo, Joseph. 'The Anattā Doctrine: A Textual and Contextual Interpretation.' Ph.D. diss., Harvard University.

Saisang, Prachaksha. 'The Impact of Buddhism upon Higher Education in Thailand' Ed.D. diss., Indiana University.

Tatz, Mark. 'Candragomin and the Bodhisattva Vow.' Ph.D. diss., University of British Columbia.

Watt, Paul. 'The Life and Thought of Jiun Sonja (1718–1804).' Ph.D. diss., Columbia University.

Childs, Margaret. '*Chigo Monogatari*: Love Stories or Buddhist Sermons.' M.A. thesis, Columbia University.

Weinstein, Lucie. 'The Hōryūji Canopies and Their Continental Antecedent.' Ph.D. diss., Yale University.

1979

Arntzen, Sonja. 'The Poetry of the Kyōunshū "Crazy Cloud Anthology".' Ph.D. diss., University of British Columbia.

Chung, Bongkil. 'The Ethics of Won Buddhism: A Conceptual Analysis of the Moral System of Won Buddhism.' Ph.D. diss., Michigan State University.

Chung, Paul Sang-wan. 'The Christian Concept of God and Zen "Nothingness" as Embodied in the Works of Tillich and Nishida.' Ph.D. diss., Temple University.

Eichenbaum, Patricia. 'The Development of a Narrative Cycle Based on the Life of the Buddha in India, Central Asia, and the Far East: Literary and Pictorial Evidence.' Ph.D. diss., New York University.

Fenner, Edward. 'Rasayana Siddhi: Medicine and Alchemy in the Buddhist Tantras.' Ph.D. diss., University of Wisconsin.

Gelfman, Wayne. 'The *Rishukyō* and Its Influence on Kūkai: The Identity of the Sentient Being with the Buddha.' Ph.D. diss., University of Wisconsin, Madison.

Groner, Paul. 'Saicho and the Bodhisattva Precepts.' Ph.D. diss., Yale University.

Grosnick, William. 'The Zen Master Dōgen's Understanding of the Buddha-Nature in Light of the Historical Development of the Buddha-Nature Concept in India, China, and Japan.' Ph.D. diss., University of Wisconsin.

Grupper, Samuel. 'The Manchu Imperial Cult of the Early Ch'ing Dynasty: Texts and Studies on the Tantric Sanctuary of Mahakala at Mukden.' Ph.D. diss., Indiana University.

Hsing, Fu-chuan. 'A Survey of Public and Popular Buddhism and Buddhist Temples in Taiwan.' Ph.D. diss., Ohio State University.

Joseph, Arthur. 'The Influence of One Form of Zen Meditation on Levels of Anxiety and Self-Actualization' Ed.D. diss., State University of New York, Albany.

Kang, Kun Ki. 'Thomas Merton and Buddhism: A Comparative Study of the Spiritual Thought of Thomas Merton and That of National Teacher Bojo.' Ph.D. diss., New York University.

Katz, Nathan. 'The Concept of the Arahant in the Sutta Pitaka, with Reference to the Bodhisattva and the Mahasiddha.' Ph.D. diss., Temple University.

Kim, Young Hwan. 'Buddhism and Its Implications for American Physical Education.' Ph.D. diss., Kent State University.

Liu, Ming-Wood. 'The Teaching of Fa-tsang: An Examination of Buddhist Metaphysics.' Ph.D. diss., University of California, Los Angeles.

Maher, Michael. 'Movement Exploration and Zazen Meditation: A Comparison of Two Methods of Personal-Growth-Group Approaches on the Self-Actualization Potential of Counselor Candidates.' Ph.D. diss., University of Idaho.

O'Malia, Edwin. 'The Transformation of Man: A Descriptive Comparative Study in the Thought of Sri Aurobindo and Zen Buddhism as Explicated in the English Language Writings of D. T. Suzuki.' Ph.D. diss., Temple University.

Padmanabhan, Pallipuram. 'The Influence of Vedanta and Buddhism on the Poetry and Drama of T. S. Eliot.' Ph.D. diss., University of Alberta.

Schwabe, Kurt. 'The Construction and Religious Meaning of the Buddhist Stupa in Solo Khumbhu, Nepal.' Ph.D. diss., Graduate Theological Union.

Shim, Jae-Ryong. 'The Philosophical Foundation of Korean Zen Buddhism: The Integration of Son and Kyo by Chinul (1158–1210).' University of Hawaii.

Shu, Wendy. 'A Zen Encounter.' M.A. thesis, California State University, Dominguez Hills.

Smisson, Peyton. 'The Mundane and Absolute in Chao lun: A Chinese Understanding of Indian Buddhism.' Senior thesis, Harvard University.

Sponberg, Alan. 'The Vijñaptimātrātā Buddhism of the Chinese Monk K'uei-chi (A.D. 632–682).' Ph.D. diss., University of British Columbia.

Staggs, Kathleen. 'In Defense of Japanese Buddhism: Essays from the Meiji Period by Inoue Enryō and Murakami Senshō.' Ph.D. diss., Princeton University.

Stilling, Stuart. 'The First Two Buddhist Council Accounts.' M.A. thesis, California State University, Fullerton.

Yoon, Byung-Yul. 'A Study of an Extended Concept of Human Intrapsychic Capacity as Expanded in D. T. Suzuki's Zen Buddhism.' Ph.D. diss., United States International University.

1980

Bastian, Edward. 'Mahayana Buddhist Religious Practice and the Perfection of Wisdom According to the Abhisamayalamkara and the Pancavimsatisahasrika Prajnaparamita.' Ph.D. diss., University of Wisconsin.

Bender, Ross. 'The Political Meaning of the Hachiman Cult in Ancient and Medieval Japan.' Ph.D. diss., Columbia University.

Bielefeldt, Carl. 'The Fukan Zazengi and the Meditation Teachings of the Japanese Zen Master Dōgen.' Ph.D. diss., University of California, Berkeley.

Draghi, Paul. 'A Comparative Study of the Theme of the Conversion of a Hunter in Tibetan, Bhutanese, and Medieval Sources.' Ph.D. diss., Indiana University.

Eckel, Malcolm David. 'A Question of Nihilism: Bhāvaviveka's Response to the Fundamental Problems of Mādhyamika Philosophy.' Ph.D. diss., Harvard University.

Fisher, Robert. 'Buddhist Architecture of Kashmir.' Ph.D. diss., University of Southern California.

Ford, Barbara. 'A Study of the Painting of Sesson Shukei.' Ph.D. diss., Columbia University.

Grotenhuis, Elizabeth ten. 'The Revival of the Taima Mandala in Medieval Japan.' Ph.D. diss., Harvard University.

Gunaratana, Henepola. 'A Critical Analysis of the Jhanas in Theravada Buddhist Meditation.' Ph.D. diss., American University.

Hallisey, Charles. 'A Trace of the Buddha: Veneration of the Footprint of the Buddha on Adam's Peak.' M.A. thesis, University of Pennsylvania.

Hanson, Mervin. 'The Trikaya: A Study of the Buddhology of the Early Vijnanavada School of Indian Buddhism.' Ph.D. diss., University of British Columbia.

Heifetz, Julie. 'The Role of the Clergy at the Vietnamese Buddhist Temple in Los Angeles as Culture Brokers in Vietnamese Refugee Resettlement.' M.A. thesis, University of Houston.

Heine, Steven. 'Existential and Ontological Dimensions of Time in Heidegger and Dōgen.' Ph.D. diss., Temple University.

Hurst, Jane. 'The Nichiren Shoshū Sokagakkai in America: The Ethos of a New Religious Movement.' Ph.D. diss., Temple University.

Jones, Richard. 'Mysticism and Science: A Comparative Study of the Claims about Reality in the Western Natural Science, Theravada Buddhism, and Advaita Vedanta.' Ph.D. diss., Columbia University.

Kaufman, Laura. '*Ippen Hijiri-e*: Artistic and Literary Sources in a Buddhist Handscroll Painting of Thirteenth-Century Japan.' Ph.D. diss., New York University.

Keenan, John. 'A Study of "Buddhabhūmyupadesa": The Doctrinal Development of the Notion of Wisdom in Yogācāra Thought.' Ph.D. diss., University of Wisconsin.

Keenan, Richard. 'Zen Buddhist Influences and Techniques in the Works of Julio Cortázar.' Ph.D. diss., University of Missouri.

Keyt, Christine. 'Dharmakirti's Concept of the "Svalaksana".' Ph.D. diss., University of Washington.

Komito, David. 'Nārārjuna's Sūnyatāptati.' Ph.D. diss., University of Indiana.
Krane, Loren. 'Personality and Socio-Political Activism in an American Buddhist Group: The Insight Meditation Society.' Ph.D. diss., California School of Professional Psychology.
Krueger, Robert. 'The Comparative Effects of Zen Focusing and Muscle Relaxation Training on Selected Experiential Variables.' Ph.D. diss., University of Iowa.
Le, Daniel Dinh Phuoc. 'Vietnamese Refugees' Perceptions and Methods for Coping with Mental Illnesses.' Ph.D. diss., United States International University.
Martin, Dorothy. 'The Life and Literature of Reinhard Goering: A Study in Contradictions.' Ph.D. diss., University of Illinois, Urbana-Champaigne.
Nakasone, Ronald. 'The "Huan-yuan-kuan": A Study of the Hua-yen Interpretation of "Pratityasamutpada".' Ph.D. diss., University of Wisconsin, Madison.
Odin, Steve. 'A. N. Whitehead's Process Metaphysics and Hua-Yen Buddhism on Interpenetration: A Critical Analysis.' Ph.D. diss., State University of New York, Stony Brook.
O'Neil, Frances. 'A Theoretical Analysis of Zen Buddhist Principles in Education and Two Cases of Their Implementation in America.' Ph.D. diss., University of Connecticut.
Pahalawattage, Don Premasiri. 'Moral Evaluation in Early Buddhism: From the Prespective of Western Philosophical Analysis.' Ph.D. diss., University of Hawaii.
Rogers, K. 'Tibetan Logic.' M.A. thesis, University of Virginia.
Shaner, David. 'The Bodymind Experience in Japanese Buddhism: A Phenomen-ological Study of Kūkai and Dōgen.' Ph.D. diss., University of Hawaii .
Steffney, John. 'Heidegger and Zen: A Study of Radicalization.' Ph.D. diss., Temple University.
Strange, Robert. 'A Buddhist View of Existence.' M.A. thesis, California Institute of Integral Studies.
Suebsonthi, Krich. 'The Influences of Buddhism and Islam on Family Planning in Thailand: Communication Implication.' Ph.D. diss., University of Minnesota.
Willson, Lawrence. 'On Being, Act or Process : A Comparative Study of the Religious Philosophies of Suzuki and Hartshorne.' Ph.D. diss., Boston University.
Witzling, Catherine. 'The Poetry of Chia Tai (779–843): A Re-examination of Critical Stereotypes.' Ph.D. diss., Stanford University.
Wright, Dale. 'Emptiness and Paradox in the Thought of Fa-tsang.' Ph.D. diss., University of Iowa.
Young, Gloria. 'The New Transcendentalism in Post-Industrial Society: Life Styles and the Search for Meaning in the New Age.' Ph.D. diss., University of Texas, Austin.

1981

Bacher, Paula Green. 'An Investigation into the Compatibility of Existential-Humanistic Psychotherapy and Buddhist Meditation.' Ed.D. diss., Boston University.
Becker, Carl. 'Survival: Death and the Afterlife in Christianity, Buddhism, and Modern Science.' Ph.D. diss., University of Hawaii.
Brown, Brian. 'The Buddha Nature: A Study of the "Tathagatagarbha" and "Alayavijnana".' Ph.D. diss., Fordham University.
Brown, Daniel. 'Mahāmudrā Meditation-Stages and Contemporary Cognitive Psychological Hermeneutics.' Ph.D. diss., University of Chicago.
Brown, Robert. 'The Dvaravati "Dharmacakras": A Study in the Transfer of Form and Meaning.' Ph.D. diss., University of Calfornia, Los Angeles.
Brown, William. 'The Distinction between "Pien-wen" and "Chiang-ching-wen": An Analysis of the Literary Forms and Preaching Methods of the "Overcoming

Demons Study" and "Exposition of the Diamond Sutra".' Ph.D. diss., University of Wisconsin.

Chhodak, Tenzing. 'Education of Tibetan Refugees: Characteristics and Conditions of Learning Environments in Selected Tibetan Schools in India.' Ed.D. diss., University of Massachusetts.

Chow, Joseph. 'Detachment in the Philosophy of Wang Yang-ming: The Concept of "Liang-chih".' Ph.D. diss., Drew University.

Dollarhide, Kenneth. 'Nichiren's Doctrine of the Age of the Last Law According to the Senji Shō.' Ph.D. diss., McMaster University.

Ebersole, Gary. 'Matsuo Bashō and the Way of Poetry in the Japanese Religious Tradition.' Ph.D. diss., University of Chicago.

Fasano, Anthony. 'The Religious Structure of Tantric Buddhism.' Ph.D. diss., Fordham University.

Gaffney, Peter. 'Myth, Dream, and Amythic Consciousness in Tibetan Buddhism.' Senior thesis, Harvard University.

Gregory, Peter. 'Tsung-mi's *Inquiry into the Origins of Man*: A Study of Chinese Buddhist Hermeneutics.' Ph.D. diss., Harvard University.

Grossberg, John. 'Formulating Attitudes toward Death: A Study of Elderly Japanese Jōdō Shin Buddhists.' Ph.D. diss., University of Illinois.

Gyatso, Janet. 'The Literary Traditions of Thang-sting rGyal-po: A Study of Visionary Buddhism in Tibet.' Ph.D. diss. University of California, Berkeley.

Hardacre, Helen. 'Reiyūkai Kyōdan and the Practice of Lay Buddhism.' Ph.D. diss., University of Chicago.

Howard, Angela. 'The Imagery of the "Cosmological Buddha".' Ph.D. diss., New York University.

Huie, Chee. 'A Study of the Chronology and Development of the Caves at Tun-Huang Executed from Northern Liang to T'ang.' Ph.D. diss., New York University.

King, Sallie. 'The Active Self: A Philosophical Study of the "Buddha Nature Treatise" and Other Chinese Buddhist Texts.' Ph.D. diss., Temple University.

Klein, Anne. 'Mind and Liberation-The Sautrantika Tenet System in Tibet: Perception, Positive and Negative Phenomena, Impermanence and the Two Truths in the Context of Buddhist Religious Insight as Presented in Ge-luk Literary and Oral Traditions.' Ph.D. diss., University of Virginia.

Kobayashi, Kazuo. 'The Effect of Zen Meditation on the Valence of Intrusive Thoughts.' Ph.D. diss., United States International University.

Kopecki, Andrew. 'Cultural Adaptation in the Chinese Acceptance of Buddhism: Selections from the "Hung-ming chi".' Ph.D. diss., Harvard University.

Lichter, David. 'Person, Action and Causation in a Bhote Ethic.' Ph.D. diss., Stanford University

Ling, Paul. 'The Intensive Buddhist Meditation Retreat and the Self: Psychological and Theravadin Considerations.' Ph.D. diss., Boston University.

Ma, Alexander. 'On the Buddhist Logical Approach to Semantics.' Ph.D. diss., Georgetown University.

Novak, Philip. 'Empty Willing: A Study of Contemplative Gesture of St. John of the Cross and Dogen Zenji.' Ph.D. diss., Syracuse University.

Orlando, Raffaello. 'A Study of Chinese Documents Concerning the Life of the Tantric Buddhist Patriarch Amoghavajra (A.D. 705–744).' Ph.D. diss., Princeton University.

Pickett, Rebecca. 'Gary Snyder and the Mythological Present.' Ph.D. diss., University of Nebraska, Lincoln.

Razzino, Andrea. "'Panna" and "Karuna" in Theravada Buddhist Ethics Compared to Love in Protestant Christian Ethics.' Ph.D. diss., Northwestern University.

Roberts, Mary Jo. 'The Meditative Mode in Gertrude Stein's Experimental Work.' Ph.D. diss., University of Texas, Austin.

Rosenthal, Joseph. 'Buddhism and Psychotherapy.' Ph.D. diss., University of Hawaii.

Shin, Hong-Shik. 'Principles of Church Planting as Illustrated in Thai Theravada Buddhist Context.' Th.D. diss., Dallas Theological Seminary.

Shirakawa, Zenryu. 'The Esotericization of Tendai in Early Heian Japan.' Ph.D. diss., Harvard University.

Tan Phat, Antoine. 'Mahayana Buddhism in Vietnam and Its Background in India and China.' Ph.D. diss., California Institute of Integral Studies.

Vryheid, Robert. 'An American Buddhist Monastery: Sociocultural Aspects of Soto Zen Training.' Ph.D. diss., University of Oregon.

Watts, Jeffrey. 'Determinism and the Path to Freedom in Early Buddhism.' Ph.D. diss., University of Hawaii.

1982

Beuscher, John. 'The Buddhist Doctrine of Two Truths in the Vaibhasika and Theravada Schools.' Ph.D. diss., University of Virginia.

Boulton, Nancy. 'Early Chinese Buddhist Travel Records as a Literary Genre.' Ph.D. diss., Georgetown University.

Christensen, Ross. 'Shinran and the Problem of Pure Land Morality.' Senior thesis, University of Hawaii.

Darling, Gregory. 'An Evaluation of the Vedantic Critique of Buddhism in Three Commentaries to the Brahma-sutras.' Ph.D. diss., Columbia University.

Hayes, Richard. 'On the Nature of Knowledge Acquired through Language: A Study of the "Apoha" Theory in Dinnaga's "Pramanasamuccaya".' Ph.D. diss., University of Toronto.

Herzberger, Radhika. 'The Development of Logic in Fifth and Sixth Century India.' Ph.D. diss., University of Toronto.

Howard, Angela. 'The Imagery of the "Cosmological Buddha".' Ph.D. diss., New York University.

Hugh, Richard. 'On the Nature of Knowledge Acquired through Language: Study of the "Apoha" Theory in Dinnaga's "Pramanasamuccaya".' Ph.D. diss., University of Toronto.

Kim, Sang Yil. 'Korean Transformation of Buddhism in the Seventh-Century: A Process View.' Ph.D. diss., Claremont Graduate School.

Lopez, Donald. 'The Svatantrika-Madhyamika School of Mahāyāna Buddhism.' Ph.D. diss., University of Virginia.

Mahony, William. 'Flying Priests, Yogins, and Shamans in Early Hinduism and Buddhism.' Ph.D. diss., University of Chicago.

Moore, Jean. 'A Study of the Thirteenth-Century Buddhist Tale Collection *Senjūshō*.' Ph.D. diss., Columbia University.

Norwood, Jean. 'An Investigation of a Zen Meditation Procedure and Its Effect on Selected Personality and Pychotherapeutic Variables.' Ph.D. diss., North Texas State University.

Oliver, Curtis. 'The Yogacara Dharma List: A Study of the Abhidharmasamuccaya and Its Commentary, Abhidharmasamuccayabhasya.' Ph.D. diss., University of Toronto.

Powell, William. 'The Record of Tung-shan: An Analysis of Pedogogical Style in Ch'an Buddhism.' Ph.D. diss., University of California, Berkeley.

Raducha, Joan. 'Iconography of Buddhist Relief Scenes from Kushan.' Ph.D. diss., University of Wisconsin.

Reed, Barbara. 'The Problem of the "Dharmakaya" as Seen by Hui-yuan and Kumarajiva.' Ph.D. diss., University of Iowa.

Routledge, Paul. 'The Role of Religion in Ethnic Identity: The Vietnamese of Oklahoma City, 1975–1982.' Ph.D. diss., University of Oklahoma.
Ryder, John. 'Ordinality, Language-Games and Sunyata: Their Implications for Religion.' Ph.D. diss., State University of New York, Stony Brook.
Sayama, Mike. 'Mushin, the Highest State of Consciousness in Zen Buddhism.' Ph.D. diss., University of Michigan.
Thompson, Heather. 'Paradox and Nirvana in the Upanishads, Buddhism, and Advaita Vedanta of Sankaracarya.' Ph.D. diss., California Institute of Integral Studies.
Tourangeau, Frank. 'Zen and the Art of Oral Interpretation: A Rational Guide to Non-Rational Discovery.' Ph.D. diss., Southern Illinois University.
Wagner, David. 'The Development of Indian Buddhism: An Ethnohistorical Perspective.' M.A. thesis, California State University, Long Beach.
Winslow, Deborah. 'Pantheon Politics: A Regional Analysis of Buddhism in Sri Lanka.' Ph.D. diss., Stanford University.

1983
Abrahams, Mark. 'A Phenomenological Adaptation of the Tibetan Buddhist Doctrine of Psychic Centers to a Metatheoretical Hierarchy of Human Motivation.' Ph.D. diss., University of Maryland.
Burford, Grace. 'The Ideal Goal According to the Atthakavagga and Its Major Pali Commentaries.' Ph.D. diss., Northwestern University.
Childs, Margaret. 'Religious Awakening Stories in Late Medieval Japan: The Dynamics of Didacticism.' Ph.D. diss., University of Pennsylvania.
Cox, Collett. 'Controversies in Dharma Theory: Sectarian Dialogue on the Nature of Enduring Reality.' Ph.D. diss., Columbia University.
Darling, Leonard. 'The Transformation of Pure Land Thought and the Development of Shinto Shrine Mandala Paintings: Kasuga and Kumano.' Ph.D. diss., University of Michigan.
Das, Rama. 'Self and Causality in Hume and Sautrantika.' Ph.D. diss., Syracuse University.
De Alwis, Tissa. 'Christian-Buddhist Dialogue in the Writings of Lynn A De Silva' Th.D. diss., Andrews University.
Dutt, Denise. 'An Integration of Zen Buddhism and the Study of Person and Environment.' Ph.D. diss., California
Institute of Integral Studies.
Edwards-Leese, Marilyn. 'The Traikutaka Dynasty and Kanheri's Second Phase of Buddhist Cave Excavation.' Ph.D. diss., University of Michigan.
Engle, Artemus. 'The Buddhist Theory of Self According to Acarya Candrakirti.' Ph.D. diss., University of Wisconsin.
Engler, John. 'Theravada Buddhist Insight Meditation and an Object Relations Model of Therapeutic-Developmental Change: A Clinical Case Study of an Ethnopsychiatric Tradition.' Ph.D. diss., University of Chicago.
Gosling, Elizabeth. 'The History of Sukhothain as a Ceremonial Center: A Study of Early Siamese Architecture and Society.' Ph.D. diss., University of Michigan.
Griffiths, Paul. 'Indian Buddhist Meditation-Theory: History, Development and Systematization.' Ph.D. diss., University of Wisconsin.
Hall, Bruce. 'Vasubandhu on "Aggregates, Spheres, and Components": Being Chapter One of the "Abhidharmakosa".' Ph.D. diss., Harvard University.
Jackson, Roger. 'Is Enlightenment Possible? An Analysis of Some Arguments in the Buddhist Philosophical Tradition with Special Attention to the "Pramanasiddhi" Chapter of Dharmakirti's "Pramanavarttika".' Ph.D. diss., University of Wisconsin.

Lang, Karen. 'Aryadeva on the Bodhisattva's Cultivation of Merit and Knowledge.' Ph.D. diss., University of Washington.

Lax, William. 'An Historical and Comparative Analysis of the Concept of Awareness in Gestalt Therapy and Mindfulness in Theravada Buddhism.' Ph.D. diss., The Fielding Institute.

Lee, Yu-Min. 'The Maitreya Cult and Its Art in Early China.' Ph.D. diss., Ohio State University.

Malandra, Geri. 'The Buddhist Caves at Ellora.' Ph.D. diss., University of Minnesota.

McRae, John. 'The Northern School of Chinese Ch'an Buddhism.' Ph.D. diss., Yale University.

Parker, Kenneth. '*Okyōsama*: Documentation of the Founding of Nyorai-kyō, Japan's First 'New Religion.' Ph.D. diss., University of Pennsylvania.

Perdue, Daniel. 'Practice and Theory of Philosophical Debate in Tibetan Buddhist Education.' Ph.D. diss., University of Virginia.

Richman, Paula. 'Religious Rhetoric in the "Manimekalai".' Ph.D. diss., University of Chicago.

Roning-Philip, Mikela. 'Transformation through Color: Buddhist Psychology and Art.' M.A. thesis, California Institute of Integral Studies.

Rosen, Elizabeth. 'The Buddhist Art of Nagarjunakonda.' Ph.D. diss., New York University.

Sano, Emily J. 'The Twenty-Eight Bushū of Sanjūsangendō.' Ph.D. diss., Columbia University.

Scales, Sandra. 'The Turquoise Sky: A Discussion of Buddhist Psychology.' Ph.D. diss., Union for Experimenting Colleges and Universities.

Sperling, Elliot. 'Early Ming China and Tibet.' Ph.D. diss., Indiana University.

Stewart, Bruce. 'A Translation and Introduction to the "Direct Perception" Chapter of Go-rams-pa's *Sde Bdun Mdo*.' Ph.D. diss., Columbia University.

Takemoto, Melvin. 'The *Kuei-shan ching-ts'e*: Morality and the Hung-chou School of Ch'an.' M.A. thesis, University of Hawaii.

Tanabe, George, Jr. 'Myōe Shōnin (1173-1232): Tradition and Reform in Early Kamakura Buddhism.' Ph.D. diss., Columbia University.

Tanabe, Willa. 'Paintings of the Lotus Sutra: The Relationship of Ritual, Text, and Picture.' Ph.D. diss., Columbia University.

Weerasingha, Tissa. 'Buddhism: A Missiological Approach.' M.A. thesis, Fuller Theological Seminary.

Wongwaisayawan, Suwanna. 'The Buddhist Comcept of Ignorance: With Special Reference to Dōgen.' Ph.D. diss., University of Hawaii.

Yusa, Michiko. 'Jinkaku and Person: Persona Originalis, According to the Philosophies of Nishida Kitaro and Jacques Maritain.' Ph.D. diss., University of California, Santa Barbara.

1984

Anderson, George. 'Buddhist Art and Mysticism in the Japanese Tea Ceremony: "Wabi-Cha-No-Yu" with its Roots and Branches.' M.A. thesis, California Institute of Integral Studies.

Barciauskas, Jonas. 'The Dynamic of Person in Eckhart's Mysticism and Its Relation to the "Sunyata" Doctrine.' Ph.D. diss., Fordham University.

Brock, Karen. '"Tales of Gisho and Gangyo": Editor, Artist, and Audience in Japanese Picture Scrolls.' Ph.D. diss., Princeton University.

Brook, Timothy. 'Gentry Dominance in Chinese Society: Monasteries and Lineages in the Structuring of Local Society, 1500–1700.' Ph.D. diss., Harvard University.

Brokaw, Cynthia. 'Determining One's Own Fate: The Ledgers of Merit and Demerit in Sixteenth- and Seventeenth-Century China.' Ph.D. diss., Harvard University.
Chang, Jiunn. 'A Study of the Relationship between the Mongol Yuan Dynasty and the Tibetan Sa-skya Sect.' Ph.D. diss., Indiana University.
Cleary, Jonathan. 'Zibo Zhenke: A Buddhist Leader in Late Ming China.' Ph.D. diss., Harvard University.
Coville, Claudia. '"Education through the Physical": A Reconceptualization Based on Analysis of Yoga, Zen, and Kendo Literature.' Ph.D. diss., Stanford University.
Dobbins, James C. 'The Emergence of Orthodoxy: A Historical Study of Heresy in the Early Jodo Shinshu.' Ph.D. diss., Yale University.
Eberhardt, Nancy. 'Knowledge, Belief, and Reasoning: Moral Developments and Cultural Acquisition in Shan Village of Northwest Thailand.' Ph.D. diss., University of Illinois, Urbana-Champaigne.
Goodman, Steven. 'The "Klong-chen Snying-thig": An Eighteenth Century Tibetan Revelation.' Ph.D. diss., University of Saskatchewan.
Goodpaster, Jeffrey. 'Theravada Buddhism and Jungian Psychology: A Comparative Study.' Ph.D. diss., California Institute of Integral Studies.
Hanson-Barber, A. W. 'The Life and Teachings of Vairocana.' Ph.D. diss., University of Wisconsin.
Hull, Monte S. '*Mujō*: The Japanese Understanding of and Engagement with Impermanence.' Ph.D. diss., University of Hawaii.
Kraft, Kenneth. 'Zen Master Daitō.' Ph.D. diss., Princeton University.
Ku, Cheng-Mei. 'The Mahayanic View of Women: A Doctrinal Study.' Ph.D. diss., University of Wisconsin.
Kwon, Yung-Hee. 'Dancing Dust on the Rafters: A Study of the "Ryojin Hisho".' Ph.D. diss., Cornell University.
Lee, Junghee. 'The Contemplating Bodhisattvas Images of Asia, with Special Emphasis on China and Korea.' Ph.D. diss., University of California, Los Angeles.
Lee, Sun-Ock. 'The Evolvement of "Yimoko III": Zen Dance Choreography.' D.A. thesis, New York University.
Lewis, Todd. 'The Tuladhars of Kathmandu: A Study of Buddhist Tradition in a Newar Merchant Community.' Ph.D. diss., Columbia University.
Marek, John. 'Thai Buddhist and People's Theories of Human Development: Implications for National Planning.' Ph.D. diss., University of California, Santa Barbara
Modlin, Robin. 'Principles and Practices of Thirty-One American Buddhist Families.' M.A. thesis, California Institute of Integral Studies.
Ochi, Reiko. 'Buddhism and Poetic Theory: An Analysis of Zeami's *Higaki* and *Takasago*.' Ph.D. diss., Cornell University.
Parks, Yoko. 'Chanting Is Efficacious: Changes in the Organization and Beliefs of the American Sokagakkai.' Ph.D. diss., University of Pennsylvania.
Poolpatarachewin, Chumpol. 'An Analysis of Buddhist Philosophy of Education in Thailand.' Ph.D. diss., University of Minnesota.
Ramaswami, Sundar. 'The Psychological and Psychotherapeutic Aspects of Buddhism.' Ph.D. diss., Marquette University.
Ramirez-Christensen, Esperanza. 'Shinkei: Poet-Priest of Medieval Japan.' Senior thesis, Harvard University.
Ryu, Kee. 'Nagarjuna's Emptiness and Paul Tillich's God: A Comparative Study for the Dialogue between Christianity and Buddhism.' Ph.D. diss., Drew University.
Shih, Heng-Ching. 'The Ch'an-Pure Land Syncretism in China: With Special Reference to Yung-ming Yen-shou.' Ph.D. diss., University of Wisconsin.

Stern, Robin. 'The Yuzu Nembutsu Engi and the Pictorialization of Popular Buddhism in Japanese Narrative Scrolls.' Ph.D. diss., University of Chicago.

Tanaka, Jon T. 'Architectural Innovation and Religious Doctrine: Shingon Temple Architecture in the Early Heian Period.' Senior thesis, Harvard University.

Urubshurow, Victoria. 'Symbolic Process on the Buddhist Path: Spiritual Development in the Biographical Tradition of Milarepa.' Ph.D. diss., University of Chicago.

Williams, Rodney. 'The Effects of Shamatha Meditation on Attentional and Imaginal Variables.' Ph.D. diss., University of Miami.

Wilson, Joe. 'The Meaning of Mind in the Mahāyāna Buddhist Philosophy of the Mind-Only (Cittamatra): A Study of a Presentation by the Tibetan Scholar Gungtang Jam-bay-yang of Asanga's Theory of Mind-Basis-of-All (Alayavijñāna) and Related Topics in Buddhist Theories of Personal Continuity, Epistemology, and Hermeneutics.' Ph.D. diss., University of Virginia.

Winnington-Ball, N. Marguerite. 'John Steinbeck and the Elevation of Ordinary Life: A Buddhist Perspective.' M.A. thesis, California Institute of Integral Studies.

Wisley, Thomas. 'Dynamic Biblical Christianity in the Buddhist/Marxist Context: Northeast Thailand.' Ph.D. diss., Fuller Theological Seminary.

1985

Abbott, Terry. 'Vasubandhu's Commentary to the "Saddhatmapundarika-sutra": A Study of Its History and Significance.' Ph.D. diss., University of California, Berkeley.

Aizawa, Yoichi. 'Almsgiving and Alms Refusal in the Fuju-Fuse Sect of Nichiren Buddhism with a Consideration of These Practices in Early Indian Buddhism.' Ph.D. diss., University of Pennsylvania.

Bernbaum, Edwin. 'The Mythic Journey and Its Symbolism: A Study of the Development of Buddhist Guidebooks to Shambhala in Relation to Their Antecedents in Hindu Mythology.' Ph.D. diss., University of California, Berkeley.

Buswell, Robert. 'The Korean Origin of the "Vajrasamadhi-sutra": A Case Study in Determining the Dating, Provenance, and Authorship of a Buddhist Apocryphal Scripture.' Ph.D. diss., University of California, Berkeley.

Bushong, Theodore. 'The "Via Mystica" and Mystical Experience: A Comparative Study of the 'The Cloud of Unknowing' and "The Path of Purification (Visuddhimagga)".' Ph.D. diss., Northwestern University.

Como, Michael. 'Contemporary Japanese Zen Buddhist Monasticism: Passage and Return in the Pilgrimage of Daily Life.' Senior thesis, Harvard University.

Cooke, Merritt. 'The People of Nyishang: Identity, Tradition and Change in the Nepal-Tibet Borderland.' Ph.D. diss., University of California, Berkeley.

Dalia, Albert. 'Social Change and the New Buddhism in South China: Fa-jung (594–657).' Ph.D. diss., University of Hawaii.

Davidson, Ronald. 'Buddhist Systems of Transformation: *Āsraya-parivrtti/parāvrtti* among the Yogācāra.' Ph.D. diss., University of California, Berkeley.

De Santis, James. 'Effects of Intensive Zen Buddhist Meditation Retreat on Rogerian Consequence as Real-Self/Ideal-Self Disparity on the California Q-Sort.' Ph.D. diss., California School of Professional Psychology.

Goldberg, Margaret. 'Argumentation and Understanding: A Study of Tibetan Religious Debate.' Ph.D. diss., University of Illinois, Urbana-Champaigne.

Goulde, John. 'Anti-Buddhist Polemic in Fourteenth- and Fifteenth-Century Korea: The Emergence of Confucian Exclusivism.' Ph.D. diss., Harvard University.

Gridley, Marilyn. 'Chinese Sculpture under the Liao: Free Standing Works in Situ and Selected Examples from Public Collections.' Ph.D. diss., University of Kansas.

Ho, Judy. 'Tunhuang Cave 249: A Representation of the Vimalakirtinirdesa.' Ph.D. diss., Yale University.

Jackson, David. 'Sa-skya Pandita on Indian and Tibetan Traditions of Philosophical Debate: The 'Mkhas pa pnams "jug pa'i sgo".' Ph.D. diss., University of Washington.

Kim, Sung-Woo. 'History and Design of the Early Buddhist Architecture in Korea.' Ph.D. diss., University of Michigan.

Kwan, Tai-Wo. 'A Study of the Teaching Regarding the Pure Land of Aksobhya Buddha in Early Mahayana.' Ph.D. diss., University of California, Los Angeles.

Liu, Xinru. 'Early Commercial and Cultural Exchanges between India and China.' Ph.D. diss., University of Pennsylvania.

Mumford, Stanley. 'Transmutation and Dialogue: Tibetan Lamaism and Gurung Shamanism in Nepal.' Ph.D. diss., Princeton University.

Napper, Elizabeth. 'Dependent-Arising and Emptiness: A Tibetan Buddhist Interpretation of Madhyamika Philosophy Emphasizing the Compatibility of Emptiness and Conventional Phenomena.' Ph.D. diss., University of Virginia.

Nguyen, Son Xuan. 'Evangelization of Vietnamese Buddhist Refugees.' Ph.D. diss., Claremont School of Theology.

Payne, Richard. 'Feeding the Gods: The Shingon Fire Ritual.' Ph.D. diss., Graduate Theological Union.

Powell, Melvin, Jr. 'Nichiren Shoshu Soka Gakkai of America in Tucson, Arizona: Portrait of an Imported Religion.' M.A. thesis, University of Arizona.

Rapp, Roger. 'Religious Responses to Modernity: A Cross-cultural Inquiry into the Philosophies of D. T. Suzuki and Romano Guardini.' Ph.D. diss., University of California, Santa Barbara.

Rhoton, Jared. 'A Study of the sDom-gSum of Sapan.' Ph.D. diss., Columbia University.

Robbins, Robert. 'The Multidimensional Character of Paticcasamuppada from an East-West Perspective.' Ph.D. diss., California Institute of Integral Studies.

Sirikanchana, Pataporn. 'The Concept of "Dhamma" in Thai Buddhism: A Study in the Thought of Vajiranana and Buddhadasa.' Ph.D. diss., University of Pennsylvania.

Swanson, Paul. 'The Two Truths Controversy in China and Chih-i's Threefold Truth Concept.' Ph.D. diss., University of Wisconsin.

Thornhill, Arthur. 'Six Circles and One Dewdrop: The Dramaturgical Treatise of Komparu Zenchiku.' Ph.D. diss., Harvard University.

Todaro, Dale. 'An Annotated Translation of the *Tattvasamgraha* (Part I) with an Explanation of the Role of the *Tattvasamgraha* Lineage in the Teachings of Kūkai.' Ph.D. diss., Columbia University.

Valby, James. 'The Life and Ideas of the Eight Century A.D. Indian Buddhist Mystic Vimalamitra: A Computer-Assisted Approach to Tibetan Texts.' Ph.D. diss., University of Saskatchewan.

Webber, Alan. 'Philosophy and Liberation: A Cross-cultural Comparison of Classical Buddhism and Platonic Philosophy.' Ph.D. diss., University of California, Irvine.

Wood, Donald. 'Eleven Faces of the Bodhisattva.' Ph.D. diss., University of Kansas.

1986

Ames, William. 'Bhavaviveka's Prajnapradipa: Six Chapters.' Ph.D. diss., University of Washington.

Barnhill, David. 'The Journey Itself Home: The Religiosity of the Literary Works of Matsuo Bashō (1644–1694).' Ph.D. diss., Stanford University.

Browning, James. 'Tarthang Tulku and the Quest for an American Buddhism.' Ph.D. diss., Baylor University.

Coats, Bruce. 'The Architecture of Zen-Sect Buddhist Monasteries in Japan, 1200–1500.' Ph.D. diss., Harvard University.

Fulton, Paul. 'The Psychological Ethnography of Anatta: Self and Selves in American Vipassana Buddhism.' Ph.D. diss., Harvard University.

Huang, Chi-Chiang. 'Experiment in Syncretism: Ch'i-sung (1007–1072) and Eleventh-Century Chinese Buddhism.' Ph.D. diss., University of Arizona.

Hubbard, James. 'Salvation in the Final Period of the Dharma: The Inexhaustible Storehouse of the San-chieh-chiao.' Ph.D. diss., University of Wisconsin.

Huntington, Claire. 'The "Akutobhaya" and Early Indian Madhyamika.' Ph.D. diss., University of Michigan.

Ishihara, John. 'The Shin Buddhist Doctrines of Amida and Self in Light of the Christian-Buddhist Dialog: Christ/Amida; Sinner/*Bombu*.' Ph.D. diss., Claremont Graduate School.

Kraus, James. 'Gary Snyder's Biopoetics: A Study of the Poet as Ecologist.' Ph.D. diss., University of Hawaii.

Kyi, Khin. 'Burmese Philosophy as Reflected in Caturangabala's "Lokaniti".' Ph.D. diss., Washington University.

Leidy, Denise. 'Northern Ch'i Buddhist Sculpture.' Ph.D. diss., Columbia University.

Mahmood, Cynthia. 'Rebellion and Response in Ancient India: Political Dynamics of the Hindu-Buddhist Tradition.' Ph.D. diss., Tulane University.

Morse, Samuel. 'The Formation of the Plain-Wood Style and the Development of Japanese Buddhist Sculpture, 760–840.' Senior thesis, Harvard University.

Orzech, Charles. 'Cosmology in Action: Recursive Cosmology, Soteriology, and Authority in Chen-yen Buddhism with Special Reference to the Monk Pu-k'ung.' Ph.D. diss., University of Chicago.

Peterman, Scott. 'The Legend of Huihai.' Ph.D. diss., Stanford University.

Rugola, Patricia. 'Japanese Buddhist Art in Context: The *Saikoku* Kannon Pilgrimage Route.' Ph.D. diss., Ohio State University.

Sutton, Florin. 'Existence and Gnosis in the "Lankavatara-Sutra": A Study in the Ontology and Epistemology of the Yogacara School of Mahayana Buddhism.' Ph.D. diss., Columbia University.

Tanaka, Kenneth. 'The "Kuan Wu-liang-shou Ching I-shu" by Ching-ying Hui-yuan (523-592) and Its Contribution to Early Chinese Pure Land Buddhism.' Ph.D. diss., University of California, Berkeley.

Teiser, Stephen. 'The Yü-lan-p'en Festival in Medieval Chinese Religion.' Ph.D. diss., Princeton University.

Tsuchida, Tomoaki. 'Mind and Reality: A Study of the "Shoulengyanjing".' Ph.D. diss., Harvard University.

Wells, Katheryn. 'The Form and Function of Dance in the Fifth SGI World Peace Youth Culture Festival.' M.A. thesis, University of Hawaii.

Yen, Chuan-ying. 'The Sculpture from the Tower of Seven Jewels: The Style, Patronage, and Iconography of the Monument.' Ph.D. diss., Harvard University.

1987

Adiele, Faith. 'Freedom without Status: Buddhist mae chi ('nuns') in Contemporary Thailand.' Senior thesis, Harvard University.

Bentel, Maria. 'The Shakaden and Shōhondō: Architectural Representations of the Reiyūkai and the Sōka Gakkai.' Senior thesis, Harvard University.

Black, John. 'Zen Practice in Transformation: A Case Study of the Cambridge Buddhist Association.' Senior thesis, Harvard University.

Blackburn, Anne. 'The Evolution of Sinhalese Buddhist Identity.' Senior thesis, Swarthmore College.

Cabezon, Jose. 'The Development of a Buddhist Philosophy of Language and Its Culmination in Tibetan Madhyamika Thought.' Ph.D. diss., University of Wisconsin.

Chao, Yun-Chung. 'The History of Tsai-Li (Abiding Principle) Sect and Its Educational Impact in Taiwan, 1950–1980.' Ed.D. diss., University of Houston.

Davis, Jonathan. 'Ego Development of Buddhist Meditators: A Qualitative Study' Ed.D. diss., Boston University.

Dreyfus, George. 'Some Considerations on Definition in Buddhism.' M.A. thesis, University of Virginia.

Dubs, John. 'Acquisition of a Novel View of Reality: A Study of Pyscho-Spiritual Development in Zen Buddhism.' Ph.D. diss., University of Michigan.

Foulk, Theodore Griffith. 'The "Ch'an School" and Its Place in the Buddhist Monastic Tradition.' Ph.D. diss., University of Michigan.

Grant, Beata. 'Buddhism and Taoism in the Poetry of Su Shi (1036–1101).' Ph.D. diss., Stanford University.

Hock, Nancy. 'Buddhist Ideology and the Sculpture of Ratnagiri, Seventh through Thirteenth Centuries.' Ph.D. diss., University of California, Berkeley.

Hulton-Baker, Robert. 'Tibetan Buddhist Drama.' Ph.D. diss., New York University.

Imamura, Ryo. 'A Comparative Study of American Temples and Non-temple Buddhist Ministers of the Jodo Shin Sect Using Jungian Psychological Type.' Ph.D. diss., San Francisco University.

Kapstein, Matthew. 'Self and Personal Identity in Indian Buddhist Scholasticism: A Philosophical Investigation.' Ph.D. diss., Brown University.

Ketelaar, James. 'Of Heretics and Matyrs: Buddhism and Persecution in Meiji Japan.' Ph.D. diss., University of Chicago.

Kotas, Frederic. '*Ōjōden*: Accounts of Rebirth in the Pure Land.' Ph.D. diss., University of Washington.

Krisiansen, Ronald. 'Creation and Emptiness: Transforming the Doctrine of Creation in Dialogue with the Kyoto School of Philosophy.' Ph.D. diss., Emory University.

Langenberg, Amy. 'The Health of the Buddhas: Health and Healing in the Tibetan Buddhist Tradition.' Senior thesis, Harvard University.

Leoshko, Janice. 'The Iconography of Buddhist Sculptures of the Pala and Sena Periods from Bodhgaya.' Ph.D. diss., Ohio State University.

Liao, Chaoyang. 'Figuralism in Chinese Narrative: Readings in the "Pancatantra," the "Lotus Sutra," and the "Jinpingmei".' Ph.D. diss., Princeton University.

Madanayake, Bandusena. 'A Study of "Sankharas" in Early Buddhism.' Ph.D. diss., University of Toronto.

Newman, John. 'The Outer Wheel of Time: Vajrayana Buddhist Cosmology in the Kalachakra Tantra.' Ph.D. diss., University of Wisconsin.

Park, Theodore. 'The Meaning of Uji in Dōgen's Thought.' Senior thesis, Harvard University.

Piggott, Joan. 'Tōdaiji and the Nara Imperium.' Ph.D. diss., Stanford University.

Pittman, Don. 'Mahayana and the Meaning of Morality: A Study of the Chinese Monk T'ai-Hsu and His Vision for a Modern Buddhism.' Ph.D. diss., University of Chicago.

Rubin, Jeffrey. 'Pathways to Transformation: An Integrative Study of Psychoanalysis and Buddhism.' Ph.D. diss., Union for Experimenting Colleges and Universities.

Ryose, Wataru. 'A Study of the "Abhidharmahrdaya": The Historical Development of the Concept of Karma in Sarvastivada Thought.' Ph.D. diss., University of Wisconsin.

Stalker, Susan. 'A Study of Dependent Origination: Vasubandhu, Buddhaghosa, and the Interpretation of "Pratityasamutpada".' Ph.D. diss., University of Pennsylvania.

Stevenson, Daniel. 'The T'ien-T'ai Four Forms of Samadhi and Late North-South Dynasties, Sui, and Early T'ang Buddhist Devotionalism.' Ph.D. diss., Columbia University.

Tarrant, John. 'The Design of Enlightenment in Koan Zen.' Ph.D. diss., Saybrook Institute.

Tatelman, Joel. 'The Glorious Deeds of Pūrna: A Translation and Study of the Pūrnāvadāna.' M.A. thesis, McMaster University.

Tuck, Andrew. 'Isogesis: Western Readings of Nagarjuna and the Philosophy of Scholarship.' Ph.D. diss., Princeton University.

Welter, Albert. 'The Meaning of Myriad Good Deeds: A Study of Yung-ming Yen-shou and the "Wan-shan T'ung-kuei chi".' Ph.D. diss., McMaster University.

Yamazato, Katsunori. 'Seeking a Fulcrum: Gary Snyder and Japan (1956–1975).' Ph.D. diss., University of California, Davis.

Yiengprukswan, Melanie. 'The Buddhist Sculpture of Chūsonji: The Meaning of Style at the Hiraizumi Temples of Ōshū Fujiwara.' Ph.D. diss., University of California, Los Angeles.

1988

Allam, Cheryl. 'The Path to Surrender: Nichiren Buddhism and Roman Catholicism Confront Japanese Nationalism, 1912–1945.' M.A. thesis, University of Hawaii

Allen, Laura. 'The Art of Persuasion: Narrative Structure, Imagery, and Meaning in the Saigyō Monogatari Emaki.' Ph.D. diss., University of California, Berkeley.

Aranow, Philip. 'Psychoanalytic Theories of the Self: A Review and Critique from a Buddhist Perspective.' Ed.D. diss., Harvard University.

Atone, Joji. 'Shan-Tao: His Life and Thought.' Ph.D. diss., University of Wisconsin.

Chiba, Yoko. 'W. B. Yeats and Noh: From "Japonisme" to Zen.' Ph.D. diss., University of Toronto.

Choi, Chong. 'Shakespearean Nothing and the Mahayana Buddhist Emptiness in the "Heart Sutra": Non-dual Visions of Reality.' Ph.D. diss., University of Michigan.

Fox, Alan. 'Elements of Omnicontextual Thought in Chinese Buddhism: Annotated Translations of Gui Feng Zong Mi's Preface to "Collection of Various Writings on the Chan Source" and His Commentary on "Meditative Approaches to the Hua Yen Dharmadhatu Thinspace".' Ph.D. diss., Temple University.

Fredericks, James. 'Alterity in the Thought of Tanabe Hajime and Karl Rahner.' Ph.D. diss., University of Chicago.

Fujieda, Mamoru. "Tengoku no Natsu' ('Summer in the Heaven') for Shomyo Voices and Reigaku Instruments.' Ph.D. diss., University of California, San Diego.

Galland, Nicole. 'Between Sacred and Profane: A Study of Japanese Religious Experience with Particular Reference to Basho.' Senior thesis, Harvard University.

Gardner, Richard. 'The Art of Nō: A Reconsideration of the Relation of Religion and Art.' Ph.D. diss., University of Chicago.

Hallisey, Charles. 'Devotion in the Buddhist Literature of Medieval Sri Lanka.' Ph.D. diss., University of Chicago.

Haner, William. 'The Body of this Death: Alterity in Nishida-Philosophy and Post-Marxism.' Ph.D. diss., University of Chicago.

Haskel, Peter. 'Bankei and His World.' Ph.D. diss., Columbia University.

Huh, Woo-sung. 'A Critical Evaluation of Nishida's Philosophy.' Ph.D. diss., University of Hawaii.

Ives, Christopher. 'A Zen Buddhist Social Ethic.' Ph.D. diss., Claremont Graduate School.

Knewitz, John. 'The Explication of Zen Buddhism as a Foundation for Counseling.' Ph.D. diss., Southern Illinois University.

Kohn, Richard. 'Mani Rimdu: Text and Tradition in a Tibetan Ritual.' Ph.D. diss., University of Wisconsin.

McTighe, Leslie. 'Mentoring in the "Majjhima Nikaya": A Study of the Canonical Buddha's Instruction of the Laity.' Ph.D. diss., Northwestern University.

Nattier, Jan. 'The Candragarbha-sūtra in Central and East Asia: Studies in a Buddhist Philosophy of Decline.' Ph.D. diss., Harvard University.

Newland, Guy. 'The Two Truths: A Study of Madhyamika Philosophy as Presented in the Monastic Textbooks of the Gel-luk-ba Order of Tibetan Buddhism.' Ph.D. diss., University of Virginia.

Oh, Young Bong. 'Wonhyo's Theory of Harmonization.' Ph.D. diss., New York University.

Putuwar, Sunanda. 'The Buddhist Sangha: Paradigm of the Ideal Human Society.' Ph.D. diss., American University.

Ra, Lang. 'The T'ien-T'ai Philosophy of Non-Duality: A Study in Chan-jan and Chih-li.' Ph.D. diss., Temple University.

Sutherland, Gail. 'The Demon and His Disguises: The Yaksa in Hindu and Buddhist Art and Literature.' Ph.D. diss., University of Chicago.

Trevithick, Alan. 'A Jerusalem of the Buddhists in British India, 1874–1949.' Ph.D. diss., Harvard University.

Vajirakachorn, Surasit. 'The Influence of Buddhism in Thai Administrative Behavior: A Q Technique Study of Thai Bureaucracy.' Ph.D. diss., University of Oklahoma.

Wells, Harry. 'The Problem of the Phenomenal Self: A Study of the Buddhist Doctrine of Anatta with Specific Regard to Buddhist-Christian Dialogue.' Ph.D. diss., Southern Baptist Theological Seminary.

1989

Abe, Stanley. 'Mogao Cave 254: A Case Study in Early Chinese Buddhist Art.' Ph.D. diss., University of California, Berkeley.

Adams, Vincanne. 'Healing Buddhas and Mountain Guides: The Production of Self within Society through Medication.' Ph.D. diss., University of California, Berkeley.

App, Urs. 'Facets of the Life and Teaching of Chan Master Yunmen Wenyan (864–949).' Ph.D. diss., Temple University.

Burke, Billy. 'An Analysis of Udayana's Arguments against the Buddhist Doctrine of "Ksanabhanga" as Presented in the "Atmatattvaviveka".' Ph.D. diss., University of Minnesota.

Cozort, Daniel. 'Unique Tenets of the Middle Way Consequence School: The Systematization of the Philosophy of the Indian Buddhist Prasanghika-Madhyamika School by the Tibetan Ge-luk-ba Scholastic Tradition.' Ph.D. diss., University of Virginia.

Deal, William. 'Ascetics, Aristocrats, and the Lotus Sutra: The Construction of the Buddhist Universe in 11th Century Japan.' Ph.D. diss., Harvard University.

Forman, Robert. 'Constructivism in Soto Zen Buddhism, Paramartha to Meister Eckhardt.' Ph.D. diss., Columbia University.

Goodman, Steven. 'A Buddhist Proof for Omniscience: The "Sarvajnasiddhi" of Ratnakirti.' Ph.D. diss., Temple University.

Hack, Sheryl. 'Collective Identity and Sacred Space: A Study of Seven Zen Communities in Northern California.' M.A. thesis, University of Delaware.

Hay, Jonathan. 'Shitao's Late Work (1697–1707): A Thematic Map.' Ph.D. diss., Yale University.

Ho, Molly. 'Gongxian and Its Pivotal Importance to the Chinese Buddhist Sculptural Tradition of the Sixth Century.' Ph.D. diss., University of Chicago.

Hunter, Jeffrey. 'The *Fuju fuse* Controversy in Nichiren Buddhism: The Debate between Busshōin Nichiō and Jakushōin Nichiken.' Ph.D. diss., University of Wisconsin.

Jan, Feei-Ching. 'Buddhism in Kurosawa's Films: A Critical Analysis.' M.A. thesis, California State University, Fresno.

Kaplan, Eric. 'Nietsche and Madhyamaka.' Senior thesis, Harvard University.

Keenan, Linda. 'En no Gyōja: The Legend of a Holy Man in Twelve Centuries of Japanese Literature.' Ph.D. diss., University of Wisconsin.

Kim, Bokin. 'Responses to Religious Pluralism: Three Case Studies and Comparative Analyses.' Ph.D. diss., Temple University.

Landenhamer, Monika. 'Personality in Theravada Buddhism.' M.A. thesis, California Institute of Integral Studies.

Lauechli, Samuel. 'Buddhist Cave Inscriptions of Western India.' Ph.D. diss., Columbia University.

Leighton, Daniel Taigen. 'Cultivating the Empty Field: Translations with Introduction from the Extensive Record of Chan Master Hongzhi Zhengjue (1091–1157).' M.A. thesis, California Institute of Integral Studies.

Lusthaus, Dan. 'A Philosophic Investigation of the "Ch'eng Wei-shih Lun": Vasubandhu, Hsuan-Tsang, and the Transmission of "Vijnapti-matra".' Ph.D. diss., Temple University.

Naughton, Alexander. 'The Buddhist Path to Omniscience.' Ph.D. diss., University of Wisconsin.

Ohsuka, Shigeru. 'Saicho (767–822) as Educator.' M.Ed. thesis, University of Hawaii.

Olson, Grant. 'A Person-Centered Ethnography of Thai Buddhism: The Life of Phra Rajavaramuni.' Ph.D. diss., Cornell University.

O'Shea, Marie. 'Development from Within: The Importance of Participation, the Sarvodaya Experience.' M.A. thesis, Carleton University.

Owens, Bruce. 'The Politics of Divinity in the Kathmandu Valley: The Festival of Bungadya/Rato Matsyendranath.' Ph.D. diss., Columbia University.

Parker, Joseph. 'Playful Nonduality: Japanese Zen Interpretations of Landscape Paintings from the Ōei Era (1394–1427).' Ph.D. diss., Harvard University.

Schober, Julianne. 'Paths to Enlightenment: Theravada Buddhism in Upper Burma.' Ph.D. diss., University of Illinois, Urbana-Champaigne

Schuler, Robert. 'Journeys toward the Original Mind: The Longer Poems of Gary Snyder.' Ph.D. diss., University of Minnesota.

Shenpen, Alexandra. 'An Inquiry into the Psychology of Innate Creativity: A Therapeutic Approach Emphasizing the Study of Buddhist Psychology, Visual Arts, and Interpersonal Dynamics.' Ph.D. diss., The Union Institute.

Sparham, Gareth. 'A Study of Haribhadra's "Abhisamayalamkaraloka Prajna-Paramita-Vyakhya".' Ph.D. diss., University of British Columbia.

Stahl, Robert. 'Psychological Aspects of Selected Cardinal Buddhist "Suttas".' Ph.D. diss., California Institute of Integral Studies.

Tiso, Francis. 'A Study of the Buddhist Saint in Relation to the Biographical Tradition of Milarepa.' Ph.D. diss., Columbia University.

Tweed, Thomas. 'The American Encounter with Buddhism, 1844–1912: Response to Buddhism, Dissent and Consent, and Victorian Religious Culture.' Ph.D. diss., Stanford University.

Zuckerman, Daniel. 'Theravada Buddhism, Psychotherapy, and American Buddhism.' Senior thesis, Harvard University.

1990

Antinoff, Steven. 'The Problem of the Human Person and the Resolution to That Problem in the Religio-Philosophical Thought of the Zen Master Shin'ichi Hisamatsu.' Ph.D. diss., Temple University.

Assavavirulhakarn, Prapod. 'The Ascendency of Theravada Buddhism in Southeast Asia.' Ph.D. diss., University of California, Berkeley.

Auerbuch, Irit. 'Yamabushi Kagura: A Study of Traditional Ritual Dance in Contemporary Japan.' Ph.D. diss., Harvard University.

Benard, Elisabeth. 'Chinnamasta: The Awful Buddhist and Hindu Tantric Goddess.' Ph.D. diss., Columbia University.

Blackstone, Katherine. 'The Struggle for Liberation in the "Therīgāthā".' M.A. thesis, McMaster University.

Blum, Mark. 'Gyōnen's *Jōdo Hōmon Genrushō* and the Importance of Lineage to the Pure Land Tradition.' Ph.D. diss., University of California, Berkeley.

Bodiford, William. 'The Growth of the Soto Zen Tradition in Japan.' Ph.D. diss., Yale University.

Chutintaranond, Sunait. '"Cakravartin": The Ideology of Traditional Welfare in Siam and Burma, 1548–1605.' Ph.D. diss., Cornell University.

Darlington, Susan. 'Buddhism, Morality, and Change: The Local Response to Development in Northern Thailand.' Ph.D. diss., University of Michigan.

Dhamabutra, Narongrit. '"Dhamachakra" and "The Dusk of the World".' Ph.D. diss., Michigan State University.

Dreifuss, Alan. 'A Phenomenological Inquiry of Six Psychotherapists Who Practice Buddhist Meditation.' Ph.D. diss., California Institute of Integral Studies.

Hall, David. 'Marishiten: Buddhism and the Warrior Goddess.' Ph.D. diss., University of California, Berkeley.

Hirsch, Peter. 'The Still Point of the Turning World: A Comparison of the Conception of Time Presented in T. S. Eliot's Four Quartets with Certain Aspects of Buddhist Philosophy.' Senior thesis, Harvard University.

Ito, Mizuko. 'Zen and Tea Ritual: A Comparative Analysis.' Senior thesis, Harvard University.

Kavirajan, Harish. 'Poetic Thinking and Wordless Awareness: The Limits of Language in the Thought of Martin Heidegger and Keiji Nishitani.' Senior thesis, Harvard University.

Law, Jane. 'Puppets of the Road: Ritual Performance in Japanese Folk Religion.' Ph.D. diss., University of Chicago.

Leech, Charles. 'Tibetan Buddhist/Newari Buddhist Interface in the Kathmandu Valley.' Ph.D. diss., University of Wisconsin.

Logreglio, John. 'Dōgen Kigen and the Poetic Function of Language.' M.A thesis, University of California, Santa Barbara.

MacWilliams, Mark. 'Kannon Engi: Strategies of Indigenization in Kannon Temple Myths of the Saikoki Sanjusansho Kannon Reijoki and the Sanjusansho Bando Kannon Reikoki.' Ph.D. diss., University of Chicago.

Makransky, John. 'Controversy over *Dharmakāya* in Indo-Tibetan Buddhism: An Historical-Critical Analysis of *Abhisamayālamkāra* Chapter 8 and Its Commentaries in Relation to the Large *Prajñāpaaramitā Sūtra* and the Yogācāra Tradition.' Ph.D. diss., University of Wisconsin.

Morgan, William. 'Change in Meditation: A Phenomenological Study of Vipassana Meditators' Views of Progress.' Psy.D. diss., Massachusetts School of Professional Psychology.

Narine, David. 'An Approach to "Vicara" in Madhyamaka Buddhism Based on a Consideration of Early Buddhist Scholasticism and the "Prasangika" Form of Polemic.' M.A. thesis, University of Manitoba.

Nasu, Eisho. 'A Christian Critic of Buddhism in Early Modern Japan: A Study of the First Volume of the Myotei Mondo.' M.A. thesis, Graduate Theological Union.

Newman, Derek. 'Exorcising the Phantom of Theology: The Implications of Deconstruction for Buddhist-Christian Dialogue.' Senior thesis, Harvard University.

Nguyen, Cuong Tu. 'Sthiramati's Interpretation of Buddhology and Soteriology.' Ph.D. diss., Harvard University.

Prothero, Stephan. 'Henry Steel Olcott (1832–1907) and the Construction of "Protestant Buddhism".' Ph.D. diss., Harvard University.

Putney, David. 'The Nature and Practice of Freedom: A Dialogue on Freedom and Determinism in Buddhist and Western Philosophy.' Ph.D. diss., University of Hawaii.

Riley, Terrance. 'A Study of the Attentional Characteristics of Long-term Zen Meditators.' Ph.D. diss., California School of Professional Pyschology at Berkeley/Alameda.

Roongrernsuke, Siriyupa. 'An Analysis of the Efficacy of Thai Buddhist Temple and the Sangha as an Informal Institution for Community Development in Northeastern Thailand.' Ph.D. diss., University of Southern California.

Rothenberg, Bonnie. 'Ksemendra's "Bodhisattvavadanakalpalata": A Text-Critical Edition and Translation of Chapters One to Five.' Ph.D. diss., University of Wisconsin.

Savvas, Carol. 'A Study of the Profound Path of God: The Mahayana Buddhist Meditation Tradition of Tibet's Great Woman Saint Machig Labdron.' Ph.D. diss., University of Wisconsin.

Sawada, Janine Anderson. 'Sekimon Shingaku: The Popularization of the Learning of the Mind in Eighteenth-Century Japan.' Ph.D. diss., Columbia University.

Schmidt, Carolyn. 'Bodhisattva Headdresses and Hairstyles in the Buddhist Art of Gandhara and Related Regions of Swat and Afghanistan.' Ph.D. diss., Ohio State University.

Scott, David. 'Yaktovil: The Cultural Poetics of a Minor Sinhala Practice.' Ph.D. diss., New School for Social Research.

Stone, Jacqueline. 'Some Disputed Writings in the Nichiren Corpus: Textual, Hermeneutical, and Historical Problems.' Ph.D. diss., University of California, Los Angeles.

Teich, Anne. 'States of Consciousness and Psychology of "Nibbana".' Ph.D. diss., California Institute of Integral Studies.

Trainor, Kevin. 'The Relics of the Buddha' A Study of the Cult of Relic Veneration in the Theravada Buddhist Tradition of Sri Lanka.' Ph.D. diss., Columbia University.

Waldron, William. 'The Alayavijnana in the Context of Indian Buddhist Thought: The Yogacara Conception of an Unconscious.' Ph.D. diss., University of Wisconsin.

Wu, Yushan. 'From Hippieism to Zen Buddhism: Counterculture Ideology and Social Change in America.' M.A. thesis, Boston College.

Young, Serenity. 'Dreams in Indo-Tibetan Buddhist Sacred Biography.' Ph.D. diss., Columbia University.

1991

Abe, Ryūichi. 'From Kūkai to Kakuban: A Study of Shingon Buddhist Dharma Transmission.' Ph.D. diss., Columbia University.

Alldritt, Leslie. 'Ontology of Love: The Religio-Philosophical Thought of Paul Tillich and Zen Buddhism.' Ph.D. diss., Temple University.

Baker, Janet. 'The Art of the Sui Dynasty Caves at Dunhuang.' Ph.D. diss., University of Kansas.

Bartholomeusz, Tessa. 'Women under the Bo Tree.' Ph.D. diss., University of Virginia.

Benton, Catherine. 'A Study of Kamadeva in Indian Story Literature.' Ph.D. diss., Columbia University.

Bentor, Yael. 'The Indo-Tibetan Buddhist Consecration Ritual for "Stupas," Images, Books and Temples.' Ph.D. diss., Indiana University.

Burns, William. 'The Doctrine of "Anatman" in Early Buddhism.' Ph.D. diss., University of Texas, Austin.

Choe, Songeun. 'Buddhist Sculpture of Wu Yueh, 907–978: Chinese Sculpture of the Tenth Century.' Ph.D. diss., University of Illinois, Urbana-Champaigne.

Codiga, Douglas. 'Mountains' Walking: The Self-Realization Approach of Ecological Philosophy and Dōgen's Zen Buddhism.' M.A. thesis, University of Hawaii .

Dreyfus, George. 'Ontology, Philosophy of Language and Epistemology in the Buddhist Tradition: A Study of Dharmakirti's Philosophy in the Light of Its Reception in the Later Indo-Tibetan Tradition.' Ph.D. diss., University of Virginia.

Haber, Melissa. 'Zen, Meditation, and "Vivid Transparence": Wallace Steven's Theory of Poetry.' Senior thesis, Harvard University.

Hall, David. 'Marishiten: Buddhism and the Warrior Goddess.' Ph.D. diss., University of California, Berkeley.

Hinz, William. 'Alan Watts' Theological Anthropology and Its Implications for Religious Education.' M.A. thesis, McGill University.

Jamspal, Lozang. 'The Range of the Bodhisattva: A Study of an Early Mahayana Sutra, "Aryasatyakaparivarta,' Discourse of the Truth Teller." Ph.D. diss., Columbia University.

Kim, Sunggon. 'Religious Pluralism and the Question of One and Many: A Study of Sot'aesan's Perspective.' Ph.D. diss., Temple University.

Lee, Kwang-Mi. '"The Lotos Rose": T. S. Eliot's "Four Quartets" and Eastern Thought.' Ph.D. diss., University of Tennessee.

Li, Terry. 'A Synthesis of Eastern and Western Time-Consciousness in T. S. Eliot's "Burnt Norton".' M.A. thesis, San Jose State University.

Lin, Chen-Kuo. '"The Samdhinirmocana Sutra": A Liberating Hermeneutic.' Ph.D. diss., Temple University.

McCagney, Nancy. 'Nagarjuna Then and Now.' Ph.D. diss., University of California, Santa Barbara.

Martin, Daniel. 'The Emergence of Bon and the Tibetan Polemical Tradition.' Ph.D. diss., Indiana University.

Powers, Chester John. 'The Concept of the Ultimate in the "Samdhinirmocana-Sutra": Analysis, Translation, and Notes.' Ph.D. diss., University of Virginia.

Rhi, Ju-Hyung. 'Gandharan Images of the "Sravasti Miracle": An Iconographic Reassessment.' Ph.D. diss., University of California, Berkeley.

Schoening, Jeffrey. 'The "Salistamba-Sutra" and Its Indian Commentaries.' Ph.D. diss., University of Washington.

Sharf, Robert. 'The "Treasure Store Treatise" (*Pao-tsang lun*) and the Sinification of Buddhism in Eight-Century China.' Ph.D. diss., University of Michigan.

Singer, Jane. 'Early Painting in Tibet.' Ph.D. diss., Harvard University.

Stevens-Guille, Max. 'Zen: An Object-Oriented Hardware Description Language' M.Sc. thesis, University of Guelph.

Styron, Charles. 'The Treatment of Strong Negative Affect in Psychotherapy: A Dialogue between Tantric Buddhist and Psychoanalytic Disciplines.' Psy.D. diss., Massachusetts School of Professional Psychology.

Tanaka, Mark. '*Mizuko Kuyō*, Memorial Rites for Aborted and Miscarried Fetuses in Japan: An Anthropological Study.' Senior thesis, Harvard University.

Williams, Duncan. 'The Interface of Buddhism and Environmentalism in North America.' Senior thesis, Reed College.

1992

Ainbinder, Lori. 'The Contributions of Zong-mi to the Hua-yen Tradition.' Senior thesis, Wellesley College.

Amstutz, Galen. 'The Honganji Institution, 1500–1570: The Politics of Pure Land Buddhism in Late Medieval Japan.' Ph.D. diss., Princeton University.

Aubry, Helene. 'Postmodernité et Bouddhisme Zen Japonais: D'une Semiotique de Lieux, Le Cas du Jardin sec Ryoan-ji.' Ph.D. diss., Université Laval.

Bantly, Francisca. 'The Dream of the Nine Clouds: A Buddhist Contribution to the Philosophy of Religions.' Ph.D. diss., University of Chicago.

Boisvert, Mathieu. 'A Study of the Five Aggregates in Theravada Buddhism: Their Order and Their Relation to the Doctrine of the Paticcasamuppada.' Ph.D. diss., McGill University.

Brereton, Bonnie. 'The Phra Malai Legend in Thai Buddhist Literature: A Study of Three Texts.' Ph.D. diss., University of Michigan.

Breyer, Chloe. 'Religious Liberty in Law and Practice: Vietnamese Home Temples in California and the First Amendment.' Senior thesis, Harvard University.

Chambers, Todd. 'Sacred Biography and Performance Community: A Dramaturgical Analysis of Urban Thai Buddhist Narrative Celebrations.' Ph.D. diss., Northwestern University.

Ch'en, Mei-Chin. 'The Eminent Monk Hsuan-Tsang: His Contributions to Buddhist Scripture Translation and to the Propagation of Buddhism in China.' Ph.D. diss., University of Wisconsin.

Choudhury, Lokananda. 'Dasavatthu and Pancavatthu: A Critical Study of Schism in Early Buddhist Monastic Traditions.' M.A. thesis, Calfornia State University, Long Beach.

Easterlin, Barbara. 'Buddhist Vipassana Meditation and Daily Living: Effect on Cognitive Style, Awareness, Affect and Acceptance.' Ph.D. diss., California Institute of Integral Studies.

Fujikawa, Robin. 'Dimensionality in Dōgen's Conception of Enlightenment.' Ph.D. diss., University of Hawaii.

Germano, David. 'Poetic Thought, The Intelligent Universe, and the Mystery of Self: The Tantric Synthesis of Rdzogzchen in Fourteenth-Century Tibet.' Ph.D. diss., University of Wisconsin.

Harding, Richard. 'An Examination of Charles Hartshorne's Process Philosophy of Religion in the Light of Abhidhamma Buddhist Philosophy.' Ph.D. diss., American University.

Harrison, Elizabeth. 'Encountering Amida: Jōdo Shinshū Sermons in Eighteenth-Century Japan.' Ph.D. diss., University of Chicago.

Hayami, Yoko. 'Ritual and Religious Transformation among Sgaw Karen of Northern Thailand: Implications on Gender and Ethnic Identity.' Ph.D. diss., Brown University.

Herron, William. 'A Questionnaire Study Comparing Mystical Experience among Zen, Yoga, Christian, and Non-Spiritual Groups.' Ph.D. diss., California Institute of Integral Studies.

Hillis, Gregory. 'An Annotated Translation of Vinitadeva's Commentary on Vasubandhu's *Twenty Stanzas*.' M.A. thesis, University of Virginia.

Hur, Nam-lin. 'Popular Buddhist Culture in the Latter Tokugawa Period: A Study of Sensōji.' Ph.D. diss., Princeton University.

Jang, Wang Shik. 'Wonhyo's Doctrines of Ultimate Reality and Faith: A Whiteheadian Evaluation.' Ph.D. diss., Claremont Graduate School.

Jones, Gayle. 'The Fabric Thanka of Tibet: Aesthetic Inquiry into a Living Tradition.' Ph.D. diss., New York University.

Kang, Sungdo. 'The Potential Contribution of Korean Buddhism: Updating Pojo Chinul through Mutual Transformation with Alfred North Whitehead.' Ph.D. diss., Claremont Graduate School.

Kim, Yong Pyo. 'Hermeneutics of the Scriptural Word in the Prajna-Madhyamika System.' Ph.D. diss., Temple University.

Lawson, Jonathan. 'The Religious Process of Wild Renewal: Buddhism, Wilderness Ethics, and Poetics in the Work of Gary Snyder.' Senior thesis, Guilford College.

Lin, Jyan-Lung. 'Gary Snyder's Poetry: A Study of the Formation and Transformation of His Enlightened Vision.' Ph.D. diss., Michigan State University.

Linrothe, Robert. 'Compassionate Malevolence: Wrathful Deities in Esoteric Buddhist Art.' Ph.D. diss., University of Chicago.

Liu, Xiaolian. 'The Odyssey of the Buddhist Mind: The Allegory of "The Later Journey to the West".' Ph.D. diss., Washington University.

Machida, Soho. 'The Specificity of Hōnen (1133-1212).' Ph.D. diss., University of Pennsylvania.

Mizuno, Kayano. 'Shinran's Pathos of the Infinite in Kierkegaard's Words.' Ph.D. diss., Boston College.

Niderost, Heather. 'The Myth of Maitreya in Modern Japan, with a History of Its Evolution.' M.A. thesis, McGill University.

Numrich, Paul. 'Americanization in Immigrant Theravada Buddhist Temples.' Ph.D. diss., Northwestern University.

Parrice, Marie. 'Buddhist Aspects of Spinoza's Thought.' Ph.D. diss., City University of New York.

Rhodes, Robert. 'Genshin and the *Ichijō yōkestsu*: A Treatise on Universal Buddhahood in Heian Japan.' Ph.D. diss., Harvard University.

Rogers, Katherine. 'A Tibetan Manual of Logic: An Introduction to Reasoning in the Ge-luk-ba Monastic Educational System.' Ph.D. diss., University of Virginia.

Salgado, Nirmala. 'The Structure of Evil and Ethical Action in the "Jatakatthavannana".' Ph.D. diss., Northwestern University.

Shahar, Meir. 'Fiction and Religion in the Early History of the Chinese God Jigong.' Ph.D. diss., Harvard University.

Shaw, Miranda. 'Passionate Enlightenment: Women in Tantric Buddhism in India.' Ph.D. diss., Harvard University.

Smythe, Norman. 'An Examination and Synthesis of the Buddhist Philosophy of Ch'an Master Hui Neng and the Existentialism of Jean-Paul Sartre.' M.A. thesis, California Institute of Integral Studies.

Snyder, Robert. 'Sudden Enlightenment and Gradual Cultivation in Early Ch'an Buddhism.' M.A. thesis, California Institute of Integral Studies.

Suh, Sang-Guk. 'Reflections of Buddhist Philosophy in Cingiz Ajtmatov's Literary Works.' Ph.D. diss., University of Wisconsin.

Tilakaratne, Asanga. 'Transcendence, Ineffability and Nirvana: An Analysis of the Relation between Religious Experience and Language According to Early Buddhism.' Ph.D. diss., University of Hawaii.

Walters, Jonathan. 'Rethinking Buddhist Missions.' Ph.D. diss., University of Chicago.

Wilson, Elizabeth. 'Charming Cadavers: Horrific Figurations of the Feminine in Post-Asokan Buddhist Literature.' Ph.D. diss., University of Chicago.

Wu, Pei-Li. 'Zen Meditation, Self-Awareness, and Autonomy.' Ph.D. diss., State University of New York, Buffalo.

1993

Abe, Nobuhiko. 'Semiotics of Self in Theology: A Comparative Study of James and Nishida.' Ph.D. diss., Harvard University.

Angurarohita, Pratoom Prasertsak. 'Soka Gakkai in Thailand: A Sociological Study of it Emergence, World View, Recruitment, Process, and Growth.' Ph.D. diss., University of Pennsylvania.

Arai, Paula. 'Sōtō Zen Nuns: Living Treasures of Japanese Buddhism.' Ph.D. diss., Harvard University.

Ariyagnana, Diwullewe. 'Freedom of Mind: A Study of the Buddhist Concept of Vimutti (Liberation) in the Pali Nikayas.' Ph.D. diss., Northwestern University.

Banerji, Naseem. 'The Architecture and Architectural Decoration of the Adina Mosque, Pandua, West Bengal, India: The Problem of the Conjoined Buddhist, Hindu and Islamic Motifs in the Mihrab Niches.' Ph.D. diss., University of Iowa.

Barat, Kahar. 'The Uygur Xuanzang Biography, Volume IX.' Ph.D. diss., Harvard University.

Baroni, Helen. 'Buddhism in Early Tokugawa Japan: The Case of Obaku Zen and the Monk Tetsugen Dōkō.' Ph.D. diss., Columbia University.

Bernard-Johnston, Jean. 'Singing the Lives of the Buddha: Lao Folk Opera as an Educational Medium' Ed.D. diss., University of Massachusetts.

Chan, Chi-Wah. 'Chih-li (960–1028) and the Formation of Orthodoxy in the Sung T'ien-Tai Tradition of Buddhism.' Ph.D. diss., University of California, Los Angeles.

Chang, Hsun. 'Incense-Offering and Obtaining the Magical Power of Qi: The Mazu (Heavenly Mother) Pilgrimage in Taiwan.' Ph.D. diss., University of California, Berkeley.

Chen, Warner. 'The Emperor Liang Wu-Ti and Buddhism.' Ph.D. diss., New York University.

Chun, Jang-Kil. 'A Study of the "Dasabhumika-Sutra": Its Relation to Previous Buddhist Traditions and the Development of Bodhisattva Practice.' Ph.D. diss., University of Wisconsin.

Cohen, Alexandra. 'Towards an Understanding of Bodymind as Expressed in the Writings of Dōgen Kigen.' Senior thesis, Brown University.

Fosmire, Edward. 'Central Asian Buddhist Painting: An Analysis of Borrowings and the Proposal of a "Central Asian Style".' M.A. thesis, California State University, Long Beach.

Fouser, Beth. 'Wat Chaiwatthanaram and the Legitimation of King Prasat Thong of Ayutthaya.' M.A. thesis, University of Victoria.

Garry, Ronald. 'The Teacher-Student Relationship: A Translation of the Root Verses and Auto-Commentary Entitled "The Explanation of the Characteristics of the Master and Student (Relationship), How to Attend (To the Master); (and How to) Explain (and) Listen to (the Dharma)" by Jam-mgon Kong-sprul Blo-'gros Mtha'-yas.' Ph.D. diss., California Institute of Integral Studies.

Goldblatt, Elizabeth. 'Vajrayana Buddhism as Viewed through a Tibetan Ritual, the Padmasambhava Ceremony.' Ph.D. diss., University of Calfornia, Los Angeles.

Goss, Robert. 'The Hermeneutics of Madness: A Literary and Hermeneutical Analysis of the "Mi-la' i-rnam-thar" by Gtsang-smyon Heruka.' Ph.D. diss., Harvard University.

Gottschall, Claudia. '"Unspeakable Visions": Beat Consciousness and Its Textual Representation.' Ph.D. diss., University of Oregon.

Hsieh, Ding-hwa. 'Yuan-wu k'o-ch'in (1063–1135) and the Practice of Ch'an Kung-an in Ch'an Pedagogy and Praxis.' Ph.D. diss., University of Calfornia, Los Angeles.

Ichimura, Elliott. 'The Hermeneutical Endeavor: Interpretation and Understanding in the Studies of Buddhism.' Senior thesis, Harvard University.

Joslyn, Marc. 'Metaphors of Mental Health: A Zen Commentary.' Ph.D. diss., The Fielding Institute.

Langford, Donald. 'The Primacy of Place in Gary Snyder's Ecological Vision.' Ph.D. diss., Ohio State University.

Li, Ming-Fen. 'The Convergence of Zen Philosophy and Habermas' Critical Theory for Designing Metacognitive Learning and Instruction.' Ph.D. diss., Indiana University.

McGinn, Molly. 'Spring in the Stone Garden: One Japanese Monastic Community's Attempts to Return to the "Original Spirit" of Zen.' Ph.D. diss., University of California, Los Angeles.

McGonigle, Marianne. 'Elements of Buddhism in the Works of Mark Tobey and Agnes Martin.' M.A. thesis, Texas Woman's University.

McLellan, Janet. 'Many Petals of the Lotus: Redefinitions of Buddhist Identity in Toronto.' Ph.D. diss., York University.

McNeill, Elizabeth. 'A Descriptive Study of Dialectical Thinking in Zen Buddhist Meditators.' Ph.D. diss., The Fielding Institute.

Merkle, William. 'Bringing Empathic Awareness beyond the Self: An Interdisciplinary Approach to the Healing Relationship.' Ph.D. diss., The Union Institute.

Miller, Stephen D. 'Shakkyō-ka: The Formation and Development of a Classical Buddhist Poetry Tradition in Early Imperial Poetry Anthologies.' Ph.D. diss., University of California, Los Angeles.

Murray, Anne. 'Jewels in the Net: Women Bringing Relation into the Light of American Buddhist Practice.' Senior thesis, Harvard University.

Newman, Jane. 'Affective Empathy Training with Senior Citizens Using Zazen (Zen) Meditation.' Ph.D. diss., University of Arizona.

Nietupski, Paul. 'The History and Development of Buddhist Monasticism.' Ph.D. diss., Columbia University.

Patt, David. '"Elucidating the Path to Liberation": A Study of the Commentary on the 'Abhidharmakosa' by the First Dalai Lama.' Ph.D. diss., University of Wisconsin.

Peng, Therese. 'Meditation and Psycho-Spiritual Transformation: A Phenomenological Study of Ch'an Buddhism and Christian Mysticism.' Ph.D. diss., California Institute of Integral Studies.

Penkower, Linda. 'T'ien-t'ai During the T'ang Dynasty: Chan-jan and the Sinification of Buddhism.' Ph.D. diss., Columbia University.

Rahula, Basnagoda. '"The Basket of Discourses": The Pali Lyric and Its Structure.' M.A. thesis, University of Houston.

Rodseth, Lars. 'Travel and Transcendence: Lamaist Expansion in the Himalayan Kingdoms.' Ph.D. diss., University of Michigan.

Rowland, Nancy. 'Buddhist-Christian Dialogue in the Global Village.' Ph.D. diss., California Institute of Integral Studies.

Smyers, Karen. 'The Fox and the Jewel: A Study of Shared Private Meanings in Japanese Inari Worship.' Ph.D. diss., Princeton University.

Song, Sung Jin. 'Saved Through Jesus Christ: An Essay on Constructive Christian Soteriology Written out of Dialogue with "The Awakening of Faith in the Mahayana".' Ph.D. diss., Southern Methodist University.

Syed-Leo, Yasmeen. 'Buddhism, Socialism, and Democracy: Democratic Kampuchea, 1975–1979.' M.A. thesis, Université Laval.

Thach, Bunroeun. 'Santiphum Khmer: A Buddhist Way to Peace.' Ph.D. diss., University of Hawaii.

Tiyavanich, Kamala. 'The Wandering Forest Monks in Thailand, 1900–1992: Ajan Mun's Lineage.' Ph.D. diss., Cornell University.

Wang, Li-Ji. 'Pointing to the Moon: Zen Influences in Three Plays by Hwang Mei-shu.' Ph.D. diss., Brigham Young University.

Watanabe, Joji. 'Karma in Theodicy.' M.A. thesis, Western Michigan University.

Watkins, Joanne. 'Spirited Women, Big-Hearted Men: A Study of Gender, Trade and Religion in the Nepal Himalaya.' Ph.D. diss., University of Wisconsin.

1994

Anderson, Carol. 'Practices of a Buddhist Doctrine: The Four Noble Truths in the Tipitaka.' Ph.D. diss., University of Chicago.

Barrett, Deborah. 'A Zen Approach to the Psychological and Pastoral Care of Dying Persons.' Ph.D. diss., United States International University.

Bedard, Stephane. 'Traduire la Parole de Sagesse Orientale: Oralité et Signifiance dans l'oeuvre de Chögyam Trungpa.' Ph.D. diss., Université Laval.

Bolick, Neil. 'The Genre of Philosophical and Religious Poetry and Intellectual Expression in the Southern Sung.' Ph.D. diss., Indiana University.

Bowers, Russell H. 'Someone or Nothing? Nishitani's "Religion and Nothingness" as a Foundation of Christian-Buddhist Dialogue.' Ph.D. diss., Dallas Theological Seminary.

Brown, Alta. 'Meditation as a Bodhisattva's Practice of Peace.' Ph.D. diss., University of Southern California.

Chirapravati, Pattaratorn. 'The Cult of Votive Tablets in Thailand.' Ph.D. diss., Cornell University.

Clark, Robert. 'Mara: Psychopathology and Evil in the Buddhism of India and Tibet.' Ph.D. diss., University of Virginia.

Cole, Alan. 'Mothers and Sons in Chinese Buddhism.' Ph.D. diss., University of Michigan.

Cyr, Tim. 'A Study in Economics and Religion: The Relationship between Buddhism and Capitalism in Thailand' M.D.E. thesis, Dalhousie University.

Disayavanish, Primprao. 'The Effect of Buddhist Insight Meditation on Stress and Anxiety.' Ph.D. diss., Illinois State University.

Dubin, Paul. 'Ambiguity Tolerance, Attribution Bias, and Meditation: A Look at Self-Schematization and Buddhist Egolessness.' Ph.D. diss., Pacific Graduate School of Psychology.

Eldershaw, Lynn. 'Refugees in the Dharma: A Study of Revitalization in the Buddhist Church of Halifax.' M.A. thesis, Acadia University.

Fenn, Mavis. 'The Concept of Poverty in the Pali Canon.' Ph.D. diss., McMaster University.

Fish, Mark. 'A Staged Revolution: The Influence of Zen Buddhism on the Living Theatre in the 1950s and 1960s.' Senior thesis, Harvard University.

Fowler, Sherry D. 'Murō-ji: A Contextual Analysis of the Temple and Its Images.' Ph.D. diss., University of California, Los Angeles.

Gayle, Robin. 'An Interaction between Western Psychotherapeutic Methodology and Eastern Buddhist Spirituality.' Ph.D. diss., California Institute of Integral Studies.

Getz, Daniel. 'Siming Zhili and Tiantai Pure Land in the Song Dynasty.' Ph.D. diss., Yale University.

Glass, Newman Robert. 'Working Emptiness: Toward a Third Reading of Emptiness in Buddhist and Postmodern Thought' Ph.D. diss., Syracuse University.

Goodman, Elizabeth. 'Dying in Japan: Japanese Folk and Religious Beliefs about Death.' Ph.D. diss., City University of New York.

Hanh, Myung-Hee. 'The Role of Women in Korean Indigenous Religion and Buddhism.' Ph.D. diss., California Institute of Integral Studies.

Hershock, Peter. 'Liberating Intimacy: Communicative Virtuosity and the Realized Sociality of Ch'an Enlightenment.' Ph.D. diss., University of Hawaii.

Heyrman, Laura. 'The Meeting of Vimalakirti and Manjusri: Chinese Innovation in Buddhist Iconography.' Ph.D. diss., University of Minnesota.

Hong, Jung Gil. 'An Effective Mission Strategy in Buddhist Cultural Society, South Korea' Th.M. thesis, Fuller Theological Seminary.

Hwang, Bong-Choul. 'Process and Harmony: A Comparison between Whitehead and Fa-Tsang's Metaphysics on the Notion of Reality.' Ph.D. diss., Illiff School of Theology.

Jintaganont, Porntip. 'Risk Factors of Diarrheal Diseases in the South of Thailand: Buddhist and Muslim Comparison.' Ph.D. diss., University of Hawaii.

Jung, Hee-Soo. 'Commentary on the "Larger-Sukhavativyuha Sutra" and the Formation of Pure Land Buddhism in Silla.' Ph.D. diss., University of Wisconsin.

Kainuma, Yoshiko. 'Kaikei and Early Kamakura Buddhism: A Study of the An'amiyo Amida Form.' Ph.D. diss., University of California, Los Angeles.

Kam, Tak Sing. 'Machu-Tibetan Relations in the Early Seventeenth Century: A Reappraisal.' Ph.D. diss., Harvard University.

Kerr, Janet. 'Precious Scrolls in Chinese Popular Religious Culture.' Ph.D. diss., University of Chicago.

Kibler, Ronald. 'Honen's Pure Land Movement: Changes in Japanese Buddhism.' M.A. thesis, California State University, Dominguez Hills.

Kim, Jongmyung. 'Buddhist Rituals in Medieval Korea (918–1392).' Ph.D. diss., University of California, Los Angeles.

Leong, Markus. 'Hanshan Deqing (1546–1623) on Buddhist Ethics.' Ph.D. diss., California Institute of Integral Studies.

Levinson, Jules. 'The Metaphors of Liberation: A Study of Grounds and Paths According to the Middle Way Schools.' Ph.D. diss., University of Virginia.

Mai, Lai Man. 'Dharmaraksa and His Work: The Input of Central Asian Buddhist Thought in Translating Buddhist Texts in the Third and Fourth-Century China.' Ph.D. diss., University of Wisconsin.

Mattis, Susan. 'Chih-i's Appropriation of Madhyamaka's Changing Conception of Truth and the Buddha's Relation to the Phenomenal World.' Ph.D. diss., Boston College.

Morris, Stephen. 'Beyond Religion: Transcendentalism and Zen Answers for Today.' Ph.D. diss., California Institute of Integral Studies.

Mullens, James. 'Principles and Practices of Buddhist Education in Asanga's "Bodhisattvabhumi".' Ph.D. diss., McMaster University.

Newland, James. 'Images and Portayals of Thai Masculinity: Through the History and Development of Politics, Buddhism, and Literature.' M.A. thesis, University of Oregon

Oxman, Daniel. 'Principal Meditative Projects in Theravada Buddhist Thought and Their Psycho-Therapeutic Implications as Experienced in the California Bay Area.' Ph.D. diss., California Institute of Integral Studies.

Pellissier, Hank. 'Jodo-Shinshu Influence in the "Insect" Haiku of Kobayashi Issa.' M.A. thesis, California State University, Dominguez Hills.

Prévèreau, Raynald, 'Dharmakīrti's Account of Yogic Intuition as a Source of Knowledge.' M.A. thesis, McGill University.

Puntarigvivat, Tavivat. 'Bhikkhu Buddhadasa's Dhammic Socialism in Dialogue with Latin American Liberation Theology.' Ph.D. diss., Temple University.

Rijssenbeek, Kamie. 'Human Nature in Hua-yen Buddhism.' Senior thesis, Brown University.

Schiller, Lauren. 'Buddhism in Contemporary America.' M.A. thesis, Southern Connecticut State University.

Sharf, Elizabeth. 'Obaku Zen Portrait Painting: A Revisionist Analysis.' Ph.D. diss., University of Michigan.

Soucy, Alexander. 'Gender and Division of Labour in a Vietnamese-Canadian Buddhist Pagoda.' M.A. thesis, Concordia University.

Suwanbubbha, Parichart. 'Grace and Kamma: A Case Study of Religio-Cultural Encounters in Protestant and Buddhist Communities in Bangkok and its Related Environs' Th.D. diss., Lutheran School of Theology.

Tokuno, Kyoko. 'Byways in Chinese Buddhism: The "Book of Trapusa" and Indigenous Scriptures.' Ph.D. diss., University of California, Berkeley.

Unno, Mark. 'As Appropriate: Myōe Kōben and the Problem of the Vinaya in Early Kamakura Buddhism.' Ph.D. diss., Stanford University .

Veidlinger, Daniel. 'Paticcasamuppada, Kamma and Freedom of Choice: A Study of the Nikayas and Some Modern Interpretation.' M.A. thesis, Carleton University.

Vowels, Yvonne. 'Toward a Third Wave Feminist Revolution: Feminists, Buddhists, and 12 Step Practitioners Encountering Difference.' Ph.D. diss., Graduate Theological Union.

Wilson, Harold. 'Charles Morris' Maitreyan Path as Via Positiva: Towards a Semiotic of Religious Symbolism.' M.A. thesis, McGill University.

Yun, Woncheol. 'On the Theory of Sudden Enlightenment and Sudden Practice in Korean Buddhism: Texts and Contexts of the Subitist/Gradualist Debates Regarding Sonmun Chongno.' Ph.D. diss., State University of New York, Stony Brook.

Zahler, Leah. 'The Concentration and Formless Absorptions in Mahayana Buddhism: Ge-luk Tibetan Interpretations.' Ph.D. diss., University of Virginia.

1995

Adolthson, Mikael. 'Monks, Courtiers, and Warriors in Premodern Japan: The Secular Powers of Enryakuji in the Heian and Kamakura Eras.' Ph.D. diss., Stanford University.

An, Ok-Sun. 'A Study of Early Buddhist Ethics: In Comparison with Classical Confucianist Ethics.' Ph.D. diss., University of Hawaii.

Bogel, Cynthea. 'Ritual and Representation in Eighth-Century Japanese Esoteric Sculpture.' Ph.D. diss., Harvard University.

Brown, Michael. 'The Myth of "Absurdity": A Critical Examination of Albert Camus' 'The Myth of Sisyphus' from a Buddhist Perspective.' M.A. thesis, Saint Mary's University.

Bryant, Gail. '*Kuhon Ojozu*: Paintings of the Nine Grades of Birth: Context and Interpretation.' Ph.D. diss., University of California, Los Angeles.

Cho, Sungtaek. 'The Rise of Mahayana Buddhism: A Self-Study of Its Self-Identity and Institutionalization through Reconstructing the Biographical Process of the Buddha.' Ph.D. diss., University of California, Berkeley.

Christoforou, Christos. 'Control of Air Exchange and Particle Deposition within the Buddhist Cave Temples at Yungang, China.' Ph.D. diss., California Institute of Technology.

Cohen, Richard. 'Setting the Three Jewels: The Complex Culture of Buddhism at the Ajanta Caves.' Ph.D. diss., University of Michigan.

Debord, Brigitte. 'West Meets East in Lucien Stryk's Poetry: A Study of Influences and a Translation of "Awakening".' Ph.D. diss., University of Arkansas.

Deegalle, Mahinda. 'Bana: Buddhist Preaching in Sri Lanka.' Ph.D. diss., University of Chicago.

Gardiner, David. 'Kūkai's and the Beginnings of Shingon Buddhism in Japan.' Ph.D. diss., Stanford University.

Goad, Angela. 'The Zen Truth in J. D. Salinger: "It's Very Hard to Meditate and Live a Spiritual Life in America".' M.A. thesis, Northeast Missouri State University.

Grady, Carla. 'A Buddhist Response to Modernization in Thailand: With Particular Reference to Conservationist Forest Monks.' Ph.D. diss., University of Hawaii.

Grumbach, Lisa. 'Dying for Your Own Good: The Kaidan Meguri of Zenkōji.' M.A. thesis, Graduate Theological Union.

Han, Bang Hee. 'A Comparartive Study of Maitreya and Jesus Christ, The Messianic Figures in Korean Buddhism and Korean Protestantism.' Ph.D. diss., Baylor University.

Hara, Maya. 'A Study and Translation of *Genku Shōnin Shi Nikki*.' M.A. thesis, Graduate Theological Union.

Heyman, Derek. 'Two Versions of the Non-Substantial Self: Sartre and Yogacara Buddhism Compared.' Ph.D. diss., State University of New York, Buffalo.

Jaffe, Richard. 'Neither Monk Nor Layman: The Debate over Clerical Marriage in Japanese Buddhism, 1868–1937.' Ph.D. diss., Yale University.

Kamberi, Dolkun. 'The Study of Medieval Uyghur Drama and Related Cultural Phenomena from "Maitrisimit" to "Qutadghu Bilik" ca. 767–1069 A.D.' Ph.D. diss., Columbia University.

Kedar, Dorit. 'Zen as a Vehicle to Increase Creativity.' Ph.D. diss., The Union Institute.

Kent, Richard. 'The Sixteen Lohans in the Pai-Miao Style: From Sung to Early Ching.' Ph.D. diss., Princeton Unversity.

Kieschnik, John. 'The Idea of the Monk in Medieval China: Asceticism, Thaumaturgy, and Scholarship in the Biographies of Eminent Monks.' Ph.D. diss., Stanford University.

Kornman, Robin. 'A Comparative Study of Buddhism Versions of the "Epic of Gesar of Ling".' Ph.D. diss., Princeton University.

Kraynak, Kenneth. 'The Buddhist Teacher-Student Relationship.' M.A. thesis, California Institute of Integral Studies.

Kritzer, Robert. 'Pratityasamutpada in the Abhidharmasamuccaya: Conditioned Origination in the Yogacara Abhidharma.' Ph.D. diss., University of California, Berkeley.

Kundert-Gibbs, John. 'No-Thing is More Real Than Nothing: Zen/Chaos Theory in the Dramatic Art of Samuel Beckett.' Ph.D. diss., Ohio State University.

Lankanavichian, Sureerat. 'The State and Buddhist Philosophy in Resource Conflicts and Conservation in Northern Thailand.' Ph.D. diss., University of California, Berkeley.

Levy, Alexander. 'The Concepts of "Paoying" and "Karma": An Example of Syncretism.' M.A. thesis, Western Michigan University.

Liu, Tannie. 'Ritual and Symbolic Function: A Biogenetic Structural Comparison of Techniques Used in Tibetan Buddhism and the Sun Dance Religion.' M.A. thesis, Carleton University.

Lyoo, Hwang Tae. 'The Life and Thought of Margaret Fuller: A Buddhist Interpretation.' Ph.D. diss., Case Western Reserve University.

Mai, Tong Ba. 'The Role of Reason in the Search for Nirvana.' M.A. thesis, McGill University.

Nelson, Mark. 'Quieting the Mind, Manifesting Mind: The Zen Buddhist Roots of John Cage's Early Chance-Determined and Indetermined Compositions.' Ph.D. diss., Princeton University.

Pepper, France. 'The Thousand Buddha Motif: A Visual Chant in Buddhist Cave-Temples along the Silk Road.' M.A. thesis, McGill University.

Prevereau, Raynald. 'Dharmakirti's Account of Yogic Intuition as a Source of Knowledge.' M.A. thesis, McGill University.

Silk, Jonathan. 'The Origins and Early History of the Maharatnakuta Tradition of Mahayana Buddhism: With a Study of the Ratnavasisutra and Related Materials.' Ph.D. diss., University of Michigan.

Sinberg, Susan. 'Tara and the "Tara-mula-kalpa": The Tara Cult's Formative Period in India.' Ph.D. diss., Columbia University.

Storch, Tanya. 'Chinese Buddhist Bibliography.' Ph.D. diss., University of Pennsylvania.

Tan, Leshan. 'Theravada Buddhism and Village Economy: A Comparative Study in Sipsong Panna of Southwest China.' Ph.D. diss., Cornell University.

Taylor, Marsha. 'How Buddhist Vietnamese Parents Make Decisions for Their Adolescent Children Who Attend Tara High School: A Case Study (Georgia).' Ph.D. diss., Georgia State University.

Tien, Po-Yao. 'A Modern Buddhist Monk-Reformer in China: The Life and Thought of Yin-Shun.' Ph.D. diss., California Institute of Integral Studies.

Tsang, Carol Richmond. 'The Development of the Ikkō Ikki, 1500–1570.' Ph.D. diss., Harvard University.

Wagner, Robin. 'Buddhism, Biography, and Power: A Study of Daozuan's Continued Lives of Eminent Monks.' Ph.D. diss., Harvard University.

Wakabayashi, Haruko. 'Tengu: Images of the Buddhist Concepts of Evil in Medieval Japan.' Ph.D. diss., Princeton University.

Wallace, Bruce. 'The Cultivation of Sustained Voluntary Attention in Indo-Tibetan Buddhism.' Ph.D. diss., Stanford University.

Wallace, Vesna. 'The Inner "Kalacakratantra": A Buddhist Tantric View of the Individual.' Ph.D. diss., University of California, Berkeley.

Wang, Dorothy. 'The Beginnings of the Buddhist Stele Tradition in China.' Ph.D. diss., Harvard University.

Wang, Xiangyun. 'Tibetan Buddhism at the Court of Qing: The Life and Work of lCang-skya Rol-pa'i-rdo-rje, 1717–86.' Ph.D. diss., Harvard University.

Welch, Matthew. 'The Painting and Calligraphy of the Japanese Zen Priest Toju Zenchu, alias Nantenbo.' Ph.D. diss., University of Kansas.

1996

Ainbinder, Lori. 'The Man in the Middle: An Introduction to the Life and Work of Gui-feng Zong-mi.' M.A. thesis, University of British Columbia.

Blackburn, Anne. 'The Play of the Teaching in the Life of the Sasana: Sararthadipani in Eighteenth-Century Sri Lanka.' Ph.D. diss., University of Chicago.

Blackstone, Kathryn. 'Standing outside the Gates: A Study of Women's Ordination in the Pāli "Vinaya".' Ph.D. diss., McMaster University.

Boucher, Daniel. 'Buddhist Translation Procedures in Third-Century China: A Study of Dharmaraksa and His Translation Idiom.' Ph.D. diss., University of Pennsylvania.

Casey, John. 'Emptiness and Actuality: The Process Philosophy of Vasubandhu's Yogacara.' Ph.D. diss., University of Hawaii.

Cayton, Lori. 'The Buddhist Stupa: Its History, Dimensions and Symbolism According to Tibetan Sources.' Ph.D. diss., University of Wisconsin.

Cha, John. 'A Study of the Dharmadharmatavibhaga: An Analysis of the Religious Philosophy of the Yogacara, Together with an Annotated Translation of Vasubandhu's Commentary.' Ph.D. diss., Northwestern University.

Chan, Beverly. 'Shuiyue Guanyin in China: The Way of Compassion.' Ph.D. diss., California Institute of Integral Studies.

Cutler, Nathan. 'Mt. Kailasa: Sources for the Sacred in Early Indian and Tibetan Tradition.' Ph.D. diss., California Institute of Integral Studies.

Feldmeier, Peter. 'Interrelatedness: A Comparison of the Spiritualities of St. John of the Cross and Buddhaghosa for the Purpose of Examing the Christian Use of Buddhist Practices.' Ph.D. diss., Graduate Theological Union.

Grabiel, Susan. 'The Hsi Lai Buddhist Temple: A New Locus for the Lotus, from Secular Space to Sacred Place.' M.A. thesis, California State University, Fullerton.

Gyori, Thomas. 'The Foundations of Mindfulness (Satipatthana) as a Microcosm of the Theravada Buddhist World View.' M.A. thesis, The American University.

Hawes, Ben. 'Take the Flagpole Down: Three Approaches to Understanding Dharma Transmission.' Senior thesis, Brown University.

Hawkins, Bradley. 'The Blending of Chinese, Indian and Indigenous Religious Traditions in Indochina from the Earliest Times to 1500 C.E.: Some New Perspectives on Religious Interaction.' Ph.D. diss., University of California, Santa Barbara.

Hur, In-Sub. 'An Analysis of the Different Way of Thinking of Indian Yogacara and Chinese Fa-Hsiang School.' Ph.D. diss., University of Hawaii.

Iibachi, Kazuko. 'Meditation in Zen Buddhism.' Ph.D. diss., The Union Institute.

Jones, Charles. 'Buddhism in Taiwan: An Historical Survey.' Ph.D. diss., University of Virginia.

Kaminishi, Ikumi. 'Etoki: The Art and Rhetoric of Pictoral Exegesis.' Ph.D. diss., University of Chicago.

Khanbaghi, Aptin. 'Early Zarathushtrianism and Early Buddhism: A Comparative Study of Religious Innovation as an Occasion for Social Reform.' M.A. thesis, McGill University.

Kinnard, Jacob 'Wisdom Divine: The Visual Representation of *Prajñā* in Pala-Period Buddhism.' Ph.D. diss., University of Chicago.

Klima, Alan. 'The Funeral Casino: Buddhist Meditation, State Terrorism, and Public Images in Thailand.' Ph.D. diss., Princeton University.

Kopf, Gereon. 'Beyond Personal Identity: Rethinking a Dominant Paradigm froma Zen Perspective.' Ph.D. diss., Temple University.

Kuo, Shun-Mei. 'The Relevance of Ch'an/Zen Buddhism to Issues in Ethical Philosophy Relative to Moral Education.' Ph.D. diss., Indiana University.

Lambert, Jerell. "Zazen' for Orchestra' D.M.A. thesis, University of Texas, Austin.

Lee, Mei-Hwa. 'The Interplay of Buddhism and Taoism in the "Dream of the Red Chamber" and Hermenn Hesse's "Demian".' Ph.D. diss., University of South Carolina.

McCarter, Bruce. 'Self or No Self: Continuity and Cohesion in Buddhist and Self Psychological Theories' Psy.D. diss., Massachusetts Schools of Professional Psychology.

McLagan, Margaret. 'Mobilizing for Tibet: Transnational Politics and Diaspora Culture in the Post-Cold War Era.' Ph.D. diss., New York University.

Mino, Katherine Tsiang. 'Bodies of Buddhas and Princes at the Xiangtangshan Caves: Image, Text, and Stupa in Buddhist Art of the Northern Qi Dynasty, 550–577.' Ph.D. diss., University of Chicago.

Moon, Simon. 'A Case Study in Comparative Monasticism: Songgwang-sa Son Buddhist Monastery, Korea and the Abbey of the Genesee, Cistercian Monastery, United States of America.' Ph.D. diss., University of Toronto.

Nasu, Eisho. 'Doctrine and Institution in Japanese Tendai Buddhism: A Study of Jie Daishi Ryōgen (912–985).' Ph.D. diss., Graduate Theological Union.

Noda, Keisuke. 'Disclosure of Presuppositions: Husserlian Phenomenology and Dogen's Zen.' Ph.D. diss., New School for Social Research.

Ohsuka, Shigeru. 'Toward a Future Buddhist Education: A Historical Study of Buddhist Morality Based on the "Fan-Wang-Ching".' Ed.D. diss., University of Hawaii.

Park, Kwangsoo. 'The Won Buddhism (Wonbulgyo) of Sot'aesan: A Twentieth-Century Religious Movement in Korea.' Ph.D. diss., University of Wisconsin.

Peng, Yunn-Ling. 'The Passage of Buddha in the Work of Odilon Redon.' M.A. thesis, Michigan State University.

Puntaniyama, Napawan. 'Temporal Awareness and Hassles Appraisal: A Comparison of Working Adults Who Practice Full Awareness of Breathing Meditation with Those Who Practice Waking Dream Imagery.' Ph.D. diss., New York University.

Rohonyi, Reka. 'Wat Phra Dhammakaya: "A Refuge in the Midst of a Turbulent World" – Analysis of a Contemporary Thai Buddhist Movement.' Senior thesis, Harvard University.

Ruppert, Brian. 'Buddha Relics and Power in Early Medieval Japan.' Ph.D. diss., Princeton University.

Sako, Toshio. 'Karman in Indian Philosophy and Vasubandhu's Exposition.' Ph.D. diss., Columbia University.

Sangay, Lobsang. 'Human Rights and Buddhism: Cultural Relativism, Individualism and Universalism' LL.M. thesis, Harvard University.

Schroeder, John. 'Nagarjuna's Unsurpassed Medicine: Emptiness and the Doctrine of Upaya.' Ph.D. diss., University of Oregon.

Sen, Tansen. 'Monks and Merchants: Sino-Indian Relations, 618–1281.' Ph.D. diss., University of Pennsylvania.

Shin, Kwangsu. 'A Study of Buddhism in North Korea in the Late Twentieth Century: An Investigation of Juche Ideology and Traditional Buddhist Thought in Korea.' Ph.D. diss., University of Southern California.

Smillie, Julia. 'A Study of Non Egalitarianism Found in Early Indian, Early Mahayana, and Vajrayana Buddhism.' M.A. thesis, California State University, Dominguez Hills.

Somaratna, Sobana. 'Witnessing to Sinhalese Buddhists through the Four Spiritual Laws of the Campus Crusade for Christ.' Th.M. thesis, Fuller Theological Seminary.

Souzis, Amy. 'The River Flows through Us: The Symbiotic Relationship of Vipassana Meditation and Authentic Movement.' M.A. thesis, Antioch University.

Stearns, Cyrus. 'The Buddha from Dol Po and His Fourth Council of the Buddhist Doctrine.' Ph.D. diss., University of Washington.

Sterling, Sean. 'Affective Change Following a Ten Day Vipassana Meditation Retreat.' Ph.D. diss., California School of Professional Psychology.

Tam, Wai-Lun. 'The Life and Thought of a Chinese Buddhist Monk: Zhiyuan (976–1022 C.E.).' Ph.D. diss., McMaster University.

Taniguchi, Masako. 'A Systematic Structure of Ethics Founded on Causal Conditionality ('Paticcasamupada'): Ethics from the Pali Nikaya Textul Point of View.' Ph.D. diss., Graduate Theological Union.

Victoria, Brian. 'Zen and Japanese Militarism: A Critical Inquiry into the Roots of "Imperial Way – Zen".' Ph.D. diss., Temple University.

Waterman, Jorie. 'Buddhist Tradition and Innovation in the Life and Teaching of Thich Nhat Hanh.' Senior thesis, Harvard University.

Wu, Chao-Ti. 'Chinese Ch'an (Zen) Buddhist Monasticism and Its Teachings.' Ph.D. diss., California Institute of Integral Studies.

Yamauchi, Jeffrey. 'The Greening of American Zen: An Historical Overview and a Specific Application.' M.A. thesis, Prescott College.

309

Yifa. 'The Rules of Purity for the Chan Monastery: An Annotated Translation and Study of the Chanyuan Qinggui.' Ph.D. diss., Yale University.

Ziporyn, Brook. 'What's So Good About Evil: Value and Anti-Value in Tiantai Thought and Its Antecedents.' Ph.D. diss., University of Michigan.

1997

Andresen, Jensine. 'Kalacakra: Mandala Rites and Empowerment in the Secret Wheel of Time.' Ph.D. diss., Harvard University.

Behrendt, Kurt. 'The Architecture of Devotion: Image and Relic Shrines of Gandhara.' Ph.D. diss., University of California, Los Angeles.

Brown, Sidney. 'Gifts of Contemplation and Action: Buddhist Nuns in Thailand.' Ph.D. diss., University of Virginia.

Causay, Joseph. 'Social and Political Struggle: Buddhism and Indigenous Beliefs in Contemporary Korean Cinema.' M.A. thesis, Ohio University.

Chen, Kai-Yu. 'Chih-Yi's Theory of "Samatha" and "Vipasyana": A Philosophical Inquiry into the "Mo-ho Chih-kuan".' Ph.D. diss., Temple University.

Coberly, Margaret. 'Transpersonal Dimensions in Hospice Care and Education: Applications of Tibetan Buddhist Psychology.' Ph.D. diss., University of Hawaii.

Dippmann, Jeffrey. 'The Emptying of Emptiness: The Chao-lun as Graduated Teachings.' Ph.D. diss., Northwestern University.

Doyle, Tara. 'Bodh Gaya: Journeys to the Diamond Throne and the Feet of Gayasur.' Ph.D. diss., Harvard University.

Grego, Richard. 'Jiddhu Krishnamurti and Thich Nhat Hanh on the Silence of God and the Human Condition.' D.A. thesis, State University of New York, Albany.

Gunn, Robert. 'The Experience of Emptiness in the Process of Self-Transformation in Zen Buddhism, Christianity and Depth Psychology as Represented by Dogen Kigen, Thomas Merton and Carl Jung.' Ph.D. diss., Union Theological Seminary.

Halperin, Mark. 'Pieties and Responsibilities: Buddhism and the Chinese Literati, 780–1280.' Ph.D. diss., University of California, Berkeley.

Hartzell, James. 'Tantric Yoga: A Study of the Vedic Precursors, Historical Evolution, Literatures, Cultures, Doctrines, and Practices of the Eleventh-Century Kashmiri Shaivite and Buddhist Unexcelled Tantric Yogas.' Ph.D. diss., Columbia University.

Hier, Grant. 'Flowers of Ink: Indirect Pointing.' M.F.A. thesis, California State University, Long Beach.

Houtkooper, Susan. 'An Exploratory Study of the Integration of Buddhism and Psychoanalytic Psychology.' Ph.D. diss., Union Institute.

Kam, C. Duh. 'Christian Mission to Buddhists in Myanmar: A Study of Past, Present, and Future Approaches by Baptists.' D. Miss., United Theological Seminary.

Lee, Chung Ok. 'Theory and Practice of Gender Equality in Won Buddhism.' Ph.D. diss., New York University.

Li, Hui. 'Traveling over the Waste Land: A Buddhist Reading of Death and Enlightenment in T. S. Eliot's Poetry.' Ph.D. diss., George Washington University.

Levine, Gregory. 'Jukoin: Art, Architecture, and Mortuary Culture at a Japanese Zen Buddhist Temple (Daitokuji).' Ph.D. diss., Princeton University.

Lwin, Tint. 'Contextualization of the Gospel: An Effective Strategy for the Evangelization of the Theravada Buddhists in Myanmar.' Ph.D. diss., Southern Baptist Theological Seminary.

Metcalf, Franz. 'Why Do Americans Practice Zen Buddhism?' Ph.D. diss., University of Chicago.

Monius, Anne. 'In Search of "Tamil Buddhism": Language, Literary Culture, and Religious Community in Tamil-Speaking South India.' Ph.D. diss., Harvard University.

Ning, Qiang. 'Art, Religion and Politics: Dunhuang Cave 220.' Ph.D. diss., Harvard University.

Ohnuma, Reiko. 'Dehadana: The "Gift of the Body" in Indian Mahayana Buddhist Narrative Literature.' Ph.D. diss., University of Michigan.

Okada, Masahiko. 'Visions and Reality: Buddhist Cosmographic Discourses in Nineteenth-Century Japan.' Ph.D. diss., Stanford University.

Pan, An-Yi. 'Li Gonglin's Buddhist Beliefs and His "Lotus Society Picture": An Iconographic Discourse on the Bodhisattva Path.' Ph.D. diss., University of Kansas.

Pibool sravut, Priyannt. 'An Outline of Buddhist Economic Theory and System.' Ph.D. diss., Simon Frasier University.

Pradel, Maria. 'The Fragments of the Tenjukoku Shucho Mandara: Reconstruction of the Iconography and the Historical Contexts.' Ph.D. Diss., University of California, Los Angeles.

Reinders, Eric. 'Buddhist Rituals of Obeisance and the Contestation of the Monk's Body in Medieval China.' Ph.D. diss., University of California, Santa Barbara.

Rohlman, Elizabeth. 'Creating One's Selves: Discovering New Foundations for the Knowing Subject.' Senior thesis, University of Dayton.

Rowan, Diana. 'Portable Buddhist Shrines of the T'ang Period.' Ph.D. diss., New York University.

Schneiderman, Sara. 'Doing/Writing Dharma: Feminist Journeys through the Tibetan Buddhist Ethnoscape.' Senior thesis, Brown University.

Seo, Audrey. 'Painting and Calligraphy Interacting in the Zen Art of Hakuin Ekaku (1685–1765).' Ph.D. diss., University of Kansas.

Shao, Ping. 'Monkey and Chinese Scriptural Traditions: A Rereading of the Novel Xiyou Ji.' Ph.D. diss., Washington University.

Shih, Jienshen. 'How Religious Professionals Learn: An Exploration on Learning by Buddhist Professionals in Taiwan.' Ph.D. diss., University of Wisconsin.

Storseth, Terri. 'On the Road with the Monkey: The Transmission of Zen Buddhism in Two Contemporary American Novels.' Ph.D. diss., University of Washington.

Suh, Jung-Hyung. 'Taoist Impact on Hua-Yen Buddhism: A Study of the Formation of Hua-Yen Worldview.' Ph.D. diss., University of Wisconsin.

Ting, Jen-Chieh. 'Helping Behavior in Social Contexts: A Case Study of the Tzu-Chi Association in Taiwan.' Ph.D. diss., University of Wisconsin.

Tu, Chung-Min. 'The World of Becoming: A Deleuzian Explication of the Middle Way in Chinese Confucianism, Buddhism, and Taoism.' Ph.D. diss., University of Georgia.

Verhoeven, Martin. '"Americanizing the Buddha": The World's Parliament of Religions, Paul Carus, and the Making of Modern Buddhism.' Ph.D. diss., University of Wisconsin.

Vorenkamp, Dirck. 'Hua-Yen Buddhism: Faith and Time in Fa-Tsang's Thought.' Ph.D. diss., University of Wisconsin.

Walser, Joseph IV. 'Logic, Scripture, and Allusion: The Recontextualization of the Canon in the Early Madhyamaka Thought of Nagarjuna.' Ph.D. diss., Northwestern University.

Walter, Mariko. 'Kingship and Buddhism in Central Asia.' Ph.D. diss., Harvard University.

Wang, Eugene Yuejin. 'Pagoda and Transformation: The Making of Medieval Chinese Visuality.' Ph.D. diss., Harvard University.

Zelinski, Daniel. 'The Meaning of Mystical Life: An Inquiry into Phenomenological and Moral Aspects of the Ways of Life Advocated by Dogen Zenji and Meister Eckhart.' Ph.D. diss., University of California, Irvine.

CONTRIBUTORS

Senryō Asai is a graduate of Tokyo University and is currently a research fellow at Aichi Gakuin University in Nagoya, Japan. On a Yokohama Zenkōji International Buddhist Study fellowship, he conducted research on Japanese American Zen temples in Hawaii and California. He has published numerous articles on American Zen Buddhism in Japanese scholarly journals.

Stuart Chandler is a Ph.D. candidate at Harvard University. He is writing his dissertation on Master Hsing Yün and Fo Kuang Buddhism. While at Harvard, he has also been involved in the Pluralism Project, a multiyear enterprise tracking the emergence of Buddhist, Hindu, Sikh, Jain, Islamic, and other religious communities in the United States.

James William Coleman is Professor of Sociology at California Polytechnic, San Luis Obispo. In addition to his research on American Buddhism, his current area of interest is white-collar crime. He is the author of *Social Problems* (6th ed. Harper Collins, 1996) and *The Criminal Elite* (4th ed. St. Martin's Press, 1998) as well as numerous articles and reviews.

Diana L. Eck is Professor of Comparative Religion and Indian Studies at Harvard University. Her work on India includes the books *Banaras: City of Light* (Knopf, 1982) and *Darsan: Seeing the Divine Image in India* (Anima, 1981; Columbia University Press, 1996). With Francois Mallison, she edited *Devotion Divine: Bhakti Traditions from the Regions of India* (Gronigen, 1991). Her work in theology includes *Encountering God: A Spiritual Journey from Bozeman to Banaras* (Beacon Press, 1993), which won the 1995 Louis Grawemeyer Award in Religion. Since 1991 she has directed the Pluralism Project, which is researching the changing religious landscape of the United States. She was chief academic advisor for the film 'Becoming the Buddha in L.A.' (WGBH 1994). In 1997, Diana L. Eck and the Pluralism Project published the multimedia CD-ROM, *On Common Ground: World Religions in America* (Columbia University Press).

Robert E. Goss teaches comparative religion at Webster University and is the Managing Editor of the *Journal of Religion and Education*. He is the author of *Jesus ACTED UP* (Harper San Francisco, 1993) and co-editor of *Our Families, Our Values: Snapshots of Queer Kinship* (Harrington Park Press, 1997).

Phillip Hammond is the D. Mackenzie Brown Chair of Religious Studies at the University of California, Santa Barbara. He is the author of *Protestant Presence in Twentieth Century America* (State University of New York Press, 1992) and *Religion and Personal Autonomy* (University of South Carolina Press, 1992); co-author of *Varieties of Civil Religion* (Harper and Row, 1980); and co-editor of *Future of New Religious Movements* (Mercer University Press, 1987). His most recent book is *With Liberty for All: Religious Freedom in the United States.*

Richard Hayes is an associate professor at McGill University who teaches classical Indian Buddhist philosophy and Sanskrit language. Since 1979 he has been involved with a variety of Buddhist groups in Canada and the United States and has participated in several conferences on Buddhism in North America.

David Machacek is a Ph.D. candidate at the University of California, Santa Barbara. He has served as an instructor at the University of California, Riverside. His interest in new religions in the United States is part of a program of research on identity, belonging, and community in contemporary urban environments. He has co-authored publications on new religions and religions in America and is currently writing up the results of the SGI-USA Membership Survey for a book on Sōka Gakkai in America.

Paul David Numrich is a research associate for the Religion in Urban America Program, University of Illinois at Chicago. His publications include *Old Wisdom in the New World: Americanization in Two Immigrant Theravada Buddhist Temples* (University of Tennessee Press, 1996) and the forthcoming essays 'Buddhism,' in *Encyclopedia of Chicago History* (University of Chicago Press), and 'Theravada Buddhism in America: Prospects for the Sangha,' in *The Faces of Buddhism in America*, edited by Charles Prebish and Kenneth Tanaka (University of California Press).

Charles S. Prebish has been a professor in the Religious Studies Program at the Pennsylvania State University since 1971. He is the author and editor of ten books, the most recent of which are *A Survey of Vinaya Literature* (Curzon Press, 1998) and *The Faces of Buddhism in America*, co-edited with Kenneth Tanaka (University of California Press, 1998); and more than fifty professional articles and chapters. He is a founding co-editor of the online *Journal of Buddhist Ethics* and editor-in-chief of *Critical Review of Books in Religion*.

Christopher S. Queen is Lecturer on the Study of Religion in the Faculty of Arts and Sciences and Dean of Students for Continuing Education at Harvard University. He is co-editor of *Engaged Buddhism: Buddhist Liberation Movements in Asia* (State University of New York Press, 1996), and editor of *Engaged Buddhism in the West*, forthcoming from Wisdom Publications. He has taught 'Buddhism in America' since 1992 and serves on the advisory board of the Pluralism Project at Harvard.

Richard Hughes Seager is Assistant Professor in Religious Studies at Hamilton College in New York. He is the author of *The World's Parliament of Religions: The East/West Encounter, Chicago 1893* (Indiana University Press, 1995) and the editor of the *The Dawn of Religious Pluralism: Voices from the World's Parliament of Religions, 1893* (Open Court Press, 1993). He is also an associate of the Pluralism Project at Harvard University.

Charles R. Strain is Professor of Religious Studies at DePaul University in Chicago, IL. He is the co-author of *Polity and Praxis: A Program for American Practical Theology* (Winston, 1985). He is the editor of *Technological Change and the Transformation of America* (Southern Illinois University Press, 1987) and of *Prophetic Visions and Economic Realities* (Eerdmans, 1989). Recently his article, 'Socially Engaged Buddhism's Contributions to the Transformation of Catholic Social Teachings on Human Rights,' was published in *Buddhism and Human Rights* edited by Damien V. Keown, Charles S. Prebish and Wayne R. Husted (Curzon Press, 1998).

Kenneth K. Tanaka is the Rev. Yoshitada Tamai Professor of Jodo-Shinshu Studies at the Graduate Theological Union. He is the author of *The Dawn of Chinese Pure Land Practice* (State University of New York Press, 1990), *Ocean: An Introduction to Jodo-Shinshu Buddhism in America* (WisdomOcean Publications, 1997) and co-editor of *Faces of Buddhism in America* (University of California Press, 1998). An ordained priest of the Buddhist Churches of America, he is an active participant in interreligious communities and with the Buddhist Council of Northern California.

Thomas A. Tweed is Associate Professor of Religious Studies at the University of North Carolina at Chapel Hill. He is the author of *The*

Contributors

American Encounter with Buddhism, 1844–1912: Victorian Culture and the Limits of Dissent (Indiana University Press, 1992) and *Our Lady of the Exile: Diasporic Religion at a Cuban Catholic Shrine in Miami* (Oxford University Press, 1997). He edited *Retelling U.S. Religious History* (University of California Press, 1997) and co-edited (with Stephan Prothero) a collecion of primary sources, *Asian Religions in America: A Documentary History* (Oxford University Press, forthcoming).

Penny Van Esterik is Professor of Anthropology at York University, Toronto, Canada. Her research interests include Theravada Buddhism and gender in Southeast Asia, with particular reference to Thailand and Lao PDR. She is also the author of *Taking Refuge: Lao Buddhism in North America* (Arizona State University, 1992).

Duncan Ryūken Williams is a Ph.D. candidate at Harvard University specializing in Japanese Buddhist history. He has been a visiting lecturer at Brown University, Trinity College, and Sophia University, Tokyo. He is the co-editor of *Buddhism and Ecology: The Interconnection of Dharma and Deeds* (Harvard University Center for the Study of World Religions, 1997) and translator of Shinichi Inoue's *Putting Buddhism to Work* (Kodansha International, 1997). He has also been a research fellow at the Harvard Pluralism Project.

INDEX

ABC News, 49
Abe, Ryuichi, 205
Abhayagiri Vihāra monastery, 133, 249
abhidharma, 144, 223
academics, academic community, 91,
    177. *See also* scholars, Buddhist
    Studies
  institutions and religious
    sectarianism, 229–232
  suspicion towards, 171–172
  societies, and Buddhist Studies,
    196–198
Adams, Henry, 82
African diaspora, 146
agape and eros, interpenetration of, 157
Ahlstrom, Sydney, 243
Aiken, Robert and Ann, 248
Albanese, Catherine, 134, 159
Alien Land Laws, 6
Amerasia Journal, 78
America, United States of, Americans,
    American society, 53, 54, 151,
    175, 185
America On Line (AOL), 178
American Academy of Religion (AAR),
    195, 197, 208
  Buddhism Section of, 192
American Buddhist Association,
    118–119
American Buddhist Congress, 129
American Civil Liberties Union (ACLU),
    48
American Oriental Society, 195–196, 198
Americanization, 245–246, 251
  and U.S. immigration history, 123

of BCA, 8, 14
of Sōka Gakkai, 249–250
of Theravāda Buddhism, 249
of Tibetan Buddhism, 247
of Zen, 247
Amherst College, 204
Amida, Amitabha, 14, 46
Angelou, Maya, 225
anattā doctrine, 60, 80
ancestral death rites, 28, 32
Anesaki, 134
Anguttara-Nikāya, 62, 170
anicca doctrine, 60
anthropologists, 60, 154
Arnold, Edwin
  The Light of Asia, 76
Ashoka (Asoka), xiv, xviii, 132, 134
Asian American(s), 45, 123, 127
  Buddhist groups ignored by
    scholarship, 30
  community, 44, 48, 129, 250, 251
  prejudice against, 48, 246
  and Euro-Americans, understanding
    between, 49
Asian Pacific American Leadership
    Council, 39, 40
astrology, 72
Augustine, 156–157
authority, religious, 170–171

baby boom generation, 94
Bali, 222
Bangladesh, 43
Baraz, James, 93
Barber, A. W., 204, 208

316

Index

Index

Index

Unno, Mark, 205
Unno, Taitetsu, 205
upāya, 158

Vajradhatu Society, 217, 219 *see also*
 Naropa Institute
Vajrayāna, 84, 92, 93, 120, 242, 247
 represented alongside other vehicles,
 123, 126, 128, 133
Van Esterik, Penny, 78
Vasubandhu, 133
Vatican, 183
vegetarianism, 174–175
Verhoeven, Martin, 186
Vietnam, Vietnamese, 77, 84, 122
Vietnam War, 186
Vietnamese Buddhist Association of
 Illinois, 119
'Village Council of All Beings,'
 153–154, 159
Vimalakīrti, 146
Vinaya, 49
Vipassana, 4, 83, 92, 93, 242, 244
Visakha, *see* Buddha, birthday of
Voltaire, 239

Wade-Giles transliteration system, 49
Waldman, Anne, 217, 223, 227
Wall Street Journal, 36, 48–50
Warren, Henry Clarke, 186
Washington Post, 40, 49–50
Wat Buddhanusorn, ix
Wat Dhammaram, 118–119
Watts, Alan, 247
Wayman, Alex, 13, 186
web browsers, 178
web pages, World Wide Web, 74, 201,
 250 *see also* Internet
Webb, Russell, 185
Webb-Boin, Sara, 183
Webster University, 220
Weight Watchers Magazine, 121
Welch, Holmes, 80
White Heron Sangha, 93
White Plum Sangha, 247
Whitman, Walt, 243
Whitney, William Dwight, 186
wild, wilderness, 155
Wiley, William, 75
Williams College, 204
Williams, Duncan Ryūken, 190
 classification of Buddhist Studies

academic programs, 202–204,
 215–16
Williams, George, 249–250
Wilson, Bryan, 108
Wilson, Pete, 38
Woo, Charlie, 40, 48
World Buddhism in North America
 Conference, Ann Arbor (1987),
 xxxi, 126
World Buddhist Conference, San
 Francisco (1915), 13
World Buddhist Sangha Council, 131
World Fellowship of Buddhists, 126,
 130
World Parliament of Religions (1893),
 117, 238–240, 244, 253
World Tribune, 101
World War II, 6, 15, 75, 118
 internment of Japanese before, 5, 7,
 128
 reparations for internment, 9
Wovoka, 145
Wulsin, Lucien, 220

Ya, Ven. Man, 40–41
Yale University, 194
Yang, X.J., 204
Yoga, 82
Young Buddhist Association, 28
Yün, Master Hsing, 36–56
 meets Al Gore, 37
 motives for planning banquet, 42–43,
 44–45, 54
 on Chinese, American identity, 54
 on the controversy, 49
 pessimism of, 54

Zangwill, Israel, 123
zazen, *see* meditation, Zen
Zen, 4, 20–35, 83, 92, 93, 120, 127,
 131, 158, 170, 177, 241, 244, 250
 see also Rinzai, Sōtō
 and the Buddhist mainstream, 246
 books on, 76
 in contemporary Japan, 27
 Korean Kwan Um school, 247
 perceived as 'the meditation school',
 20, 30
 Rinzai, 247
 Zen Boom, 20, 247, 252
Zen Buddhist Temple of Chicago,
 118–119

Zen Center of Los Angeles, 23, 30–32
Zen centers, 153, 171
  Euro-American, 23, 30–31
  proliferation of, 20

Zen Mountain Monastery, 224
Zendo e-mail discussion list, 177
Zensheji temple, 21, 27–30, 32
  economics of, 23